Selections from the Paston Letters

"*The classics are always modern.*"

EDWARD BULWER-LYTTON

The Paston Letters

THE HOLBORN LIBRARY

Selections from

The Paston Letters

AS TRANSCRIBED BY

Sir John Fenn

Arranged and Edited by

ALBERT H. R. BALL M.A.

George G. Harrap & Co. Ltd.

LONDON SYDNEY TORONTO BOMBAY

First published 1949
by George G. Harrap & Co. Ltd.
182 High Holborn, London, W.C.1

Dewey Decimal classification: 826·2

Composed in Imprint type and printed by
The Pitman Press, Bath
Made in Great Britain

CONTENTS

TABLES AND MAP

THE PASTON FAMILY

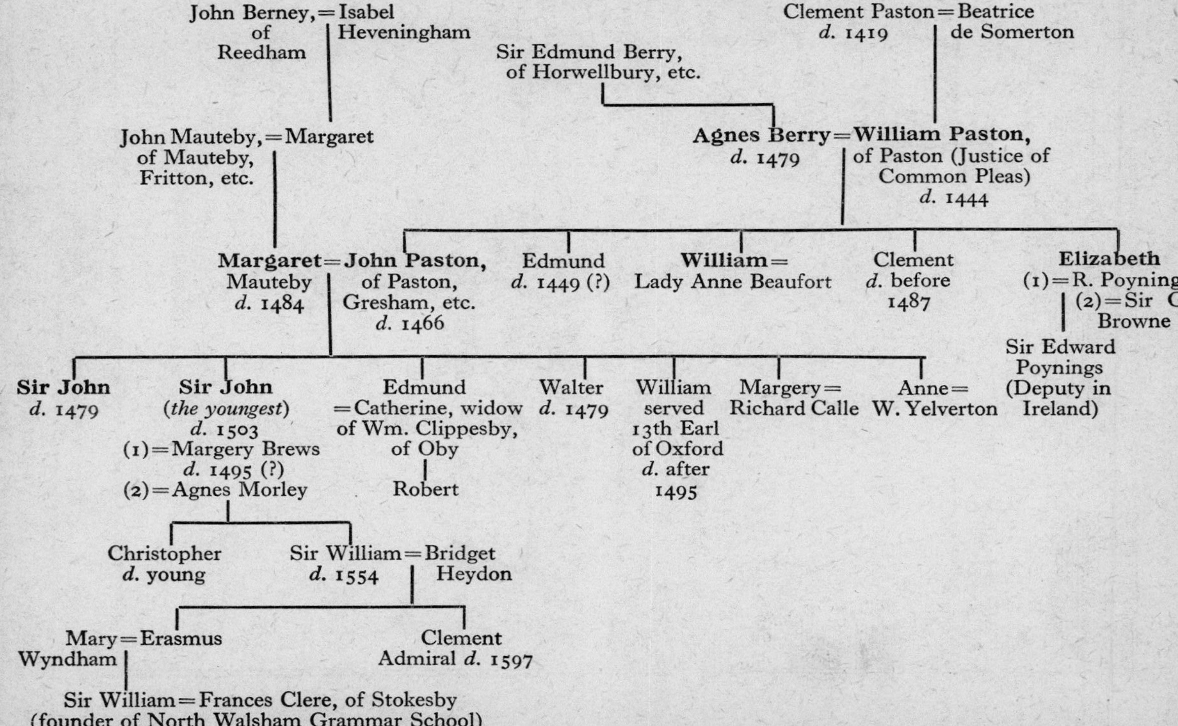

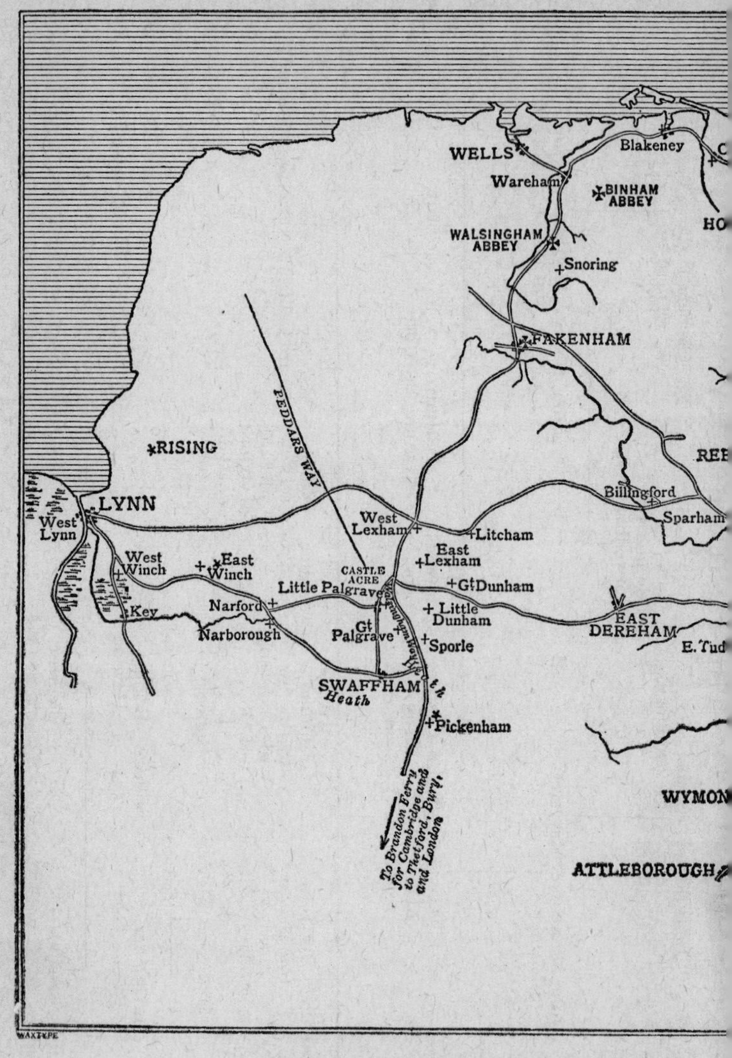
WELLS
Blakeney
Wareham
BINHAM ABBEY
WALSINGHAM ABBEY
Snoring
FAKENHAM
PEDDARS WAY
RISING
LYNN
West Lynn
Billingford
Sparham
West Lexham
Litcham
East Lexham
West Winch
East Winch
CASTLE ACRE
Little Palgrave
Gt Dunham
Narford
Little Dunham
Key
EAST DEREHAM
Gt Palgrave
Narborough
Sporle
SWAFFHAM
Heath
Pickenham
To Brandon Ferry for Cambridge and to Thetford, Bury, and London
ATTLEBOROUGH
WAXTYPE

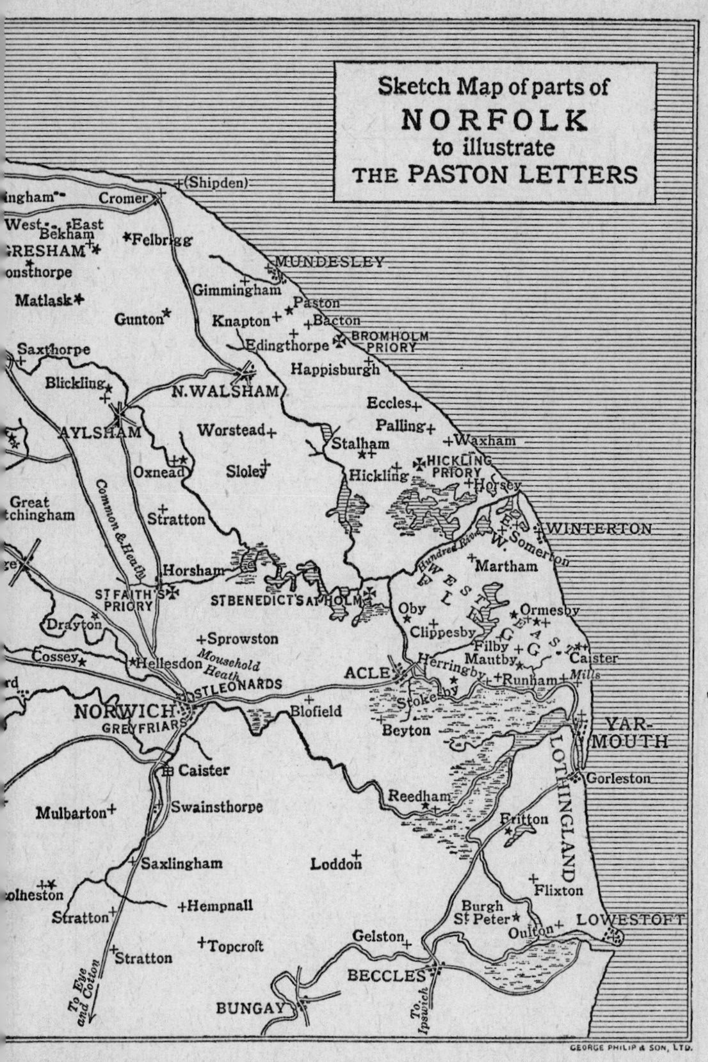

he Paston Letters," by Alice D. Greenwood (G. Bell and Sons.)

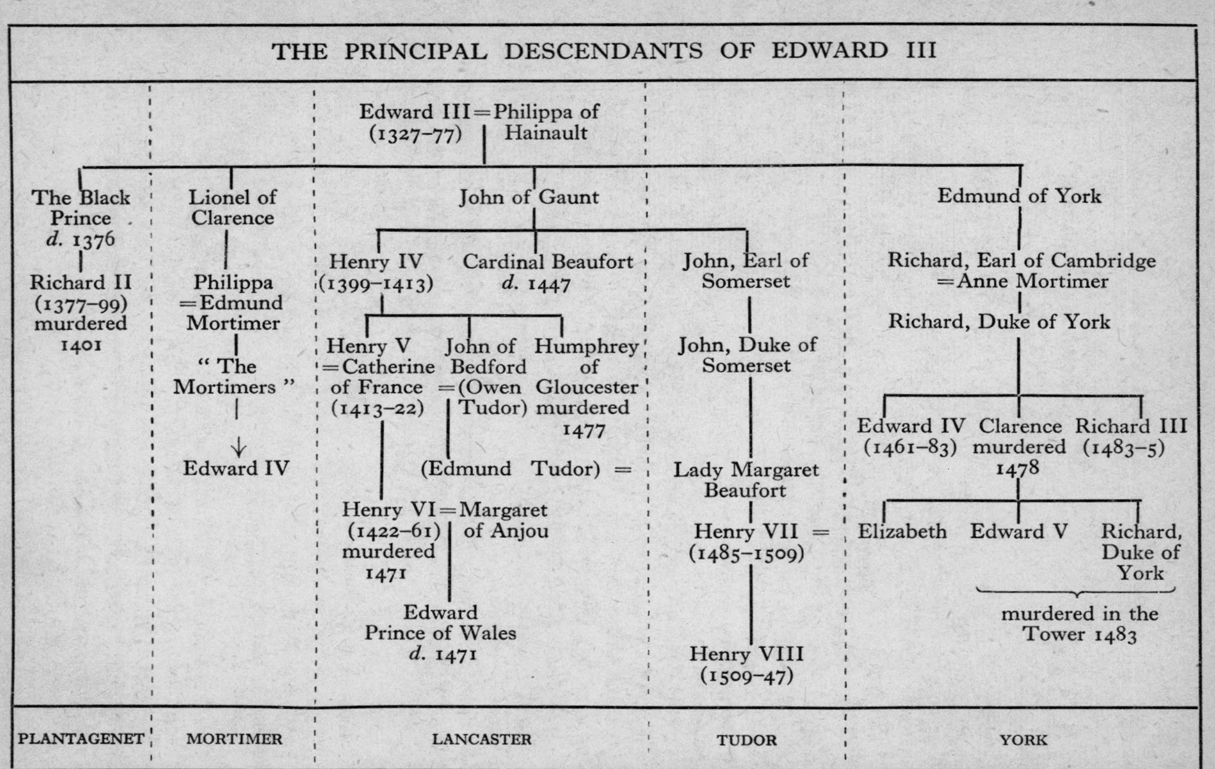
THE PRINCIPAL DESCENDANTS OF EDWARD III
Edward III = Philippa of Hainault
(1327–77)
The Black Prince d. 1376
Richard II (1377–99) murdered 1401
Lionel of Clarence
Philippa = Edmund Mortimer
" The Mortimers "
Edward IV
John of Gaunt
Henry IV (1399–1413)
Cardinal Beaufort d. 1447
Henry V = Catherine of France (1413–22)
John of Bedford
= (Owen Tudor)
Humphrey of Gloucester murdered 1477
(Edmund Tudor) =
Henry VI (1422–61) murdered 1471
= Margaret of Anjou
Edward Prince of Wales d. 1471
John, Earl of Somerset
John, Duke of Somerset
Lady Margaret Beaufort
Henry VII (1485–1509) =
Henry VIII (1509–47)
Edmund of York
Richard, Earl of Cambridge = Anne Mortimer
Richard, Duke of York
Edward IV (1461–83)
Clarence murdered 1478
Richard III (1483–5)
Elizabeth
Edward V
Richard, Duke of York
murdered in the Tower 1483
PLANTAGENET
MORTIMER
LANCASTER
TUDOR
YORK

INTRODUCTION

I. The Paston Letters

PRIVATE letters, interspersed with public and legal papers, have no pretensions to be regarded as literature, and in any case collections of such scope and completeness as to compel literature to take cognizance of them are rare. But if not literature they are the stuff of which both literature and history are made, in the same way as the private diary which Samuel Pepys wrote for no one's reading but his own; and it is, therefore, regrettable that a work of such outstanding interest as *The Paston Letters* should have remained in comparative obscurity. Their fifteenth-century background is doubtless largely responsible. The general reader is deterred, unnecessarily in a modern edition, by anticipated difficulties of language and reference.

To the student of literature Chaucer is raised by his genius on a peak above the rich fecundity of the fourteenth century; the age of Elizabeth is a period of profuseness and intense originality; and the intermediary fifteenth century seems singularly unproductive. For the historian it is the tangled era of the Wars of the Roses—a time of evil and decay: inglorious wars abroad; at home England wasting in the convulsions of civil war; the feudal system tottering to its fall through the selfishness and greed of turbulent nobles, with private disputes carried on by violence and armed force, and the forms of law often merely instruments of oppression. From these gloomy but deeply interesting days, when original literary production lacked inspiration not only in England but in all the countries of Western Europe except Italy, there comes, more or less accidentally, a most vivid contemporary picture in *The Paston Letters*. They are the main source of much of our knowledge of fifteenth-century social life. And though they sought no place in the story of English prose, they have a significant and important literary interest in a period when prose was better produced than it had been since the Conquest.

Prose, after all, is just the common speech purged of the defects of haste, gradually becoming more careful and deliberate, yet always suited to the needs of life. It lacks the emotional appeal given by metre and rhyme: it is the literature of knowledge, not power. There is artistic, almost poetical prose, for reason and emotion are rarely wholly divorced; there is the prose of simple, natural talk about the interesting things of ordinary life, where the homely phrase of the family or the street is the instrument of literary expression. It is in the latter kind that *The Paston Letters* have a place of perennial interest. Though our own age is steeped in a different spirit, though we think in different forms, we can find in these letters not only a mirror of the life and society of another age, but many of the enduring qualities of our common humanity.

In the development of English poetry there is a distinct break in the early fourteenth century, between Chaucer and Old English. In prose there is no such break in the continuity, though naturally there are differences of vocabulary and forms and external impressions. Prose suffered severely from the Conquest, for, with French as the language of the Court, and no standard English dialect, writers turned to French or Latin for cultured expression and neglected the vernacular. In the eleventh century there are some good homilies; in the twelfth the *Anglo-Saxon Chronicle* is still running; in the thirteenth there is some admirable writing, clear, graceful, and homely, as in *The Ancren Riwle*; but not until the fourteenth century, when, with the growing importance of the Commons, French decayed and a standard English dialect became the language of the law courts, did it become worth while to write in the vernacular. Mandeville, John de Trevisa, Wycliffe, and Chaucer, all write with confidence in English prose, but the period is dominated by Chaucer as a poet. In the next century, however, prose in the vernacular becomes really important, with works pouring from Caxton's new press. But whereas Caxton, though he keeps to popular material, sets out to create a literary prose style similar to the French, and Malory produces good narrative, with a mixture of purple patches and naïve, unconscious style, it is in *The Paston Letters* that we can see the extent of literary ability among all classes of people—noblemen, gentry, priests, yeomen, and servants. Here are ordinary men and women using the vernacular as a means of expressing themselves: factual, simple, straightforward, vigorous, and often with rare grace.

The Paston Letters first became known in 1787, when a Mr Fenn, of East Dereham, in Norfolk, issued a first collection of letters in his possession, written by or to members of a family named Paston, of the same county. The Pastons, who were not noblemen but landed proprietors of some importance in the county, carefully preserved their correspondence for several generations, and as the family, apart from its local connexions, played a prominent part in the great legal controversy of the Fastolf will, in bickering with noblemen whose names are synonymous with the last days of the feudal system, in the Wars of the Roses, and in much political controversy of the times, we have here not only a detailed picture of the personal and business life of a characteristic well-to-do English family, but State papers and historical letters of unique interest.

The original publication in 1787 aroused the enthusiasm of Horace Walpole, literary magnate of the day, and the King accepted not only the dedication, but a gift of two bound volumes of the autograph letters for the Royal Library, rewarding the editor with a knighthood. Unfortunately the volumes disappeared from that date until the year 1889, when they were accidentally found at Orwell Park, in Suffolk. The two volumes, however, contained only a selection from the very large number of fifteenth-century letters in Fenn's possession, and three further volumes were issued in 1789 and 1823. The originals of these, too, had a strange history, owing to the dispersal of Fenn's property after his death in 1794: they were missing for long periods, but many have since been found and have been safely housed in the British Museum, the Bodleian at Oxford, or in private collections. If it were necessary these sufficiently establish the authenticity of the letters, for a comparison of the available originals with Fenn's edition reveals a care and accuracy in transcription which gives every reason to suppose that the remaining copies are not less accurate. The Society of Antiquaries compared minutely the printed text with the originals of Fenn's fifth volume; errors were found to be few and for the most part trivial.

Sir John Fenn issued two versions of *The Paston Letters*, one in the exact spelling and punctuation of the originals, the other in more modern orthography. Again investigation has shown that the modern versions interpreted with meticulous accuracy the antique spelling and the peculiarly crabbed contractions of the manuscript copies. In the present selection, intended for general readers, the modern version is followed, and the letters have been arranged in groups to illustrate the main topics—Family Letters, The Fastolf Inheritance, Local Affairs, and Political Events—which provide continuity of themes and ease of reference. The student of literature and history is already provided for by the scholarly definitive edition, in six volumes, edited by James Gairdner in 1904,[1] and the large modern edition of selections by Miss Alice D. Greenwood,[2] while further information on the background of *The Paston Letters* will be found in *The Pastons and their England*, by H. S. Bennett.[3]

II. The Paston Family

The Pastons lived in the village of the same name, near the coast some twenty miles north of Norwich. Little is known of them until the fifteenth century, when they appear as industrious peasants, tilling their own land—at the best, small local gentry. One of these managed to educate his son for the profession of law, in which he achieved distinction, becoming a justice of the Common Pleas in the reign of Henry VI. *The Paston Letters* begin in the last years of this " Good Judge," William Paston. Improving his fortunes by marriage with a wealthy heiress, Agnes Berry, he set out to establish for the family a position in the county as landed proprietors, purchasing various manors in the neighbourhood—Bacton, Oxnead, Gresham, and Shipden. Rights of property, however, with the weight and influence in local affairs accompanying them, were complicated matters in those unsettled times—a particular subject of jealousy and cupidity among the local aristocracy—and in 1444 Judge William transmitted to his descendants a troubled inheritance. The early letters, immediately after his death, are much occupied by disputes about the family property: the vicar of Paston pulls up the

[1] Chatto and Windus. [2] G. Bell and Sons. [3] Cambridge University Press.

landmarks of a highway diverted, with due agreement, by the Judge; when Agnes Paston builds a wall it is thrown down before completion; Oxnead is claimed by one John Hauteyn; Lord Molynes asserts his right to Gresham by armed attack. Apart from violent defence, in justice alone lay any remedy, and it was, therefore, appropriate that the Judge's eldest son, John, should also be trained in the law. " Whosoever should dwell at Paston," the old Judge said, " should have need to defend himself."

John Paston, the protagonist of the early correspondence, appears first on the arrival of his wife-to-be, the " Gentlewoman from Reedham," Margaret Mauteby, of Mauteby, in Norfolk, who brought to the family not only additional property, but character and devotion. Her letters form a large portion of the correspondence, for, with her husband in London during the law terms, the local management of the estates fell mainly to her: she negotiates with neighbours and dependants, holds courts and collects rents, defends the property against lawsuits and violence, and faithfully reports to her husband all that affects his interests, together with news of local events and people. From Gresham, when further resistance to Lord Molynes is useless, she has to be carried by force, and later, with the same intrepid courage, she endures the more bitter siege of Caister. Deeply religious, she admonishes her husband over an unpaid bequest for masses for the soul of a relative; the influence of her chaplain in later years is such as to discommode her children; and her own will provides for an aisle and a tomb in Mauteby Church. As a mother she retains the affection of her large family, in spite of the conventionally strict upbringing of children: she has little patience with the thoughtlessness and extravagance of her eldest son; the two younger brothers suffer continual remonstrance and reproach; the door is closed on daughter Margery when she seeks an unfavoured match with a dependant. Through the formal humility and matter-of-factness of her letters we see a woman of forceful character, a skilled business manager, a devoted wife and mother. In all the vicissitudes of the family fortunes her guiding hand is obvious, until her death in 1484, in the reign of Richard III.

John Paston, her husband, succeeded to the estates at the age of twenty-four, and, learning early through his inheritance the need for wariness and shrewd policy, he displays undaunted determination and a capacity for sound business. That the position of importance in Norfolk which he plans for his family turns out to be unstable and perilous is no fault of his. While his wife literally holds the fort at home, he, by all legal and political means in his power, deals with the London end, and, in the changing fortunes of his affairs, is three times imprisoned there. The outstanding effort of his policy, however, is the cultivation of a friendship with Sir John Fastolf, a wealthy and childless kinsman, in such wise that he later becomes executor to Fastolf's will and heir to much of his property. Fastolf, not the most amiable of men, seems to have a genuine regard for him: "God send me soon my good cousin Paston, for I hold him a faithful man, and ever one man." For good and ill the Fastolf inheritance dominates the family fortunes for two generations, and its story is told later. More immediately, the leading position of the Pastons in Norfolk comes to be acknowledged. In 1460, a few months before Henry VI was deposed, John Paston is returned to Parliament, as a supporter of the Duke of York. He enters quietly into his possession of the Fastolf manors, in one of which, Hellesdon, his wife resides, on intimate terms with the Mayor and Mayoress of Norwich. With the advent of Edward IV in 1461 he is still in favour, a member of the King's household, and he is able to place his eldest son there too. But the renewal of the civil war brings opportunities for unscrupulous and covetous nobles. The royal favour wavers, exasperated by the Norfolk feuds, and John Paston is imprisoned. Debenham seizes the manor of Cotton; the Duke of Suffolk attacks Drayton and captures Hellesdon; Lord Scales, the Queen's brother, casts envious eyes on the magnificent castle of Caister. With the quasi-legal warfare over these Fastolf estates all John Paston's later years are occupied. His three imprisonments and the loss of Hellesdon affected him seriously, and he died in London in 1466. He was buried with great magnificence in Bromholm Abbey.

The preservation of the Paston collection begins with the businesslike character of John Paston, but, though the letters of the first twenty years are concerned almost wholly with his affairs, we obtain surprisingly few positive impressions of him.

The picture of an absentee husband, an unamiable and cold-hearted parent, and a grasping landlord is doubtless incomplete. Family life in the fifteenth century is notably lacking in sentiment, and among his fellows he seems highly popular—his wife relates how his imprisonment excited much sympathy in Norwich. Against the malicious ingenuity of his enemies he fights with unflinching energy, but for him the times are out of joint. Once only, in writing from the Fleet Prison, is there a suggestion of buoyant spirits and a sense of humour. All in all, it is a somewhat negative portrait that we have, but undoubtedly he and his wife are the soundest and most reliable characters of the Paston family.

John Paston and Margaret had seven children, the two oldest both bearing their father's Christian name. John the Eldest is attached for a time to the household of Edward IV, and in 1463, at the age of twenty-one, receives the dignity of knighthood. At that time, however, a friend writes to his father complaining that Sir John is living a life of inglorious ease at home. Nevertheless we hear of his foresight and determination in withstanding the first attack of Suffolk's men at Hellesdon, and after his father's death he is again much at Court, evidently in high favour and a special friend of Lord Scales. He takes part in tournaments, and he attends the King's sister, Margaret, to Flanders for her marriage with Duke Charles of Burgundy. There he becomes engaged to Anne Haute, a relation of Lord Scales; but the engagement is eventually broken off, and Sir John died a bachelor. On his return from abroad the troubles of the Fastolf inheritance fall thickly about him, though, as his father did, he remains in London, trusting to his influence at Court, over-optimistic about the prospects of defence, and neglecting the appeals of his mother and younger brother, who bear the brunt of violence and abuse in Norfolk. Hellesdon, Cotton, Caister—all are lost, and at a time when it can be least excused his own extravagance brings the family fortunes to their lowest ebb. Disgusted with the failure of Edward IV to protect them from armed agression, the Pastons, like all men who desired a steady Government, are now committed to the Lancastrian cause. The brief restoration of Henry VI in 1470, and the powerful friendship of the Earl of Oxford, temporarily restore Sir John's influence at Court, but he fights against Edward IV at Barnet in the next year, and with the success of the Yorkist king he has to sue for pardon. His later years are taken up with lawsuits, debts, and serious money difficulties. His mother expresses her discontent at his thriftless extravagance with some bitterness: Sir John is neglecting to provide even his father's gravestone; the property is running through his hands; and all her ingenuity is required to defend the family interests from his neglect. But after four years of negotiation, chiefly through the Duchess of Norfolk, he secures the restoration of Caister on the death of the Duke in 1476, and an agreement with Bishop Waynflete ends the long controversy over the Fastolf inheritance. After some further service in France with Charles the Bold, where he takes part in the Siege of Neuss, he contracted various illnesses, and died in London in 1479, a year of great mortality from pestilence, which also carried off his grandmother, Agnes Paston. Though softer and more pleasure-loving, Sir John appears as a character of much wider interest than his father. An adventurous soldier, a careless business man, a patron of literature, possessing a lively sense of humour—though unsuccessful in love himself he is willing to go courting on behalf of his brother—he is the most human figure in *The Paston Letters*.

John the Youngest, the second son, begins life well. He is early placed in the household of the young Duke of Norfolk—doubtless to obtain influence in the disputes over the Fastolf manors; he is familiar with Court life, and he has many powerful friends. He too has his share of adventure: he helps his mother to seize and hold the manor of Cotton, though this leads to the loss of Hellesdon; he accompanies his brother to the Court of Burgundy and gives a vivid account of its splendours; he sustains the siege of Caister in 1469; two years later he is wounded fighting for Henry VI at Barnet, but is pardoned like his brother; and he serves in France with the King's army at Calais. His love affairs occupy many letters, for he had several strings to his bow, courting in turn Lady Bourchier, Mrs Eberton, a Miss Stockton, and Lady Walgrave. Eventually, however, in 1477 he marries Margery Brews, whose warm and ardent letters form a human and delightful interlude in the correspondence. They had several children, the second being William, the forbear of the first Earl of Yarmouth. On the death of his brother in 1479 John sets out determinedly to restore the family property, and secures the manors of Marlingford and Oxnead. He appears to be suspected by the King of doubtful faith at Lambert Simnel's rebellion, but we find him in the royal army when the Pretender is defeated at Stoke, and he is knighted on the battlefield. Thenceforward his fortunes flourish: he is deputy to the Earl of Oxford as Lord High Admiral; it is to him that the town of Yarmouth appeals for help when a landing by Perkin Warbeck is feared; and in our last reference he is commanded to attend at the reception for Catherine of Aragon, the affianced bride of the Prince of Wales in 1501.

The remaining members of the family appear more casually. Of the older generation, John Paston's sister Elizabeth married first Richard Poynings, the sword-bearer to Jack Cade, whose seditious activities ended with his death at the second battle of St Albans, and later Sir George Browne, by whom she became the wealthy member of the family. She is chiefly interesting for the account of the rough domestic discipline of the times in the description of her home life before marriage: she is secluded, forbidden visitors, and regularly beaten. Her elder brother, William, who assisted John Paston in the early stages of the Fastolf controversy, also became a rich man. He married a daughter of the Duke of Somerset, provided a home for his mother, Agnes Paston, and gave much financial assistance to his impecunious nephew, Sir John the Eldest, in particular helping to save the manor of Sporle—an interest which aroused the jealousy of Margaret Paston.

John Paston and Margaret had five children in addition to the two Johns. We meet them mainly over their love affairs. Edmund, the third son, after a somewhat unhappy life at home, served like his brother in the army at Calais; held the manors of Marlingford and Oxnead for Sir John the Youngest; and, after unsuccessful negotiations for the hand of a wealthy mercer's daughter, married the widow Catherine Clippesby. Walter, the mother's favourite, was educated for the priesthood, though Margaret was unable to get him accepted by the Church. His letters give a lively account of life at Oxford, but after graduating in 1479 he succumbed to a sudden illness. William, the youngest, whose life at Eton appears as a mixture of Latin verses and calf love, had a successful career in the service of the Earl of Oxford. Margery fell into disgrace with the family after a clandestine engagement with Richard Calle, John Paston's bailiff and general agent. She was disavowed by her brothers and turned from home by her mother, so that the fall of Caister came opportunely for her—Sir John, unwilling to lose Calle's services, agreed to the marriage. The story of Anne, her youngest sister, is less romantic. In 1477 she seems to have been disposed of by marriage to William Yelverton, a grandson of the Judge who had caused much trouble to her father, and she disappears rapidly from the correspondence.

The Paston Letters leave the family, with Sir John the Youngest at the head, firmly established among the principal gentry of Norfolk. Of their subsequent history it may be mentioned that the son of Sir John the Youngest, Sir William Paston, became, like his grandfather, an eminent lawyer. A century later the family fought for Charles I in the Civil War, and on the return of Charles II was rewarded with the earldom of Yarmouth. The second earl, however, in the attempt to sustain a magnificent alliance with a natural daughter of the King, dissipated the family fortunes, ruined himself, and lost the estates. The Pastons sank again into obscurity, and, the earl having no male heirs, the title lapsed after his death in 1732.

III. The Fastolf Inheritance

The Paston Letters are concerned with the death rather than the life of Sir John Fastolf, but the popular conception of him, based on the Shakespearian burlesque of a fat, disorderly knight needs correction. He was actually a redoubtable warrior and a notable captain of the French wars, who had served with Henry V at Agincourt, again in France under the Regent Bedford, and finally as Governor of several conquered districts. When we meet him in the letters he has retired to London, and later, at seventy years of age, he returns to his own county of Norfolk, much occupied with the building of a great fortified castle on the manor of Caister, where he spends his last days formulating a huge claim against the Crown for losses incurred in the French War, and meditating on the foundation of a College of Priests. He died at Caister in November 1459.

In spite of his soldier-like qualities he was generally unpopular: he is accused by the populace of diminishing the garrisons in France and causing the loss of the empire there; his servant John Payn is violently attacked. In his later years he seems to have been an irascible old gentleman, vehement, intolerant, and a trifle miserly. His servant Windsor describes him as "cruel and vengeable . . . for the most part without pity and mercy," and his secretary, Worcester, a man of culture and refinement who had devoted a lifetime of service to Fastolf, complains bitterly of the shabby and niggardly treatment he received. Stephen Scrope, his stepson and ward, writes also of the mercenary and unfeeling way in which Sir John managed his affairs. Like all men of property, he had a comprehensive knowledge of litigation, and his letters are full of references to all sorts of legal processes. He is mentioned also as a merchant, his ships trading between Yarmouth and London.

John Paston was apparently related to Fastolf through his wife, Margaret Paston, and the knight had a high regard for his business capacity and integrity. In Fastolf's later years they were in continual contact. "He saith," wrote William Paston to his brother, "ye are the heartiest kinsman and friend that he knoweth. He would have you at Mauteby dwelling." Paston certainly lived for considerable periods with him, and at the end was entrusted with the drawing up of his will, which, subject to the obligation to endow the College of Priests at Caister and a few other bequests, gave to John Paston all Fastolf's manors and property in Norfolk and Suffolk—Caister, Drayton, Hellesdon, Cotton, and Calcotes.

The consequences of this will dominate a large part of *The Paston Letters.* The struggle for the inheritance falls generally into two parts: the dispute and litigation concerning the authenticity of the will, and the quasi-legal attempts of envious rivals to obtain and hold the property by force. To comprehend fully the whole amazing story it is necessary to keep in mind the background of late fifteenth-century history, on which these letters throw the clearest and most appalling light. The deciding factor throughout is the Civil War, when, with the fortunes of the King continually changing, with the influence of favourites waxing and waning, the lack of any central authority to repress disorder gave the powerful opportunists—nobles, churchmen, and local gentry—the chance to disregard law and justice, and to seize by force any desirable property they coveted.

Under the feudal system, property of a deceased nobleman was liable to be attached, at his death, by a King's officer, called the Escheator, until a jury of the county decided the legal heir. To avoid this it was the common practice to vest the property, before death, in trustees with stated powers and obligations. By the last will of Sir John Fastolf, drawn up by John Paston immediately before the knight's death, and sealed but not signed by him, a body of ten trustees was constituted, of whom two, John Paston and Sir Thomas Howes, the priest, were to have sole and absolute administration, the other eight having nominal powers only. Two of these, Sir William Yelverton, the Judge, and William Jenney, challenged the claim of John Paston to be chief executor and main beneficiary, accused him of trespass in taking possession of the manors, and took upon themselves to dispose of some of them to the Duke of Norfolk and others. The resulting actions lasted from 1464 to 1470, and they provide an interesting commentary on the vacillating fortunes of favourites. Testamentary assignment of property was in these times a complex business, generally best accomplished by compromise with the rival claimants, and above all, with the Crown. Paston, himself a Member of Parliament, trusted at varying times to the King's favour; both he and his eldest son served in the household of Edward IV; and during the suit the machinations of powerful influences brought him alternate support and disgrace.

Yelverton claimed simply that the last will drawn up by Paston, when Fastolf was too ill to sign, was nothing more than a forgery, and not the testator's genuine will. Partial records only of the lawsuit are extant, and it is impossible to assess the true facts. Against Paston is the testimony of Sir Thomas Howes, his co-executor and partner in the will, who, at the end of his life, confessed an uneasiness of conscience at his part in the fabrication of the document. On the other hand, Friar Brackley, Fastolf's friend and an eminent divine, gave unsolicited dying testimony that the document produced was genuine, and that Paston was not present when it was sealed. It is undoubtedly true that, with the extreme debility of Fastolf in his last days, Paston had ample opportunities of inserting at least his own interpretations of the dying man's instructions, and this may be the extent of his guilt. In any case John Paston died in 1466, and it was left to his son, Sir John the Eldest, to negotiate a settlement. In 1470, during the brief restoration of Henry VI, Bishop Waynflete was recognized as the sole executor; Sir John Paston, whose title to the estates had already been confirmed in 1467 by the King's Council, divided the much-wasted property with the Bishop, and surrendered the deeds of all but Caister, which the Duke of Norfolk agreed to give up, though he did not do so until three years later.

John Paston was chiefly concerned with the rich benefactions which came to him under the will, but the major project of Fastolf himself was the establishment at Caister Castle, after his death, of a "College of seven religious men, monks, or secular priests, and seven poor folk, to pray for his soul and the souls of his wife, his father and mother, and other that he was behold to, in perpetuity." This project, however, required both the goodwill of the executors, and a licence from the Crown to avoid the laws of Mortmain. The licence was obtained in 1464, but Caister was destined for a much stormier history. There were practical difficulties, too, in the attainment of Fastolf's wishes, and Worcester, the secretary, at one time proposed to transfer the foundation to Cambridge, as nearer to Norfolk, if Caister were impossible. Finally, in the 1470 settlement, it was agreed that the legacy should be applied to Waynflete's new college at Oxford—Magdalen—and that seven poor priests and seven poor scholars should be endowed there.

The territorial questions of the will provide a more sordid story. Caister, the chief prize and the main issue, was claimed first by the Duke of Norfolk as an alleged gift from Fastolf, but the intervention of the King restored it to Paston. Next Lord Scales, the Queen's brother, coveted it, and threatened action, but apparently relinquished his claim. In 1467 Sir John Paston's possession was confirmed by a Court of Audience, but meantime, during the litigation over the will, Yelverton and Howes assumed the right to sell Caister, with other estates, to the Duke of Norfolk, and in 1469 the Duke besieged the castle for five weeks. In spite of the reinforcement of the garrison and a fierce resistance under Margaret Paston and John the Youngest, it was forced to surrender, and the family were ejected. Under the will settlement of 1470, when the Earl of Oxford, Paston's patron, was in power, the Duke agreed to release the castle, but with the return of Edward IV in the next year, he took it again. Thenceforward Sir John Paston proceeded by peaceful, though fruitless, negotiation. Eventually, however, when the Duke died in 1476, Sir John again entered the Castle, and his title was finally established by the King's Council in 1477—seven years after the great siege.

The fate of the smaller manors was no less violent, and it illustrates well the system of 'Maintenance,' by which great lords 'maintained' factions which, under this protection, were able to incite violence and to oppress the countryside. Unhappy was the lot of the tenants, who, with the rapid and doubtful changes of ownership, were called to the manor courts to pay rents first to one claimant and then another, and often to both. Of the Fastolf lands, Cotton, after a determined stand by Richard Calle against Yelverton, was sold by the Judge to Gilbert Debenham, who seized and fortified it, and resided there until it was regained some years later by Margaret Paston, following a compromise with the Duke of Suffolk. Even more bitter was the conflict at Drayton and Hellesdon, which were claimed and savagely despoiled by the Duke. Sir John Paston acquired merit by one vigorous repulse of the Duke's men, but the manors were captured and wrecked. At Saxthorpe, which with Titchwell was sold over Sir John's head, there is an interesting account of "interrupting the Manor Court" by John the Youngest, in an endeavour to protect the rents. Typical of the times is the agreement with Bishop Waynflete in 1474, by which Sir John was allowed the manors in Norfolk "if he could recover them from the Duke." By the same agreement he gave up Drayton to the Bishop. Right up to 1478, however, the Duke of Suffolk gave trouble over Hellesdon and Drayton, attaching the property and selling the wood. By that time the Pastons were again high in the royal favour, and, with the advent of more settled government, they were left to enjoy what remained of the much wasted Fastolf inheritance.

IV. The Political Scene, 1440–90

Two main themes emerge from the tangled historical background of *The Paston Letters*—the closing years of the long war with France, barren and profitless for England, and the Yorkist-Lancastrian struggle at home, with its rapidly changing panorama of kings and nobles. The glories of Crécy and Agincourt had departed. They rested on French disunity; and the great house of Burgundy, which had given its support to the English cause, now made its peace with the French Crown. Shaken by the military success of Joan of Arc and disturbed by the marriages of the Dukes of Gloucester and Bedford, the alliance with Burgundy ended with the Treaty of Arras in 1435, when the French factions were reconciled, and King Charles returned to Paris, which had been Burgundian rather than French during the war. The Hundred Years War ceased to further any essential English interest.

In England the eighteen-year-old Henry VI, last and weakest of the Lancastrian kings, was quite unable to control the bitter strife which rent the Privy Council, in whose hands lay the governing power. Historians talk about the Lancastrian "constitutional experiment," for the House of Lancaster, which owed the throne to the revolution of 1399, when Richard II was deposed, was so closely controlled by Parliament, and above all by the Council, that in a way their rule seems to anticipate our modern system. In 1440 the outstanding question was the conduct of the French war. The peace party was led by Cardinal Beaufort, son of John of Gaunt, who saw in a policy of compromise the only hope of retaining any of the conquests in France. Humphrey of Gloucester, the King's uncle, clamoured for a more vigorous prosecution of the war. At the height of the struggle between these contending interests Henry VI came of age in 1437, and as he inclined towards the peace policy Beaufort gained a temporary ascendancy, though after 1441 his place was gradually taken by his nephew, Edmund Beaufort, Duke of Somerset, and William de la Pole, Earl of Suffolk. The latter negotiated the treaty with France in 1445, whereby Henry VI married Margaret of Anjou, a young, active, handsome, and vigorous princess, who soon gained a complete ascendancy over her husband, and was not slow to use it in the interests of the men who had brought about her marriage. Suffolk and Somerset sought to make their triumph over their opponents complete at a Parliament held at Bury St Edmunds in 1447. They had Gloucester arrested on a charge of treason, and ten days later, with suspicious convenience for his enemies, he died in prison.

If, however, Somerset and Suffolk did bring about the untimely end of Gloucester they made a grave error, for his death opened up the whole question of succession to the throne. So long as Henry VI and Margaret remained childless the next in succession was Richard, Duke of York, a descendant of Edward III. York and Somerset were thus rivals not only in politics, but also as claimants to the throne, failing a direct heir, and in the fierce quarrels which resulted the Wars of the Roses were already casting their bitter shadows before.

In 1449 the war in France was renewed with disastrous consequences for English arms. The French invaded Normandy and rapidly overran the province which had been conquered by Henry V thirty years earlier. Guienne and Gascony were next attacked, and soon Bordeaux and Bayonne opened their gates to the armies of Charles VII of France. The blame was put on Suffolk and Somerset, and in 1450, before the final military collapse, Suffolk was impeached. The King tried to save his friend by sending him into exile, but the ship in which he was crossing the Channel was intercepted, and he was put to death at sea by an angry crew amid jeers and cries of "Traitor." The complete powerlessness of the King's Government is well illustrated by Jack Cade's Rebellion. It was no disorderly rabble that the pretender led to Blackheath, but an organized force which reflected the general feeling of disgust with the incapacity of the Court and the misconduct of the war with France. In 1451 a member of the House of Commons made the suggestion that the Duke of York should be recognized as Henry's heir, but the proposal was not carried, and the Court's reaction is shown by the fact that the unfortunate mover of the original motion was thrown into prison.

The English defeat at Castillon, in Guienne, in 1453 brought the Hundred Years War virtually to an end. Of the once wide territories held in France by the English kings Calais alone was left. At home Bedford, Gloucester, Suffolk, and Cardinal Beaufort were dead, and the leading parts were now played by Richard, Duke of York, Somerset, and Queen Margaret. The birth in 1453 of Edward, Prince of Wales, was a bitter blow to the hopes of Richard of York. In the next year, however, Henry VI became insane, and, to Margaret's disgust, Parliament passed over her claims and chose York as Protector of England during the incapacity of the King. With Henry's restoration to health York's protectorate came to an end, and Margaret and Somerset regained power. Faced with complete exclusion from political life, if not, indeed, with a harsher fate, York decided to appeal to arms, and the Wars of the Roses began. With an army recruited in the north York advanced on London, and at the first battle of St Albans he was completely victorious. Somerset was killed, Henry VI taken prisoner, and the protectorate restored.

The subsequent period is a time of extreme confusion. The Central Government was relatively impotent, private wars were common, and the French ravaged the Channel coast. The most powerful supporter of the Yorkist cause was Richard Neville, Earl of Warwick, soon to be a maker and unmaker of kings. With the second recovery of Henry VI in 1456 a great reconciliation between the parties was arranged in St Paul's, and two years of comparative peace followed. In 1459, however, York again took up arms, but the Queen, who had bided her time, routed his forces at Ludlow. The Yorkists were attainted, and fled from the country. In the following summer they returned, entered London, and defeated the King at the battle of Northampton. Henry again was taken prisoner, and the Queen sought refuge in Scotland. York was now convinced that his only hope of lasting triumph lay in the removal from the throne of both Henry and his son, but this was too startling even to his followers, and he had to accept a compromise by which he was named as Henry's successor—a proposal which could not fail to lead again to war.

The two parties were able to raise troops only through the great nobles whose bands of liveried retainers were augmented by the troops returning in search of fresh employment from the French wars. These were simply mercenaries; they had no stake in the country as tenants; and the Wars of the Roses thus caused comparatively little economic upheaval in England, though the disturbances consequent upon the lack of a strong Central Government seriously affected local life. The geographical distribution of support for the parties was determined by the influence of the great families. The Midlands and the North were naturally for Lancaster; York, the inheritor of the old Mortimer claim, had the Welsh marches, Ireland, and, most important of all, the South-east and London, where the merchants wanted effective government.

Queen Margaret, who had refused to recognize the displacement of her son from the succession, left her refuge in Scotland in 1460, raised an army in Wales, and advanced against the Yorkists. She won a decisive victory at Wakefield, York himself being slain. Warwick, however, still held London and the King, and Margaret retired again to the North. Edward of York, son of the late Duke Richard, entered London, was proclaimed king as Edward IV, and at Towton in 1461 completely defeated the Lancastrians. The queen escaped and for four years carried on a desultory war in the North, but by 1465 Henry was still a prisoner, and Margaret an exile begging help in France from her cousin, Louis XI.

The throne of Edward IV was neither comfortable nor secure. Dependent entirely on the power of the great nobles, especially the House of Neville, he grew resentful of any suggestion of control by the over-presumptuous Warwick. The earl worked for an alliance with France to deprive Queen Margaret of any hope of help there: Edward showed his independence and spoiled Warwick's plans by his own marriage to Elizabeth Woodville and his sister's betrothal to Charles of Burgundy—a revival of the old alliance which forced Louis XI to support Lancaster, and led to the renewal of the war in 1469.

With the decline in Warwick's influence at Court, King and King-maker soon became bitter enemies. In 1470 Warwick and his son-in-law Clarence, the King's brother, fled to France, where Louis XI effected a reconciliation between them and Margaret of Anjou, who had been a refugee there for the past four years, and a marriage was arranged between Anne Neville, Warwick's daughter, and the young Prince of Wales. Louis equipped a small army, which crossed to England under the leadership of Warwick. Edward IV was absent in the North; the King-maker marched to London, brought the unhappy Henry VI from his prison in the Tower, and placed him again on the throne. Edward had now, in his turn, to flee to Flanders for shelter with his brother-in-law, Charles the Bold of Burgundy. Henry VI, however, his reason permanently affected, was a mere puppet in the hands of Warwick, who became a kind of dictator.

Though Charles the Bold was but lukewarm in support of Edward he aided him secretly with men and ships, and in March 1471 Edward IV landed at Ravenspur, on the Humber. His triumph was startling and rapid. Meeting with no opposition, he marched south. London welcomed him; his enemies were divided among themselves. Warwick, fighting for his own hand, could not wait for the arrival of French help, and after the defection of Clarence he fell at the bloody battle of Barnet. Margaret of Anjou, who had landed at Weymouth, was decisively beaten by Edward at Tewkesbury. The Queen was taken prisoner; the Prince of Wales was killed; Somerset, like his father and his brother earlier, fell to Yorkist swords of vengeance; and on the day that Edward returned in triumph to London Henry VI "died" in the Tower! The whole House of Lancaster was gone, and Lady Margaret Beaufort was the only descendant of John of Gaunt left in England. Her son was in Brittany, whence he was to come in 1485 as Henry VII.

After Barnet and Tewkesbury Edward IV was king, secure and absolute—the triumph of monarchy over oligarchy and the beginning of personal rule in England. The confiscation of Lancastrian estates freed him from the control of Parliament. He raised forced loans and benevolences—an especially popular form of taxation because the bulk of the people did not have to pay them. He engaged profitably in the wool trade and in foreign war, allowing himself to be bought off by Louis before his attack on France had developed. He was a despot rather than a popular ruler. He made no real reforms, and on his unexpectedly early death in 1483 the old factions broke out again.

Edward's elder son became king as Edward V, but the unpopularity of his mother and her relatives caused their uncle, Richard of Gloucester to be made Protector. Within three months the young King, with his brother, Richard, Duke of York, was put to death in the Tower, and Gloucester, basing his claim on the invalidity of Edward's marriage, was crowned king as Richard III. Though ruthless and violent Richard was not the monster of iniquity that he is usually made out to be. His ability was undoubted, but his finances were in a hopeless state, and he had to face the active dislike of most of the nobility, both old and new. In 1485 they gave their support to Henry Tudor, whose claim they deemed to be weak enough to make him a satisfactory puppet in their hands. Richard's short reign came to an end at the battle of Bosworth in August 1485. He was killed, fighting desperately; and the throne passed to the victor, who was crowned king as Henry VII.

Henry VII was the son of Edmund Tudor, Earl of Richmond, and the grandson of Owen Tudor, a Welsh gentleman who had married Catherine of France, the widow of Henry V. His mother, Lady Margaret Beaufort, was a great-granddaughter of John of Gaunt, the fourth son of Edward III. No one expected him to reign long, since he owed his throne to a coalition of half-hearted nobles, most of whom had no real loyalty to him. Henry, however, discarded the old ' Lancastrian ' principles, and resolutely excluded the remaining nobles from political power. Neither popular nor even very well known, he ruled in the interests of his people as a whole. He had to deal with rebellions and plots, the last flickers of the old faction strifes, like the risings of Lambert Simnel and Perkin Warbeck. To restore order he used the Court of the Star Chamber, a court so powerful that the greatest noble could not defy it or hope to corrupt it, a court which in very truth did " keep all England quiet." His laws struck at the roots of baronial independence and overweening power. Livery was forbidden and Maintenance rendered impossible. Henry VII, the first, and in many ways the greatest of the House of Tudor, was to leave England united and prosperous where he found it divided and anarchical. The processes by which he effected that transformation were all in train in 1490, when his reign was but five years old.

SECTION I

THE PASTON FAMILY

(DOMESTIC LETTERS)

I. The Older Pastons

I. MARGARET MAUTEBY COMES TO PASTON

To my Worshipful Husband William Paston, be this Letter taken

DEAR Husband, I recommend me to you, etc. Blessed be God I send you good tidings of the coming, and the bringing home, of the Gentlewoman,[1] that ye weeten [2] of from Reedham, this same night according to appointment, that ye made there for yourself.

And as for the first acquaintance between John Paston and the said Gentlewoman, she made him Gentle cheer in Gentle wise, and said, he was verily your son; and so I hope there shall need no great Treaty between them.

The Parson of Stockton told me, if ye would buy her a Gown, her mother would give thereto a goodly Fur; the Gown needeth for to be had; and of colour it would be a goodly blew, or else a bright sanguine.

I pray you do buy for me two pipes [3] of gold [thread]. Your [fish] stews [4] do well. The Holy Trinity have you in governance.

Written at Paston in haste the Wednesday next after "Deus qui errantibus" [5]; for default of a good secretary, etc.

Yours
AGNES PASTON

[1440]

[1] Margaret Mauteby. [2] Know. [3] Rolls. [4] Ponds.
[5] Collect for Third Sunday after Easter.

2. JOHN PASTON ILL IN LONDON

To my right worshipful husband John Paston, dwelling in the Inner Temple at London, in haste

RIGHT worshipful husband, I recommend me to you, desiring heartily to hear of your welfare, thanking God of your amending of the great disease that ye have had, and I thank you for the letter that ye sent me, for by my troth my mother and I were nought in heart's ease from the time that we wist of your sickness, till we wist verily of your amending.

My Mother behested [1] another Image of Wax of the weight of you to our Lady of Walsingham, and she sent four Nobles [2] to the four Orders of Friars at Norwich to pray for you, and I have behested to go on Pilgrimage to Walsingham, and to St Leonard's for you; by my troth I had never so heavy a season as I had from the time that I wist of your sickness, till I wist of your amending, and yet my heart is in no great ease, nor nought shall be, till I weet that ye be very whole. Your Father and mine was this day sev'night at Beccles, for a matter of the Prior of Bromholm, and he lay at Gelderstone [3] that night, and was there till it was 9 of the clock, and the other day. And I sent thither for a gown, and my mother said that I should none have then, till I had been there anon, and so they could none get.

My [step] Father Garneys sent me word that he should have been here the next week, and mine Emme [4] also, and play them here with their Hawks, and they should have me home with them; and so God help me, I shall excuse me of my going thither if I may, for I suppose that I shall readilier have tidings from you here than I should have there. I shall send my Mother a Token that she took [5] me, for I suppose the time is come that I should send it her, if I keep the behest that I have made; I suppose I have told you what it was; I pray you heartily that [ye] will vouchsafe to send me a Letter, as hastily as ye may, if writing be none disease to you, and that ye will vouchsafe to send me word how your sore do. If I might have had my will, I should have

[1] Promised. [2] £1 6*s*. 8*d*. [3] Home of Margaret's mother.
[4] Uncle. [5] Brought.

seen you ere this time; I would ye were at home, if it were your ease, and your sore might be as well looked to here as it is there ye be, now lever [1] than a new Gown though it were of Scarlet. I pray you if your sore be whole, and so that ye may endure to ride, when my father come to London, that ye will ask leave and come home when the horse should be sent home again, for I hope ye shall be kept as tenderly here as ye be at London. I may none leisure have to do write half a quarter so much as I should say to you if I might speak with you. I shall send you another Letter as hastily as I may. I thank you that ye would vouchsafe to remember my girdle, and that ye would write to me at the time, for I suppose that writing was none ease to you. Almighty God have you in his keeping, and send you health. Written at Oxnead, in right great haste, on St Michael's Even.

Yours,
MARGARET PASTON

OXNEAD
Saturday, September 28, 1443

My Mother greet you well, and sendeth you God's blessing and hers; and she prayeth you, and I pray you also, that ye be well dieted of meat and drink, for that is the greatest help that ye may have now to your healthward. Your Son fareth well, blessed be God!

3. TROUBLE AFTER THE JUDGE'S DEATH

To Edmund Paston, of Clifford's Inn, in London, be this Letter taken

To mine well beloved Son, I greet you well, and advise you to think once of the day of your father's counsel to learn the law, for he said many times that whosoever should dwell at Paston, should have need to con [2] defend himself.

The Vicar of Paston and your Father, in Lent last was, were thorough and accorded,[3] and doles [4] set how broad the way

[1] Rather.
[2] Know how to.
[3] Agreed.
[4] Landmarks.

should be,[1] and now he hath pulled up the doles, and saith he will make a ditch from the corner of his wall, right over the way to the new ditch of the great close. And there is a man in Trunch hight [2] Palmer, that had of your father certain lands in Trunch over seven years, or eight years agone, for corn, and truly hath paid all the years; and now he hath suffered the corn to be withset [3] for eight shillings of rent to Gimmingham, which your father paid never; Geoffry asked Palmer why the rent was not asked in mine husband's time, and Palmer said, for he was a great man, and a wise man of the law, and that was the cause men would not ask him the rent.

I send you the names of the men, that cast down the pit, that was in Genney's Close, written in a bill closed in this Letter.

I send you not this Letter to make you weary of Paston, for I live in hope and [4] ye will learn that they shall be made weary of their work, for in good faith I dare well say it was your father's last will to have done right well to that place, and that can I shew of good proof though men would say nay. God make you right a good man, and send God's blessing and mine. Written in haste at Norwich, the Thursday after Candlemas-day.

Weet of your brother John how many joists will serve the parlour and the chapel at Paston, and what length they must be, and what breadth and thickness they must be, for your father's will was, as I ween verily, that they should be nine inches one way, and seven another way, and purvey therefore that they may be squared there, and sent hither, for here can none such be had in this country; and say to your brother John it were done to think on Stansted church; and I pray you to send me Tidings from beyond sea, for here they are afraid to tell such as be reported.

By your Mother,

AGNES PASTON

NORWICH

Thursday, February 4

[1] A licence was granted to William Paston in 1443 to enclose a portion of the highways at Paston and Oxnead.

[2] Called. [3] Pledged. [4] That.

4. ESTATE AFFAIRS

To my right worshipful husband, John Paston, be this Letter delivered in haste

RIGHT worshipful husband, I recommend me to you, desiring heartily to hear of your welfare, praying you to weet that I was with my Lady Morley [1] on the Saturday next after that ye departed from hence, and told her what answer that ye had of John Butt, and she took it right strangely, and said that she had told you and shewed you enough, whereby ye might have knowledge that the relief [2] ought to be paid to her; and she said she wist well that ye delay it for that she should not have that [be]longeth to her right; and she told me how it was paid in Thomas Chamber's time, when her daughter Hastyngs was wedded; and she said, since that ye will make none end with her, she will sue therefore as law will.

I conceived by her that she had counsel to labour against you therein within right short time, and then I prayed her that she would vouchsafe not to labour against you in this matter till ye came home, and she said nay by her faith, she would no more days give you therein; she said she had set you so many days to accord [3] with her, and ye had broke them, that she was right weary thereof; and she said she was but a woman, she must do by her counsel, and [as] her counsel had advised her, so she said she will do; then I prayed her again that she would tarry till ye came home, and I said I trusted verily that ye would do when ye came home, as it longeth to you to do, and if ye might have very knowledge that she ought of right for to have it, I said I wist well that ye would pay it with right good will; and told her that ye had searched to have found writing thereof, and ye could none find in none wise; and she said she wist well there was writing thereof enough, and she hath writing thereof how Sir Robert of Mawteby, and Sir John, and my Grandsire and divers other of my ancestors paid it, and said never nay thereto; and in no wise I could not get no

[1] Widow of Thomas, Lord Morley (died 1435), and daughter of the Earl of Suffolk.

[2] Payment made to the overlord by the heir of a feudal tenant on taking up possession of an estate.

[3] Come to an agreement.

grant of her to cease till ye came home; and she bad me that I should do an errand to my mother, and when I came home I did mine errand to her, and she asked me if I had spoken to my Lady of this foresaid matter, and I told her how I had done, and what answer I had; and she said she should go to my Lady Morley's on the next day, and she should speak to her thereof, and assay to get grant of her to cease of the foresaid matter till that ye come home; and truly my mother did her devour [1] right faithfully therein, as my Cousin Clere shall tell you when that he speak with you; and she got grant of my said Lady that there should nought be done against you therein, and ye would accord with her, and do as ye ought to do betwixt this time and Trinity Sunday.

Laurence Reed of Mawteby recommendeth him to you, and prayeth you that ye will vouchsafe to let him buy of you the farm barley [2] that ye should have of him, and if ye will let him have it to a reasonable price, he will have it with right a good will, and he prayeth you if ye will that he have it, that ye will vouchsafe to send him word at what price he should have the Comb [3] as hastily as ye may, and else he must be purveyed in other place. . . .

It is said in this Country that Daniel [4] is out of the King's good grace, and he shall down and all his men, and all that be his well willers, there shall no man be so hardy to do neither say against my Lord of Suffolk, nor none that longeth to him, and all that have done and said against him, they shall sore repent them. Katharine Walsham shall be wedded on the Monday next after Trinity Sunday, as it is told me, to the galant with the great chain; and there is purveyed for her much good array of Gowns, Girdles, and Attires, and much other good array, and he hath purchased a great purchase of five marks [5] by the year to give her to her jointure.

I am afraid that John of Sparham is so shuttlewitted, that he will set his goods to mortgage to Heydon,[6] or to some other of your good friends, but if I can hold him in the better, ere ye come home; he hath been arrested since that ye went, and hath had

[1] Best endeavour.
[2] Barley paid as rent.
[3] A measure of cereals and fruit.
[4] Thomas Daniel, one of Suffolk's party.
[5] £3 6*s*. 8*d*.
[6] A lawyer and recorder of Norwich.

much sorrow at the suit of Master John Stokes of London for ten marks that Sparham owed to him; and in good faith he hath had so much sorrow and heaviness that he wist not what he might do; I feel him so disposed that he would have sold and have set to mortgage all that he hath, he had not ruth to whom, so that he might have had money to have holpen himself with; and I entreated him so, that I suppose he will neither sell nor set to mortgage, neither cattle nor other goods of his, till he speak with you; he supposeth that all that is done to him is at the request of the parson of Sparham and Knatysale. I suppose it is alms to comfort him, for in good faith he is right heavy, and his wife also; he is not now under arrest, he hath paid his fees, and goeth at large; he was arrested at Sparham, of one of Knatysale's men.

Hodge Feke told me that Sym Shepherd is still with Wylly, and if ye will I shall purvey that he shall be brought home ere ye come home. It is told me that he that kept your sheep, was outlawed on Monday, at the suit of Sir Thomas Todenham,[1] and if it be so, ye are not like to keep him long. And as touching that, that ye bad me speak for to Bacton, he saith he is well advised that she said she would never have to do withal, nor he cannot pick that she hath none right to have it, and he will say like as he hath heard her say, and if she speak to him thereof, he will rather hold with you than with her. I pray you that ye will vouchsafe to send me word how ye speed in your matter touching Gresham, and how Daniel is in grace. Harry Goneld hath brought to me 40*s.* of Gresham since ye went, and he saith I shall have more ere Whitsuntide, if he may pick it up.

I suppose James Gresham have told you of other things that I have sped since ye went hence. If I hear any strange tidings in this country I shall send you word. I pray you that I may be recommended to my lord Daniel.

The holy Trinity have you in his keeping, and send you health and good speed in all your matters touching your right. Written at Norwich, on the Wednesday next after that ye parted hence.

Yours,

[1448] MARGARET PASTON

[1] A neighbour and patron of John Heydon, who persuaded Lord Molynes to claim the estate of Gresham from John Paston.

5. PROVISIONS FOR LENT

To my right worshipful Husband, John Paston, be this delivered in haste

RIGHT worshipful husband, I recommend me to you, beseeching you that ye be not displeased with me, though my simpleness caused you for to be displeased with me; by my truth it is not my will neither to do nor say that should cause you for to be displeased, and if I have done, I am sorry thereof, and will amend it; wherefore I beseech you to forgive me, and that ye bear none heaviness in your heart against me, for your displeasure should be too heavy to me to endure with.

I send you the Roll that ye sent for, ensealed by the bringer hereof; it was found in your trussing Coffer. As for Herring, I have bought a horse-load for 4*s.* and 6*d.* I can get none Eels yet; as for Bever [1] there is promised me some, but I might not get it yet. I sent to Joan Petche to have an answer for the windows, for she might not come to me; and she sent me word that she had spoken thereof to Thomas Ingham, and he said that he should speak with you himself, and he should accord with you well enough, and said to her it was not her part to desire of him to stop the lights; and also he said it was not his part to do it, because the place is his but for years.

And as for all other errands that ye have commanded for to be done, they shall be done as soon as they may be done. The blessed Trinity have you in his keeping.

Written at Norwich, on the Monday next after Saint Edward.

Yours,

MARGARET PASTON

[1451]

[1] Beverage, light drink.

6. THE HIGHWAY DISPUTE

To John Paston, dwelling in the Temple at London, be this Letter delivered in haste

I GREET you well, and let you weet, that, on the Sunday before Saint Edmond, after even Song, Agnes Ball [1] come to me to my closet [2] and bad me good even, and Clement Spicer with her; and I asked him what he would; and he asked me why I had stopped in the King's way; and I said to him, I stopped no way but mine own, and asked him why he had sold my land to John Ball, and he swore he was never accorded with your father; and I told him if his father had done as he did, he would have been ashamed to have said as he said; and all that time Waryn Herman leaned over the parclose [3] and listened what we said; and said that the change was a rewly change, for the town [4] was undo thereby, and is the worse by an 100*l.* And I told him it was no courtesy to meddle him in a matter, but if [5] he were called to council; and proudly going forth with me in the church, he said, the stopping of the way should cost me twenty nobles and yet it should down again. And I let him weet, he that put it down should pay therefore.

Also he said that it was well done that I set men to work to owl [6] many while I was here, but in the end I shall lose my cost. Then he asked me why I had away his hay at Walsham, saying to me he would he had wist it, when it was carried, and he should a letted it; and I told him it was mine own ground, and for mine own I would hold it; and he bad me take four acres and go no farther; and thus churtly he departed from me in the churchyard. And since I spake with a certain man, and asked him if he heard ought say why the dinner was made at Norfolk's house, and he told me, [he] heard say that certain men had sent to London to get a Commission out of the Chancery to put down again the wall and the dyke. I received your letter by Robert Repps this day, after this Letter written thus far; I have read it, but I can give you none answer more than I have written, save the wife of

[1] A neighbour. [2] Pew. [3] Park close.
[4] The village of Paston (*cf.* Letter 3).
[5] Unless. [6] Deceive.

Harman hath the name of our Lady, whose blessing ye have and mine. Written at Paston, on the day after Saint Edmond.

By your Mother,

AGNES PASTON

[1451]

7. A TOWN HOUSE IN NORWICH

To my right worshipful Husband John Paston be this delivered in haste

RIGHT worshipful husband, I recommend me to you desiring heartily to hear of your welfare, praying you to weet that it was told me this week that there is a fair place to sell in St Laurence's parish, and standeth near the church, and by the water side, the which place Topps hath to sell, Pyte a Lyster [1] bought it of Topps, and now for default of payment Topps hath entered again therein, and shall sell it in haste, as it is told me, the said Lyster dwelleth therein at this time, but he shall out, for he is held right a poor man; I suppose if ye like to buy it, when ye come home ye shall mow [2] have it of Topps as good cheap or better than another should.

As for tidings we have none good in this country, I pray God send us good; it was told me that Richard Southwell hath entered in the manor of Hale, the which is the Lady Boys', and keepeth it with strength with such another Fellowship as it hath been at Braston, and wasteth and despoileth all that there is; and the Lady Boys, as it is told me, is to London to complain to the King and to the Lords thereof; it seemeth it was not for nought that he held with Charles and his Fellowship.[3]

I pray you that ye will vouchsafe to speak to James Gloys [4] to buy the Unguentum Album [5] that I spake to him for; and that ye will remember your fair Daughter's Girdle.

[1] A dyer. [2] Be able to.

[3] Charles Nowell, who, with a band of lawless companions, caused much violence and disorder in Norfolk.

[4] The chaplain and secretary. [5] White ointment.

I hope ye shall be at home so soon that I will write no more tidings to you. The blessed Trinity have you in his keeping, and send you good speed in all that ye will speed well in. Written at Norwich on the Ascension day.

Yours
MARGARET PASTON

[1451]

8. LOCAL NEWS

To my right worshipful husband, John Paston, be this delivered in haste

RIGHT worshipful husband, I recommend me to you, desiring heartily to hear of your welfare, praying you to weet that I have spoken with my Lady Felbrigg [1] of that ye bade me speak to her of, and she said plainly to me, that she would not, nor never was advised, neither to let the Lord Molyns nor none other to have their intents as for that matter, while that she liveth; and she was right evil paid with [2] Sauter that should report as it was told you that he should have reported; and she made right much of you, and said that she would not that no servant of hers should report nothing that should be against you, otherwise than she would that your servants should do or say against her; and if either your servants did against her, or any of hers against you, she would that it should be reformed betwixt you and her, and that ye might be all one; for she said in good faith she desired your friendship; and as for the report of Sauter, she said, she supposed that he would not report so, and if she might know that he did, she would blame him therefore; I told her that it was told me since that ye rode, and that it grieved me more that the said Sauter should report as he did, than it had been reported of another, inasmuch as I had ought him good will before; and she prayed me that I should not believe such reports till I know the truth.

[1] The family of Sir S. Felbrygg were friendly neighbours. Robert Molynes, afterwards Baron Hungerford, was Paston's enemy, and had seized Paston's manor of Gresham in 1448.

[2] Was badly treated by.

I was at Topps's at dinner on saint Peter's day, there my Lady Felbrigg and other Gentlewomen desired to have had you there; they said, they should all have been the merrier if ye had been there. My Cousin Topps hath much care till she hears good tidings of her brother's matter, she told me that they should keep a day on Monday next coming betwixt her brother and Sir Andrew Ogarde and Wyndham; I pray you send me word how they speed, and how ye speed in your own matters also.

Also, I pray you heartily that ye will send me a pot with Treacle in haste, for I have been right evil at ease, and your Daughter both, since that ye yeden [1] hence, and one of the tallest young men of this parish lyeth sick, and hath a great Myrr [2] how he shall do God knoweth.

I have sent my Uncle Berney the pot with treacle that ye did buy for him, mine aunt recommendeth her to you, and prayeth you to do for her as the bill maketh mention of, that I send you with this letter, and as ye think best for to do therein. Sir Harry Inglos is passed to God this night, whose soul God assoil [3]; and was carried forth this day at nine of the clock to Saint Faith's, and there shall be buried.

If ye desire to buy any of his stuff, I pray you send me word thereof in haste, and I shall speak to Robert Inglos, and to Wichingham thereof; I suppose they be Executors. The Blessed Trinity have you in his keeping. Written at Norwich in haste on the Thursday next after Saint Peter.[4]

I pray you trust not to the Sheriff for no fair language.

Yours, M. P.

[MARGARET PASTON]

[1451]

9. NEWS FROM NORWICH

This Letter be delivered to John Paston, being at London, in the Inner Inn of the Temple

I GREET you well, and send you God's blessing and mine, and as touching the matter which ye desired my Cousin Clere should

[1] Departed. [2] Murrain. [3] Pardon. [4] June 29.

write for, she hath done, and I send you the copy closed in this Letter. As for the enquiry, I have sent by Pynchemore to enquire and sent mine own man to William Bacton, and done him enquire in divers places, and I can hear no word of none such enquirance, I wot not what it meaneth. Robert Hill was at Paston this week, and the man that dwelled in Bowers place is out thereof, and said to Robert he durst no longer abide therein, for Waryn Herman sayeth to him it is his place. . . .

Bertholomew White is condemned in Forncet Court in 40 marks [1] as it is said.

Item, as for Talfas, the Sheriffs have behest to do all the favour they may, I sent the parson of St Edmund's to Gilbert, and he said there was come a new writ for to have him up by the 15th day of Saint Martin, and how Caly had been at home, and desired to carry up Talfas on his own cost, and give him good wages.

Item, John Osbern said to me this day that he supposed they will not have him up before Easter, and Margaret Talfas said to me the same day, that men told her that he should never have end till he were at London, and asked me counsel, whether she might give the Sheriffs silver, or none, and I told her if she did, I supposed she should find them the more friendly.

Item, as for Horwelbury I send you a bill of all the receipts since the death of your father, and a copy written on the back how your father let it to farm to the said Gurney; I would ye should write Gurney and charge him to meet with you from Londonward, and at the least way let him purvey ten pounds for [he] oweth by my reckoning at Michaelmas last past, beside your father's debt 18*l.* 14*s.* 8*d.* If ye would write to him to bring surety both for your father's debt and mine, and pay by days, so that the man might live and pay us, I would forgive him of the old arrearages ten pounds and he might be made to pay 20 marks by year, on that condition I would forgive him ten pounds, and so thinketh me he should have cause to pray for your father and me, and [so] it was let in my father's time. I feel by Robert, his wife is right loth to go thence, she said that she had lever I

[1] £26 13*s.* 4*d.*

should have all her goods after her day than they should go out thereof.

Item, John Dam told me that the Lady Boys will sell a place called Hales,[1] but he saith she speaketh it privily, and saith it is not [en]tayled, as John Dam know, which will she hath said as largely of other things that hath not been so.

Item, he told me as he heard said, Sir John Fastolf hath sold Hellesden to Boleyn of London, and if it be so, it seemeth he will sell more, wherefore I pray you, as ye will have my love and my blessing, that ye will help and do your devoir that some thing were purchased for your two brethen; I suppose that Sir John Fastolf, and he were spoke to, would be gladder to let his Kinsmen have part than strange men; assay him in my name of such places as ye suppose is most clear.

It is said in this country that my Lord of Norfolk saith Sir John Fastolf hath given him Caister, and he will have [it] plainly. I send you a bill of Osbern's hand, which was the answer of the Sheriff and John of Dam.

John, bring me my Letter home with you, and my cousin Clere's copy of her Letter, and the copy of the receipt of Horwellbury, and recommend me to Lomner, and tell him his best beloved fareth well, but she is not yet come to Norwich, for they die yet, but not so sore as they did, and God be with you. Written at Norwich, in right great haste, the 16th day of November.

By your Mother,

AGNES PASTON

[1452]

10. DEATHS

To my well beloved Son John Paston

SON I greet you well, and send you God's blessing and mine, and let you weet that Robert Hill came homeward by Orwellbury, and Gurney telled him he had been at London for money and could not speeden, and behested Robert that he should send me money by you; I pray forget it not as ye come homeward, and speak sadly [2] for another Farmer.

[1] Holm Hale.

[2] Seriously.

And as for tydings Philip Berney [1] is passed to God on Monday last past with the greatest pain that ever I saw man; and on Tuesday Sir John Heveningham yede [2] to his church and heard three masses, and came home again, never merrier, and said to his wife that he would go say a little devotion in his garden, and then he would dine; and forthwith he felt a fainting in his leg and sit down; this was at nine of the clock, and he was dead ere noon.

My Cousin Clere prays you that ye let no man see her Letter, which is ensealed under my seal. I pray you that you will pay your brother William for four ounces and an half of silk as he paid, which he sent me by William Taverner, and bring with you a quarter of an ounce even like of the same that I send you closed in this Letter; and say your brother William that his horse hath one sarcy [3] and great running sores in his legs. God have you in keeping. Written at Norwich, on Saint Thomas's even [4] in great haste.

By your Mother,
AGNES PASTON

[1453]

11. CLEMENT'S EDUCATION

Errands to London of Agnes Paston, the 28th day of January, the year of King Henry VI the 36th (1458)

To pray Greenfield to send me faithfully word by writing, how Clement Paston hath done his devoir [5] in Learning. And if he hath not done well, nor will not amend, pray him that he will truly belash him, till he will amend; and so did the last Master, and the best that ever he had at Cambridge.

And say Greenfield, that if he will take upon him to bring him into good Rule and Learning, that I may verily know he doth his devoir, I will give him 10 Marks [6] for his labour, for I had lever he were fairly buried than lost for default.

Item, to see how many Gowns Clement hath, and they that be bare, let them be raised.

[1] Uncle to Margaret Paston.
[2] Went.
[3] Fleshy growth.
[4] July 6.
[5] Duty.
[6] £6 13*s.* 4*d.*

He hath a short green Gown and a short muster-develers Gown [1] were never raised.

And a short blue Gown, that was raised, and made of a side [2] Gown, when I was last at London; and a side Russet Gown furred with beaver was made this time two years. And a side Murrey [3] Gown was made this time twelvemonth.

Item, to do make me six Spoons of eight ounces of troy weight, well fashioned and double gilt.

And say Elizabeth Paston that she must use herself to work readily, as other Gentlewomen do, and somewhat to help herself therewith.

Item, to pay the Lady Pole 26*s.* and 8*d.* for her board.

And if Greenfield have done well his devoir to Clement, or will do his devoir, give him the noble.

AGNES PASTON

[1458]

12. AGNES PASTON'S BLESSING

To my well beloved Son, John Paston, be this delivered in haste

SON, I greet you well, and let you weet, that for as much as your brother Clement letteth me weet that ye desire faithfully my blessing; that blessing that I prayed your father to give you the last day that ever he spake, and the blessing of all saints under heaven, and mine mote come to you all days and times; and think verily none other but that ye have it, and shall have it, with that [4] that I find you kind and willing to the weal of your Father's soul, and to the welfare of your brethren.

By my counsel dispose yourself as much as ye may to have less to do in the world; your Father said, "In little business lyeth much rest." This world is but a thoroughfare, and full of woe; and, when we depart therefrom, right nought bear with us, but our good deeds and ill; and there knoweth no man how soon

[1] A kind of mixed grey woollen cloth. [2] Long.
[3] Dark red. [4] On condition.

God will clepe him; and therefore it is good for every creature to be ready. Whom God visiteth him he loveth.

And as for your brethern they will I know certainly labour all that in them lyeth for you. Our Lord have you in his blessed keeping, body and soul. Written at Norwich, the 29th day of October.

By your Mother,
AGNES PASTON

[1458]

13. A PROPOSAL OF MARRIAGE

To my right worshipful Husband John Paston, be this Letter delivered in haste

RIGHT worshipful Husband, I recommend me to you, please you to weet that I was at Norwich this week to purvey such things as needeth me against this winter; and I was at my Mother's, and while I was there, there came in one Wrothe, a kinsman of Elizabeth Clere's and he saw your Daughter and praised her to my Mother, and said that she was a goodly young woman; and my Mother prayed him for to get for her one good marriage if he knew any; and he said he knew one should be of a 300 marks [1] by year, the which is Sir John Cley's Son, that is Chamberlayn with my Lady of York, and he is of age of 18 years old; if ye think it be for to be spoken of, my Mother thinks that it should be got for less money now in this world than it should be hereafter, either that one, or some other good marriage. . . .

As for answer [of] other matters, Daubeney [2] telleth me he wrote to you. I beseech Almighty God have you in his keeping. Written at Caister, the Sunday next after Saint Martin.

By your
MARGARET PASTON

[*about* 1465]

[1] Two hundred pounds. [2] Paston's agent.

II. *Elizabeth Paston*

14. STEPHEN SCROPE OFFERS MARRIAGE

To John Paston be this Letter delivered

SON, I greet you well, with God's blessing and mine, and I let you weet that my Cousin Clere [1] writted to me that she spake with Scroope [2] after that he had been with me at Norwich, and told her what cheer that I had made him; and he said to her he liked well by the cheer that I made him.

He had such words to my Cousin Clere, that, less than [3] ye made him good cheer and gave him words of comfort at London, he would no more speak of the matter.

My Cousin Clere thinketh that it were a folly to forsake him less than ye know of one other as good or better; and I have assayed your Sister [4] and I found her never so willing to none as she is to him: if it be so that his land stand clear.

I sent you a Letter by Brawnton for silk, and for this matter before my Cousin Clere wrote to me, the which was written on the Wednesday next after Midsummer day.

Sir Harry Inglose is right busy about Scroope for one of his daughters.

I pray you forget not to bring me my money from Horwelberry, as ye come from London, either all or a great part; the due debt was at Christmas last past, nothing allowed, 7*l*. 14*s*. 8*d*. and at this Midsummer it is 5*l*. more; and though I allow him all his asking, it is but 1*l*. 6*s*. 6*d*. less, but I am not so advised yet. As for the Friar [5] he hath been at St Benet's,[6] and at Norwich, and made great boast of the suit that he hath against me, and bought many boxes,[7] to what intent I weet never; it is

[1] Elizabeth, widow of Robert Clere of Ormesby.

[2] Stephen Scrope, a stepson of Sir John Fastolf.

[3] Unless.

[4] Elizabeth Paston.

[5] Friar Hauteyn had a quarrel with Judge Paston and the Priory of Bromholm, and pretended a claim on Paston's manor of Oxnead.

[6] Abbey of St Benet at Holme.

[7] Writs were carried in special boxes.

well done to beware at London, in dread if he bring any syse [1] at Saint Margaret's time.[2]

I can no more, but Almighty God be our good Lord, who have you ever in keeping. Written at Oxnead in great haste, on the Saturday next after Midsummer.

By your Mother,
AGNES PASTON

[1449]

15. A COUSIN'S ADVICE

To my Cousin John Paston be this Letter delivered

TRUSTY and well beloved Cousin, I commend me to you, desiring to hear of your welfare and good speed in your matters, the which I pray God send you to his plesaunce and to your heart's ease.

Cousin, I let you weet that Scroope [3] hath been in this Country to see my Cousin [4] your Sister, and he hath spoken with my Cousin your Mother, and she desireth of him that he should shew you the Indentures made between the Knight that hath his Daughter and him, whether that Scroope, if he were married and fortuned to have children, if those children should inherit his land, or his Daughter, the which is married.

Cousin, for this cause take good heed to his Indentures, for he is glad to show you them, or whom ye will assign with you; and he saith to me he is the last in the [en]tail of his livelihood, the which is 350 marks [5] and better for he hath taken an account of his livelihood divers times; and Scroope saith to me if he be married and have a Son, an heir, his Daughter that is married shall have of his livelihood 50 marks and no more; and therefore, Cousin, me seemeth he were good for my Cousin your Sister without that ye might get her a better; and if ye can get a better I would advise you to labour it in as short time as ye may goodly, for she was never in so great sorrow as she is now a days, for she may not speak with no man, whosoever come, ne not may

[1] Writ of Assize. [2] July 20. [3] Stephen Scrope (see Letter 14)
[4] Used for any near relative. [5] £234 6*s*. 8*d*.

see nor speak with any man, nor with servants of her Mother's, but that she beareth her an hand [1] otherwise than she meaneth; and she hath since Easter the most part been beaten once in the week or twice, and sometimes twice on a day, and her head broken in two or three places. Wherefore, Cousin, she hath sent to me by Friar Newton in great counsel, and prayeth me that I would send to you a Letter of her heaviness, and pray you to be her good brother, as her trust is in you; and she saith if ye may see by his Evidences that his children and hers may inherit, and she to have reasonable jointure, she hath heard so much of his birth and his conditions, that, and ye will, she will have him, whether that her mother will or will not, notwithstanding it is told her his person is simple, for she saith men shall have the more duty [2] of her, if she rule her to him as she ought to do.

Cousin, it is told me there is a goodly man in your Inn, of the which the father died lately, and if ye think that he were better for her than Scroope, it would be laboured,[3] and give Scroope a goodly answer, that he be not put off till ye be sure of a better; for he said when he was with me but if he have some comfortable answer of you, he will no more labour in this matter, because he might not see my Cousin your Sister, and he saith, he might have seen her and she had been better than she is; and that causeth him to deem that her mother was not well willing and so have I sent my Cousin your mother word; wherefore, Cousin, think on this matter, for sorrow often time causeth women to beset them otherwise than they should do, and if she were in that case, I wot well ye would be sorry: Cousin, I pray you burn this Letter, that your men nor none other men see it; for and my Cousin your Mother knew that I had sent you this Letter, she should never love me. No more I write to you at this time, but Holy Ghost have you in keeping. Written in haste, on Saint Peter's day,[4] by candle light.

By your Cousin,

ELIZABETH CLERE

[1449]

[1] Accuses her wrongly.

[2] Respect.

[3] Tried.

[4] June 29,

16. ELIZABETH UNHAPPY

To my right worshipful husband John Paston, be this delivered in haste

RIGHT worshipful husband, I recommend me to you, praying you to weet that I spake yesterday with my sister, and she told me that she was sorry that she might not speak with you ere ye yede [1]; and she desired, if it pleased you, that ye should give the Gentleman, that ye know of, such language as he might feel by you, that ye will be well willing to the matter that ye know of; for she told me that he hath said before this time that he conceived that ye have set but little thereby; wherefore she prayeth you that ye will be her good brother, and that ye might have a full answer at this time whether it shall be yea or nay; for her mother hath said to her since that ye ridden hence, that she hath no fantasy therein, but that it shall come to a jape [2]; and saith to her that there is good craft in daubing; and hath such language to her that she thinketh right strange, and so that she is right weary thereof; wherefore she desireth the rather to have a full conclusion therein. She saith her full trust is in you, and as ye do therein, she will agree her thereto.

Master Brackley [3] was here yesterday to have spoken with you; I spake with him, but he would not tell me what his errand was.

It is said here that the Sessions shall be at Thetford on Saturday next coming, and there shall be my Lord of Norfolk and others with great people, as it is said.

Other tidings have we none yet, the blissful Trinity have you in his keeping. Written at Norwich on the Tuesday next before Candlemas.[4]

I pray you that you will vouchsafe to remember to purvey a thing for my neck, and to do make my girdle.

Yours

MARGARET PASTON

[1452]

[1] Left. [2] To nothing.

[3] John Brackley, of the Convent of Grey Friars at Norwich, a notable preacher. [4] February 2.

17. BUILDING AT CAISTER. ELIZABETH STILL UNMARRIED

To my right worshipful husband, John Paston, be this delivered in haste

RIGHT worshipful husband, I recommend me to you, desiring to hear of your welfare; Praying you to weet that Sir Thomas Howes hath purveyed four Dormants [1] for the draught Chamber, and the Malthouse, and the Brewery, whereof he hath bought three, and the fourth, that shall be the longest and greatest of all, he shall have from Heylesdon, which he saith my master Fastolf shall give me, because my chamber shall be made therewith. As for laying of the said Dormants, they shall be laid this next week because of the Malthouse, and as for the remanant I trow it shall abide till ye come home, because I can neither be purveyed of posts, nor of boards, not yet.

I have taken the measure in the draught chamber, there as ye would your coffers and your Cowntewery [2] should be set for the while, and there is no space beside the bed, though the bed were removed to the door, for to set both your Board and your Coffers there, and to have space to go and sit beside; wherefore I have purveyed that ye shall have the same draught chamber that ye had before, there as ye shall lye to yourself; and when your gear is removed out of your little house, the door shall be locked, and your bags laid in one of the great Coffers, so that they shall be safe, I trust. . . .

My Mother prayeth you for to remember my Sister, and to do your part faithfully ere ye come home to help to get her a good marriage; it seemeth by my mother's language that she would never so fain to have be delivered of her as she will now.

I was told here that Knivet the heir is for to marry; both his wife and child be dead, and it was told here; wherefore she would that ye should enquire whether it be so or no, and what his livelihood is, and if ye think that it be for to do, to let him be spoken with thereof.

[1] Beams.

[2] His counter-board, with a device to help the reckoning of figures. A man's money-chest was usually in his bedroom.

I pray you that ye be not strange [1] of writing of Letters to me betwixt this and that ye come home, if I might I would have every day one from you. The blessed Trinity have you in his keeping. Written at Norwich, on the Tuesday next after the Conversion [of] Saint Paul.[2]

By yours,

[1453] MARGARET PASTON

18. TRYING FOR SIR WILLIAM OLDHALL

This Letter be delivered to John Paston dwelling in the Inner Inn of the Temple at London, in haste

I GREET you well and let you weet, that this day I was with my Daughter your wife, and she was in good heel [3] at the making of this letter, thanked be God! and she let your Sister and me weet of a letter which ye sent her, that ye have been laboured to for Sir William Oldhall [4] to have your Sister, and desiring in the said letter to have an answer in short time, how she will be demeaned in this matter.

Your Sister recommendeth her to you, and thanketh you heartily that ye will remember her, and let her have knowledge thereof, and prayeth you that ye will do your endeavour to bring it to a good conclusion, for she saith to me, that she trusteth that ye will do so, that it shall be both for her worship and profit; and, as for me, if ye can think that his Land standeth clear, in as much as I feel your Sister well willed thereto, I hold me well content.

And as for the Obligation of the Parson of Marlingford, which I sent you by John Newman, I pray you let it be sued; and as for the Parson and Lyndesey they be accorded, and God have you in his keeping, and send you his blessing and mine. Written at Norwich on Pulver-Wednesday.[5]

By your Mother,

[1454] AGNES PASTON

[1] Chary. [2] January 25. [3] Health.

[4] A prominent Yorkist, Speaker of the 1450 Parliament and owner of much property in Norfolk.

[5] Ash Wednesday.

19. JOHN CLOPTON'S SUIT[1]

Unto [my] right reverend Sir, and my good Master, John Paston

RIGHT worthy and worshipful Sir, and my right good master, I recommend me unto you, thanking you evermore of your great gentleness and good masterhood shewed unto me at all times, and specially now to my heart's ease, which on my part cannot be rewarded, but my simple service is ever ready at your commandment; furthermore as for the matter that ye weet of, I have laboured to my father that your intent as for the jointure shall be fulfilled; and Sir I beseech you since I do my part to fulfil your will, that ye will show me your good masterhood in her chamber[2] as my full trust is, insomuch that it shall nought hurt you nor none of yours, and the profit thereof shall be unto the avail of my mistress your sister, and to me, and to none other creature.

And also my mistress your mother shall not be charged with her board after the day of the marriage, but I to discharge her of her person; and to ease me, that hath her chamber, may be none contradiction.

And Sir I am ready, and always will to perform that I have said unto you, etc.

Furthermore liketh you to weet, I was on Thursday last past at Cavendish to deliver an estate to Wentworth in the land that was my brother Cavendish's, as I told you when I was last with you, and there I spake with Crane, and he besought me that I would send over to my mistress your mother for his excuse, for he might not be with her at this time; but on the Saturday in Easter-week he will not fail to be with her, so he counselled me that I and my brother [-in-law] Denton should meet with him there, and so without your better advice, I and my brother purpose us to be

[1] John Clopton, Sheriff of Norfolk (1451–2). This suit came to nothing.

[2] Perhaps it means, some Expenses for the accommodation of the Bride. [F.] It was a very usual arrangement for a parent to lodge and board a newly married couple for the first year, or even longer, as the equivalent of a dowry. Clopton apparently asks that Elizabeth, should he marry her, may have some outfit instead. [Gr.]

with you there at that time, for the sooner, the lever me, for, as to my conceit, the days be waxed wonderly long in a short time, wherefore I beseech you send me your advice how ye will have me ruled, etc.

No more I write to you at this present time, but beseeching you to recommend [me] in the lowliest wise, and the Trinity preserve you body and soul.

Written with my chancery hand in right great haste on the Friday before Palm Sunday.

Your
JOHN CLOPTON

[1454]

20. A MARRIAGE SETTLEMENT

Marriage Articles betwixt Agnes Paston, etc., on the one part and William Clopton, Esq., on the other part

THIS Indenture, made betwixt Agnes that was the wife of William Paston, John Paston her son, and John Damme [1] on the one part, and William Clopton, Esquire, on the other part, witnesseth that accord is taken atween the said parties, that John Clopton, son and heir of the said William Clopton, by the grace of God shall wed Elizabeth the daughter of the said Agnes, for which marriage the said Agnes, etc. shall pay to the said John Clopton 400 marks [2] in hand of lawful money of England, and over that if the said marriage be holden with the said Agnes, the said Agnes shall bear the costages thereof the day of the wedding, with such chambering as shall be to the pleasure of the said Agnes; And the said William Clopton shall do [3] his Foeffees make a lawful estate to the said William of lands, tenements, rents, and services to the yearly value of 40*l.* over all charges borne, to have and hold to him [for the] term of his life without impeachment of waste, the remainder thereof to the said John and Elizabeth, and to his heirs male of her body lawfully begotten, without impeachment of waste, within twelve days after the said wedding.

[1] A friend of the Pastons, Burgess in Parliament for the City of Norwich. He acts as Trustee.

[2] £266 13*s.* 4*d.*

[3] Ensure that.

And over that, within the said twelve days the said John shall do lawful estate to be made to the said William of lands, tenements, rents, and services to the yearly value of 40 marks over all charges borne to have and hold to the said William [for] term of his life, without impeachment of waste, the remainder thereof to the said Elizabeth to have and hold to her [for] term of her life, without impeachment of waste.

Also it is accorded that the said William shall make estate of all the residue of his lands which he is seized of, or any other man to his use to such persons as the said John shall name, to the use of the said John.

Also the said John Clopton shall do lawful estate to be made to the said Elizabeth of lands, tenements, rents, and services to the yearly value of 30*l.* over all charges borne, to have and hold to her during the life of the said William.

And moreover the said John promiseth and ensureth by the faith of his body that he shall leave, over the 40*l.* worth land abovesaid, to his heirs and issue male of the body of the said Elizabeth begotten, lands in fee simple or in tail to the yearly value of 40 marks in case the same male issue be governed to the said John as the son oweth to be to the father. And, etc.

[1454?]

21. GREY OF RUTHYN [1] OFFERS HELP

To my trusty and well beloved John Paston, Esquire, be this Letter delivered

TRUSTY and well beloved Friend, I commend me to you, certifying you that and your Sister be not yet married, I trust to God I know that where she may be married to a gentleman of 300 marks [2] of livelihood, the which is a great gentleman born, and of good blood, and if ye think that I shall labour any farther therein,

[1] Edmund, Lord Grey of Ruthyn, one of the most violent of the nobility; betrayed Henry VI at Northampton; created Earl of Kent by Edward IV.

[2] Two hundred pounds.

I pray you send me word by the bringer of this Letter, for I have spoken with the parties, and they have granted me that they will proceed no farther therein till I speak with them again, and therefore I pray you send me word in haste how that ye will be disposed therein, and God have you in his keeping. Written at Ampthill, the 11th day of July last past.

By EDMOND GREY, LORD OF HASTYNGS,
WAIFFORD, and RUTHYN

[1454]

22. JOHN PASTON'S REPLY

The Lord Grey

RIGHT worshipful and my right good Lord, I recommend me to our Lordship, and whereas it pleased your Lordship to direct your Letter to me for a marriage for my poor Sister to a Gentleman of your knowledge of 300 marks livelihood, in case she were not married; wherefore I am greatly bound to do your lordship service; for sooth my Lord she is not married, nor insured to no man; there is and hath been, divers times and late, communication of such marriages with divers gentlemen not determined as yet, and whether the gentleman that your Lordship meaneth of be one of them or nay I doubt; and whereas your said Letter specifieth that I should send you word whether I thought you should labour farther in the matter or nay; in that my Lord I dare not presume to write so to you without I know the gentleman's name; notwithstanding, my Lord, I shall take upon me with the advice of other of her friends, that she shall neither be married nor insured to no creature, nor farther proceed in no such matter before the feast of the Assumption of our Lady [1] next coming, during which time your Lordship may send me, if it please you, certain information of the said gentleman's name, and of the place and country where his livelihood lieth, and whether he hath any children; and after I shall demean me in the matter as your Lordship shall be pleased; for in good faith, my Lord, it were to me great joy that my said poor sister were, according to her poor

[1] August 15.

degree, married by your advice, trusting then that ye would be her good Lord.

Right worshipful and my right good Lord I beseech Almighty God to have you in his keeping. Written at Norwich, the 15th day of July.

This letter, being only a Copy, has no concluding Subscription. [F.]

[1454]

23. WILLIAM PASTON'S OPINION

To my right worshipful brother John Paston, be this delivered

RIGHT worshipful brother I recommend me to you, desiring to hear of your welfare. Billing the Serjeant [1] hath been in his country, and he came to London this week; he sent for me and asked me how I fared; I told him here is Pestilence; and said I fared the better [that] he was in good health for it was noised that he was dead; a took me to him, and asked how my Sister did, and I answered, well, never better; he said he was with the Lord Grey, [2] and they talked of a gentleman which is Ward to my Lord, I remember he said it was Harry Grey that they talked of; and my Lord said, " I was busy within this few days to a married him to a gentlewoman in Norfolk, that shall have 400 marks to her marriage, and now he will not by me, for 400 marks would do me ease, and now he would have his marriage money himself, and therefore, quoth he, he shall marry himself for me." [3]

These words had my Lord to Billing, as he told me, he understood that my Lord laboured for his own avail; and counselled to bid her be wise; and I thanked him for his good counsel.

I sent you an answer of your Letter of Sir John Fastolf's coming home as he told me himself, nevertheless he bode longer than he said himself he should a do.

[1] Thomas Billing, afterwards Chief Justice of the King's Bench.

[2] Lord Grey of Ruthyn (see Letter 21).

[3] *I.e.*, Lord Grey meant to pocket Elizabeth's dowry, but his ward refused consent—so the marriage was off.

He told me he should make an end betwixt Scroop [1] and my Sister while he is in Norfolk; many would it should not prove, for they say it is an unlikely marriage.

In case Cressener be talked of any more, he is counted a gentlemanly man and a worshipful, ye know who is most worshipful better than I; at the reverence of God draw to some conclusion, it is time.

My Lord Chancellor [2] come not here, since I came to London, neither my Lord of York.

My Lord of Canterbury [3] hath received his Cross, and I was with him in the King's Chamber when he made his homage; I told Harry Wilton the demeaning betwixt the King and him, it were too long to write. . . .

Here is great Pestilence, I purpose to flee into the Country. My Lord of Oxford is come again fro the sea, and he hath gotten him little thank in this country; much more thing I would write to you, but I lack leisure.

Harry Wilton saw the King. My Lord of Ely hath done his fealty. God have you in his blessed keeping.

Written at London, on the Friday before our Lady's-day the nativity [4] in great haste. I pray recommend me to my Sister and to my Cousin Clere.

By your Brother

[1454] WILLIAM PASTON [5]

24. ELIZABETH MARRIED [6]

To my right worshipful Mother, Agnes Paston

RIGHT worshipful and my most entirely beloved mother, in the most lowly manner I recommend me unto your good mother-

[1] Stephen Scrope (see Letter 14).

[2] Richard Neville, Earl of Salisbury. Lord Chancellor, 1454.

[3] Thomas Bourchier, translated from Ely to Canterbury, April 1454.

[4] September 8.

[5] William Paston, the fourth son of the Judge, was a steady Lancastrian and had a pardon for all treasons, etc., under the great seal, dated July 16, 1468.

[6] In 1459 Elizabeth married Robert Poynings, younger brother of Robert, Lord Poynings. He was deeply concerned in Cade's Rebellion.

hood, beseeching you daily and nightly of your motherly blessing, evermore desiring to hear of your welfare and prosperity, the which I pray God to continue and increase to your heart's desire; and if it liked your motherhood to hear of me and how I do at the making of this letter, I was in good health of body thanked be Jesu; and as for my master, my best beloved that ye call, and I must needs call him so now, for I find none other cause, and as I trust to Jesu never shall, for he is full kind unto me, and is as busy as he can to make me sure of my Jointure, whereto he is bound in a Bond of a thousand pounds to you mother, and to my brother John, and to my brother William, and to Edmund Clere, the which needed so such bond; wherefore, I beseech your good mother, as our most singular trust is in your good motherhood, that my master, my best beloved, fail not of the hundred marks [1] at the beginning of this term, the which ye promised him to his marriage, with the remanant of the money of father's will; for I have promised faithfully to a Gentleman called Bain, that was one of my best beloved's sureties, and was bound for him in two hundred pounds, of which he rehearseth for to receive at the beginning of this term one hundred and twenty pounds, and if he fail thereof at this time, he will claim the whole of us, the which were to us too great an hurt; and he cannot make an end with none of his other sureties without this said silver, and that can my brother John tell you well enough and it lusteth him to do so, and in all other things. As to my Lady Pool, with whom I sojourned, that ye will be my tender and good mother, that she may be paid for all the costs done to me before my marriage, as ye wrote unto my brother John, that it should have been so; and that it please your good motherhood to give credence to William Worcester [2]; and Jesu for his great mercy save you; Written at London, the Wednesday the 3 day of January.

By your humble Daughter,

ELIZABETH PONYNGGS

[1459]

[1] £66 13*s*. 4*d*.

[2] William Worcester negotiated the marriage, at a fee of ten shillings.

25. ELIZABETH WIDOWED

To the worshipful Sir John Paston, Knight, be this delivered in haste

WORSHIPFUL and with all mine heart entirely well-beloved Nephew, I recommend me to you, desiring to hear of your prosperity and welfare, which I pray Almighty God maintain and increase to his pleasure, and your heart's desire, thanking God of your amending and health. Furthermore certifying you that Sir Robert Fynes hath done great hurt in the livelihood which pertained to my Husband and me, in the Shire of Kent, wherein William Keene and other persons are enfeoffed, and greatly troubleth it, and receiveth the issues and profits of great part of them, and as of my said Husband's livelihood, as well in the same Shire as in other Shires.

Beside mine jointure, my said Husband, when he departed towards the field of St Alban's,[1] made and ordained his will, that I should have the rule of all his livelihood, and of Edward his son and mine, and to take the issues and profits of the said livelihood, to the finding of his and mine said son, to pay his debts, and to keep the right and title of the same livelihood, which I might not accordingly occupy for Sir Edward Poynings, mine said Husband's Brother, and so since my said Husband's departing, I assigned that the said Sir Edward for certain years should have and take the revenues of the Manors at Westwood, Eastwell, Loneland, Horsemonden, Totingdon, Eccles, Standon, and Combesden, parcel of the said livelihood, which are clearly yearly worth 76*l.* 13*s.* 4*d.* to the intent that the said Sir Edward should pay mine Husband's debts, for he would not suffer me to be in rest without that he might have a rule in the livelihood; and after the said assignment made, the said Robert Fynes, contrary to truth, and without cause of right, interrupted me and the said Sir Edward, as well of and in the said manors as of other manors underwritten, whereupon the same Sir Edward sued unto the King's Highness,[2] and had the King's honourable Letters under

[1] Robert Poynings was slain in the second battle of St Albans, 1461. The Earl of Northumberland married his sister and claimed his property.

[2] Edward IV.

his signet, directed to the said Sir Robert Fynes, the tenour whereof I send unto you herein enclosed; and as for residue of the livelihood of mine said Husband's and mine, within the same Shire of Kent, wherein the said William Keene and other are enfeoffed, that is to say, the manor of Tyrlingham, Wolverton, Halton, Newington, Bartram, Rokesley and Northcray, with the appurtenances, I of them, by mine said Husband's will, should have residue, and take the issues and profits of them, contrary to right and conscience, taking away my right, and breaking my said Husband's will, the said Robert Fynes hath done great waste and hurt there, and long time hath taken up the revenues and profits of the same, where thorough I have not my right, and the said will may not be performed.

Wherefore I heartily pray you that ye will labour unto the King's Highness, that it liketh him address his honourable Letters to be directed to the said Robert Fynes, discharging him utterly of the menurance,[1] occupation, and receipt of the revenues of the said manors of Tyrlingham and other, according to the tenour of the letters laboured by Sir Edward, for the manors assigned to him from the King's Highness, directed to the same Robert Fynes, or straiter if it may be, and that I and mine assigns may peaceably re-enjoy them; and if any person would attempt to do the contrary, that a commandment, if it please the King's Highness, by him might be given to my Lord Chancellor to seal writings sufficient with his Great Seal, in aiding and assisting me and mine assigns in the same.

And as for the manors of Easthall, Faulkham, Asslie, Chelsfield, with the appurtenances in the said Shire of Kent, whereof my Husband at his departure was seised,[2] and my Son since, unto the time that the Earl of Kent [3] without any inquisition or title of right for the King, by colour of the King's Letters Patents, entered into them, and him thereof put out, and now my Lord of Essex occupieth them in like manner and form; if any remedy therein will be had, I pray you attempt it.

Also, furthermore I heartily pray you that if any general pardon

[1] Tenure. [2] Possessed.

[3] Lord Grey of Ruthyn (Kent) and Henry, Lord Bourchier (Essex) were creations of Edward IV.

be granted, that I may have one for John Dane my servant, whom the said Robert Fynes of great malice had endicted of felony, and that ye secretly labour this, and send me an answer in writing in as goodly haste as ye may; as soon as it may please you to send me parcels of costs and expenses ye bear and pay for the said causes, I will truly content you it of the same, and over that reward you to your pleasure, by the grace of Jesu, who have you in his blessed keeping. Written in Southwark, the 15th day of December,

By your aunt

ELIZABETH POYNINGS

[1468]

26. ELIZABETH REMARRIED [1]

To my Right Worshipful and heartily beloved Nephew, John Paston, Esq. [*her younger nephew*]

RIGHT worshipful and my right heartily beloved nephew I recommend me to you; and whereas ye desire me to send you word, whether my brother John Paston, your father, was with my father and his, whom God assoil! during his last sickness and at the time of his decease at St Bride's or not.

Nephew, I ascertain you upon my faith and poor honour, that I was 14, 15 year, or 16 year old, and at St Bride's with my father and my mother, when my father's last sickness took him, and till he was deceased; and I dare depose before any person honourable, that when my father's last sickness took him, my brother your father was in Norfolk, and he came not to London till after that my father was deceased; and that can Sir William Cooting and James Gresham record, for they both were my father's clerks at that time; and I remember and wot well, that James Gresham was with my father at St Bride's during all his sickness, and at his decease, and this I will witness while I live for a truth, as knoweth God, whom I beseech to preserve you and yours.

And, Nephew, I pray you recommend [me] to my niece your wife, whom I would be glad to see once again in London, where

[1] Elizabeth, before 1472, married Sir George Browne, of Beechworth, Surrey, a gentleman of the household of Edward IV.

this bill was written, signed with mine hand and sealed with my seal (the Thursday next before Whitsunday, the second year of King Richard the Third), the 23rd day of September, the first year of the reign of King Henry the VIIth.

Your loving Aunt,

ELIZABETH BROWNE [1]

[1485]

[1] Elizabeth, now the wealthy woman of the family, died in 1487.

III. *Sir John and his Brother*

27. JOHN THE ELDEST [1] AT THE COURT OF EDWARD IV

To my right reverend and worshipful Father John Paston, Esquire, dwelling in Hellesdon, be this letter delivered in haste

MOST reverend and worshipful Father, I recommend me heartily, and submit me lowlily to your good fatherhood, beseeching you for charity of your daily blessing; I beseech you to hold me excused that I sent to you none erst [2] no writing, for I could not speed to mine intent, that ye sent to me for. I have laboured daily my Lord of Essex, Treasurer of England, to have moved the King, both of the Manor [of] Dedham, and of the Bill, copied of the Court Roll, every morning afore he went to the King, and often times enquired of him, and he had moved the King in these matters; he answered me nay, saying it was no time and said he would it were as fain sped as I myself; so oft times delaying me that in truth I thought to have sent you word, that I feeled by him that he was not willing to move the King therein; nevertheless I laboured to him continually, and prayed Berners his man to remember him of it. I told often times to my said Lord that I had a man tarrying in town, that I should have sent to you for other sundry matters, and he tarryed for nothing, but that I might send you by him an answer of the said matters; other times beseeching him to speed me in those matters for this cause that ye should think no default in me for remembering in the said matters.

And now of late, I remembering him of the same matter, inquired if he had moved the King's Highness therein, and he answered me, that he had felt and moved the King therein, rehearsing the King's answer therein, how that when he had

[1] John, the eldest son of John Paston and Margaret, was knighted by Edward IV in 1463, became head of the family on the death of his father in 1466, and died, unmarried, in 1479.

[2] No earlier.

moved the King in the said manor of Dedham, beseeching him to be your good Lord therein, considering the service and true heart that ye have done, and owe to him, and in especial the right that ye have thereto; he said, he would be your good Lord therein, as he would be to the poorest man in England, he would hold with you in your right, and as for favour, he will not be understood that he shall show favour more to one man than to another, not to one in England.

And as for the Bill, copied of the court roll, when he moved to him of it, he smiled, and said, that such a bill there was, saying that ye would have oppressed sundry of your countrymen of worshipful men, and therefore he kept it still, nevertheless he said he should look it up in haste, and ye should have it.

Berners undertook to me twice or thrice, that he should so have remembered his Lord and Master, that I should have had it within two or three days; he is often times absent, and therefore I have it not yet, when I can get it, I shall send it you, and of the King's mouth, his name that take it him.

I send you home Peacock again, he is not for me; God send grace that he may do you good service, that by estimation is not likely; ye shall have knowledge afterward how he hath demeaned him here with me; I would, saving your displeasure, that ye were delivered of him, for he shall never do you profit nor worship.

I suppose ye understand that the money that I had of you at London may not endure with me till that the King go into Wales and come again, for I understand it shall be long ere he come again, wherefore I have sent to London to mine Uncle Clement to get an hundred Shillings of Christopher Hanson your servant, and send it me by my said Servant, and mine harness with it, which I left at London to make clean.

I beseech you not to be displeased with it, for I could make none other chevisance [1] but I should have borrowed it of a strange man, some of my fellows, who I suppose should not like you, and ye heard of it another time.[2] I am in surety whereas I shall have another man in the stead of Peacock.

My Lord of Essex saith he will do as much for you as for any

[1] Arrangement; borrowing.

[2] Which you would dislike if you heard, etc.

Esquire in England, and Berners his man telleth me, saying, "your Father is much beholden to my Lord, for he loveth him well;" Berners moved me once, and said that ye must needs do somewhat for my Lord and his; and I said I wist well, that ye would do for him that lay in your power; and he said that there was a little money betwixt you and a Gentleman of Essex called Dyrward, saying, that there is as much between my said Lord and the said Gentleman, of the which money he desireth your part.[1]

It is talked here how that ye and Howard [2] should have striven together on the Shire day, and one of Howard's men should have stricken you twice with a dagger, and so ye should have been hurt, but for a good doublet, that ye had on at that time; blessed be God, that ye had it on. No more I write to your good fatherhood at this time, but Almighty God have you in his keeping, and send you victory of your Enemies, and worship increasing to your life's ending.

Written at Lewes, on Saint Bartholomew's Even.[3]

By your Servant and Elder Son,

JOHN PASTON

[1461]

28. YOUNG JOHN AT COURT

To my right worshipful and reverend Master John Paston, at Norwich

RIGHT worshipful and my right honourable Master, I recommend me lowly to you, and please your mastership to weet that my Master Clement your brother and Playters [4] wrote a letter to my master your son [5] yesterday, the tenor of which was how ye were entreated there, and as ye desired me, so I informed them the matter along, for they wist not of it till I told them, and they wrote the more plainerly in as much as a worshipful man rode the same day, and bare the letter to my said master, your son. . . .

[1] That you should pay.
[2] Sir John Howard (Duke of Norfolk, 1483).
[3] August 23.
[4] Servant to the Pastons.
[5] John, the eldest son.

Item, Sir this day came one John Waynfleet from the King strait way, and he is of mine acquaintance; and he told me there was no voice nor speaking about the King of that matter, and I told him all the matter along how ye were entreated, which he will put in remembrance in any place that he cometh in in Suffolk or Essex as he goeth homewards, for he oweth no good will to your adversary. And the said Waynfleet told me that he knoweth for certain the King cometh not into Norfolk till he hath been upon the Marches of Wales,[1] and so there is no certainty of his coming this many days; he told me he left the King with a small fellowship about him.

And I enquired [of] him of the guiding of my master, your son, which he commended greatly, and said that he stood well in conceit, and daily should increase; and he was well in acquaintance, and beloved with gentlemen about the King; but he said there shall nothing hurt him, but your straitness of money to him, for without he have money in his purse, so as he may reasonably spend among them, else they will not set by him; and there be Gentlemen's sons of less reputation, that hath money more liberal ten times than he hath; and so in that the said Waynfleet said it were full necessary for you to remember, etc.

As for tidings here be none new, etc. I trust I shall bring you a letter from my Master your son, or than [2] I come, for which I shall rather than fail abide one day the longer; and Jesu have you, my right honourable Master, in his merciful governance, and preserve you from adversity. Written at London on St Bartholomew's even.

I can speak with no man but that think the guiding of your adversary [3] hath been in many causes right strange, and as it is supposed, that he shall understand at the Parliament, but for God's sake have men enough about you, for ye understand his unmannerly disposition.

Your beadsman and servant,

John Russe [4]

[1461]

[1] Edward IV went to Wales in the autumn of 1461.
[2] When.
[3] Howard (see Letter 27).
[4] One of Paston's servants.

29. UNCLE CLEMENT'S OPINION

To his right reverend and worshipful Brother
John Paston

RIGHT reverend and worshipful brother I recommend me to your good brotherhood, desiring to hear of your welfare and good prosperity, the which I pray God increase to his pleasure and your heart's ease, certifying you that I have spoken with John Russe, and Playters spoke with him both [1] on Friday before Saint Bartholomew; he told us of Howard's guiding, which made us right sorry, till we heard the conclusion that ye had none harm.

Also I understand by William Peacock that my Nephew had knowledge thereof also upon Saturday next before Saint Bartholomew, in the King's House; notwithstanding upon the same day Playters and I wrote Letters unto him, rehearsing all the matter for cause if there were any questions moved to him thereof, that he should tell the truth, in case that the questions were moved by any worshipful man, and [we] named my Lord Bourchier [2] for my Lord Bourchier was with the King at that time.

I feel by William Peacock that my Nephew is not yet verily acquainted in the King's House; nor with the Officers of the King's House; he is not taken as none of that House, for the Cooks be not charged to serve him, nor the Sewer [3] to give him no dish, for the Sewer will not take no men no dishes 'till they be commanded by the Controller; also he is not acquainted with nobody but with Wykes,[4] and Wykes had told him that he would bring him to the King, but he hath not yet done so; wherefore it were best for him to take his leave and come home, till ye had spoken with some body to help him forth, for he is not bold enough to put forth himself; but then I considered that if he should now come home, the King would think that when he should do him any service, it were that then ye would have him home, the which should cause him not to be had in favour; and

[1] Also. [2] Eldest son of the Earl of Essex and cousin to Edward IV.

[3] An officer who had the ordering of the dishes, etc.

[4] An usher of the King's chamber and a friend and cousin of John Paston's.

also men would think that he were put out of service. Also William Peacock telleth me that his money is spent, and not riotously, but wisely and discreetly, for the costs is greater in the King's House when he rideth [1] than ye weened it had been, as William Peacock can tell you; and therefore we must get him one hundred Shillings at the least as by William Peacock's saying, and yet that will be too little, and I wot well we cannot get forty pence of Christopher Hanson, so I shall be fain to lend it him of mine own silver; if I knew verily your intent were that he should come home, I would send him none; therefore I will do as me thinketh ye should be best pleased, and that me thinketh is to send him the silver; therefore I pray you [as] hastily as ye may send me again five marks [2] and the remanent I trow I shall get upon Christopher Hanson and Loket. I pray you send me it as hastily as ye may, for I shall leave my self right bare, and I pray you send me a Letter how ye will that he shall be demeaned. Written on Tuesday after Saint Bartholomew, etc. Christus vos conservet!

By

CLEMENT PASTON

[1461]

30. JOHN STILL SHORT OF MONEY

To mine right reverend and worshipful Father John Paston, being in the Inner Temple

RIGHT reverend and worshipful Father, I recommend me unto you, beseeching you of your blessing and good fatherhood. Please it you to understand the great expense that I have daily travelling with the King, as the bearer hereof can inform you, and how long that I am like to tarry here in this country ere I may speak with you again, and how I am charged to have mine horse and harness ready, and in hasty wise, beseeching you to consider these causes, and so to remember me that I may have such things as I may do my master service with and pleasure, trusting in God it shall be

[1] Travels.

[2] £3 6*s*. 8*d*.

to your worship and to mine avail, in especial I beseech you, that I may be sure where to have money somewhat before Easter either of you, or by mine Uncle Clement when need is, of other causes the bearer hereof can inform you. No more to you at this time, but God have you in his keeping.

Written at Samford, the 13th day of March.

By your Son and Servant

JOHN PASTON, the older

[1462]

31. TREACLE OF GENOA

To Mistress Margaret Paston, be this delivered

PLEASE it you to weet that I send you by Barker, the bearer hereof, three treacle pots of Geane[1] as my Apothecary sweareth unto me, and moreover that they were never undone since they came from Geane, whereof ye shall take as many as pleaseth you, nevertheless my Brother John sent to me for two, therefore I must beseech you that he may have at the least one; there is one pot that is marked under the bottom two times, with these letters M. P. which pot I have best trust unto, and next him to the wry[2] pot, and I mistrust most the pot that hath a krott[3] above on the top, lest that he hath been undone; and also the other two pots be printed with the Merchant's mark two times over the covering and that other pot is but once marked but with one print, notwithstanding I had like oath and promise for one as well as for all.

JOHN PASTON

32. MARGARET PASTON'S ANXIETY

To my right worshipful Husband John Paston, be this Letter delivered in haste

RIGHT worshipful husband, I recommend me to you, please you to weet that I received a Letter from you on the Sunday next

[1] Genoa. [2] Crooked. [3] Small piece.

after Twelfth day,[1] which was sent by a Priest of St Gregory's parish of Norwich; and whereas ye marvelled I sent you no writings of such Letters as ye sent me before, I send you an answer of the substance of such matters as ye have written of to me before. And as touching the errands that ye sent to me for to do to Richard Calle,[2] I have done as ye commanded me to do, and called upon him therefore, both before your writing, and sithen [3]; he therefore have none excuse for default of leisure for he hath been but right little here since ye departed hence; he is out at this time, and when that he cometh home I shall make him make you a clear bill of the receipt of your livelihood,[4] and Fastolf's both; and I shall send you a clear bill of my receipts, and also of my payments out thereof again; and as for such errands that should be done to Sir Thomas Howes, I have shewed Richard Calle your writing, and told him your intent, as for such things as ye would he should say to him on his own head. Also I have done your errands to my mother and to my Cousin Clere [5] after your writing. Item, I have spoken to John Adam and to Playters of your intent of the last bill that ye sent me, and they say they will do after your intent as much as they may, and ye shall have an answer thereof in haste.

Item, Sir Robert Coniers dined with me this day, and shewed me a letter that came from the King to him, desiring him that he should await upon his well-beloved brother the Duke of Suffolk, at Norwich on Monday next coming, for to be at the Election of Knights of the Shire [6]; and he told me that every gentleman of Norfolk and Suffolk that are of any reputation hath writing from the King in likewise as he had. I feel him by his saying, that he is right well disposed to you ward; he saith there shall no man make him to be against you in no manner. . . .

I thank you heartily of your writing to me before that John Paston came home, for God knoweth I thought right long till I heard from you; I shall send word in writing of such tidings as we have here on Monday in haste. Dawbeney desireth to weet

[1] January 9.
[2] Bailiff to the Paston family.
[3] Since.
[4] Property.
[5] Elizabeth, widow of Robert Clere of Ormesby.
[6] Probably for the Parliament which met on April 29, 1463.

what time that it please you, that he should come again to you.

My mother and many other folks maketh much of your son John, the elder and [are] right glad of his coming home, and liketh right well his demeaning. Heydon's son [Harry] [1] hath borne out the side stoutly here this Christmas, and when that he rideth, he hath four or five men with him in Clothing [2]; but he hath but little favour in this country, but if it be of the Bishop and of the Prior of Norwich, the said Prior hath granted him the stewardship that his father had, he hath it under the Convent Seal, and Spilman [is] his tutor to learn him how he should be demeaned therein. It is said about Baconsthorp that Harry Heydon should have said, that it were well done that men of the Country should make ready their bald batts and their clouted shoon,[3] and go fetch home their Knights of Shire [Paston and] Berney; and it is promised him that he shall be met withal because of his language. Pray God send us a good world and a peaceable. I shall purvey for all things that ye have sent to me for, so that I ween ye shall be pleased. The blessed Trinity have you in his keeping. Written in haste, the Wednesday next before Saint Agnes.[4]

Your

MARGARET PASTON [5]

[1463]

33. SIR JOHN KEPT AT HOME

To my worshipful Master, Master Paston the eldest

RIGHT worshipful Master, I recommend me unto your Mastership, and of one matter at reverence of God take heed, for in truth I hear much talking thereof, and that is both in Norfolk, Suffolk, and Norwich among all men of worship, as well that love you as others, and that is of my master, your son Sir John,

[1] Son of John Heydon, Recorder of Norwich. [2] Livery.

[3] *Bald batts* seem to mean here ball batts, or batts to play at ball with. *Clouted shoon*, shoes shod with thin plates of iron. [F.]

[4] January 21.

[5] *N.B.* A part of the original letter is torn off, which makes it defective in two or three sentences. [F.]

because he is so at home, and none other wise set for.[1] Some say that ye and he both stand out of the King's good grace, and some say that ye keep him at home for niggardship, and will no thing ware [2] upon him, and so each man say his advice as it please him to talk; and I have enquired, and said the most cause is in part, for cause ye are so much out, that he is the rather at home for the safeguard of the coasts. But at the reverence of God, for eschewing of common language, see that he may worshipfully be set for, either in the King's service, or in marriage; for as for touching the Lady Chamberlayne [3] that matter is done for, I spake with the parson thereof, and I heard by him, that that matter will not pre.[4]

No more but God speed you as well in all matters, as I would ye should do, I beseech you that this letter be kept secret.

By your beadsman,

R. C. V. C.

[1463]

34. SIR JOHN RUNS AWAY FROM HOME

To my well-beloved Son, Sir John Paston, be this delivered in haste

I GREET you well, and send you God's blessing and mine, letting you weet that I have received a Letter from you whereby I conceive that ye think ye did not well that ye departed hence without my knowledge,[5] wherefore I let you weet I was right evil paid with you; your father thought, and thinketh yet, that I was assented to your departing, and that hath caused me to have great heaviness; I hope he will be your good father hereafter, if ye demean you well, and do as ye ought to do to him; and I charge you upon my blessing that in any thing touching your father that should be [to] his worship, profit, or avail, that ye do your devoir and diligent labour to the furtherance therein, as ye

[1] Provided for. [2] Spend.

[3] A wealthy widow, nearly double Sir John's age. [4] Proceed.

[5] Sir John had apparently left home without informing his mother of his intention, probably to join the King, Edward IV, in Yorkshire.

will have my good will, and that shall cause your father to be better father to you.

It was told me ye sent him a Letter to London; what the intent thereof was I wot not, but though he take it but lightly, I would ye should not spare to write to him again as lowly as ye can, beseeching him to be your good father; and send him such tidings as be in the country there ye be in, and that ye be ware of your expences better and [1] ye have been before this time, and be your own purse-bearer, I trow ye shall find it most profitable to you.

I would ye should send me word how ye do, and how ye have shifted for yourself since ye departed hence, by some trusty man, and that your father have no knowledge thereof; I durst not let him know of the last Letter that ye wrote to me, because he was so sore displeased with me at that time.

Item, I would ye should speak with Wykes,[2] and know his disposition to Jane Walsham, she hath said since he departed hence, but [3] she might have him, she would never [be] married, her heart is sore set on him; she told me that he said to her, that there was no woman in the world he loved so well; I would not he should jape [4] her, for she meaneth good faith; and if he will not have her, let me weet in haste, for I shall purvey for her in other wise.

As for your harness and geer that ye left here, it is in Daubeney's keeping, it was never removed since your departing, because that he had not the keys, I trow it shall apeyer,[5] but if it be taken heed at betimes; your father knoweth not where it is.

I sent your grey horse to Ruston to the farrier, and he saith he shall never be nought to ride, neither right good to plough nor to cart, he said he was splayed, and his shoulder rent from the body, I wot not what to do with him.

Your Grandam would fain hear some tidings from you; it were well done that ye sent a Letter to her how ye do, as hastily as ye may, and God have you in his keeping, and make you a good man, and give you grace to do well, as I would ye should do.

[1] Than.
[2] A servant of Paston's.
[3] Unless.
[4] Deceive.
[5] Deteriorate.

Written at Caister, the Tuesday next before Saint Edmund the King.[1]

Your Mother

MARGARET PASTON

[1463]

35. SIR JOHN AT HOME

To my right worshipful Husband John Paston, in haste

RIGHT worshipful husband, I recommend me unto you, pleaseth you to weet, that on Thursday last was, there were brought unto this town many Privy Seals, and one of them was indorsed to you and to five or six other Gentlemen; and another was sent unto your Son, and indorsed to himself alone, and assigned [2] within with the King's own hand; and so were but few that were sent, as it was told me; and also, there were more special terms in his than were in others; I saw a Copy of those that were sent unto other Gentlemen; the intent of the writing was, that they should be with the King at Leicester the 10th day of May, with as many persons defensibly arrayed, as they might according to their degree, and that they should bring with them for their expences for two months. . . .

I pray you that ye vouchsafe to send word in haste, how ye will that your Son be demeaned herein. Men think here, that be your well willers, that ye may no less do than to send him forth.

As for his demeaning since ye departed, in good faith, it hath been right good, and lowly, and diligent, in oversight of your servants, and other things, the which I hope ye would have been pleased with, and ye had been at home; I hope he will be well demeaned to please you hereafterward.

He desired Arblaster to be a mean [3] to you for him; and was right heavy of his demeaning to you, as I sent you word also by Arblaster, how I did to him after that ye were gone; and I beseech you heartily, that ye vouchsafe to be his good Father, for I hope he is chastised, and will be the worthier hereafter.

As for all other things at home, I hope that I and others shall

[1] November 20. [2] Signed. [3] Mediator.

do our part therein, as well as we may; but as for money it cometh but slowly, and God have you in his keeping, and send you good speed in all your matters.

Written in haste at Norwich on the Sunday next before the Ascension-day.

Sir, I would be right glad to hear some good tidings from you,

By yours,

MARGARET PASTON

[1463]

36. SIR JOHN APOLOGIZES

To my right worshipful Father, John Paston, Esquire, be this Letter delivered in hasty wise

RIGHT worshipful Sir, in the most lowly wise I commend me to your good fatherhood, beseeching you of your blessing; might it please your fatherhood to remember and consider the pain and heaviness that it hath been to me since your departing out of this country, here abiding till the time it please you to shew me grace, and till the time that by report my demeaning be to your pleasing; beseeching you to consider that I may not, nor have no mean to seek you as I ought to do, saving under this form, which I beseech you be not taken to no displeasure, nor am not of power to do any thing in this country for worship or profit of you, nor ease of your tenants which might and should be to your pleasing; wherefore I beseech you of your fatherly pity to tender the more this simple writing; as I shall out of doubt hereafter do that shall please you to the uttermost of my power and labour; and if there be any service that I may do, if it please you to command me, or if I may understand it, I will be as glad to do it as any thing earthly, if it were any thing that might be to your pleasing. And no more, but Almighty God have you in keeping. Written at Norwich, the 5th day of March.

By your elder Son,

JOHN PASTON

[1464]

37. JOHN THE YOUNGEST IN THE DUKE OF NORFOLK'S HOUSEHOLD

To my right reverend and worshipful Father, John Paston, be this delivered in haste

RIGHT reverend and worshipful Father, I recommend me unto you, beseeching you lowly of your blessing. Please it you to have knowledge, that my Lord is purposed to send for my Lady, and is like to keep his Christmas here in Wales; for the King hath desired him to do the same, wherefore I beseech you, that you would vouchsafe to send me some money by the bearer hereof: for, in good faith, as it is not unknown to you, that I had but two Nobles in my purse, which that Richard Calle took me by your commandment, when I departed from you out of Norwich.

The Bearer hereof should buy me a Gown with part of the money, if it please you to deliver him as much money as he may buy it with; for I have but one gown at Framlingham and another here, and that is my Livery Gown, and we must wear them every day for the more part, and one Gown without change will soon be done.

As for tidings, my Lord of Warwick yede forwards into Scotland, as on Saturday last past, with twenty thousand men, and Sir William Tunstall is taken with the garrison of Bamborough [1] and is like to be headed, and by the means of Sir Richard Tunstall his own brother.

As soon as I hear any more tidings, I shall send them you by the grace of God, who have you in his keeping. Written in haste at the Castle of the Holt,[2] upon Holymas day.[3]

Your Son and lowly Servant,

J. PASTON, Junior

[1462]

[1] Margaret of Anjou, coming from France in October 1462, besieged and captured Bamborough Castle, in Northumberland. Sir William Tunstall was in the garrison for King Edward; his brother, Sir Richard, was in Queen Margaret's army.

[2] Denbighshire.

[3] November 1.

38. COMMISSIONS FOR JOHN THE YOUNGEST

To my Mistress Margaret Paston, be this delivered in haste, at London [1]

AFTER all humble and most due recommendation, as lowly as I can, I beseech you of your blessing, please it you to weet that I have sent to my Father to have an answer of such matters as I have sent to him for in haste, of which matters the greatest of substance is for the Manor of Cotton, beseeching you to remember him of the same matter, that I may have an answer in the most hasty wise.

Also I pray you that mine Aunt Poynings [2] may be desired to send me an answer of such matters as she woteth of, by him that shall bring me an answer of the matter of Cotton.

Also Mother, I beseech you that there may be purveyed some mean that I might have sent me home by the same messenger two pair of Hose, one pair black, and another pair of russet, which be ready made for me at the Hosier's with the crooked back, next to the Black Friar's-Gate, within Ludgate; John Pamping [3] knoweth him well enough I suppose, and the black hose be paid for he will send me the russet unpaid for; I beseech you that this gear be not forgotten, for I have not an whole hose for to do on; I trow they shall cost both pair 8*s*.

My Brother, and my Sister Anne, and all the garrison of Hellesdon fare well, blessed be God, and recommend them to you ever each one.

I pray you visit the Rood of Northdoor [4] and St Saviour, at Bermondsey, among while ye abide in London, and let my Sister Margery go with you to pray to them that she may have a good Husband ere she come home again and now I pray you send us some tidings, as ye were wont to command me; and the Holy

[1] It appears that Margaret Paston was visiting her husband in the Fleet Prison, London; her sons holding Hellesdon at the time.

[2] Elizabeth Poynings.

[3] Paston's servant.

[4] The cross at the north door of St Paul's.

Trinity have you in keeping; and my fair Mistress of the Fleet. Written at Norwich, on Holy Rood Day.[1]

Your Son and lowly Servant

JOHN PASTON, the youngest

[1465]

39. ORDERS FROM THE DUKE OF NORFOLK

To our trusty and entirely beloved Servant John Paston, Esq. [*the youngest*]

The Duke of Norfolk

RIGHT well-beloved Servant, I greet you heartily well, certifying that we shall be at full age on Friday next coming, wherefore, well counselled by the Lords of our Counsel and other of our Counsel, that ye, one of our Servants of household, with others, be with us at London on Friday or Saturday next coming at the furthest to accompany us then to our worship, for we shall have then livery of our Lands and Offices, and that ye fail us not, as ye will have our good Lordship in time coming, and also that ye do warn our Feedmen and Servants, such as be nigh to you, that they be there then in our Livery. Written the 12th day of October.

NORFOLK

[1465]

40. A MOTHER'S ADVICE

To my right worshipful Master, Sir John Paston, Knight, be this Letter delivered in haste

I GREET you well, and send you God's blessing and mine, desiring you to send me word how that ye speed in your matters, for I think right long till I hear tidings from you; and in all wise I advise you for to beware that ye keep wisely your writings that be of charge, that it come not in their hands that may hurt you hereafter; your Father,[2] whom God assoil! in his trouble's

[1] September 14.

[2] John Paston, husband of Margaret, died in 1466, and was buried magnificently at Bromholm Priory.

season, set more by his writings and evidence than he did by any of his moveable goods; remember, that if they were had from you, ye could never get no more such as they be for your part, etc.

Item, I would ye should take heed that if any Process come out against me, or against any of those that were indicted afore the Coroner, that I might have knowledge thereof, and to purvey a remedy therefore.

Item, as for your Father's will, I would ye should take right good counsel therein, as I am informed it may be proved, though no man take no charge this twelvemonth; ye may have a Letter of administration to such as ye will, and administer the goods and take no charge; I advise you that ye in no wise take no charge thereof till ye know more than ye do yet, for ye may verily know, by that your Uncle William said to you and to me, that they will lay the charge upon you and me for more things than is expressed in your Father's will, the which should be too great for you or me to bear, but as for me I will not be too hasty to take it upon me I assure you; and at the reverence of God, speed your matters so this term, that we may be in rest hereafter, and let not for no labour for the season, and remember the great cost and charge that we have had hithertoward, and think verily it may not long endure; ye know what [money] ye left when ye were last at home, and weet it verily, there is no more in this country to bear out no charge with. I advise you to enquire wisely if ye can get any more there as ye be, for else by my faith, I fear else it will not be well with us; and send me word in haste how ye do, and whether ye have your last deeds that ye failed, for plainly they are not in this country; it is told me in counsel that Richard Calle hath near conquered your Uncle William with fair promise, touching his livelihood and other things, the which should prevail him greatly as he saith; beware of him and of his Fellow by mine advice. God send you good speed in all your matters. Written at Caister, the morrow next after Symon and Jude,[1] where as I would not be at this time but for your sake, so might I choose.

By your Mother

MARGARET PASTON

[1466]

[1] October 28.

41. ADVICE ON COURTING

To my Brother, John Paston

RIGHT worshipful and verily well-beloved Brother, I heartily commend me to you, thanking you of your labour and diligence that ye have in keeping of my place at Caister, so surely both with your heart and mind, to your great business and trouble; and I againward have had so little leisure that I have not sped but few of your errands, nor cannot before this time.

As for my Lady Boleyn's [1] disposition to you ward, I cannot in no wise find her agreeable that ye should have her daughter, for all the privy means that I could make, insomuch I had so little comfort by all the means that I could make, that I disdained in mine own person to commune with her therein; nevertheless I understand that she sayeth, " what if he and she can agree I will not let it, but I will never advise her thereto in no wise." And upon Tuesday last past she rode home into Norfolk; wherefore as ye think ye may find the mean to speak with her yourself, for without that in mine conceit it will not be; and as for Crosby, I understand not that there is no marriage concluded between them, nevertheless there is great language that it is like to be; ye be personable, and peradventure your being once in the sight of the maid, and a little discovering of your good will to her, binding her to keep it secret, and that ye can find ih your heart with some comfort to her, to find the mean to bring such a matter about, as shall be her pleasure and yours, but that this ye cannot do without some comfort of her in no wise; and bear yourself as lowly to the Mother as ye list, but to the maid not too lowly nor that ye be too glad to speed, nor too sorry to fail; and I always shall be your herald both here, if she come hither, and at home, when I come home, which I hope hastily, within forty days at the farthest; my Mother hath a Letter which can tell you more, and ye may let Daubeney see it.

JOHN PASTON, Knight

[1] Anne, widow of Sir Geoffrey Boleyn, Lord Mayor of London 1457–58. John Paston wished to pay his addresses to the youngest of Anne's three daughters.

I suppose and ye call well upon R. Calle he shall purvey your money, I have written to him enough.

[1467]

42. SIR JOHN COURTING

To Mistress Anne [1]

SINCE it is so, that I may not, as oft as I would, be there as I might do my message myself, mine own fair Mistress Anne, I pray you to accept this bill for my messenger to recommend me to you in my most faithful wise, as he that fainest of all other desireth to know of your welfare, which I pray God increase to your most pleasure.

And Mistress, though so be, that I as yet, have given you but easy [2] cause to remember me for lack of acquaintance, yet I beseech you let me not be forgotten, when ye reckon up all your Servants, to be set in the number with others.

And I pray you, Mistress Anne, for that service that I owe you, that in as short time, as ye goodly may, that I might be ascertained of your intent, and of your best Friends, in such matters as I have broken to you of; which both your and mine right trusty Friends John Lee, or else my Mistress his Wife, promised before you and me at our first and last being together, that as soon as they, or either of them knew your intent, and your Friends, that they should send me word, and if they so do, I trust soon after to see you.

And now farewell, mine own fair Lady, and God give you good rest, for in faith I trow ye be in bed.

Written in my way homeward, on Mary Magdalen's day at Midnight.[3]

Your own,

JOHN PASTON

Mistress Anne, I am proud that ye can read English, wherefore

[1] Apparently Mrs Anne Haute, a court lady, to whom Sir John was for a long time engaged. She seems to have been born abroad, or to have lived there for most of her life. The engagement was later broken off.

[2] Little.

[3] July 22.

I pray you acquaint yourself with this my lewd [1] hand, for my purpose is, that ye shall be more acquainted with it, or else it shall be against my will; but yet and when ye have read this bill, I pray you burn it, or keep it secret to yourself, as my faithful trust is in you.

[1468]

43. SIR JOHN EXTRAVAGANT

To Sir John Paston

I GREET you well, and send you God's blessing and mine, thanking you for my Seal that ye sent me, but I am right sorry that ye did so great cost thereupon, for one of forty pence should have served me right well; send me word what it cost you, and I shall send you money therefore; I sent you a Letter by a man of Yarmouth, send me word if ye have it, for I marvel ye sent me none answer thereof by Juddy.

I have none very [2] knowledge of your insurance [3] but if ye be insured, I pray God send you joy and worship together, and so I trust ye shall have, if it be as it is reported of her [4]; and anenst [5] God, ye are as greatly bound to her, as ye were married, and therefore I charge you upon my blessing, that ye be as true to her as she were married unto you in all degrees, and ye shall have the more grace and the better speed in all other things.

Also, I would that ye should not be too hasty to be married till ye were sure of your livelihood, for ye must remember what charge ye shall have, and if ye have not [wherewithal] to maintain it, it will be a great rebuke; and therefore labour that ye may have releases of the lands, and be in more surety of your land, or than ye be married. . . .

Your enemies be as bold here as they were before, wherefore I cannot think but that they have some comfort; I sent to Caister that they should beware in keeping of the place, as ye did write to me; haste you to speed your matters as speedily as ye can, that

[1] Unlearned, clumsy. [2] Certain. [3] Engagement.
[4] Anne Haute (see Letter 42). [5] Before.

ye may have less fellowship at Caister, for the expenses and costs be great, and ye have no need thereof and ye remember you well what charges ye have beside, and how your livelihood is dispoiled and wasted by your adversaries.

Also I would ye should purvey for your Sister [1] to be with my Lady of Oxford or with my Lady of Bedford, or in some other worshipful place, whereas ye think best, and I will help to her finding, for we be either of us weary of other; I shall tell you more when I speak with you; I pray you do your devyr [2] herein as ye will my comfort and welfare, and your worship, for divers causes which ye shall understand afterwards, etc.

I spake with the Lord Scales at Norwich, and thanked him for the good Lordship that he had shewed to you, and desired his Lordship to be your continual good Lord; and he swore by his troth he would do that he might do for you, and he told me that Yelverton the Justice had spoken to him in your matter, but he told me not what; but I trow, and ye desired him to tell you, he would. Ye are beholden to my Lord of his good report of you in this country, for he reported better of you than I trow ye deserve. I felt by him that there hath been proffered him large proffers on your adversaries part again you.

Send me word as hastily as ye may after the beginning of the term, how ye have sped in all your matters, for I shall think right long till I hear some good tidings.

Item, I pray you recommend me to the good Master that ye gave to the Chapel of Caister, and thank him for the great cost that he did on me at Norwich; and if I were a great Lady he should understand that he should fare the better for me, for me seemeth by his demeaning he should be right a good man.

Item, I send you the nowche [3] with the diamond, by the bearer hereof. I pray you forget not to send me a kerchief of Cremelle [4] for neckerchiefs for your sister Anne, for I am shent [5] of the good Lady she is with, because she hath none, and I can none get in all this town.

[1] Margery Paston, with whom the family were displeased owing to her engagement, without their consent, with Richard Calle.

[2] Endeavour.

[3] Brooch.

[4] A fabric with openwork edging.

[5] Blamed.

I should write more to you but for lack of leisure; God have you in his keeping, and send you good speed in all your matters. Written in haste, on Easter Monday.

By your Mother

MARGARET PASTON

[1469]

IV. Margery Paston

44. A PROPOSAL OF MARRIAGE

To my right worshipful and good Master,
Sir John Paston, Knight

RIGHT worshipful Sir, after due recommendation, please it you to understand the cause of my writing is for a marriage for my Mistress Margery your Sister; for my Nephew John Straunge would make her sure of forty pounds jointure, and two hundred marks [1] by year of inheritance; and if ye and your friends will agree thereto, I trust to God it shall take a conclusion to the pleasure of God and worship to both parties.

Moreover, and it pleaseth you to weet, I am sore troubled with Bedston, as well by the way of attachment out of the Chancery as otherwise; I must beseech you of your good mastership and help in secret manner, as Sir Thomas Lynes the bringer of this shall inform you. I shall be at London in the beginning of this term by the grace of God, which preserve you. Written at Norwich, in haste, the Monday after Twelfth-day.

By your

J. STRANGE [2]

[1467–69]

45. THE BROTHERS ANGRY WITH THEIR SISTER

To Sir John Paston, Knight

SIR, pleaseth it to understand, that I conceive, by your Letter which that ye sent me by Jude, that ye have heard of Richard

[1] *£133 6s. 8d.*

[2] The Stranges were a knightly family of Hunstanton, in Norfolk. This proposal for the marriage of Margery came to nothing.

Calle's [1] labour which he maketh by our ungracious sister's assent, but whereas they write that they have my good will therein, saving your reverence, they falsly lie of it, for they never spake to me of that matter, nor none other body in their name. Lovell asked me once a question, whether that I understood how it was betwixt R^d^ Calle and my sister; I can think that it was by Calle's means, for when I asked him whether Calle desired him to move me that question or not, he would have gotten it away by hums and by hays, but I would not so be answered; wherefore at the last he told me that his eldest son desired him to spere [2] whether that Richard Calle were sure of her or not, for he said that he knew a good marriage for her, but I wot he lied, for he is whole with Richard Calle in that matter; wherefore to that intent that he nor they should pick no comfort of me, I answered him, that and my Father, whom God assoil! were alive, and had consented thereto, and my Mother and ye both, he should never have my good will for to make my Sister to sell candle and mustard in Framlingham, and thus, with more which were too long to write to you, we departed.

And whereas it pleaseth you in your Letter to cry me mercy, for that ye sent me not such gear as I sent you money for; I cry you mercy that I was so lewd [3] to encumber you with any so simple a matter, considering the great matters and weighty that ye have to do; but need compelled me, for in this country is no such stuff as I sent to you for.

Also, whereas it pleaseth you to send to Richard Calle to deliver me money, so God help me, I will none ask him for myself, nor none had I of him, nor of none other man but of mine own since ye departed, but that little that I might forbear of mine own, I have delivered to Dawbeney for household, and paid it for you in men's wages, and therefore whoever sendeth you word that I have spent you any money since ye went hence, they must give you another reckoning, saving in meat and drink, for I eat like an horse, of purpose to eat you out at the doors,

[1] Richard Calle, head bailiff to John Paston, married Margery Paston, after much family displeasure, in 1469. Later he seems to have had a manor of his own, and to have become a person of county standing.

[2] Inquire.

[3] Troublesome.

but that needeth not, for you come not within them, wherefore, so God help me, the fellowship here [1] thinks that ye have forgotten us all, and any thing be ill ruled when ye come home wite [2] it [on] yourself for default of oversight.

Also, I understand for very certain, and it is sent me so word out of my Lord's house, that this Pentecost is my Lord's Counsel at Framlingham, and they purpose this week and the next to hold courts here at Caister, and at all other manors that were Sir John Fastolf's, purchased of Yelverton and of Sir Thomas Howes, whom God assoil, and how that my demeaning shall be, it is too late to send to you for advice, wherefore, and I do well I ask no thank, and if I do ill, I pray you lay the default on over little wit, but I purpose to use the first point of hawking, to hold fast and I may; but so God help me, and they might pull down the house on our heads, I wite them not, which I trust to God to keep them from; for by God that bought me, the best Earl in England would not deal so with my Lord and my Lady as ye do, without making of some means to them [3] so God help me, whosoever advise you to do so, he is not your friend; and I may, I trust to God to see you about Midsummer or before, for in good faith I ween ye purpose you that it shall be Easter ere ye come home, for all your servants here ween that ye purpose no more to deal with them, but to leave them here in hostage to my Lord of Norfolk.

Also, Sir, I pray you purvey what Inn that my brother Edmund shall be in, for he loseth sore his time here I promise you; I pray you send me word by the next messenger that cometh, and I shall either send him or bring him up with me to London.

Also, Sir, we poor sans deniers [4] of Caister have broken three or four steel bows,[5] wherefore we beseech you and there be any maker of steel-bows in London which is very cunning, that ye will send me word, and I shall send you the bows that be broken, which be your own great bow, and Robert Jackson's bow, and

[1] Caister. The Duke of Norfolk was making a claim to the manor of Caister, which he besieged and took in September 1469.

[2] Blame.

[3] Some advances to them.

[4] Moneyless men.

[5] Cross-bows.

John Pamping's bow; these three have cast so many calves, that they shall never cast quarrels [1] till they be new made.

I pray you find the means that my Lord may have some reasonable mean proffered, so that he and my Lady may understand that ye desire to have his good Lordship; I promise you it shall do you ease and your tenants both, and God preserve [you].

JOHN PASTON

[1469]

46. A LOVE-LETTER FROM RICHARD CALLE TO MARGERY PASTON

To Mistress Margery Paston

MINE own Lady and Mistress, and, before God, very true wife,[2] I with heart full sorrowful recommend me unto you, as he that cannot be merry, nor nought shall be till it be otherwise with us than it is yet, for this life that we lead now is neither pleasure to God nor to the world, considering the great bond of matrimony that is made betwixt us, and also the great love that hath been, and as I trust, yet is betwixt us, and as on my part never greater; wherefore I beseech Almighty God comfort us as soon as it pleaseth him, for we that ought of very right to be most together, are most asunder, me seemeth it is a thousand year ago since that I spake with you, I had liever than all the good in the world I might be with you; alas, alas! good Lady, full little remember they what they do that keep us thus asunder, four times in the year are they accursed that let [3] matrimony; it causeth many men to deem in them they have large conscience in other matters as well as herein, but what Lady suffer as ye have done. And make you as merry as ye can, for I wis, lady, at the long way God will of his rightwiseness help his servants that mean truly, and would live according to his laws, etc.

I understand, Lady, ye have had as much sorrow for me as any Gentlewoman hath had in the world, as would God all that

[1] Bolts for cross-bows.

[2] Margery had, at this time, solemnly betrothed herself to Calle, which was regarded almost as binding as matrimony.

[3] Hinder.

sorrow that ye have had had rested upon me and that ye had been discharged of it, for I wis, Lady, it is to me a death to hear that ye be entreated otherwise than ye ought to be; this is a painful life that we lead, I cannot live thus without it be a great displeasure to God.

Also like you to weet that I had sent you a Letter by my lad from London, and he told me he might not speak with you, there was made so great await upon him and upon you both; he told me John Thresher come to him in your name, and said that ye sent him to my lad for a Letter or a token, which I should have sent you, but he trust him not, he would not deliver him none; after that he brought him a ring, saying that ye sent in him, commanding him that he should deliver the Letter or token to him, which I conceive since by my lad it was not by your sending, it was by my Mistress and Sir James's [1] advice; Alas, what mean they? I suppose they deem we be not ensured together, and if they so do I marvel, for then they are not well advised, remembering the plainness that I brake to my Mistress at the beginning, and I suppose by you both,[2] and ye did as ye ought to do of very right, and if ye have done the contrary, as I have been informed ye have done, ye did neither consciencely nor to the pleasure of God, without ye did it for fear, and for the time to please such as were at that time about you; and if ye did it for this cause it was a reasonable cause, considering the great and importable calling upon that ye had, and many an untrue tale was made to you of me, which, God know it, I was never guilty of.

My Lad told me that my Mistress your mother asked him, if he had brought any Letter to you, and many other things she bare him on hand, and among all other at the last she said to him that I would not make her privy to the beginning, but she supposed I would at the ending; and as to that, God know it, she knew it first of me and none other, I wot not what her mistresship meaneth, for by my troth there is no gentlewoman alive that my heart tendereth more than it doth her, nor is loather to displease, saving only your person, which of very right I ought to tender and love best, for I am bound thereto by the

[1] Sir James Gloys, a priest. [2] Also.

law of God, and so will do while that I live, whatsoever fall of it; I suppose and ye tell them sadly the truth, they will not damn their souls for us; though I tell them the truth they will not believe me as well as they will do you, and therefore, good Lady, at the reverence of God be plain to them and tell the truth, and if they will in no wise agree thereto, betwixt God, the Devil, and them be it, and that peril that we should be in, I beseech God it may lie upon them and not upon us; I am heavy and sorry to remember their disposition, God send them grace to guide all things well, as well [as] I would they did; God be their guide and send them peace and rest, etc.

I marvel much that they should take this matter so heedely [1] as I understand they do, remembering it is in such case as it cannot be remedied, and [remembering] my desert upon every behalf, it is for to be thought there should be none obstacle against it; and also the worshipful that is in them, is not in your marriage, it is in their own marriage, which I beseech God send them such as may be to their worship and pleasure to God and to their hearts ease, for else were it great pity. Mistress I am afraid to write to you for I understand ye have shewed my letters that I have sent you before this time ; but I pray you let no creature see this Letter, as soon as ye have read it let it be burnt, for I would no man should see it in no wise. Ye had no writing from me this two year, nor I will not send you no more, therefore I remit all this matter to your wisdom; Almighty Jesu preserve, keep, and [give] you your heart's desire, which I wot well should be to God's pleasure, etc.

This Letter was written with as great pain as ever wrote I thing in my life, for in good faith I have been right sick, and yet am not verily at ease, God amend it, etc.

RICHARD CALLE

[1469]

[1] Grievously.

47. MARGARET PASTON CASTS OUT HER DAUGHTER

To Sir John Paston, Knight

I GREET you well, and send you God's blessing and mine, letting you weet that on Thursday last was, my mother and I were with my Lord of Norwich, and desired him that he would no more do in the matter touching your sister, till that ye and my brother and others that were Executors to your father might be here together, for they had the rule of her as well as I; and he said plainly that he had been required so often to examine her, that he might not, nor would no longer delay it, and charged me in pain of cursing that she should not be deferred, but that she should appear before him the next day; and I said plainly that I would neither bring her nor send her; and then he said that he would send for her himself; and charged that she should be at her liberty to come when he sent for her; and he said by his troth that he would be as sorry for her, and she did not well,[1] as he would be and she were right near of his kin, both for my mother's sake, and mine, and other of her friends, for he wist well that her demeaning had sticked sore at our hearts.

My mother and I informed him that we could never understand by her saying, by no language that ever she had to him, that neither of them were bound to other, but that they might choose both; then he said that he would say to her as well as he could, before that he examined her; and so it was told me by divers persons that he did as well and as plainly as she had been right near to him, which were too long to write at this time, hereafter ye shall weet, and who were labourers therein; the Chancellor was not so guilty therein as I weened he had been.

On Friday the Bishop sent for her by Ashfield and other that are right sorry of her demeaning, and the Bishop said to her right plainly, and put her in remembrance how she was born, what kin and friends that she had, and should have more if she were ruled and guided after them; and if she did not, what rebuke, and shame, and loss should be to her, if she were not guided by

[1] If she did not marry well.

them, and cause of forsaking of her for any good, or help, or comfort that she should have of them; and said that he had heard say, that she loved such one that her friends were not pleased with that she should have, and therefore he bad her be right well advised how she did; and said that he would understand the words that she had said to him, whether it made matrimony or not, and she rehearsed what she had said, and said, if those words made it not sure, she said boldly, that she would make it surer ere than she went thence, for she said she thought in her conscience she was bound whatsoever the words were; these lewd words grieveth me and her grandam as much as all the remanent; and then the Bishop and the Chancellor both said that there was neither I nor no friend of hers would receive [her].

And then Calle was examined apart by himself, that her words and his accorded, and the time, and where it should have been done; and then the Bishop said that he supposed that there should be found other things against him that might cause the letting thereof,[1] and therefore he said he would not be too hasty to give sentence thereupon, and said that he would give over day till the Wednesday or Thursday after Michaelmas, and so it is delayed; they would have had her [2] will performed in haste, but the Bishop said he would none otherwise than he had said.

I was with my Mother, at her place [in Norwich], when she was examined, and when I heard say what her demeaning was, I charged my servants that she should not be received in mine house; I had given her warning, she might have been ware afore, if she had been gracious; and I sent to one or two more that they should not receive her if she came; she was brought again to my place for to have been received, and Sir James told them that brought her, that I had charged them all, and she should not be received; and so my Lord of Norwich hath set [3] her at Roger Best's, to be there till the day before said, God knoweth full evil against his will and his wife's, if they durst do otherwise; I am sorry that they are a-cumbered with her, but yet I am better paid [4] that she is there for the while, than she had been in

[1] *I.e.*, if he had done any such wrongs as gave the Church jurisdiction over him, it might be undone, as a punishment. [Gr.]

[2] Their. [3] Boarded. [4] Satisfied.

other place, because of the sadness and good disposition of himself and his wife; I pray you and require you that ye take it not pensily [1] for I wot well it goeth right near your heart, and so doth it to mine and to others, but remember you, and so do I, that we have lost of her but a brethel,[2] and set it the less to heart, for and she had been good wheresoever she had been, it should not have been as it is, for and she were dead at this hour, she should never be at mine heart as she was. As for the divorce that ye write to me of, I suppose [3] what ye meant, but I charge you upon my blessing that ye do not, nor cause none other to do, that should offend God and your conscience, for and ye do, or cause for to be done, God will take vengeance thereupon, and ye should put yourself and others in great jeopardy, for wot it well, she shall full sore repent her lewdness hereafter, and I pray God she might; so I pray you for mine heart's ease be ye of a good comfort in all things; I trust God shall help right well, and I pray God so do in all our matters; I would ye took heed if there were any labour made in the court of Canterbury for the lewd matter aforesaid.

But if the Duke [4] be purveyed for, he and his wise counsel shall leave this country; it is told me that he saith that he will not spare to do that he is purposed [at Caister], for no Duke in England. God help at need.[5]

[1469]

[1] Heavily.
[2] A worthless person.
[3] Understand.
[4] The Duke of Norfolk.
[5] The letter is unsigned, but a note on the back of the original states that it is to Sir John Paston from his mother.

V. Sir John Paston

48. SIR JOHN'S EXTRAVAGANCE

To my Right Worshipful Brother, Sir John Paston, Knight

RIGHT worshipful Sir, I recommend me to you, certifying that I have spoken with Master John Smyth [1] for Sir Thomas Lynde's will, and he hath showed me your bill which ye ask to be content of,[2] your bill alone draweth four marks and odd money, for ye have set in your bill, for wax alone, 20*s.* which to Master John Smyth's imagination, and to all other Officers of the Court, should not draw past 20*d.* at his burying.[3] The bills that be put into the Court of Sir T. Lynde's debts draw 30*l.* 18*s.* 6*d.* and all the money that can be made of his house and goods in this country draweth but 5*l.* Master J. Smyth would ye should send him into the Court an inventory of such goods as Sir Thomas had at London when he died, and that inventory once had, ye shall have as cometh to your part and more also; ye must send the certainty whether the wax be 20*s.* or 20*d.*; and as for the Friars, Master John will not allow them a penny, for he saith, " where the debts may not be paid, set the bequests at nought "; he is agreed to pay the Apothecary, after that he have the inventory from you.

Item, as for John Maryot, I have sent to him for the 40*s.* but have none answer.

Item, I have spoken with Barker, and he hath no money nor none can get till harvest, when he may distrain the crop upon the ground; he saith there is not owing past five marks and on Saturday next coming he shall send me a view of his account, which I shall send you, as soon as I have it; as for Fastolf's five marks, J. Wyndham hath been spoken to by me half-a-dozen times to send to him for it, and he saith he hath done so.

[1] An officer in the Bishop's Court; afterwards Chancellor of the Diocese of Norwich.

[2] Paid.

[3] *I.e.*, for wax candles.

Item, Sir John Styll hath told Jude when ye shall have the chalice, ask Jude of your cruets also.

Item, the proud, peevish, evil-disposed priest to us all, Sir James,[1] saith, that ye commanded him to deliver the book of Seven Sages to my brother Walter, and he hath it.

Item, I send you the certainty herewith of as much as can be inquired for my uncle William's claim in Caister; these articles that fail,[2] the tenants of Caister shall inquire them, and send them to me hastily; they have promised, and they come, ye shall have them sent you by the next messenger that cometh to London.

Item, my mother would ye should in all haste get her acquittance of the Bishop of Winchester for Sir John Fastolf's goods, she prayed you to make it sure by the advice of your counsel, and she will pay for the costs.

Item, she prayeth you to speak to the said Bishop for to get Master Clement Felmingham the eight marks by year during his life that Sir John Fastolf beset him; she prayed you to get him an assignment for it to some manor in Norfolk or in Lothingland.[3]

Item, she would ye should get you another house to lay in your stuff, such as came from Caister, she thinketh one of the Friars is a fair house [4]; she purposeth to go into the country, and there to sojourn once a year. Many quarrels are picked to get my brother Edmund and me out of her house; we go not to bed unchidden lightly [5]; all that we do is ill done, and all that Sir James and Peacock doth is well done; Sir James and I be twain: we fell out before my mother, with "thou proud priest," and "thou proud squire," my mother taking his part, so I have almost beshut the bolt,[6] as for my mother's house; yet summer shall be done, ere I get me any master.

My mother proposeth hastily to take estate in all her lands, and upon that estate to make her will of the said lands, part to give to my younger brethren for term of their lives, and after to remain to you; part to my sister Anne's marriage, till an hundred pounds be paid; part for to make her aisle at Mawtby; [7]

[1] Sir James Gloys. [2] Are missing. [3] In Suffolk.
[4] *I.e.*, to rent. [5] Easily. [6] Shut myself out.
[7] Margaret Paston endowed a South aisle at Mawtby Church, and her tomb was made there.

part for a priest to sing for her, and my father, and their ancestors; and in this anger between Sir James and me, she hath promised me that my part shall be nought; what yours shall be I cannot say; God speed the plough. I'faith ye must purvey for my brother Edmund to go over with you,[1] or he is undone; he will bring twenty nobles [2] in his purse. My mother will neither give nor lend none of you both a penny forward; purvey a mean to have Caister again ere ye go over; my Lord and my Lady,[3] which for certain is great with child, be weary thereof, and all the household also.

If ye will any other thing to be done in this country, send me word, and I shall do as well as I can with God's grace, who preserve you.

Written the 8th day of July.

I pray burn this before losing [it].

Your,
JOHN PASTON

[1472]

49. SIR JOHN TRIES TO GET INTO PARLIAMENT

To my right worshipful Brother Sir John Paston, Knight

RIGHT worshipful Sir, I recommend me to you, letting you weet, that your desire, as for the Knights of the Shire, was an impossible [thing] to be brought about; for my Lord of Norfolk and my Lord of Suffolk, were agreed, more than a fortnight ago, to have Sir Robert Wingfield, and Sir Richard Harcourt, and that knew I not till Friday last past. I had sent, ere I went to Framlingham, to warn as many of your friends, to be at Norwich, as this Monday, to serve your intent, as I could; but when I came to Framlingham, and knew the appointment that was taken for the two Knights, I sent warning again to as many as I might, to tarry at home; and yet there came to Norwich this day as many as their costs drew to 9*s.* 1½*d.* paid and reckoned by Peacock

[1] *I.e.*, to Calais.
[2] Ten pounds.
[3] The Duke and Duchess of Norfolk.

and R. Capron; and yet they did but break their fasts and departed; and I thanked them in your name, and told them that ye would have no voice [1] as this day, for ye supposed not to be in England when the Parliament should be; and so they came not at the Shire-house, for if they had, it was thought by such as be your friends here, that your Adversaries would have reported, that ye had made labour to have been one, and that ye could not bring your purpose about.

I sent to Yarmouth, and they have promised also to Doctor Aleyn and John Russe to be [Burgesses] more then three week ago.

James Arblaster hath written a Letter to the Bailiff of Maldon, in Essex, to have you a Burgess there, how Jude shall speed, let him tell you, when ye speak together.

Sir, I have been twice at Framlingham, since your departing, but now the last time the Council was there; I saw your Letter which was better than well endited . . . my words were well taken, but your Letter a thousand fold better; when they had read it, they showed it to my Lady; after that my Lady had seen it, I speak with my Lady, offering to my Lord and her your service, and besides that, ye to do my Lord a pleasure [2] and her a better, so as ye might depart without any sum specified; she would not tell in that matter, but remitted me again to the Council, for she said, and she spoke in it, till my Lord and the Council were agreed, they would lay the weight of all the matter on her, . . . then I went to the Council, and offered them your service to my Lord, and to do him a pleasure, for the having again of your Place and Lands in Caister, 40*l.*, not speaking of your Stuff nor thing else; so they answered me your offer was more than reasonable, and if the matter were theirs, they said, they wist what Conscience would drive them to. They said they would move my Lord with it, and so they did; but then the Tempest arose, and he gave them such an answer, that none of them all would tell it me; but when I asked an answer of them they said; " And some Lords or greater men moved my Lord with it, the matter were yours ";—(Keep counsel)—and with this answer I departed. . . .

If ye miss to be Burgess of Maldon, and my Lord Chamberlain

[1] Vote. [2] *I.e.*, give him a present.

will, ye may be in another place; there be a dozen Towns in England that choose no Burgess, which ought to do it, ye may be set in for one of those Towns, and ye be friended. Also in any wise forget not in all haste to get some goodly ring [at the] price of 20*s.* or some pretty Flower of the same price, and not under, to give to Jane Rodon; for she hath been the most special labourer in your matter, and hath promised her good will forth [1]; and she doth all with her Mistress. . . . I profered but 40*l.* and if my Lord Chamberlain profer my Lady the remanent, I can think it shall be taken; my Lady must have somewhat to buy her a Coverchief [2] besides my Lord. . . .

I ask no more good of you for all the service, that I shall do you while the world standeth, but a Goss Hawk,[3] if any of my Lord Chamberlain's men or yours go to Calais, or if any be to get in London, that is, a mewed Hawk, for she may make you sport when ye come into England a dozen years hence. . . . Now think on me, good Lord, for if I have not an Hawk, I shall wax fat for default of Labour, and dead for default of company by my truth. No more but I pray God send you all your desires, and me my mewed Goss Hawk in haste, or rather then fail, a Soar Hawk, there is a Grosser [4] dwelling right over against the Well with two Buckets [5] a little from Saint Helen's hath ever Hawks to sell.

Written at Norwich the 21st day of September, in the 12th year of Ed. IV.

JOHN PASTON

Rather then fail a Tarssel [6] proved will occupy the time till I come to Calais.

[1472]

[1] In future. [2] Headdress.

[3] A mewed gosshawk was a large, short-winged hawk that had changed her feathers once or more; a soar hawk was one who began to prey for himself; a tiercel hawk was the male of the gosshawk kind. The gosshawk was the most esteemed.

[4] A dealer in foreign fruits and an importer of various luxuries who sold hawks.

[5] The name of an inn. [6] Tiercel.

50. THE CHAPLAIN INTERFERING

To Sir John Paston, Knight

. . . I SEND you herewith the Indenture between you and Townshend [1]; my Mother hath heard of that matter, and taketh on marvellously, for she saith she weeteth well it shall never be pledged out; wherefore she saith that she will purvey for her land, that ye shall never sell of it, for she thinks ye would, and it came to your hands; as for her Will, and all such matters as were in hand at your last being here, they think that it shall not lie in all our powers to let it in one point.

Sir James [Gloys] [2] is ever chopping at me, when my Mother is present, with such words as he thinks wrath me, and also cause my Mother to be displeased with me, even as who saith, he would I wist that he setteth not by the best of us; and when he hath most unfitting words to me, I smile a little, and tell him, "it is good hearing of these old tales."

Sir James is parson of Stokesby by J. Berney's gift; I trow he beareth him the higher.

Item, ye must send in haste to W. Baker a warrant to pay John Cook 30*s.*, and to the woman of Yarmouth, for oats, 20*s.*, and Sir John Styll [3] his money, for they all call daily upon it.

Item, I pray you send me some tidings how the world goeth, and whether ye have sent any of your folk to Calais: me thinks it costeth you too much money for to keep them all in London at your charge.

Item, whether ye have any thing spoken of my going to Calais.

Item, as for a Goshawk or a Tersel, I weened to have had one of yours in keeping long ere this time, but "far from eye far from heart"; by my troth I die for default of labour [4]; and it may be by any mean possible, for God's sake let one be sent me in all haste, for if it be not had by Hallowmas, the season shall pass

[1] The indenture was for a mortgage.

[2] The priest on whom Margaret Paston largely relied after the death of her husband.

[3] The chaplain at Caister who had stood the siege.

[4] Lack of exercise.

anon, memento mei, and in faith ye shall not lose on it, nor yet much win on it, by God, who preserve you. Written on Saint Michael's day [1] in monte tomba.[2]

JOHN PASTON

[1472]

51. A RING AND A HAWK

à Johan Paston Equyer soit doné

WORSHIPFUL and well beloved Brother, I recommend me to you, letting you weet, that I send you a Letter, and a Ring with a Diamond; in which Letter ye might well conceive, what I would ye should do with the same Ring, with many other tidings and things which I prayed you to have done for me; which letter Botoner [3] had the bearing of. It is so now that I understand that he is either dead or else hard escaped; whereof I am right heavy; and am not certain whether the said Letter and Ring came to your hands or not.

I would not that Letter were seen with some folks, wherefore I pray you take good heed, how that letter cometh to your hands, whole or broken, and in especial I pray you get it, if ye have it not . . . I sent you word of a Hawk, I heard not from you since, I do and shall do that is possible in such a need.

Also I cannot understand that my Lord of Norfolk shall come here this time, wherefore I am in a great agony, how is best for me to sue to him for rehaving of my place [4]; that good Lord weet full little how much harm he doth me, and how little good or worship it doth him. I pray you send me your advice. No more to you this time, but God have you in his keeping.

Written at London the 4th day of November in the 12th year of Edward IVth. . . .

JOHN PASTON, Knight

[1472]

[1] September 29. [2] Tombland, in Norwich.

[3] William Botoner, otherwise Worcester. He was not dead, and later became secretary to John the Youngest.

[4] Manor of Caister. It was seized by Norfolk in 1469.

52. THE DISAPPOINTING HAWK

To Master Sir John Paston, Knight

RIGHT worshipful Sir, I recommend me to you, thanking you most heartily of your diligence and cost which ye had in getting of the Hawk, which ye sent me, for well I wot your labour and trouble in that matter was as much as though she had been the best of the world, but so God help me as forsooth as the most cunning falconers that ever I speak with can imagine, she shall never serve but to lay eggs, for she is both a muer-de-haye, and also she hath been so bruised with carnage of fowl, that she is as good as lame in both her legs, as every man may see at eye; wherefore all such folk, as have seen her, advise me to cast her into some wood whereas I will have her to eyer [1]; but I will do therein as ye will; whether ye will I send her you again, or cast her into Thorp wood, and a Tarsel with her; for I weet where one is: but now I dare no more put you to the cost of an hawk; but for God's sake, and there be any Tarsel, or good cheap Goshawk that might be gotten, that the bearer hereof may have her to bring me, and I ensure you, by my troth, ye shall have Dolly's and Brown's bond to pay you at Candlemas the price of the hawk; now and [2] ye have as many ladies as ye were wont to have, I require you for her sake that ye best love of them all, once trouble yourself for me in this matter, and be out of my clamour.

Item, as for the ring, it is delivered; but I had as great pain to make her [3] take it as ever I had in such a matter: but I have promised you to be her knight, and she hath promised me to be more at your commandment than at any knight's in England, my Lord reserved; and that ye shall well understand, if ye have ought to do, wherein she may be an helper, for there was never knight did so much cost on her as ye have done.

I marvel that I hear no word of the letters that my Lord Chamberlain [4] should send to my Lord and my Lady for Caister:

[1] Lay eggs. [2] If. [3] Jane Rodon (see Letter 49).

[4] William, Lord Hastings, Lord Chamberlain and Lieutenant of Calais. A patron of Sir John Paston.

it is best that my Lord Chamberlain write to my Lady by some privy token betwixt them, and let a man of his come with the letters; my Lord Chamberlain may speed with my Lady what matters he will, saving the great matter; and ye inbill me for a solicitor, I shall be à votre commandement à toujours.

Item, methinketh that ye do evil that ye go not through with my Lady of Suffolk for Hellesdon and Drayton; for there should grow money to you, which would quit you against R. C. [1] and set you before for ever.

I pray you for your ease, and all others to you ward, ply these matters; as for all other things, I shall send you an answer when I come to Norwich, which shall be on Thursday, with God's grace. I have tarried here at Framlingham this sev'night for [my] Lady took not her chamber till yesterday. Adieu. Written on Saint Catherine's even.[2]

JOHN PASTON

I saw the pie, and heard it speak; and by God it is not worth a crow; it is far worse than ye weened: by God it were shame to keep it in a cage.

[1472]

53. MARGARET PASTON'S PRIVATE CHAPEL

To Sir John Paston, Knight

SYM recommendeth him to your good mastership, and prayeth you that ye will not forget, though he be a boy, to let him wear the same livery that your men do; and if it pleased you to let his gown cloth be sent him home, that it might be made against your coming into this country, he would be as proud as any man ye have.

Sir, as heartily as I can I thank you for the hat, which is coming, as I understand by your writing sent by John the Abbot's man of Saint Benet's.[3]

My mother sends you God's blessing and her's, and prays you

[1] Richard Calle. [2] November 24. [3] At Holme.

to get a new licence of my Lord of Norwich, that she may have the Sacrament in her Chapel [1]: I got a licence of him for a year, and it is nigh worn out; ye may get it for the Bishop's life, an ye will. . . .

JOHN PASTON

[1472]

In another letter Margaret writes:

And for the Licence that I speak to you, for to have the Sacrament in my Chapel, if ye cannot get it of the Bishop of Norwich, get it of the Bishop of Canterbury, for that is most sure for all places.

God keep you. Written on Midlent Sunday.

54. SIR JOHN GOING TO FRANCE [2]

To John Paston, Esquire, in Norfolk

WORSHIPFUL and right heartily beloved Brother, I recommend me unto you, letting you weet, that on Wednesday last past I wrote you a Letter, whereof John Carbalde had the bearing, promising me that ye should have it at Norwich this day, or else to-morrow in the morning; wherein I pray you to take a labour according after the tenure of the same, and that I may have an answer at London to Hoxon, if any messenger come, as [ever?] I may do for you.

As for tidings, there was a Truce taken at Brussels about the 26th day of March last past, between the Duke of Burgundy and the French King's Ambassadors, and Mr William at Clyff for the King here; which is a Peace by land and water till the first day of April now next coming, between France and England, and also the Duke's land; God hold it for ever, and Grace be!

Item, the Earl of Oxford was Saturday at Dieppe, and is purposed into Scotland with a 12 Ships; I mistrust that work.

[1] For Margaret's chapel see Letter 48.

[2] In 1473 Edward IV allied himself with Duke Charles of Burgundy, and in 1474 prepared at Calais to invade France. Calais became the centre of fashion and intrigue.

Item, there be in London many flying Tales, saying, that there should be a work [1] and yet they wot not how.

Item, my Lord Chamberlain sendeth, now at this time to Calais, the young Lord Zouch and Sir Thomas Hungerford's Daughter and Heir, and some say, the young Lady Harrington, these be three great Jewels; Calais is a merry town, they shall dwell there I wot not while.[2]

No more, but I have been, and am troubled with mine over large and courteous dealing with my servants, and now with their unkindness; Platting your man would this day bid me farewell to to-morrow at Dover, notwithstanding Thyrston your other man is from me, and John Myryel, and W. Woode, which promised you and Dawbeney, God have his Soul, at Caister, that if ye would take him in to be again with me, and then he would never go from me; and thereupon I have kept him this three years to play Saint George and Robin Hood, and the Sheriff of Nottingham, and now when I would have good horse, he is "gone into Bernysdale" and I without a [horse] Keeper.[3]

Written at Canterbury, to Calais ward on Tuesday and hap be, upon Good Friday the 16th day of April, in the 13th year of Edward IV.

Your,
JOHN PASTON, Knight

[1473]

55. SERVANT TROUBLES

To John Paston, Esquire, be this delivered

RIGHT worshipful Brother, I recommend me to you, letting you weet, that this day I was in very purpose to Calais ward, all ready to have gone to the Barge; save I tarried for a young man, that I thought to have had with me thither, one that was with Rows which is in the country; and because I could not get him, and

[1] Rising. [2] How long.

[3] Sir John apparently patronized acting. The quotation is from a ballad of Robin Hood. Hastings married the heiress of Hungerford to his son, Edward.

that I have no more here with me but Pampyng, Edward, and Jack, therefore Pampyng remembered me, that at Calais he told me that he purposed to be with the Duchess of Norfolk, my Lady and yours; and Edward is sick, and seemeth not abiding, he would see what shall fall of this world, and so I am as he that saith; " come hither, John, my man "; And as hap was yesterday Juddy went afore to Calais ward, wherefore I am now ill purveyed; which for ought that I know yet, is like to keep me here this Whitsuntide, wherefore if ye know any likely men, and fair conditioned, and good Archers, send them to me, though it be four, and I will have them, and they shall have four Marks by the year, and my Livery. . . .

Item, I pray you send me a new Vestment of white Damask for a Deacon, which is amongst mine other Gear at Norwich, for he shall thereto as ye wot of; I will make an arming Doublet of it, though I should another time give a long Gown of velvet for another vestment; and send it in all haste to Hoxon to send me.

I hoped to have been very merry at Calais this Whitsuntide, and am well apparelled and appointed, save that these folks fail me so, and I have matter there to make of right excellent. Some man would have hastened him to Calais, though he had no better errand, and some men think it wisdom and profit to be there now well out of the way.

Item, as for the Bishop [1] and I, we be nearer to a point than we were, so that my part is now all the Lands in Flegg wholly, the Manor of Hellesdon, Tolthorpe, and Tenements in Norwich and Earlham, except Fairchild's; but farewell Drayton, the Devil doytt [2] them.

Item, large and fair communication hath been between Sir John Fagge and Richard Haulte for their Sister and me, before Doctor Wyntborne and elsewhere, so that I am in better hope than I was by St Lawrence [3] that I shall have a deliverance.[4]

Item, as for tidings here, I trow ye have heard your part, how

[1] Waynflete, Bishop of Winchester. He was unravelling the complications of Fastolf's will.

[2] Pay.

[3] August 10.

[4] *I.e.*, from his betrothal. Sir John and Anne Haute were endeavouring to get the ecclesiastical authorities to cancel their betrothal.

that the Earl of Oxford landed by St Osyth's in Essex, the 28th day of May, save he tarried not long; for if he had, the Earl of Essex rode to him wards, and the Lords Denham and Duras, and other more, which by likelihood should have distressed him; but yet his coming saved Hogan his head; and his Prophesy is the more believed; for he said, that this trouble should begin in May, and that the King should Northwards, and that the Scots should make us work, and him battle.

Men look after they wot not what, but men buy Harness fast; the King's menial men, and the Duke of Clarence's, are many in this town, the Lord Rivers came to day, men say, to purvey in likewise.

Item, how that the Countess of Warwick [1] is now out of Beverley Sanctuary and Sir James Tyrell conveyeth her Northwards, men say, by the King's assent, whereto some men say, that the Duke of Clarence is not agreed.

Item, men say, that the Earl of Oxford is about the Isle of Thanet, hovering, some say, with great company, and some say, with few.

No more but God keep you. Written at London the 3rd day of June, in the 13th year of Edward IV.

John Paston, Knight

[1473]

56. LORD HASTINGS THANKS SIR JOHN

To my right heartily beloved friends and fellows, Sir John of Middleton and Sir John Paston, Knights

After hearty Recommendation, I thank you of the good attendance that ye gave unto the King's Counsel at Calais; and the good and effectual Devoirs, that ye put you in to assist my Deputy Sir John Scot, in all such things as might concern the safeguard of my charge there. Letting you weet, that if there be any thing that I can and may do for you, I shall with right good will perform it to my power. And I pray you to recommend me to my Lady

[1] Anne, widow of Richard Neville, the King-maker.

Howard,[1] my Lady Bourchier,[2] and all other Ladies and Gentlewomen, of the said town. And in like wise to the Mayor, Lieutenant and Fellowship of the Staple; my fellows the Soldiers, and all other such as [to] you shall seem good. And our Lord send you your desires. Written at Nottingham, the 16th day of September. Sir John Paston I pray you to give credence to such things as my Deputy shall shew you from me, and conform you to the same.

Your Fellow,

HASTYNGS [3]

[1473]

57. MORE TROUBLES

To John Paston, Esquire, at Norwich, be this delivered

WORSHIPFUL and well beloved Brother, I commend me to you, letting you weet, that the World seemeth queasy [4] here; for the most part that be about the King have sent hither for their Harness, and it [is] said for certain, that the Duke of Clarence maketh him big in that he can, shewing as he would but deal with the Duke of Gloucester; but the King intendeth, in eschewing all Inconvenience, to be as big as they both, and to be a Stiffler [5] atween them; and some men think, that under this, there should be some other thing intended, and some Treason conspired; so what shall fall, can I not say.

Item, it is said that yesterday two Passagers [6] of Dover were taken; I fear that if Juddy had no hasty passage, so that if he passed not on Sunday or Monday, that he is taken, and some Gear of mine, I would not for 20*l.*

I hope and purpose to go to Calais ward on Sunday or Monday or nigh by, for I came not accompanied to do any service here; wherefore it were better for me to be out of sight.

[1] Wife of John, Lord Howard, late Duke of Norfolk.

[2] Probably daughter-in-law of Sir John Bourchier, Lord Berners.

[3] Supporter of Edward IV, Lord Chamberlain and Lieutenant of Calais.

[4] Unsettled. [5] Mediator. [6] Passage boats.

[*Here follow some money transactions relative to Dr Pykenham, Chancellor of Norwich, his Mother, and others.*]

Item, Spring, that waited on my father when he was in Gaol house, whom my father, at his dying beset [1] 40*s*. he cryeth ever on me for it, and in way of Alms he would be eased, though it were but xxs. or xs. wherefore he hath written to my Mother, and must have an answer again; I would that my Mother send him, as though she lend him somewhat, and he will be pleased, and else he can say as shrewdly as any man in England.

Item, the King hath sent for his Great Seal; some say, we shall have a new Chancellor, but some think that the King doth as he did at the last Fields,[2] he will have the Seal with him, but this day Doctor Morton, Master of the Rolls, rideth to the King, and beareth the Seals with him.

Item, I had never more need of money than now, wherefore Fastolf's 5 marks, and the money of Master John Smythe would make me whole, etc.

Written on St Leonard's day [3] in the 13th year of the reign of Edward IVth.

Item, send me my vestments, according to the Letter I sent you by Symond Dam, in all haste.

JOHN PASTON, Knight

[1473]

58. SIR JOHN PEEVISH

To John Paston, Esq., be this delivered

RIGHT worshipful and heartily beloved brother, I commend me to you, letting you weet that I received a letter that came from you, written circa viii Michælis [4] wherein ye let me weet of the decease of Sir James [Gloys] [5] and that my mother is in purpose to be at Norwich, and I am right glad that she will now do some-

[1] Bequeathed. [2] Battlefields. [3] November 6.

[4] *Circa octabas Michælis*—about the octaves of Michaelmas—*i.e.*, October 6.

[5] The priest.

what by your advice, wherefore beware from henceforth that no such fellow creep in between her and you; and if ye list to take a little labour, ye may live right well, if she pleased: it is as good that ye ride with a couple of horses at her cost, as Sir James or Richard Calle. Ye send me word also, that she in no wise will purvey the 100*l.* for the redeeming of Sporle; let it go: as touching that matter, John Osbern told me that he communed with you at Sporle of that matter; farther, he devised that Cocket, or such another man should, to have it the better cheap, lay out the value of six years for to have it seven years, whereto I would agree; and for God's sake, if that may be brought about, let it be done: as ye wot of, it is let for 22*l.* by the year, yet the farmer grant but 21*l.*; but to Cocket it would be worth 25*l.*; yea, and better: nevertheless, if Cocket will deliver six score pounds, I would he had it for seven years, with this, that my mother be agreeable to the same, because of the interest that she hath for my brother William, which shall not be of age this seven years; nevertheless, as ye know my old intent, I purpose to purvey for him in another place better than there; of which grant of my mother, I pray you to be my solicitor; in which, and it be brought about, Sporle shall be in as good case as ever he was.

John Osbern willed me to make you a sufficient warrant to sell and fell wood at Sporle, which I remember ye have in as ample form as can be: nevertheless, if this mean above written, of letting to farm, may be had, it shall, I hope, not need to fell nor sell much; but I remit that gear to your discretion: but if ye have such comfort, I pray you send me word.

I may say to you John Osbern flattered me, for he would have borrowed money of me. Item, in retailing of wood there, it were hard to trust him; he is needy. If Cocket, or whosoever had that manor to farm for seven years, and paid therefore but six score pounds, he should, to let it again, win 36*l.* which be much; wherefore if it might be, it were more reasonable six score and seven pounds to be received, and yet is there lost 29*l.* or else if ye take less money and fewer years, so it be after the rate, so there be paid 100*l.* at the least, send word.

Item, ye wrote that like a true man ye sent me 18*s.* by Richard Raddle; ye were too true: but he seems to be a false shrew, for he brought me none yet; whether he be out of town or not can I not say. Ye prayed me also to send you tidings how I sped in my matters, and in chief of Mistress Ann Hault: I have answer again from Rome, that there is the Well of Grace and salve sufficient for such a sore, and that I may be dispensed with: nevertheless my Proctor there asketh a 1000 ducats, as he deemeth; but Master Lacey, another Rome runner here, which knoweth my said Proctor there, as he saith, as well as Bernard knew his shield, saith that he meaneth but an 100 ducats, or 200 at the most. . . .

Item, as touching Caister, I trust to God that ye shall be in it to mine use, ere Christmas be past.

Item, your host Brigham recommends him to you, and when he and I reckoned, I gave him two nobles for your board, while ye were there in his absence; but in faith he would, for nought that I could do, take a penny; wherefore ye must thank him, or charge me to thank him on your behalf, in some next epistle that ye write to me to Calais: he let me weet that he would do more for you than so. . . .

As for other tidings, I trust to God that the two Dukes of Clarence and Gloucester shall be set at one by the award of the King.

Item, I hope by the means of the Duke of Gloucester, that my Lord Archbishop [1] shall come home.

Item, as touching my sister Ann,[2] I understand she hath been passing sick; but I weened that she had been wedded: as for Yelverton, he said but late, that he would have her if she had her money, and else not; wherefore methinketh that they be not very sure: but, among all other things, I pray you beware that the old love of Pampyng renew not; he is now from me: I wot not what he will do.

No more. Written at London the 22d day of November, the 13th year of Edward IV.

JOHN PASTON, Knt

[1473]

[1] George Neville, Archbishop of York, imprisoned at Guines for corresponding with the Earl of Oxford.

[2] Anne Paston, married William Yelverton, grandson of the judge.

59. SIR JOHN'S REMINDERS

To John Paston, Esq.

RIGHT worshipful and well-beloved brother, I recommend me to you, letting you weet that I send you herewith one citation, wherein be my mother and ye, whereof I pray you that I may have hasty answer; the effect thereof is no more, but ye both must send answer, and make you a Proctor here; and that must come hither under a Notary's sign, affirming that ye make such a man, Master John Halsnothe, or else, if ye will do the cost to send some other hither; your Proctor to take administration, or to refuse; and what so he doth, ye to hold it for firm and stable: then must my mother and ye write a letter, under my mother's seal and your sign manual, to me and Master John Halsnothe, in this form.

"We greet you well, letting you weet that we have made you, Master John Halesnothe, our Proctor, in the Testament of John Paston, husband and father to you,[1] wherein we will that on our behalf ye refuse the administration of the said Testament, and this writing is to you warrant and discharge, and also the very will of us."

This must we have for our discharge.

Item, I pray you take good heed to my sister Anne, lest the old love atween her and Pamping renew.

Item, I pray you send me word how my mother is disposed to her wards; and, if so were that a good marriage might be had, what she would depart with.

Item, I pray you that ye remember her for the tomb of my father at Bromholm, and also the chapel at Mauteby; and send me word how she is disposed herein.

Item, if I have Caister again, whether she will dwell there or not, and I will find her a priest towards at my charge, and give her the dove-house, and other commodities there; and if any horsekeeper of mine lie there, I will pay for his board also, as well as for the priest's.

Item, if my mother should have a new priest, I think that my

[1] "Father to us," this should be.

brother, Sir J. Goos were a meetly man to be there; he would also do as ye would have him, " now bear the cup even," as What-call-ye-him said to Aslake.

Beware of Minors [1] from henceforth, and send me word how ye trust Doctor Pykenham: I would, if he would do aught for my mother, that he hasted the sooner to pay me the 100*l.* so that I might pledge out Sporle.

Item, as for other tidings, the Earl of Oxford is still besieged; nevertheless once he issued out, and took a gentleman, and has him within: but now of late he was busy, and one espied him, and shot at him, and struck him in the very face with an arrow. I saw this day the same man, and there I leave him.[2]

If Arblaster come to you, ye may see his letter sent to him by me, wherein I have written that he should take your advice; but I pray you, above all things, that ye make haste, so that I hear from you again by this day sev'night. At London, the 25th day of November.

JOHN PASTON, Knight

[1473]

60. SIR JOHN TO HIS MOTHER

Mrs Margaret Paston, at Norwich

RIGHT honourable and most tender good Mother, I recommend me to you, beseeching you to have, as my trust is that I have, your daily Blessing; and thank you of your good Motherhood, kindness, cheer, charge, and costs, which I had, and put you to, at my last being with you, which God give me Grace hereafter to deserve!

Please it you to weet, that I think long that I hear not from you, or from Peacock your Servant, for the knowledge how he hath

[1] Minor friars.

[2] The Earl of Oxford fled abroad on Warwick's defeat in 1471, then took by surprise St Michael's Mount, where, after a siege he surrendered. After his surrender his Estates were confiscated, his Countess left destitute, and he was conveyed to the Castle of Hammes, near Calais, in Picardy, where he remained a Prisoner many years, namely, till 1484, 2 R. III. when he escaped, and joined the Earl of Richmond. [F.]

done in the sale of my farm barley [1] nor what is made thereof; wherefore I beseech you, if it be not answered by that time this bill cometh to you, to haste him and it hitherward; for if that had not tarried me, I deem I had been at Calais by this day; for it is so, as men say, that the French King with a great Host is at Amiens, but three-score miles from Calais; and if he, or his, rode before Calais, and I not there, I would be sorry.

Item, men say, that the Earl of Oxford hath been constrained to sue for his Pardon only of his Life; and his Body, Goods, Lands, with all the remanent, at the King's Will, and so should in all haste now come in to the King; and some men say, that he is gone out of the Mount,[2] men wot not to what place, and yet left a great Garrison there, well furnished in victual, and all other thing.

Item, as for the having again of Caister, I trust to have good tidings thereof hastily.

Item, my Brother John fareth well, and hath done right diligently in my Cousin Elizabeth Berney's matter, whereof hastily I trust he shall send her tidings, that shall please her; and as to morrow he purposeth to take his Journey to Wales ward to the Lord Rivers.

No more at this time, but Jesu have you in his keeping.

Written at London the 20th day of February, in the 13th year of Edward IV.

Your Son,

J. Paston, Knight

[1474]

61. UNCLE WILLIAM

To Mistress Margaret Paston at Norwich, or to J. Paston in her absence

Right worshipful and my most kind and tender mother, I recommend me to you, thanking you of the great cost, and of the great cheer, that ye did to me at my last being with you; which cheer also had made me perfectly whole, I thank God and

[1] Rent in kind. [2] St Michael's Mount, Cornwall.

you; insomuch that, whereas I feared me that for weakness, and so green [1] recovered of my sickness, that I should have apeyred [2] by the way; but, God thank you, I took so my crumbs, while I was with you, that I feeled myself by the way that God and ye have made me stronger than I weened that I had been insomuch that I feel myself every day wholer than other.

It was so that I met with mine uncle William by the way, and there in the field [3] paid him the 4*l.* which I had borrowed of him; and he was passing inquisitive how that I was purveyed for recompensing of Townshend: I told him I hoped well; and he told me that he understood that I had the 100*l.* of the Bishop's executors and he had heard say that I had also borrowed another 100*l.* of a merchant, and so I lacked but an 100 marks. I deem he heard this of T. Lovel, for I told him that I was in hope to find such a friend that would lend me an 100*l.* He asked me who was that? I answered him, an old merchant, a friend of mine; but mine uncle thought that should be by way of chevisance,[4] and to mine hurt; wherefore I was plain to him, and told him that ye were surety therefore, and purveyed it of such as would do for you; and as for the fourth hundred marks, he said to me that as for that he would, rather than jeopardy should be, purvey it by way of chevisance at London; insomuch that, ere he came from London, he had for my sake laid 500 marks [5] worth of plate with Hugh Fenn: the place at Warwick's inn is large, and my grandam is aged; it had been jeopardous to leave much plate with her, though half were her own: but, if I may do otherwise, I purpose not to chevise any money by his mean.

Item, I have delivered your bottle to Courby the carrier this same day, and he promised me to be with you on Monday night, or else on Tuesday timely; he hath also 40*d.* to pay for the third hired horse, and he bringeth the three horses with him, and is content [6] for the labour, and for the meat largely: they be delivered him in as good, or rather better plight than when I had them forth, and not galled nor hurt; he hath also two saddles, one of my brother's, and another hired, as ye wot of.

Item, he hath a pair of boots of Edmund Reed's, the shoemaker,

[1] Lately. [2] Grown worse. [3] Open country.
[4] Usury. [5] £333 6*s.* 8*d.* [6] Paid.

which Saunders borrowed of him: I beseech you that William Millisent or Sym may see that every man have his own.

Item, as for my brother Edmund, blessed be God, he is well amended.

Item, as for Hankin our dog, I am afraid never to see him, but if your good help be.

Item, as for the books that were Sir James's,[1] if it like you that I may have them, I am not able to buy them; but somewhat would I give, and the remanent, with a good devout heart, by my troth, I will pray for his soul; wherefore if it like you, by the next messenger or carrier, to send them in a day, I shall have them dressed [2] here; and if any of them be claimed hereafter, in faith I will restore it.

Written on Saturday.

JOHN PASTON, Kt

[1474]

62. DEBTS, BOOKS, AND HEALTH

To Mistress Margaret Paston, or to Roos dwelling before her gate at Norwich

AFTER due recommendation, my most tender and kind mother, I beseech you of your daily blessing: please it you to weet that I received a letter that came from you, written the 26th of October, none erst, but on Wednesday last past; whereby I conceived that, at the writing of that letter, ye were not certain of the dealing between Townshend and me. It was so that, God thank you, I received the 20*l.* brought by Sym, and also the money brought by my brother; with which money, and with more that I had myself, I redeemed the manor of Sporle, and paid Townshend both the 400 marks therefore, and also 10*l.* that I owed him beside, and have of him an acquittance of all bargains of all other debts: nevertheless I assayed him, if he would, if need had been, have given me a twelve-month's longer respite, which he granted to do; but in conclusion I cannot entreat him, but that he will have the uttermost of his bargain, and this 20*l.* payable at Candlemas

[1] Sir James Floys, the priest. [2] Set in order.

and Easter: I can entreat him none otherwise as yet; wherefore I think, if I had passed my day, it had been hard to have trusted to his courtesy; insomuch I find him also right loose in the tongue. . . .

Item, as for Caister, it needeth not to spur nor prick me to do ought therein; I do that I can with good will, and somewhat I hope to do hastily therein that shall do good.

Item, as for the books that were Sir James's, God have his soul! which it liketh you that I shall have them I beseech you that I may have them hither by the next messenger; and, if I be gone, yet that they be delivered to mine hostess at the George, at Paul's Wharf, which will keep them safe; and that it like you to write to me what my pain [1] or payment shall be for them.

Item, it liked you to weet of mine heal, I thank God that I am not greatly sick nor sore, but in my heel, wherein all men know not what pain I feel; and where ye advised me to hasten me out of this town, I would full fain be hence: I spend daily more than I should do if I were hence, and I am not well purveyed.

Item, blessed be God, my grandam is amended by such time as mine uncle William come hither; but my youngest cousin Margaret, his daughter, is dead and buried ere he come home.

I am as much afraid of this land that is in his hand, as I was of that that was in Townshend's hand.

I hope to write you more certainties within four or five days. No more, etc. Written the 20th day of November, in the 14th of Edward IV.

Your Son, JOHN PASTON, Kt

[1474]

63. SIR JOHN AT CALAIS

To the right worshipful John Paston, Esquire, at Norwich, or To his Mother Margaret Paston, in his absence, in haste

I RECOMMEND me to you, praying you heartily, that I may have weeting when that my Lord and Lady of Norfolk shall be at

[1] Return, responsibility.

London, and how long they shall tarry there, and in especial my Lord of Norfolk; for upon their coming to London were it for me to be guided; . . . it is so that as to-morrow I purpose to ride into Flanders to purvey me of Horse and Harness, and per case [1] I shall see the Siege of Neuss [2] ere I come again, if I have time; wherefore, if I so do, by likelihood it will be a 14 days ere I be here again; and after, as I hear from you and others thereupon, that at the next passage, and God will, I purpose to come to London ward: God send me good speed; in chief for the matter above written; and secondly, for to appoint with the King and my Lord, for such Retinue as I should have now in these wars into France; wherefore I pray you in Norfolk, and other places, commune with such as ye think likely for you and me, that are disposed to take wages in Gentlemen's Houses and elsewhere, so that we may be the more ready, when that need is; nevertheless at this hour, I would be glad to have with me daily three or four more than I have, such as were likely; for I lack of my Retinue, that I have here, so many.

I pray you send me some tidings, such as ye hear, and how that my brother Edmund doth; for as for tidings here, there be but few, save that the Siege lasteth still by the Duke of Burgundy afore Neuss, and the Emperor hath besieged also, not far from thence, a Castle, and another Town in like wise, wherein the Duke's men be.

And also, the French King, men say, is coming nigh to the water of Somme with 4000 Spears, and some men trow that he will, the day of breaking of Truce,[3] or else before, set upon the Duke's Countries here.

When I hear more, I shall send you more tidings.

The King's Ambassador Sir Thomas Montgomery and the Master of the Rolls be coming homeward from Neuss, and as for me, I think that I should be sick but if I see it.

Sir John of Parre [4] and William Berkeley come this way to

[1] Perhaps.

[2] Neuss, near Düsseldorf, was at this time besieged by Charles the Bold, Duke of Burgundy.

[3] The truce between Louis XI and Charles the Bold came to an end in the summer of 1475.

[4] Father of Queen Catherine Parr.

Flanders ward to buy them Horse and Harness [1] and [I] made Sir J. Parr [as] good cheer as I could for your sake; and he told me, that ye made him haulte [2] cheer, etc. at Norwich; no more. Written at Calais, the 17th day of January, in the 14th year of Edward IV.

[1475]

64. MARGARET PASTON AND UNCLE WILLIAM

To John Paston, Esq., be this delivered by haste

IHS [3]

I GREET you well, and send you God's blessing and mine, letting you weet that my cousin Robert Clere was here with me this week, and told me that he was not paid of the money, that ye know that was borrowed of his mother and of him, but fourscore pounds; the 20*l.* that my pledges lie for is unpaid; he said that he was desired to deliver my pledges, and to have been paid the 20*l.*; but he would not, till he had spoken with me, because of the promise that he had made to me before, that he should not deliver them to none without my assent. I said to him that I suppose verily that your brother is agreed with your uncle, that he should pay all the whole, for I suppose he hath a surety for all that and more; I would understand how it is, and how that my said cousin shall be content, for I were loath to lose my pledges; I wot it well your good uncle would be in possession with good will, but I would not so: I would that ye should speak with your uncle therein, and send me word in haste what he said.

I marvel, by my troth, that I had no writing from your brother, ere he departed from London, as he promised in the last letter that he sent to me, the which was written before the King's coming to Norwich; I weened verily to have heard from him at this time: I would ye should send him word of your uncle's dealing in this said matter, and send me an answer thereof.

[1] Armour. [2] High.

[3] This customary contraction of the name Jesus was frequently written at the head of a letter.

Recommend me to your grandam; I would she were here in Norfolk, as well at ease as ever I saw her, and as little ruled by her son as ever she was; and then I would hope that we all should fare the better for her. It is told me that your uncle hath made great means and large proffers to John Bacton, to make a release to him of Oxnead; whether it be done or not, I wot not yet, but I shall wot in haste, if I may.

I would ye should speak with my Lord of Norwich, and assay to get a licence of him, that I may have the Sacrament here in the chapel, because it is far to the church, and I am sickly, and the parson is often out: for all manner of casualties of me and mine I would have it granted, if I might.

Send me word if you hear any tidings from your brother, how he doth of his sickness, and in other things, as far forth as you know, as hastily as ye may. I think long till I hear from him, for divers causes. God keep you.

Written on haste at Mawteby, on the Saturday next before Candlemas day. Send me an answer of this letter in haste, and other tidings, etc.

My cousin Robert told me that there was more than 7*l.* of the money that was paid him that was right rusty [1] and he could not have it changed: he was ungoodly served therein.

By your Mother,

MARGARET PASTON

[1475]

65. A KITCHEN CLERK FOR LORD HASTINGS

To my Lord Hastyngs [2]

MY most redoubted and singular good Lord, after most humble and due recommendation, please it your good Lordship to have knowledge, that according to your commandment, in my way homeward, I remembered me of a person, which to my thinking is meet to be clerk of your kitchen; which person is now in

[1] Bad.

[2] For Lord Hastings see Letters 52 and 56. Hastings, a patron of Sir John, was preparing to leave for Calais in March 1476.

service with Master Fitzwalter, and was before that with Whethill at Guisnes, and purveyor for his house, and at such time as the King's grace was there last, in his voyage towards France. This man is mean [1] of stature, young enough, well witted, well mannered; a goodly young man on horse and foot; he is well spoken in English, meetly well in French, and very perfect in Flemish; he can write and read; his name is Richard Stratton ; his mother is Mistress Grame of Calais; and when I had showed him mine intent, he was agreeable and very glad, if that it might please your Lordship to accept him into your service: whereto I promised him my poor help, as far forth as I durst move your good Lordship for him, trusting that I should have knowledge of your pleasure herein, ere I departed towards your Lordship out of this country, wherefore I advised him to be ready within fourteen days of March at the farthest; that if it pleased your Lordship to accept him, or to have a sight of him before your departing to Calais, that there should be no sloth in him.

He desired me to move Master Fitzwalter to be good master to him in this behalf, and so I did, and he was very glad and agreeable thereto, saying if his son had been of age, and all the servants he hath might be in any wise acceptable to your Lordship, that they all and himself in like wise, shall be at your commandment, while he liveth.

And at my coming home to my poor house, I sent for Robert Bernard, and showed unto him that I had moved your Lordship for him; and he in like form is agreeable to be ready, by the 14th day of March, to await on your Lordship, be it to Calais or elsewhere, and from that day so forth for ever, while his life will last, without drudging or contrarying your commandment and pleasure, in any wise that is in him possible to accomplish. . . .

My Lord, I trust that your Lordship shall like both their persons and their conditions; and as for their truth, if it may please your good Lordship to accept my poor word with their's, I will depose largely for that; and as it pleaseth your good Lordship to command me in these matters, and all other, if it may please your Lordship to show the same to my brother Nessfield, he knoweth who shall soonest be with me to put me in knowledge

[1] Moderate.

of your pleasure, which I shall be at all seasons ready to accomplish to my poor power with God's grace, whom I beseech long to continue the prosperous estate of your good Lordship.

From Norwich, the second day of March, with the hand of your most humble servant and beadsman,

JOHN PASTON

[1476]

66. MARGARET PASTON ANGRY

The Copy of a Letter to Sir John Paston, Knt, from his Mother

IT is so that I understand by your letter, written the Thursday next before Saint Laurence, that ye would have knowledge how that I would be demeaned in Kocket's [1] matter, which I send you hereunder written: I put you in certain that I will never pay him [a] penny of that duty that is owing to him, though he sue me for it, not of mine own purse; for I will not be compelled to pay your debts against my will, and though I would, I may not: wherefore I advise you to see me saved harmless against him for your own advantage in time coming; for, if I pay it, at long way ye shall bear the loss. And whereas ye write to me that I gave you 20*l.* and promised other 20*l.* that is not so, for I wot well if I had so done, ye would not [have] assigned me by your letters of your own hand writing, the which I have to shew, that I should receive again the same sum of William Peacock, and of your farmers, and buyers of your wood of Sporle; and take this for a full conclusion in this matter, for it shall be none otherwise for me than I write here to you.

I marvel much that ye have dealt again so simply with Sporle, considering that ye and your friends had so much to do for to get it you again once, and ye having no greater matters of charge than ye have had since it was last pledged out, it causeth me to be in great doubt of you, what your disposition will be hereafter for such livelihood as I have been disposed, before this time, to leave you after my decease; for I think verily that ye will be disposed

[1] For Kocket (or Cocket) see Letter 58.

hereafter to sell or set to mortgage the land, that ye should have after me your mother, as gladly and rather than that livelihood that ye have after your father; it grieveth me to think upon your guiding, after the great good [1] that ye had in your rule, since your father died, whom God assoil, and so simply spent as it hath been; God give you grace to be of sad [2] and good disposition hereafter to his pleasance and comfort to me, and to all your friends, and to your worship and profit hereafter.

And as for your brother William, I would ye should purvey for his finding, for as I told you the last time ye were at home, I would no longer find him at my cost and charge; his board and his school hire is owing since Saint Thomas's day afore Christmas; and he hath great need of gowns, and other gear, that were necessary for him to have in haste. I would ye should remember it, and purvey them, for as for me I will not. I think ye set but little by my blessing, and if ye did ye would have desired it in your writing to me: God make you a good man to his pleasance.

Written at Maultby the day after Saint Laurence,[3] the year of the reign of King Edward IV, the 17th year.

your Mother,

MARGARET PASTON

[1477]

67. THE CLOTH OF GOLD

To my right worshipful Mother Margaret Paston, be this delivered

PLEASE it you to weet, that whereas I intended to have been at home this Midsummer, and purposed with your good help to have begun upon my Father's Tomb, so that it might have been ended this Summer; it is so, that for such causes as are now begun between my Lord of Suffolk and me, for the Manors of Heylesdon, Drayton, etc., for which matters I must needs be here this next term; therefore I deem it would be after Midsummer, ere than I can see you.

Please it you also to weet that I communed with Master

[1] Property. [2] Serious. [3] February 2.

Pykenham to weet if he would buy the Cloth of Gold for so much as he desired once to have bought it, and he offered me once 20 marks [1]; therefore, nevertheless it cost me 24*l.* yet now, when I speak to him thereof, he refused to buy it; and said, that he had now so many charges that he may not.

But it is so that the King doth make certain Copes and Vestments of like Cloth, which he intendeth to give to the College of Fotheringhay, where my Lord his Father is now buried, and he buyeth at a great price; I communed with the vestment maker for to help me forth with 12 yards, and he hath granted to do, as Wheatley can tell you; wherefore, if it please you that it be bestowed for to make a Tomb for my father at Bromholm, if ye like to send it hither, if it be sold I undertake ere Michælmas, that there shall be a Tomb, and somewhat else over my Father's grave, on whose Soul God have mercy, that there shall none be like it in Norfolk; and as ye shall be glad hereafter to see it; and God send me leisure that I may come home, and if I do not, yet the money shall be put to none other use, but kept by some other that ye trust, till that it may be bestowed according as is above written, and else I give you cause never to trust me while ye and I live.[2]

When I was last with you, ye granted, that the said Cloth of Gold should be wared [3] about this work, that is above written, which if ye will perform, I undertake that there shall be such a Tomb, as ye shall be pleased with, though it cost me 20 marks of mine own purse beside, if I once set upon it.

No more, but I beseech God have you in his keeping.

Written at London the Wednesday in Whitsun-week, in the 18th year of Edward IV.

Please you to send me word by Wheatley of your pleasure herein.

By your Son,
JOHN PASTON, Knight

[1478]

[1] £13 6*s.* 8*d.*
[2] It was twelve years since his father's burial.
[3] Used in exchange.

68. GOOD ADVICE

To the Right Worshipful Sir John Paston, Knight

I GREET you well and send you God's blessing and mine, letting you weet that I have sent you by Wheatley the Cloth of Gold, charging you that it be not sold to none other use than to the performing of your Father's Tomb, as ye send me word in writing; if ye sell it to any other use, by my truth, I shall never trust you while I live.

Remember that it cost me 20 marks, the pledging out of it, and if I were not glad to see that [tomb] made, I would not depart from it. Remember you what charge I have had with you of late, which will not be for my ease this two years; when ye may better, I trust ye will remember it.

My Cousin Clere doth as much cost at Bromholm as will draw an 100*l.* upon the Desks in the Choir, and in other places, at Heydon in likewise, and if there should nothing be done for your Father, it would be too great a shame for us all, and in chief to see him lie as he doth.

Also as I understand that my Cousin Robert Clere thinketh great unkindness in dealing with him of Peacock, for certain Pasture that ye granted him to have, and Peacock hath let it to others, such as he list to let it to, notwithstanding my Cousin hath laid the pasture with his Cattle, and Peacock hath distrained them. I think this dealing is not as it should be: I would that each of you should do for other, and live as Kinsmen and Friends; for such Servants may make trouble betwixt you, which were against courtesy, so near neighbours as ye be. He is a man of substance and worship, and so will be taken in this shire; and I were loath that ye should lose the good will of such as may do for you.

Item, whereas ye have begun your claim in Hellesdon and Drayton, I pray God send you good speed and furtherance in it; ye have as good a season as ye would wish, considering that your Adversary stands not in best favour with the King.

Also ye have the voice in this Country, that ye may do as much with the King, as any Knight that is belonging to the Court; if it be so, I pray God continue it; and also that ye should marry right nigh of the Queen's blood; what she is we are not as certain, but if it be so, that your Land should come again by the reason of your marriage, and to be set in rest, at the reverence of God forsake it not, if ye can find in your heart to love her, so that she be such one as ye can think to have Issue by, or else by my truth, I had rather that ye never married in your life.

Also, if your matter take not now to good effect, ye and all your Friends may repent them that ye began your claim, without that ye have taken such a sure way, as may be to your intent, for many inconveniences that may fall thereof; God send you good speed in all your matters.

Written at Mawteby the day after Saint Austin in May [1] the 18th year of King Edward the IVth.

By your Mother

[1478]

69. SIR JOHN'S BOOK BILL

To my most worshipful Master, Sir John Paston, Knight [2]

MY most worshipful and most special Master, with all my service, most lowly I recommend [me] unto your good Mastership, beseeching you most tenderly to see me somewhat rewarded for my labour in the Great Book [3] which I wrote unto your said good Mastership. I have often times written to Pampyng, according to your desire, to inform you how I have laboured in writings for you. . . .

And in especial I beseech you to send me for Alms one of your old Gowns, which will countervail much of the premises I wot well; and I shall be yours while I live, and at your commandment; I have greatly missed of it God knows, whom I beseech preserve you from all adversity; I am somewhat acquainted with it.

Your very man,

WM EBESHAM

[1] May 25.

[2] Sir John Paston died on November 15, 1479.

[3] *I.e.*, a large volume containing several works.

Following appeareth, parcelly, divers and sundry manner of Writings, which I William Ebesham have written for my good and worshipful Master, Sir John Paston, and what money I have received, and what is unpaid.

	s.	*d.*
First, I did write to his Mastership a little Book of Physic, for which I had paid by Sir Thomas Lewis, in Westminster		20
Item, I had for the writing of half the Privy Seal, of Pampyng		8
Item, for the writing of the said whole Privy Seal of Sir Thomas	2	
Item, I wrote eight of the Witnesses in Parchment but after 14*d.* a-piece, for which I was paid of Sir Thomas	10	
Item, while my said Master was over the sea in Midsummer term, Calle set me at work to write two times the Privy Seal in paper, and then after clearly in parchment .	4	8
And also I wrote at the same time one or more of the longest Witnesses, and other diverse and necessary Writings, for which he promised me 10*s.* (whereof I had of Calle but 4*s.* 8*d.*) due 5*s.* 4*s.*	5	4
Item, I received of Sir Thomas at Westminster 30 October 8 E. IV. 1468	3	4
Item, I did write two Quires of paper of Witnesses, every Quire containing 14 leaves after 2*d.* a leaf . .	4	8
Item, as to the Great Book		
First, for writing of the Coronation; and other Treatises of Knighthood, in that quire which containeth a 13 leaves and more, 2*d.* a leaf	2	2
Item, for the Treatise of War in four books, which containeth 60 leaves after 2*d.* a leaf	10	
Item, for Othea,[1] an Epistle, which containeth 43 leaves	7	2
Item, for the Challenges, and the Acts of Arms which is 28 leaves	4	8

[1] *Othea* means a treatise on wisdom. The word is used as a book title.

	s.	d.
Item, for De Regimine Principum, which containeth 45 leaves, after 1 penny a leaf, which it is right well worth	3	9
Item, for Rubrishing [1] of all the Book	3	4
	63	5

	£	s.	d
Sum received		22	4
Sum unpaid		41	1
Sum Total	3	3	5

WILLIAM EBESHAM

[1469?]

70. SIR JOHN'S BOOKS

The Inventory of English Books, of John Paston, made the 5th day of November, in the . . . year of the reign of Edward IV

1. A BOOK had of my Hostess at the George, of the Death of Arthur, beginning at Cassibelan, Guy Earl of Warwick, King Richard Cœur de Lyon, a Chronicle to Edward the III. price.
2. Item, a Book of Troilus, which William Br[andon?] hath had near ten years, and lent it to Dame. . . . Wyngfeld, and there I saw it . . . worth
3. Item, a black Book, with the Legend of Ladies; [La Belle Dame] sans Mercy; The Parliament of Birds; The Temple of Glass [2]; Palatyse and Scitacus [3]; the Meditations of . .; [Sir Gawain and the] Green Knight . . . worth
4. Item, a Book in print of the play of [the Chess].[4]
5. Item, a Book lent Midelton, and therein is: Belle Dame sans

[1] This either means ornamenting the whole with red capital letters, or writing the heads of the several treatises or chapters in red letters. [F.]

[2] Probably the four ballads of Lydgate, with these titles.

[3] Possibly *Palamon and Arcite.*

[4] The second book from Caxton's press, 1474.

Mercy[1]; the Parliament of Birds; Ballad of Guy and Colbrond; . . . the Goose [The Horse the Sheep and]; The Disputing between Hope and Despair; . . . Merchants; The Life of Saint Cry[stopher].

6. A red Book that Percival Robsart gave me, of the Meeds of the Mass[2]; the Lamentation of Child Ipotis[3]; A Prayer to the Vernicle; . . . called the Abbey of the Holy Ghost.[4]
7. Item, in quires Tully de Senectute in diverse . . . whereof there is no more clear writing.
8. Item, in quires Tully or Cypio de Amicitia,[5] left with William Worcester . . . worth
9. Item, in quires, a Book of the Policy of In. . . .
10. Item, in quires, a Book de Sapientiâ,[6] wherein the second person is likened to Sapience.
11. Item a Book de Othea text and gloss, worth in quires.

Memorandum; mine old Book of Blazonings of Arms.

Item, the new Book portrayed and blazoned.

Item, a Copy of Blazonings of Arms, and the names to be found by Letter.[7]

Item, a Book with Arms portrayed in paper.

Memorandum; my Book of Knighthood; and the manner of making of Knights; of Jousts, of Tournaments; fighting in Lists; paces holden by Soldiers; Challenges; Statutes of War; and de Regimine Principum[8] . . . worth

Item, a Book of new Statutes from Edward the iiii.[9]

[1479?]

[1] By Richard Ross.
[2] Possibly *The Neglicentes happying in the Mass.*
[3] Epictetus.
[4] A well-known devotional work.
[5] Cicero's *De Amicitia.*
[6] Lydgate's *Court of Sapience.*
[7] Alphabetically.
[8] By Thomas Occleve.
[9] If this is not an error for Edward III these last items seem to have been added at a period later than the main list.

VI. *John the Youngest*

71. JOHN THE YOUNGEST SEEKING A WIFE

To Sir John Paston, Knight, or to his Brother Edmund in his absence, lodged at the George, by Paul's Wharf, in London

RIGHT worshipful sir, I recommend me to you, praying you to remember, ere ye depart out of London, to speak with Harry Eberton's wife, draper, and to inform her that I am proffered a marriage in London, which is worth 600 marks [1] and better, with whom I prayed you to commune, inasmuch as I might not tarry in London myself; always reserving, that if so be that Mistress Eberton will deal with me, that ye should not conclude in the other place; though so were that Eberton would not give so much with Mistress Elizabeth his daughter, as I might have with the other, for such fantasy as I have in the said Mistress Elizabeth Eberton; and that it like you to say to Eberton's wife, that such as I spake to her of shall be bettered rather than impaired as for my part; and if it like her to deal with me, I will be at London for that cause only within fourteen days after the writing of this letter, with God's grace, who preserve you and yours. Written at Norwich, on Saint James's day.

Also, Sir, I pray you that ye will, as I desired you, commune with John Lee, or his wife, or both, and to understand how the matter at the Black Friars doth, and that ye will see and speak with the thing yourself, and with her father and her mother, ere ye depart; and that it like you to desire John Lee's wife to send me a bill in all haste possible, how far forth the matter is, and whether it shall be necessary for me to come up to London hastily or not, or else to cast all at the Cock.[2] Also, I pray you that Pitt may truss in a mail, which I left in your chamber at London, my tawny gown furred with black, and the doublet of purple satin, and the doublet of black satin, and my writing box of cypress, and my "Book of the Meeting of the Duke and of

[1] 400 pounds.

[2] Throw it all up?

the Emperor "[1]; and when all this gear is trussed in the mail, to deliver it to the bearer hereof, to bring me to Norwich.

Item, I send you herewith the pillion for the mail, and 10*s.* for the hire, which is usury, I take God to record.

Also, that it like you to speak to your apothecary, which was sometime the Earl of Warwick's apothecary, and to weet of him what the widow of the Black Friars is worth, and what her husband's name was: he can tell all, for he is executor to the widow's husband. I pray you forget me not, no more than I do you. . . .

Also, brother Edmund, I pray you, and my brother Sir John be not in London, that ye will labour all these matters with effect, as my trust is in you in every point as is above written. . . .

Also I sent John Lee's wife a letter by one Crawthorn, dwelling in Wood Street, or else in Silver Street, at the end of Wood Street: I pray you weet whether she had it or not; and she had it not, brother Edmund, I pray you go to the same Crawthorn, and take the letter of him, and deliver it her in all haste.

JOHN PASTON

[1474]

72. DISCOURAGEMENT

To John Paston, Esquire, at Norwich, or to Roose, dwelling afore Mrs Paston's Gate, in Norwich

RIGHT worshipful and well beloved Brother, I recommend me to you, letting you weet, that I have communed with your friend Dawnson, and have received your Ring of him, and he hath by mine advice spoken with her [2] two times; he telleth me of her dealing and answers, which if they were according to his saying, a fainter Lover than ye, would and well ought to take therein great comfort, so that he might haply sleep the worse three nights after.

[1] His book most probably contained an account of some meeting between Charles, Duke of Burgundy, and the Emperor Frederick III. [F.]

[2] Lady Walgrave, widow of Sir Richard Walgrave. Her brother-in-law, a lawyer of the Norfolk connexion, seems to have been a friend of John the Youngest, but had lately died.

And such dealing in part as between my lady W. and your friend Dawnson he wrote me a bill thereof, which I send you herewith; and that that longeth to me to do therein, it shall not fail to leave all other business apart; nevertheless within three days, I hope so to deal herein, that I suppose to set you in certainty how that ye shall find her for ever hereafter.

It is so, as I understand, that ye be as busy on your side for your friend Dawnson, whereas [1] ye be, I pray God send you both good speed in these works, which if they be brought about, each of you is much beholden to other; yet were it pity that such crafty Woers, as ye be both, should speed well, but if ye love truly.

Item, as for Stocton's Daughter, she shall be wedded in haste to Skeerne, as she told herself to my Silkmaid, which maketh part of such as she shall wear, to whom she broke [2] her heart, and told her, that she should have had Master Paston, and my Maid weened it hath been I that she spoke of; and with more, that the same Master Paston came where she was with 20 men, and would have taken her away; I told my Maid that she lied of me, and that I never spoke with her in my life, nor that I would not wed her to have with her 3000 Marks.[3]

Item, as for Eberton's Daughter, my brother Edmond saith, that he heard never more speech thereof since your departing, and that ye would that he should not break, nor do nothing therein but if it came of their beginning. . . .

Written at London, the Sunday the 20th of November, in the 14th year of Edward IV.

JOHN PASTON, Knight

[1474]

73. LADY WALGRAVE DECLINES

To John Paston, Esquire

BROTHER, I recommend me to you, letting you weet, that I have, like as I promised you I have, done my endeavour to know my Lady Walgrave's stomach,[4] which, as God help me, and to be

[1] If. [2] Opened. [3] £2000. [4] Mind.

plain to you, I find in her no matter nor cause, that I might take comfort of.

She will in no wise receive, nor keep your Ring with her, and yet I told her that she should not be any thing bound thereby; but that I knew by your heart of old, that I wist well ye would be glad to forbear the lievest [1] thing that ye had in the world, which might be daily in her presence, that should cause her once on a day to remember you; but it would not be, she would not thereby as she said, put you nor keep you in any comfort thereby.

And moreover she prayed me, that I should never take labour more herein, for she would hold her to such answer as she had given you tofore; wherewith she thought both ye and I would have held us content, had [it] not been [for] the words of her Sister Genevieve.

When I understood all this, and that over night she bad her that went between her and me, bid me bring with me her Muskball [2] which, etc., then I after all this asked if she were displeased with me for it, and she said, nay.

Then I told her, that I had not sent it you, for sin of my soul; and so I told her all, how I had written to you, why that I would not send it to you, because I wist well ye should have sleeped the worse; but now, I told her, as God help me, that I would send it you, and give you mine advice not to hope over much on her, which is over hard on hearted Lady for a young man to trust unto; which, I thought, that for all my words, ye could not nor would not do, for all mine advice.

Yet againwards, she is not displeased, nor forbid me not but that ye should have the keeping of her Muskball; wherefore do ye with it as ye like; I would it had done well by Good, I speak for you so, that in faith I trow I could not say so well again wherefore I send you herewith your Ring, and the unhappy Muskball; also make ye matter of it hereafter as ye can, I am not happy to woo,[3] neither for myself nor none other. . . .

John Paston, Knight

[1474]

[1] Dearest.

[2] This Muskball, or ball of perfume, seems to have been taken from Lady Walgrave by Sir John Paston in a jesting manner, to send to his brother, as a present from her. [F.]

[3] Fortunate in wooing.

74. SIR THOMAS AND DAME BREWS NEGOTIATE

Unto my Right Worshipful Cousin John Paston, be this Letter delivered, etc.[1]

RIGHT worshipful Cousin, I recommend me unto you, etc. And I sent mine husband a bill of the matter that ye know of, and he wrote another bill to me again touching the same matter, and he would that ye should go unto my mistress your mother, and assay if ye might get the whole 20*l.* into your hands, and then he would be more glad to marry with you, and will give you an 100*l.*, and, Cousin, that day that she is married, my father [2] will give her 50 marks. But and we accord, I shall give you a great treasure, that is, a witty gentlewoman, and if I say it, both good and virtuous; for if I should take money for her, I would not give her for a 1000*l.*; but, Cousin, I trust you so much, that I would think her well beset on you, and ye were worth much more. And, Cousin, a little after that ye were gone, came a man from my Cousin Derby, and brought me word that such a chance fell, that he might not come at the day that was set, as I shall let you understand more plainly, when I speak with you, etc. But, Cousin, and it would please you to come again, what day that ye will set, I dare undertake that they shall keep the same day, for I would be glad that, and mine husband and ye might accord in this marriage, that it might be my fortune to make an end of this matter between my cousins and you,[3] that each of you might love other in friendly wise, etc. And, Cousin, if this bill please not your intent, I pray you that it may be burnt, etc. No more unto you at this time, but Almighty Jesu preserve you, etc.

By your Cousin,

DAME ELIZABETH BREWS

[1476]

1 This is the first of a series of letters relating to the engagement of John Paston to Margery Brews.

2 Sir G. Debenham.

3 The ancient quarrel between the Pastons and the Debenhams and Heydons (see Letter 130).

75. CHOOSING A VALENTINE

To my worshipful Cousin John Paston, Be this Bill delivered, etc.

COUSIN, I recommend me unto you, Thanking you heartily for the great cheer ye made me, and all my Folks, the last time that I was at Norwich; and ye promised me, that ye would never break the matter to Margery unto such time, as ye and I were at a point. But ye have made her such [an] Advocate for you, that I may never have rest night nor day, for calling and crying upon me to bring the said matter to effect, etc.

And, Cousin, upon Friday is Saint Valentine's day, and every Bird chooseth him a Mate; and if it like you to come on Thursday at night, and so purvey you, that ye may abide there till Monday, I trust to God, that ye shall so speak to mine husband, and I shall pray, that we shall bring the matter to a conclusion, etc. For, Cousin,

> It is but a simple Oak,
> That is cut down at the first stroke,

for ye will be reasonable I trust to God, which have you ever in his merciful keeping, etc.

By your Cousin Dame ELIZABETH BREWS,
otherwise shall be called by God's Grace

[1477]

76. MARGERY'S VALENTINE

Unto my right well beloved Valentine, John Paston, Esquire, be this Bill delivered, etc.

RIGHT reverend and worshipful, and my right well beloved Valentine, I recommend me unto you, full heartily desiring to hear of your welfare, which I beseech Almighty God long for to preserve unto his pleasure, and your heart's desire.

And if it please you to hear of my welfare, I am not in good hele of body, nor of heart, nor shall be till I hear from you;

For there wots no creature, what pain that I endure,
And for to be dead I dare it not discure.[1]

And my Lady my Mother hath laboured the matter to my father full diligently, but she can no more get than ye know of, for the which God knoweth I am full sorry. But if that ye love me, as I trust verily that ye do, ye will not leave me therefore.

And if ye command me to keep me true wherever I go,
I wis I will do all my might you to love, and never no mo.
And if my Friends say, that I do amiss,
They shall not let me so for to do,
Mine heart me bids evermore to love you,
Truly over all earthly thing,
And if they be never so wrath,
I trust it shall be better in time coming.

No more to you at this time, but the Holy Trinity have you in keeping; and I beseech you that this bill be not seen of none earthly Creature save only yourself, etc.

And this Letter was endited at Topcroft, with full heavy heart, etc.

By your own,
MARGERY BREWS

[1477]

77. A LOVE-LETTER

To my Right Well beloved Cousin John Paston, Esquire, be this Letter delivered, etc.

RIGHT worshipful and well beloved Valentine, in my most humble wise, I recommend me unto you, etc. And heartily I thank you for the Letter, which that ye send me by John Beckerton, whereby I understand and know, that ye be purposed to come to Topcroft in short time, and without any errand or matter, but only to have a conclusion of the matter betwixt my father and you; I would be most glad of any Creature alive, so that the matter might grow to effect. And thereas ye say, and ye come and find the matter no more towards you than ye did aforetime, ye

[1] Discover.

would no more put my father and my Lady my Mother to no cost nor business for that cause a good while after, which causeth my heart to be full heavy; and if that ye come, and the matter take to none effect, then should I be much more sorry, and full of heaviness.

And as for myself I have done and understand in the matter [all] that I can or may, as God knoweth; and I let you plainly understand, that my father will no more money part withal in that behalf, but an 100*l.* and 50 marks, which is right far from the accomplishment of your desire.

Wherefore, if that ye could be content with that Good, and my poor Person, I would be the merriest maiden on ground; and if ye think not yourself so satisfied, or that ye might have much more Good, as I have understood by you afore; good, true, and loving Valentine, that ye take no such labour upon you, as to come more for that matter, But let [what] is, pass, and never more to be spoken of, as I may be your true Lover and Beadwoman during my life.

No more unto you at this time, but Almighty Jesu preserve you both body and soul, etc.

By your Valentine,
MARGERY BREWS

78. ONE ENCOURAGEMENT

Unto my right worshipful Master, John Paston, Esquire, be this bill delivered, etc.

RIGHT worshipful Sir, I recommend me unto you, letting you know, as for the young Gentlewoman, she oweth you her good heart and love; as I know by the communication that I have had with her for the same.

And Sir, ye know what my Master and my Lady have proffered with her 200 Marks [1] and I dare say, that her Chamber and Arayment shall be worth 100 Marks.[2] And I heard my Lady

[1] £133 6*s.* 8*d.*

[2] It was customary for the bride's parents to offer board and lodging for the first few years of a marriage.

say, that and the case required, both ye and she should have your board with my Lady three years after.

And I understand by my Lady, that she would that ye should labour the matter to my Master, for it should be the better.

And I heard my Lady say,

> "That it was a feeble Oak,
> That was cut down at the first stroke."

And ye be beholden unto my Lady for her good word, for she hath never praised you too much.

Sir, like as I promised you, I am your man, and my good will ye shall have in word and deed, etc.

And Jesu have you in his merciful keeping, etc.

By your man,
THOMAS KELA [1]

[1477]

79. THREE PROPOSITIONS

To John Paston, Esq., in haste

I HAVE received your letter, and your man Bykerton, by whom I know all the matter of Mistress Brews, which if it be as he saith, I pray God bring it to a good end.

Item, as for this matter of Mistress Barley, I hold it but a bare thing; I feel well that it passeth not . . . marks; I saw her for your sake; she is a little one, she may be a woman hereafter, if she be not old now; her person seemeth 13 years of age, her years, men say, be full 18; she knoweth not of the matter I suppose, nevertheless she desired to see me, as glad as I was to see her.

I pray you send me some writing to Calais of your speed with Mistress Brews; Bykerton telleth me that she loveth you well; if I died, I had lever ye had her than the Lady Walgrave, nevertheless she singeth well with an harp.

Clopton is afraid of Sir T. Grey, for he is a widower now late, and, men say, that he is acquainted with her of old.

[1] Possibly a chaplain of the Brews.

No more. Written on Sunday the 9th day of March, in the 17th year of Edward IV to Calais ward.

If ye have Mistress Brews, and E. Paston Mistress Bylingford, ye be like to be brethren.

JOHN PASTON, Kt

[1477]

80. JOHN PASTON IS UNCERTAIN

This Bill be delivered to Thomas Grene, Goodman of the George by Paul's Wharf, or to his Wife, to send to Sir John Paston, wheresoever he be, at Calais, London, or other places

RIGHT worshipful Sir, and my most good and kind Brother, in as humble wise as I can, I recommend me to you; Sir, it is so that I have, since John Bykerton departed from home, been at Topcroft at Sir Thomas Brews's, and as for the matter that I sent you word of by John Bykerton, touching myselfe and Mistress Margery Brews, I am yet at no certainty; her father is so hard; but I trow, I have the good will of my Lady her mother and her; but as the matter proveth, I shall send you word with God's grace in short time.

But as for John Bykerton, I pray you deal with him for surety as a soldier should be dealt with, trust him never the more for the bill that I sent you by him but as a man at wild, for every thing that he told me is not true; for he departed without license of his master Sir Thomas Brews, and is sore endangered [1] to divers in this country; I pray God that I write not to you of him too late; but for all this I know none untruth in him, but yet I pray you trust him not over much upon my word.

Sir, Perse Moody [2] recommendeth him to your mastership, and beseecheth you to send him word in haste, how he shall be demeaned at your place at Caister; for he is assigned to nobody as yet, to take of meat and drink, nor yet where that he shall have money to pay for his meat and drink; and now is the chief replenishing of your warren there; the advantage of the Dove house were well for him, till ye come home yourself.

[1] In debt. [2] A servant of Sir John Paston's.

Sir, I pray you pardon me of my writing, howsoever it be, for Carpenters of my craft, that I use now [lovers] have not alder-best their wits their own; and Jesu preserve you.

Written at Norwich, the 9th day of March, in the 17th year of Edward IV.

JOHN PASTON

[1477]

81. DAME BREWS TO MEET MISTRESS PASTON

To my right worshipful Mother Margaret Paston

RIGHT worshipful Mother, after all duties of recommendation, in as humble wise as I can, I beseech you of your daily blessing. Mother, please it you to weet, that the cause that Dame Elizabeth Brews desireth to meet with you at Norwich, and not at Langley, as I appointed with you at my last being at Mawtby, is by my means, for my brother Thomas Jermyn, which knoweth nought of the match telleth me, that the Causey ere ye can come to Bokenham Ferry is so overflown that there is no man that may unethe [1] pass it, though he be right well horsed; which is no meet way for you to pass over, God defend [2] it. But all things reckoned, it shall be less cost to you to be at Norwich, as for a day or tweyn and pass not, than to meet at Langley, where every thing is dear; and your horse may be sent home again the same Wednesday.

Mother, I beseech you for diverse causes, that my Sister Anne may come with you to Norwich; Mother, the matter is in a reasonable good way, and I trust with God's mercy, and with your good help, that it shall take effect better to mine advantage than I told you of at Norwich; for I trow there is not a kinder woman living than I shall have to my Mother in law, if the matter take, nor yet a kinder Father in law than I shall have, though he be hard to me as yet.

All the circumstances of the matter, which I trust to tell you at your coming to Norwich, could not be written in three leaves

[1] Scarcely. [2] Forbid.

of paper, and ye know my lewd [1] head well enough, I may not write long, wherefore I ferry over all things till I may await on you myself. I shall do tun [2] into your place a dozen Ale, and Bread according, against Wednesday. If Sym might be forborne [3] it were well done, that he were at Norwich on Wednesday in the morning at market. Dame Elizabeth Brews shall lie at John Cook's [4]; if it might please you, I would be glad that she might dine in your house on Thursday, for there should you have most secret talking.

And mother, at the reverence of God, beware that ye be so purveyed for, that ye take no cold by the way towards Norwich, for it is the most perilous March that ever was seen by any man's days now living; and I pray to Jesu preserve you and yours.

Written at Topcroft, the 8th day of March.

Your Son and humble Servant,

JOHN PASTON

[1477]

82. SIR THOMAS BREWS

To my right worshipful Cousin Sir John Paston, Knight, be this Letter delivered, etc.

RIGHT worshipful, and my heartily well beloved Cousin I recommend me unto you, desiring to hear of your welfare, which I pray God may be as continually good as I would have mine own; and Cousin, the cause of my writing unto you, at this time, is I feel well by my Cousin John Paston your Brother, that ye have understanding of a matter, which is in communication touching a Marriage, with God's Grace, to be concluded betwixt my said Cousin your Brother, and my Daughter Margery, which is far communed, and not yet concluded, nor neither shall nor may be, till I have answer from you again of your good will and assent to the said matter; and also of the obligation which that I send you herewith; for Cousin I would be sorry to see either my Cousin your Brother, or my Daughter, driven to live so mean a life as

[1] Stupid. [2] Have placed in tuns. [3] Spared.
[4] Cooke was a wealthy citizen, afterwards Mayor of Norwich.

they should do, if the six score pounds [1] should be paid of their marriage money; and Cousin, I have taken myself so near in leaving of [2] this said six score pounds, that whereas I had laid up an 100*l.* for the marriage of a younger Daughter of mine, I have now lent the said 100*l.* and 20*l.* over that, to my Cousin your Brother, to be paid again by such easy days as the obligation, which I send you herewith specifies.

And Cousin, I were right loath to bestow so much upon one daughter, that the other her Sisters should fare the worse; wherefore, Cousin, if ye will that this matter shall take effect under such form as my Cousin your brother hath written unto you, I pray you put thereto your good will, and some of your Cost, as I have done of mine more largely than ever I purpose to do to any two of her Sisters, as God knoweth mine intent, whom I beseech to send you your levest heart's desire.

Written at Topcroft, the 8th day of March, etc.

By your Cousin,

THOMAS BREWS, Knight

[1477]

83. SIR THOMAS'S PROPOSALS

A Determination of Sir Thomas Brews how much he would give with his Daughter Margery in Marriage

MEMORANDUM, To let my Cousin Margaret Paston understand, that for a jointure to be made in Swainsthorp in hand, and for a jointure of no more but 10 marks [3] out of Sparham, I will depart with 200 marks in hand, and to give them their board free as for two or three years in certain, or else 300 marks without their board, payable by 50 marks yearly, till the sum of 300 marks be full paid.

Item, I will give 400 marks payable 50*l.* in hand at the day of marriage, and 50*l.* yearly, till the sum of 400 marks be full paid, upon these conditions following.

[1] John the Youngest had mortgaged the estate of Swainsthorpe for £120, which fell to be redeemed.

[2] Parting with.

[3] £6 13*s.* 4*d.*

Whereof one condition is this,

That I will lend my Cousin John Paston sixscore pounds, besides his marriage money, to pledge out the manor of Swainsthorp, so that [1] he may find such a friend as will pay me again the said sixscore pounds by 20 marks a year, so that it be not paid of the marriage money, nor of the proper goods of my said cousin John.

Or else, another condition is this,

If it be so that my said Cousin John may be suffered, from the day of his marriage to my daughter, to take the whole profits of the manor of Sparham, besides the manor of Swainsthorp, for term of their two lives, and the longest of them living, yet will I be agreeable to depart with the said 400 marks payable again in form above-said.

And if these or any of the conclusions may be taken, I am agreeable to make the bargain sure, or else no moreto be spoken of.

[1477]

84. JOHN'S NOTES OF THE TERMS

Notes touching the Marriage between John Paston, Esq., and Margery Brews

MEMORANDUM, To keep secret from my mother that the bargain is full concluded.

Item, to let her have first, knowledge that in the chapel [2] (whereas ye would had been no book nigh by ten miles) that when Master Brews said that he would shortly have either more land in jointure than Swainsthorp and ten marks out of Spar-

[1] On condition.

[2] It appears that these conditions were discussed in the chapel, where J. Paston swore on one of the service books, that he never would consent to the endangering of any of his friends by their entering into an obligation for the repayment of the sixscore pounds.

This condition, by what follows, seems to have been given up and the agreement appears to be, that the sixscore pounds should be repayed by him by £10 every year on his own security only. [F.]

ham,[1] or else that some friend of mine should pay the sixscore pounds, so that it should not be paid of the marriage money, that then I swore on a [sacred] book to him, that I would never of my motion endanger mother nor brother farther than I had done; for I thought that my mother had done much for me to give me the manor of Sparham in such form as she had done; but Master Brews will not agree, without that my mistress his daughter and I be made sure of it now in hand, and that we may take the whole profits, whatsoever fortune.

Item, to inform my mother that if so be that we may be put in possession of all the whole manor during our two lives, and the longest of us living, that then Master Brews will give me in marriage with my mistress his daughter 400 marks (266*l.* 13*s.* 4*d.*) payable in hand 50*l.* and so yearly 50*l.* till the sum of 400 marks be full paid.

Item, that whereas he had laid up 100*l.* for the marriage of a younger daughter of his, he will lend me the same 100*l.* and 20*l.* more, to pledge out my land, and he to be paid again his 100*l.* and 20*l.* by 10*l.* by year.

Item, to advise my mother that she break not for the yearly value of Sparham above the ten marks during her life.

[1477]

85. SIR JOHN'S OBJECTIONS

To my right Worshipful Mother, Margaret Paston

PLEASE it you to weet, that I have received your Letter, wherein is remembered the great hurt, that by likelihood might fall to my brother, if so be that this matter between him, and Sir Thomas Brews's Daughter take not effect; whereof I would be as sorry as himself reasonably; and also the wealthy and convenient marriage, that should be if it take effect; whereof I would be as glad as any man; and am better content now, that he should have her, than any other that ever he was heretofore about to have

[1] Margaret Paston had given the manor of Sparham to her son.

had. Considered her Person, her Youth, and the stock that she is come of, the Love on both sides, the tender favour that she is in with her father and mother; the kindness of her father and mother to her in departing with her, the favour also, and good conceit that they have in my Brother, the worshipful and virtuous disposition of her father and mother, which prognosticateth that, of likelihood, the maid should be virtuous and good, all which considered, and the necessary relief that my Brother must have, I marvel the less, that ye have departed,[1] and given him the manor of Sparham, in such form as I have knowledge of by W. Gornay, Lomner, and Skipwith; and I am right glad to see in you such kindness unto my Brother as ye have done to him; and would by my truth lever than an 100*l.* that it were fee simple land, as it is intailed, which by likelihood should prosper with him and his blood the better in time to come, and should also never cause debate in our blood in time to come, which God defend,[2] for that were unnatural.[3]

Item, another inconvenience is, whereas I understand that the manor is given to my Brother, and to his Wife, and to the Issue between them begotten; if the case were so, that he and she had issue together a Daughter or more, and his wife died, and he married after another, and had issue a Son, that Son should have none land, and he being his father's Heir, and for the inconvenience that I have known late enure in case like, and yet endureth in Kent, between a Gentleman and his Sister, I would ye took the advice of your counsel in this point, and that [which] is past you by writing or by promise, I deem verily in you, that ye did it of kindness, and in eschewing of a more ill that might befall.

Item, whereas it pleaseth you that I should ratify, grant, and confirm the said gift unto my Brother, it is so, that with mine honesty, I may not, and for other causes.

The Pope will suffer a thing to be used, but he will not license nor grant it to be used nor done, and so I.

My Brother John knoweth mine intent well enough heretofore

[1] Parted with (a gift). [2] Forbid.

[3] *I.e.*, Sparham was entailed on himself, and his mother can only give the income to John, but, without promising anything, he will not disturb his brother in possession.

in this matter; I will be found to him as kind a Brother as I may be.

Item, if it be so that Sir Thomas Brews and his Wife think that I would trouble my Brother and his Wife in the said Manor, I can find no means to put them in surety thereof, but if it need, to be bound in an obligation with a condition that I shall not trouble nor infest them therein.

Item, I think that she is made sure enough in estate in the land, and that of right I deem they shall make none obstacles at my writing, for I had never none estate in the land, nor I would not that I had.

No more to you at this time, but Almighty God have you in keeping.

Written at Calais, the 28th day of March in the 17th year of Edward IV.

By your Son,

JOHN PASTON, Knight

[1477]

86. SIR JOHN'S SYMPATHY

To John Paston, Esquire

RIGHT worshipful and heartily beloved Brother, I recommend me to you, letting you weet, that as by Peirse Moody, when he was here, I had no leisure to send answer in writing to you, and to my Cousin Gurney, of your Letters, but for a conclusion ye shall find me to you as kind as I may be, my conscience and worship saved, which, when I speak with you and them, ye both shall well understand; and I pray God send you as good speed in that matter as I would ye had and as I hope ye shall have ere this Letter come to you; and I pray God send you Issue between you, that may be as honourable as ever was any of your Ancestors and theirs, whereof I would be as glad in manner as of mine own; wherefore I pray you send me word how ye do, and if God fortune me to do well, and be of any power, I will be to Sir Thomas Brewse, and my Lady his wife, a very Son-in-law for your sake, and take them as ye do, and do for them as if I were in case like with them as ye be.

No more, but Jesu have you in keeping.

Written at Calais, the 14th day of April, in the 17th year of Edward IV. . . .

JOHN PASTON, Knight

[1477]

87. SIR JOHN IS ANGRY

To his well-beloved Brother, John Paston, Esq.[1]

I RECOMMEND me to you, letting you weet that I received a letter of yours by Edward Hensted two days after that Wheatley was departed from me, which he had forgotten in his casket, as he said, whereof I should have sent you answer by Wheatley, if I had had it before he went: notwithstanding I am right loath to write in that matter oft; for a conclusion, I wrote to my Mother by Perse Moody all that I might and would do therein; ye have also now written again: You need not to pray me to do that might be to your profit and worship, that I might do, oftener than once, or to let me weet thereof, for to my power I would do for you, and take as much pain for your weal, and remember it when per case [2] ye should not think on it yourself. I would be as glad that one gave you a manor of 20*l.* by year, as if he gave it to myself by my troth.

Item, where[as] ye think that I may with conscience recompense it again unto our stock of other lands that I have of that value in fee simple, it is so that Snailwell by my grandfather's will once, and by father's will secondly, is entailed to the issue of my father's body.

Item, as for Sporle 20*l.* by year, I had thereof but 20 marks by year, which 20 marks by year and the 10 marks over, I have endangered, as ye well know of the bargain; which, if it be not redeemed, I must recompense some other manor of mine to one

[1] Clearly in answer to an application by John Paston to his brother to aid him in making arrangements with Sir T. Brews.

[2] Perchance.

of my brethren for the said 10 marks and 20 marks that longeth to me, wherefore I keep the manor of Runham; then have I fee simple land the manor of Winterton with Bastwick and Billys, which in all is not 20 marks by year, which is not to the value of the manor of Sparham. And as for Caister, it were no convenient land to exchange for such a thing; nor it were not policy for me to set that manor in such case for all manner of haps. I need not to make this excuse to you, but that your mind is troubled; I pray you not to rejoice yourself too much in hope to obtain a thing that all your friends may not ease you of, for if my mother were disposed to give me and any woman in England the best manor that she hath to have it to me and my wife, and to the heirs of our two bodies begotten, I would not take it of her by God. Stablish yourself upon a good ground, and grace shall follow; your matter is far spoken of and blown wide, and if it prove no better, I would that it had never been spoken of. Also that matter noiseth me, that I am so unkind that I let [1] altogether. I think not a matter happy nor well handled nor politically dealt with, when it can never be finished without an inconvenience, and to any such bargain, I keep never to be condescending nor of counsel; if I were at the beginning of such a matter, I would have hoped to have made a better conclusion, if they mock you not. This matter is driven thus far forth without my counsel; I pray you make an end without my counsel: if it be well, I would be glad; if it be otherwise, it is pity; I pray you trouble me no more in this matter.

JOHN PASTON, Kt

[1477]

88. MARGARET PASTON'S FINAL EFFORT

To the Right Worshipful and my very good Lady and Cousin Dame Elizabeth Brews

RIGHT worshipful, and my chief Lady and Cousin, as heartily as I can I recommend me to you; Madam, liketh you to understand that the chief cause of my writing to you at this season is this;

[1] Hinder it.

I wot well it is not unremembered with you the large communication that divers times hath been had touching the marriage of my Cousin Margery your daughter and my son John, of which I have been as glad, and now latewards as sorry, as ever I was for any marriage in my life; and where or in whom the default of the breach is, I can have no perfect knowledge; but, Madam, if it be in me or any of mine, I pray you assign a day, when my Cousin your husband and ye think to be at Norwich towards Sall, and I will come thither to you, and I think, ere ye and I depart, that the default shall be known where it is, and also that with your advice and help, and mine together, we shall take some way that it shall not break; for if it did, it were none honour to neither parties, and in chief to them in whom the default is, considering that it is so far spoken.

And Madam, I pray you that I may have perfect knowledge by my son [in law] Yelverton,[1] bearer hereof, when this meeting shall be, if ye think it expedient, and the sooner the better in eschewing of worse; for, Madam, I know well if it be not concluded in right short time, that as for my son he intendeth to do right well by my Counsin Margery and not so well by himself, and that should be to me, nor I trust to you, no great pleasure, if it so fortuned, as God defend, whom I beseech to send you your levest desires.

Madam, I beseech you that I may be recommended by this bill to my cousin your husband, and to my Cousin Margery,[2] to whom I supposed to have given another name ere this time. Written at Mawtby on Saint Barnabas's day.[3]

By your

MARGARET PASTON

[1477]

[1] Husband of Anne Paston.

[2] John Paston married Margery Brews the same year, 1477.

[3] June 11.

VII. *The Younger Brothers*

89. EDMUND PASTON

To John Paston, or to his Brother Edmund Paston, at the George, at Paul's Wharf

BROTHER Edmund, it is so that I hear tell that ye be in hope to come hither, and to be in such wages as ye shall come [and] live like a gentleman, whereof I would be glad; wherefore for your better speed, I let you weet that Hugh Beaumont is dead; wherefore I would ye had his room [1] now or never, if ye can bring it about; else, if ye dispose you to abide in England, since it is so that the Bishop of Lincoln [2] is Chancellor, his service is the meeter for you, he is next neighbour to Norfolk of any estate: God send you some good ward of his.

I pray you, if your leisure be thereafter to remember Townshend, that he, with the advice and assistance of my Master of the Rolls, have one day of march [3] with the slow Bishop of Winchester, that he may keep his promise, that is to say, to entreat the Duke and Duchess of Norfolk for Caister; he promised to do it, and to lay out an 100*l.* for the same.

Item, I pray you send me some tidings within five days after that you see this bill. Written at Calais, the 13th day of June.

JOHN PASTON, Kt

[1473]

90. EDMUND AT CALAIS

To Edmund Paston, Esquire, at Calais, be this delivered

BROTHER Edmund, I greet you well, letting you weet, that about this day sev'night I sent you a Letter by Nicholas Bardesley a Soldier . . . and also an Hosecloth [4] of black for you; I weened

[1] Place. [2] Thomas Rotherham, officially Chancellor, May 1474.
[3] Bargaining. [4] Cloth for hose.

that ye should have it within two days, but I am afeared that he deceived me.

Item, I let you weet that Plattyng is coming hither, and he saith, that ye gave him leave to fetch his gear and Pytt's; and that is his errand hither and none other, nor he thought never to go from me, nor he will not go from me, as he saith; wherefore I pray you send me word of his conditions, and why ye think that he should never do me worship.

He saith also, that he and Pytt were at the taking of the Easterlings,[1] and that he was in the Packer, and Pytt in the Christopher; I pray you send me word how both he and Pytt quit them, by the report of some indifferent true man that was there; if they quit them well, I would love them the better; wherefore the next day after the sight of this letter, I pray you write again, and send it by the next passage.

Item, I send you a little pretty Box herewith, which I would that Juddy should deliver to the woman that he weeteth of, and pray her to take it to the man that she weeteth of; that is to say, as much as ye know all well enough, but ye may not make you wise, in no wise.

Item, I pray you send me word as ye were wont to do, of her welfare; and whether I were out and other in or not; and whether ye shall forsake Calais as soon as she sent me word of, or not.

By God I would be with you as fain as yourself, and shall be in haste with God's grace.

Item, as for my brother John, I hope within this month to see him in Calais; for by likelihood to-morrow, or else the next day, he taketh ship at Yarmouth, and goeth to Saint James ward [2]: and he hath written to me that he will come homeward by Calais. . . .

Item, Mistress Elizabeth fareth well, but as yet Songer knoweth not so perfectly all that ye would weet, that he would not write to

[1] German Hanse fleet.

[2] To St James of Compostella, in Spain, perhaps in the suite of some nobleman. The phrase also meant to get out of England.

you of these two days, till he know more; but if she had been bold, and durst have abiden still at her gate, and spoken with me, so God help me, she had had this same that I send now, where ye wot of, which ye shall see worn hereafter, it is a pretty ribbon with pretty Aglets [1] and goodly.

Make you not wise to Juddy neither, not that ye would weet any thing, for I may say to you, at his coming over he brought goodly gear reasonably.

Item, as for my Bill,[2] that is gilt, I would it were taken heed to, there is one in the town, that can glaze well enough, as I heard say; also there is one cometh every market day from St Omer's to Calais, and he bringeth Daggers and fetcheth also, he may have it with him, and bring it again the next market day for 12*d.* or 16*d.* at the most; and else, let it be well oiled and kept till I come.

No more. Written at London the 5th day of July, in the 13th year of Edward IV.

John Paston, Knight

[1473]

91. WALTER PASTON

Margaret Paston to [James Gloys?]

I recommend me to you, and thank you heartily of your letters, and diligent labour that ye have had in those matters that ye have written to me of, and in all other, to my profit and worship, and in especial at this season, touching the matter that I sent you the Indenture of; ye have lightened my heart therein by a pound, for I was in fear that it would not have been done so hastily without danger.[3] And as for the letters that Thomas Holler's son should have brought me, I see neither him, nor the letters that he should have brought; wherefore I pray you heartily, if it be no disease to you, that ye will take the labour to bring Walter where he should be, and to purvey for him, that he may be set in good and sad rule, for I were loath to lose him, for I trust to have more

[1] Points. [2] Battle-axe. [3] Of borrowing.

joy of him than I have of them that be older; though it be more cost to me to send you forth with him, I hold me pleased, for I wot well ye shall best purvey for him, and for such things as is necessary to him, than another should do, after mine intent. As for any horse to lead his gear, methink it were best ye purvey one at Cambridge, less than[1] ye can get any carrier thence to Oxford more hastily, and I marvel that the letters come not to me, and whether I may lay the default to the father or to the son, thereof. And I would Walter should be coupled with a better than Holler's son is, there as he shall be; how be it I would not that he shall make never the less of him, because he is his countryman and neighbour; and also I pray you write a letter in my name to Walter, after that[2] ye have known mine intent before this to him ward; so that he do well, learn well, and be of good rule and disposition, there shall nothing fail him that I may help with, so that it be necessary to him; and bid him that he be not too hasty of taking of orders that should bind him, till that he be of twenty-four years of age or more, though he be counselled the contrary, for *Often rape rueth*[3]: I will love him better to be a good secular man than to be a lewd[4] priest.

And I am sorry that my cousin Berney is sick; and I pray you if my white wine, or any of my waters, or any other thing that I have, that is in your award, may do him comfort, let him have it, for I would be right sorry if any thing should come to him but good; and for God's sake advise him to do make his will, if it be not done, and to do well to my cousin his wife, and else it were pity; and I pray you to recommend me to her, and to my aunt, and to all the gentlemen and gentlewomen there. And as for John Day, if he be dead I would be sorry, for I know not how to come by my money that he oweth me; and I purpose Peacock shall have less to do for me another year than he hath had, if I may be better purveyed with your help, for he is for himself, but not for me.

And as for any merchants to my corn, I can get none here, therefore I pray you do ye as well therein as ye can. Also I send you, by the bearer hereof, the bill of mine receipts; and if ye go

[1] Unless.
[2] According to what.
[3] Haste repents.
[4] Stupid.

forth with Walter, I pray you come to me as soon as ye may after ye be come home; and me liketh mine abiding and the country here right well, and I trust when summer cometh and fair weather, I shall like it better, for I am cherished here but too well; and I construe your letters into other matters well enough, whereof I thank you, and if it need not to send forth Walter hastily, I would ye might come to me, though ye should come upon one day, and go again on the next day, then should I commune with you in all matters; and I hold best if ye have not the letters that Holler's son should have brought me, that ye send Sym over for them this night, that I may have them to-morrow, and if ye may come yourself I would be the better pleased; and I remember that water of mint or water of milfoil [1] were good for my cousin Berney to drink for to make him to brook [2]; and if they send to Dame Elizabeth Calthorpe, there ye shall not fail of one or of both; she hath other waters to make folks to brook. God keep you; written on the Monday next after Saint Hilary.[3]

I have no longer leisure at this time.

MARGARET PASTON

[1473]

92. WALTER AT OXFORD

To his Worshipful Mother, Margaret Paston, dwelling in Maultby, be this Letter delivered in haste

RIGHT Reverend and Worshipful Mother, I recommend me unto your good Mothership, beseeching you to give me your daily benediction, desiring heartily to hear of your prosperity, which God preserve to his pleasure and to your heart's desire, etc. I marvel sore that you sent me no word of the letter which I sent to you by Master William Brown at Easter: I sent you word that time that I should send you mine expenses particularly; but as at this time the bearer hereof had a letter suddenly that he should come home, and therefore I could have no leisure to send them you on that wise, and therefore I shall write to you in this letter

[1] A medicinal plant. [2] Digest. [3] January 13.

the whole sum of my expenses since I was with you till Easter last past, and also the receipts, reckoning the 20*s.* that I had of you to Oxon wards with the Bishop's finding.

	£	*s.*	*d.*
The whole sum of receipts is . . .	5	17	6
And the whole sum of expenses is . .	6	5	$5\frac{3}{4}$
And that [which] cometh over the receipts in my expenses, I have borrowed of Master Edmund, and it draweth to . . .	0	8	0

and yet I reckon none expenses since Easter, but as for them they be not great, and therefore I beseech you to send me money by Sir Richard Cotman, bringer of this letter, or else by the next messenger that you can have to me.

I beseech you that he that I sent by this letter to you, may have good cheer, if he bring it himself, as he telleth me that he will, for he is a good lover of mine. Master Edmund Alyard recommend him specially to you, and to all my brethren and sisters and to all your household; and I beseech you that I may be recommended to all them also, and specially to my brother John the younger. No more to you at this time, but Almighty Jesus have you in his keeping Amen.

Written at Oxonforth [1] on Saint Dunstan's day, and the 19th day of May.

By your son and scholar,

WALTER PASTON

[1478]

93. WALTER AND THE CHURCH

To my Mistress Margaret Paston at Norwich

MY worshipful Mistress, I recommend me unto you, and thank you of your approved ensured kindness evermore shewed, and so I pray you to continue. I have received your letter and understand your desire, which is against the law for three causes; one

[1] Walter Paston took a degree at Oxford in 1479, and died later in the same year.

is, for your son Walter is not tonsured; another cause, he is not twenty-four years of age, which is required compleat. The third, he ought of right to be priest within twelvemonths after that he is parson, without so were he had a dispensation from Rome, by our Holy Father the Pope, which I am certain cannot be had; therefore I present not your desire unto my lord,[1] lest he would have taken it to a displeasure; or else to take a great simpleness in your desire, which should cause him, in such matters as shall fortune you to speed with him another time, to shew unto you the rigour of the law, which I would be loth; therefore present another man able; ask counsel of Master John Smyth, and cease of your desire in this part, for it is not goodly neither godly; and let not your desire be known, after my advice: be not wroth, though I send unto you thus plainly in the matter, for I would ye did as well, as any woman in Norfolk, that is, with right, to your honour, prosperity, and to the pleasure of God, with you and all yours, who have you in his blessed keeping. From Hoxne on Candlemas day.

I send you your present again in the box.

William Pykenham
[Chancellor of Norwich]

[1479]

94. WALTER AND THE LAW

To his worshipful Mistress, Mistress Margaret Paston

Right worshipful Mistress, I recommend me unto you as lowly as I can, thanking you for your goodness at all times, God grant me to deserve it and do that may please you.

As for your son Walter, his labour and learning hath been, and is, in the faculty of art, and is well sped therein: and [he] may be bachelor [2] at such time as shall like you, and then to go to law, I can think it to his preferring, but it is not good he know it unto the time he shall change; and as I conceive there shall none have that exhibition to the faculty of law, therefore move ye the

[1] The Bishop of Norwich. [2] *I.e.*, graduate.

executors that at such time as he shall leave it, ye may put another in his place, such as shall like you to prefer. If he shall go to law, and be made bachelor of arts before, and ye will have him home this year, then may he be bachelor at Midsummer, and be with you in the vacation and go to law at Michaelmas.

What it shall like you to command me in this or any other, ye shall have mine service ready.

I pray you by the next messenger to send me your intent, that such as shall be necessary may be purveyed in season, and Jesu preserve you. At Oxinforth the 4th day of March.

Your Scholar,

EDMUND ALYARD

[1479]

95. WALTER'S GRADUATION

To his Right Reverend Brother Sir John Paston, at Caistor Hall in Norfolk

AFTER all due reverence, and recommendations, liketh it you to understand that I received a letter from my brother John, whereby I understood that my mother and you would know what the costs of my proceeding should be; I sent a letter to my brother John certifying my costs, and the causes why that I would proceed, but as I have sent word to my mother, I purpose to tarry now till it be Michaelmas, for if I tarry till then, some of my costs shall be paid, for I supposed, when that I sent the letter to my brother John, that the queen's brother [1] should have proceeded at Midsummer, but he will tarry now till Michaelmas, but as I sent word to my mother, I would be Inceptor before Midsummer, and therefore I beseeched her to send me some money, for it will be some cost to me, but not much.

Sir, I beseech you to send me word what answer ye have of the Bishop of Winchester for that matter which ye spake to him of for me, when I was with you at London: I thought for to have

[1] When a person of royal or very great family took a degree in the university he bore a part of the expenses of those who became graduates at the same time.

had word thereof ere this time: I would it would come, for our finding of the Bishop of Norwich beginneth to be slack in payment [1]; and if ye know not what this term meaneth "Inceptor," Master Edmund, that was my ruler at Oxford, bearer hereof, can tell you, or else any other graduate.

Also, I pray you send me word what is done with the horse I left at Tottenham, and whether the man be content that I had it of or not. Jesu preserve you to his pleasure, and to your most heart's desire. Written at Oxford the Saturday next after the Ascension of our Lord.

WALTER PASTON

[1479]

96. WALTER'S GRADUATION FEAST

To his right trusty and heartily beloved Brother, John Paston, abiding at the George at Paul's Wharf in London, be this Letter delivered

RIGHT worshipful and heartily beloved Brother, I recommend me unto you, desiring faithfully to hear of your prosperity, which God preserve, thanking you of divers letters that you sent me.

In the last letter that you sent to me, ye writ that you should have writ in the letter that you sent by Master Brown, how that I should send you word what time that I should proceed,[2] but there was none such writing in that letter; the letter is yet to show, and if you come to Oxon, ye shall see the letter, and all the letters that you sent me since I came to Oxon.

And also Master Brown had that same time much money in a bag, so that he durst not bring it with him, and that same letter was in that same bag, and he had forgotten to take out the letter, and he sent all together by London, so that it was the next day after that I was made bachelor ere than the letter came, and so the fault was not in me.

[1] Evidently the Bishop of Norwich was responsible for some Exhibitions which he did not pay punctually. Walter would Incept as M.A. soon after he had Proceeded as B.A. The term is still used at Cambridge, where the older Pastons had studied. [Gr.]

[2] To the bachelor's degree.

And if ye will know what day I was made bachelor, I was made on Friday was sev'night, and I made my feast on the Monday after. I was promised venison against my feast, of my Lady Harcourt, and of another person too, but I was deceived of both; but my guests held them pleased with such meat as they had, blessed be God, who have you in his keeping. Amen.

Written at Oxon, on the Wednesday next after Saint Peter.

WALTER PASTON

[1479]

97. DEATH OF WALTER AND HIS GRANDMOTHER

SURE tidings are come to Norwich that my Grandam [1] is deceased, whom God assoil: my Uncle had a messenger yesterday that she should not escape, and this day came another, at such time as we were at mass for my brother Walter, whom God assoil! [2] My Uncle was coming to have offered, but the last messenger returned him hastily, so that he took his horse incontinent to inform more of our heaviness.

My Sister is delivered, and the child passed to God, who send us of his grace.

Docking told me secretly that, for any haste [3] my Uncle [William] should ride by my Lady of Norfolk to have a threescore persons, whether it is to convey my Grandam hither or not he could not say: I deem it is rather to put them in possession of some of her lands.

Written the Saturday the 21st of August, in the 19th year of Edward IV.

EDMUND TO JOHN

[1479]

[1] Agnes Paston.

[2] Walter Paston died soon after his return from Oxford, in the town residence of the Pastons, in Norwich.

[3] In spite of his haste.

98. AN ACCOUNT OF JOHN PASTON, ESQ.[1]

	£	s.	d.
RECEIVED at Cressingham the Thursday after Saint Edmund[2] at the court there, by the hands of me John Paston Esq.	5	10	0
Whereof paid to my mother,			
For costs done upon the burying of Walter Paston, and while he lay sick;			
And for the hire of a man coming with the said Walter from Oxon, 20*d*.	1	9	11
Item, paid to William Gibson for one horse, saddle and bridle lent to Walter Paston by the said William.	0	16	0
Item, given the said man coming from Oxon with the said Walter, by the hands of John Paston . .	0	1	8
Item, paid for divers things while Walter Paston lay sick	0	0	4
Item, for the costs of John Paston riding to keep the court at Cressingham anno supradicto, which was four days in doing, for the steward might not be there at the day prefixed	0	3	4
Total paid . .	2	11	3

[1479]

99. WILLIAM AT ETON[3]

To his worshipful Brother John Paston, be this delivered in haste

RIGHT reverend and worshipful brother, I recommend me unto you, desiring to hear of your welfare and prosperity, letting you weet that I have received of Alweder a letter and a noble in gold therein; furthermore my creanser[4] Master Thomas [Stevenson]

[1] For the burial of Walter Paston. [2] November 25, 1479.

[3] William, younger son of old John Paston, now nineteen years of age, and at Eton.

[4] Creditor.

heartily recommended him to you, and he prayeth you to send him some money for my commons, for he saith ye be 20*s.* in his debt, for a month was to pay for, when he had money last; also I beseech you to send me a hose cloth, one for the holydays of some colour, and another for the working days how coarse soever it be it maketh no matter, and a stomacher, and two shirts, and a pair of slippers: and if it like you that I may come with Alweder by water, and sport me with you at London a day or two this term time, then ye may let all this be till the time that I come, and then I will tell you when I shall be ready to come from Eton by the grace of God, who have you in his keeping. Written the Saturday next after Allhallows day with the hand of your brother.

WILLIAM PASTON

[1478]

100. DIVERSIONS AT ETON

To his Worshipful Brother, John Paston, be this delivered in haste

RIGHT reverend and worshipful Brother, after all duties of recommendation, I recommend me to you, desiring to hear of your prosperity and welfare, which I pray God long to continue to his pleasure, and to your heart's desire; letting you weet that I received a letter from you, in the which Letter was 8*d.* with the which I should buy a pair of slippers.

Farthermore certifying you as for the 13*s.* 4*d.* which ye sent by a Gentleman's man, for my board, called Thomas Newton, was delivered to mine Hostess, and so to my Creanser Mr Thomas Stevenson; and he heartily recommended him to you; also ye sent me word in the letter of 12*lb.* of Figgs and 8*lb.* of Raisins, I have them not delivered, but I doubt not I shall have, for Alweder told me of them, and he said, that they came after in another Barge.

And as for the young Gentlewoman, I will certify you how I first fell in acquaintance with her; her father is dead, there be two sisters of them, the elder is just wedded; at which wedding I was with mine hostess, and also desired [1] by the Gentleman himself, called William Swan, whose dwelling is in Eton. So it fortuned that mine hostess reported on me otherwise than I was worthy; so that her Mother commanded her to make me good Cheer; and so in good faith she did; she is not abiding where she is now, her dwelling is in London; but her Mother and she came to a place of hers five miles from Eton, where the wedding was, for because it was nigh to the Gentleman, which wedded her Daughter; and on Monday next coming, that is to say, the first Monday of Lent, her Mother and she will go to the Pardon at Sheene [2] and so forth to London, and there to abide in a place of hers in Bow Church-Yard; and if it please you to enquire of her, her Mother's name is Mistress Alborow, the name of the Daughter is Margaret Alborow, the age of her is, by all likelyhood, 18 or 19 years at the farthest; and as for the money and plate it is ready whensoever she were wedded; but as for the Livelihood [3] I trow not till after her mother's decease, but I cannot tell you for very certain, but you may know by enquiring.

And as for her Beauty, judge you that, when you see her, if so be that ye take the labour; and specially behold her hands, for and if it be, as it is told me, she is disposed to be thick.

And as for my coming from Eton, I lack nothing but versifying, which I trust to have with a little continuance.

Quœritur, Quomodo nonvalet hora, valet mora? Unde dicitur?

> Arbore jam videas exemplum. Non die possunt
> Omnia suppleri; sed tamen illa mora.

And these two verses aforesaid be of mine own making.

No more to you at this time, but God have you in his keeping.

Written at Eton the even of Saint Mathias the Apostle, in haste, with the hand of your Brother.

WILLIAM PASTON, Junior

[1479]

[1] Invited. [2] Richmond. [3] Property.

101. EDMUND AND THE WIDOW CLIPPESBY

To Sir John Paston, Knight

SIR, after all duties of recommendation, please it [you] to understand, that, according to your letter sent me by Wilson, Lomner and I met at Norwich and drew out a formable bill out of yours, and sent it again to the Escheator Palmer by my brother Edmund, which had another errand into that country to speak with H. Spilman, to get his good will towards the bargain like to be finished hastily betwixt Mistress Clippesby [1] and him.

And, Sir, at the delivery of the Bill of Inquisition to the Escheator,[2] my brother Edmund told him that according to your writing to me, I spake with mine uncle William [3] wherefore ye had need to beware that the Escheator skips not from you, when he cometh to London, and certify it, ere ye speak with him.

The Escheator shall be at London by Tuesday or Wednesday next coming, at John Lewis's house, for he shall ride forwards as on Monday next coming betimes.

Sir, your tenants at Cromer say that they know not who shall be their lord, they marvel that ye nor no man for you hath not yet been there. . . .

Also, Sir, ye must of right, considering my brother Edmund's diligence in your matters, since your departing, help him forwards to mine uncle Sir George Brown, as my brother Edmund prayed you in his letter that he sent unto you by Mond's son of Norwich, dwelling with Thomas Jenney, that mine uncle Sir George may get to my brother Edmund of the king the wardship of John Clippesby, son and heir to [William] Clippesby, late of Oby, in the county of Norfolk, esquire, during the nonage [4] of my lord and lady of York, though it cost four or five marks the suit; let mine uncle Sir George be clerk of the hanaper,[5] and keep the

[1] Catherine, widow of William Clippesby of Stow Bekerton, who soon afterwards married Edmund Paston.

[2] The officer who collected the king's dues on the death of a landowner.

[3] *I.e.*, about the estates of Agnes Paston.

[4] Childhood.

[5] The Clerk of the Hanaper registered and kept grants and patents. The wardship of little Clippesby belonged to the Duke of Norfolk—Richard, Duke of York, Edward IV's younger son married to the little

patent, if it be granted, till he have his money, and that shall not be long to. Mine uncle Sir George may inform the king for truth, that the child shall have no land during his young mother's life, and there is no man here that will marry with him without they have some land with him, and so the gift shall not be great that the king should give him; and yet I trow he [1] should get the mother by that mean; and in my conceit the king doth but right if he grant my brother Edmund, Clippesby's son in recompense for taking my brother Edmund's son, otherwise called Dyxson's, the child's father being alive; Dyxson is dead, God have his soul, whom I beseech to send you your most desired joy.

Written at Norwich on Saint Leonard's day.[2]

JOHN PASTON

Sir, it is told me that Nicholas Barley the squire hath taken an action of debt against me this term, I pray you let Wheatley or somebody speak with him, and let him weet that if he sue me softly this term, that he shall be paid ere the next term be at an end; it is about six pounds, and in faith he should have had it ere this time and our threshers of Swainsthorp had not died upon [me], and if I might have paid it him a year ago, as well as I trust I shall soon after Christmas, I would not for twelve pounds have broken him so many promises as I have.

Also, Sir, I pray you send me by the next man that cometh from London two pots of treacle of Genoa, they shall cost 16*d.* for I have spent out that I had with my young wife, and my young folks, and myself; and I shall pay him that shall bring them to me, and for his carriage; I pray you let it be sped.

The people dieth sore in Norwich, and specially about my house, but my wife and my women come not out, and flee farther we cannot, for at Swainsthorp, since my departing thence, they have died, and been sick nigh in every house of the town.[3]

[1479]

Mowbray heiress: the king would exercise his son's rights while the latter was a minor. The sale of the marriage was the most profitable part of wardship. [Gr.]

[1] Edmund. [2] November 6.

[3] Sir John himself died shortly after receiving this letter.

102. EDMUND'S MARRIAGE

To my Right Worshipful and especial good Mother, Margaret Paston

RIGHT worshipful and most especial good mother, in my most humble wise, with all my duty and service, I recommend me to you, beseeching you of your blessing, which is to me most joy of earthly thing; and it please you to be so good and kind, mother, to me, to forgive me, and also my wife [1] of our lewd [2] offence, that we have not done our duty, which was to have seen you and have waited upon you ere now. My huswife trusteth to lay to you her houswifry for her excuse, which I must beseech you not to accept, for in good faith, I deem her mind hath been otherwise occupied than as to houswifry, which seemeth well by the lacheness [3] of the tilth of her lands. I beseech God, for the furtherance of them as now reward you, and the good parson of Maultby and also Master Baily, who I weened would not have baulked this poor lodging to Norwich ward.

I understand by the bringer hereof that ye intend to ride to Walsingham, if it please you that I may weet the season, as my duty is, I shall be ready to await upon you.

Please it you, that the bringer hereof came to me for 10*s*. 8*d*. which I should owe his father; true it was at my last departing from him, I owed him so much, but certainly ere I came at Thetford homewards, I thought of conscience he ought to have restored me as much; I had my horses with him at livery, and among all, one of them was put to grass and to labour, so that he died of a lax by the way; I paid for hard meat ever to him.

Please it you to deliver Katharine 5*s*. which I send you in this bill. I am not ascertained how she is purveyed of money towards her journey. If her father could not have claimed one penny of me, I would not see her dispurveyed [4] if I might, nor the poorest child that is belonging to his lodging.

Mother, my wife is bold to send you a token; I beseech you

[1] Edmund married the widow Clippesby possibly in 1480.
[2] Discourteous. [3] Negligence. [4] Unprovided.

pardon all things not done according to duty. I beseech God send you the accomplishment of your most worshipful desires. At Oby, the Saturday next before Candlemas.

Your humble Son
and Servant,
EDMUND PASTON

[1480?]

VIII. John, Head of the Family

103. MARGERY PASTON

To my right reverend and worshipful Husband,
John Paston

RIGHT reverend and worshipful Husband,[1] I recommend me to you, desiring heartily to hear of your welfare, thanking you for the Token that ye sent me by Edmund Perys, praying you to weet that my Mother sent to my father to London for a Gown cloth of Muster develers [2] to make of a Gown for me; and he told my Mother and me when he came home, that he charged you to buy it, after that he was come out of London.

I pray you, if it be not bought, that you will vouchsafe to buy it, and send it home as soon as ye may, for I have no gown to wear this winter but my black and my green-a-lyer, and that is so cumberous that I am weary to wear it.

. . . Of all other things that ye desired that I should send you word of, I have sent you word of in a letter that I did write on Our Lady's day last was: the Holy Trinity have you in his keeping.

Written at Oxnead, in right great haste on the Thursday next before Saint Thomas's day.

I pray you that ye will wear the Ring with the Image of St Margaret that I sent you, for a Remembrance, till ye come home. . . .

Yours,
MARGERY PASTON

[1477]

[1] After so much correspondence in negotiating the marriage of John Paston and Margery Brews it is strange that there is no record in the letters of the actual marriage, which must have taken place in 1477. She was a Debenham, and with the end of the ancient family quarrels and the return of the main Fastolf estates, the Pastons, with John the Youngest as head of the family, now occupied an important position in the county.

[2] A grey woollen cloth.

104. CAREFUL ARRANGEMENTS OF JOHN PASTON

To my Right Worshipful Mother Margaret Paston

RIGHT Worshipful Mother, after all duties of humble recommendation, in as humble a wise as I can, I beseech you of your daily blessing; please it you to weet that at my being now at London, like as ye gave me in commandment, I moved to Master Pykenham and to James Hobart for their being at Norwich this Lent, that ye might have their advices in such matters as ye let me have understanding of. And as for Master Pykenham he is now Judge of the Arches, and also he hath another office which is called Auditor Causarum, and his business is so great in both these offices, that he cannot tell the season when that he shall have leisure to come into Norfolk; but I left not till I had gotten James Hobart and him together, and then I told them your intent; and then Master Pykenham told James and me his intent; and he prayed James that he should in no wise fail to be with you this Lent; notwithstanding it was no great need to pray him much, for he told Doctor Pykenham that there was no gentlewoman in England, of so little acquaintance as he had with you, that he would be gladder to do service unto, and much the gladder, for he proposeth from henceforth during his life to be a Norfolk man, and to lie within two miles of Loddon, which is but eight or ten miles at the most from Maultby; and in conclusion he hath appointed to await on you at Norwich the week next after Midlent Sunday, all the whole week, if need be, all other matters laid apart.

Also I communed with my brother Sir John at London of such matters as ye would have amended in the bill that he sent unto you, and he stuck not greatly at it.

Also, Mother, I heard while I was in London, where was a goodly young woman to marry, which was daughter to one Seff, a mercer, and she shall have 200*l.* in money to her marriage, and 20 marks by year of land after the decease of a step-mother of hers, which is upon fifty years of age and ere I departed out of London, I spake with some of the maid's friends, and have gotten their good wills to have her married to my brother Edmund, notwithstanding, those friends of the maid's, that I communed with, advised me to get the good will of one Sturmyn, which is in Master Pykenham's danger so much that he is glad to please him; and so I moved this matter to Master Pykenham, and incontinent he sent for Sturmyn, and desired his good will for my brother Edmund, and he granted him his good will, so that he could get the good will of the remanent that were executors to Seff, as well as the said Sturmyn was; and thus far forth is the matter; wherefore Mother we must beseech you to help us forward with a letter from you to Master Pykenham to remember him for to handle well and diligently this matter now this Lent; and, for I am acquainted with your conditions of old, that ye reck not, who enditeth more letters than ye, therefore I have drawn a note to your Secretary's hand, Friar Perse, which letter we must pray you to send us, by the bearer hereof, and I trust it shall not be long from Master Pykenham.

Your daughter of Swainsthorp,[1] and her sojournant, Edmund Paston, recommendeth them to you in their most humble wise, lowly beseeching you of your blessing; and as for my brother Edmund, Swainsthorp, for none intreat that his hostess your daughter nor I could intreat him, might not keep him, but that he would have been at home with you at Maultby on Sunday last part at night; and as he was departing from hence, had we word from French's wife, that, God yield [2] you, Mother, ye had given him leave to disport him here with us for a seven or eight days; and so the drevyll [3] lost his thank of us, and yet abode nevertheless. Your daughter sendeth you part of such poor stuff as I sent her from London, beseeching you to take it in gree,[4] though it be little plenty that she sendeth you; but as for Dates I will say truth, ye have not so many by two pounds, as were meant unto you, for she thinks at this season Dates right good meat, whatsoever it meaneth, I pray God send us good tidings, whom I beseech to preserve you and yours, and to send you your most desired joy.

At Swainsthorp on Ash Wednesday.

Your Son and humble servant,

[1478] JOHN PASTON

[1] Margery Paston, his wife, apparently staying at Swainsthorpe.
[2] Thank. [3] Simpleton. [4] Favour.

105. A SON AND HEIR

To John Paston, Esquire, be this Letter delivered, or to my Mistress his Wife at Norwich, to deliver to him

BROTHER John, I recommend me to you, and I thank God, my Sister your Wife, and you, of my fair Nephew Christopher, which I understand ye have, whereof I am right glad, and I pray God send you many, if it be his pleasure; nevertheless ye be not kind, that ye send me no weeting thereof; I had knowledge by Footmen, or ever ye could find any messenger on horseback to bring me word thereof.

Sir, it is so, that the Duke of Buckingham shall come on Pilgrimage to Walsingham, and so to Bokenham Castle to my Lady his Sister; and then it is supposed, that he shall to my Lady of Norfolk, and mine Uncle William cometh with him; and he telleth me, that there is like to be trouble in the Manor of Oxnead; wherefore I pray you take heed, lest that the Duke of Suffolk's Council play therewith now at the Vacation of the Benefice,[1] as they did with the Benefice of Drayton, which by the help of Master John Salett and Donne his man, there was a Quest made by the said Donne, that found that the Duke of Suffold was very Patron, which was false, yet they did it for an evidence; but now if any such practice should be laboured, it is I hope in better case, for such a thing must needs be found before Master John Smyth, who is our old Friend; wherefore I pray you labour him, that, if need be, he may do us a friend's turn therein.

Item, both ye and I must needs take this matter as our own, and it were for none other cause, but for our Good Grandam's sake; nevertheless ye wote well, that there is another Interest longing to us after her decease; if there be any such thing begun there by such a Frier or Priest, as it is said, I marvel that ye sent me no word thereof; but ye have now Wife and Child, and so much to care for, that ye forget me.

As for tidings here, I hear tell that my Cousin Sir Robert

[1] Agnes Paston, grandmother of Sir John, made various presentations to the Rectory of Oxnead, apparently without interference from the Duke of Suffolk.

Chamberlain hath entered the Manor of Scolton upon your Bedfellow [1] Conyers, whereof ye send me no word.

Item, as for the Pageant that men say that the Earl of Oxford hath played at Hammes,[2] I suppose ye have heard thereof; it is so long ago, I was not in this Country when the tidings came, therefore I sent you no word thereof, but for conclusion, as I hear say, he leaped the Walls, and went to the Dyke, and into the Dyke to the chin; to what intent I cannot tell; some say, to steal away, and some think he would have drowned himself, and so it is deemed.

No more, but I am not certain whether I shall come home in haste or not.

Written at London, the day next Saint Bartholomew [3] in the 18th year of Edward IV.

John Paston, Knight

[1478]

106. SIR JOHN'S DEATH

To my right worshipful Mother, Margaret Paston, at St Peter's of Hungate

Right worshipful Mother, after all duties of humble recommendation, as lowly as I can, I beseech you of your daily blessing and prayers; and Mother, John Clement, Bearer hereof, can tell you the more pity is, if it pleased God, that my Brother is buried in the White Fryers at London,[4] which I thought should not have been; for I supposed that he would have been buried at Bromholm, and that caused me so soon to ride to London, to have purveyed his bringing home; and if it had been his will to have lain at Bromholm, I had purposed all the way as I have ridden, to have brought home my Grandam and him together

[1] Intimate friend.

[2] For this episode see note to Letter 60. The Earl of Oxford escaped from Hammes in 1484.

[3] August 24.

[4] For the death of Walter Paston see Letter 97. Sir John Paston died in London on November 15, 1479. His grandmother, Agnes, widow of William Paston, the Judge, died in the same year.

but that purpose is void as now; but this I think to do when I come to London, to speak with by Lord Chamberlain, and to win by his means my Lord of Ely if I can; and if I may, by any of their means, cause the King to take my service and my quarrel together, I will; and I think that Sir George Brown, Sir James Radcliff, and others of mine acquaintance, which wait most upon the King, will put to their good wills: this is my way as yet.

I have much more to write, but my empty head will not remember it.

Also Mother I pray that my brother Edmund may ride to Marlingford, Oxnead, Paston, Cromer, and Caister, and in all these Manors to enter in my name, and to let the Tenants of Oxnead and Marlingford know, that I sent no word to him to take no money of them, but their Attornment; wherefore he will not, till he hear from me again, ask them none, but let him command them to pay to [no] Servants of mine Uncle, nor to himself, nor to none other to his use, in pain of payment again to me; I think if there should be any money asked in my name, peradventure it would make my Lady of Norfolk against me, and cause her to think I dealt more contrary to her pleasure than did my brother, whom God pardon of his great mercy!

I have sent to enter at Stansted and at Orwellbury; and have written a bill to Anne Montgomery and Jane Rodon, to make [to] my Lady of Norfolk if it will be.

Your Son, and humble Servant,

JOHN PASTON

[1479]

107. DIFFICULTIES WITH UNCLE WILLIAM

To the Right Worshipful John Paston, Esq., in haste

MY Master Paston I recommend me to you, praying God to have mercy on my master your brother's soul, to whom ye are heir, and also to my mistress your grandam; wherefore by the advice of my mistress your careful mother, your brother Edmund, on Sunday next before Saint Andrew, rode to Marlingford, and before all the tenants examined one James, keeper there for

William Paston, where he was the week next before Saint Andrew, and there he said, that he was not at Marlingford from the Monday unto the Thursday at even, and so there was no man there but your brother's man at the time of his decease; so by that your brother [1] died seized [2]; and your brother Edmund bad your man keep possession to your behest, and warned the tenants to pay no man, till you had spoken them; so meseemeth that is a remitter to the old tailed title: commune with your counsel. Further, at afternoon he was at Oxnead, to understand how they had done; and Piers kept your brother's possession at that time, and your uncle his man was not there, but he assigned another poor man to be there, whether that continued the possession of W. Paston or not be remembered, etc.

And after the decease, etc. W. Paston sent the man that kept possession tofore, to enter and keep possession, which was no warrant by that appointment, for ye stand at your liberty as for any appointment or communication had before, and so men seem it were good for you to stand at large, till ye hear more; if ye might have my Lord Chamberlain's good favour and lordship, it were right expedient; as for my Lord of Ely, deal not with him by our advice, for he will move for treaty,[3] and else be displeased. Your brother Edmund sent to John Wymondham, and he sent word he would be a mean of treaty, but would take no part, and as I suppose that was by Heydon's advice, for your uncle sent to me to be with him, and also the same man rode to Heydon and Wymondham, etc. the bringer of this letter can tell, for he was with your brother Edmund at these places.

Further, my mistress your mother greeteth you well, and sendeth you her blessing, requiring you to come once of that here, as soon as ye may: and your brother Edmund commended him to you, and he doth his diligence and part for you full well and sadly in many behalves; and hath brought my mistress your wife to Topcroft on Friday last, and they fare all well there; and he

[1] Sir John Paston.

[2] In possession. If Sir John was in possession on Dame Agnes's death his brother John was heir; if not William could claim as nearer in relation to his mother.

[3] Compromise.

intendeth to see my master Fitzwalter, which lyeth at Freton, near Long Stratton, etc. and God be your guide in all matters, and bring you soon home.

By your
WILLIAM LOMNER

[1479]

108. JOHN NOT NERVOUS

To my right worshipful and most kind Mother, Margaret Paston

RIGHT worshipful mother, after all duties of humble recommendation, as lowly as I can, I beseech you of your daily blessing and prayer.

Please it you to understand that whereas ye willed me by Paines, to haste me out of the air that I am in [1]; it is so that I must put me in God, for here must I be for a season, and in good faith I shall never, while God sendeth me life, dread more death than shame; and thanked be God, the sickness is well ceased here, and also my business putteth away my fear. I am driven to labour in letting of [2] the execution of mine unkind uncle's intent, wherein I have as yet none other discourage, but that I trust in God he shall fail of it.

I have spoken to my Lord of Ely divers times, which hath put me in certainty by his words, that he will be with me against my uncle, in each matter that I can shew that he intendeth to wrong me in; and he would fain have a reasonable end betwixt us, whereto he will help, as he saith; and it is certain, my brother, God have his soul! had promised to abide the rule of my Lord Chamberlain and of my Lord of Ely; but I am not yet so far forth; nor not will be, till I know my Lord Chamberlain's intent, and that I purpose to do to-morrow, for then I think to be with him, with God's leave. And since it is so that God hath purveyed me to be the solicitor of this matter, I thank him of his grace for the good lords, masters, and friends that he hath sent me, which have perfectly

[1] The year 1479 was a year of great mortality from pestilence.
[2] Hindering.

promised me to take my cause as their own, and these friends be not a few.

And mother, as I best can and may, I thank you and my cousin Lomnor of the good advice that ye have sent me, and I shall apply me to do thereafter; also, mother, I shall beseech you on my behalf to thank mine cousin Lomnor for the kindness that he hath shewed unto me in giving of his answer to mine uncle's servant, which was with him.

Mother, I write not so largely to you as I would do, for I have not most leisure; and also when I have been with my Lord Chamberlain, I purpose not to tarry long after in London, but to dress me to you wards, at which time I trust I shall bring you more certainty of all the fardel [1] that I have in my business than I can as yet write.

I am put in certainty by my most special good master, my Master of the Rolls, that my Lord of Ely is and shall be better lord to me than he hath shewed as yet, and yet hath he dealt with me right well and honourably.

Mother, I beseech you that Peacock may be sent to purvey me as much money as is possible for him to make against my coming home, for I have much to pay here in London, what for the funeral costs, debts, and legacies, that must be content [2] in greater haste than shall be mine ease. Also I would the farm barley in Flegg, as well as at Paston, if there be any, were gathered, and if it may be reasonably sold, then to be sold, or put to the malting; but I would at Caister that it were out of the tenants' hands, for things that I hear: keep ye counsel this from Peacock and from all folks, which matter I shall appease, if God will give me leave.

JOHN PASTON

109. MARGERY AND UNCLE WILLIAM

To my Right Worshipful Master, John Paston, in haste

RIGHT reverend worshipful sir, in my most humble wise, I recommend me unto you as lowly as I can, etc. Please you to weet

[1] Burden. [2] Paid.

John Howes, Alexander Wharton, John Fille, with the parson and the new miller of Marlingford, have gotten Thomas at Well's cart of East Todenham, farmer; and mine uncle William Paston, Harry Hervey of Melton Magna, farmer, and bailiff to my said uncle, Richard Barker's cart of the said town of Melton, late farmer, and yet is in danger [1] to my said uncle, and William Smyth's cart of Brandon juxta Barnham Broom, late farmer, and bailiff, and also in danger to my said uncle, on Monday and Tuesday last past carried away from Marlingford into the place at Saint Edmund's in Norwich, twelve of your great planks, of the which they made six loads, bearing about the said carts bows and glaives [2] for fear of taking away. Sir, as for your tenants of Marlingford, they withhold their cattle and themselves both from the court, and come not within the lordship, nor make none attournment,[3] except Thomas Davy and John Water, which absenting of the tenants is to them a great hurt and loss, for lack of seeding of their lands with their winter corn; beseeching you for God's sake to remember some remedy for them.

My Lady Calthorpe has been at Ipswich on pilgrimage, and came home by my Lady of Norfolk, and there was much communication of your matter betwixt you and mine uncle, saying to my Lady Calthorpe, ye need not have gone to London, ye might have had an end at home; remembering to my said Lady Calthorpe of the motion that he made touching the manor of Sporle, promising to my Lady to abide that, and to write and seal as largely as any man will desire him.

And at his departing from my Lady he was not merry, what the cause was I wot not. My Lady Calthorpe desired me to write to you to have end, for he intends largely to have a peace with you, as he saith; but trust him not too much, for he is not good. My mother-in-law thinketh long she hear no word from you; she is in good health, blessed be God, and all your babes also. I marvel I hear no word from you, which grieveth me full evil; I sent you a letter by [the] brasier's son of Norwich, whereof I hear no word. No more to you at this time, but Almighty Jesu have

[1] Debt. [2] Carrying bows and bills.
[3] Transference of service by a tenant to a new feudal lord.

you in his blessed keeping. Written at Norwich on Hallowmass day at night.

By your servant and beadswoman
MARGERY PASTON

Sir, I pray you, if ye tarry long at London, that it will please [you] to send for me for I think long since I lay in your arms.

[1482]

110. THE OLD QUARREL WEARING OUT

To my Right Worshipful Master, John Paston, Esq., be this letter delivered in haste

MINE own sweet heart, in my most humble wise, I recommend me unto you, desiring heartily to hear of your welfare, the which I beseech Almighty God preserve and keep to His pleasure and your heart's desire.

Sir, the cause of my writing to you at this time, on Friday at night last past came Alexander Wharton, John Howse, and John Fille, with two good carts well manned and horsed with them to Marlingford, and there at the manor of Marlingford and at the mill loaded both carts with mestlyon [1] and wheat, and betimes on Saturday in the morning they departed from Marlingford towards Bungay, as it is said; for the said carts came from Bungay, as I suppose, by the sending of Bryon, for he goeth hastily over the sea, as it is said, and as I suppose he will have the mestlyon over with him, for the most part of the cart loads was mestlyon, etc.

Sir, on Saturday last past, I spake with my cousin Gornay, and he said if I would go to my Lady of Norfolk and beseech her good Grace to be your good and gracious lady, she would so be, for, he said, that one word of a woman should do more than the words of twenty men, if I would rule my tongue, and speak none harm of mine uncle; and if ye command me so for to do, I trust I shall say nothing to my Lady's displeasure, but to your profit; for me thinketh by the words of them, and of your good farmer of

[1] Mixed corn—rye and wheat.

Oxnead, that they will soon draw to an end, for he curseth the time that ever he came in the farm of Oxnead, for he saith that he weeteth well that he shall have a great loss, and yet he will not be aknowyn [1] whether he hath paid or not; but when he seeth his time, he will say truth.

I understand by my said cousin Gornay that my Lady is near weary of her part; and he saith my Lady shall come on pilgrimage into this town, but he knoweth not whether afore Christmas or after, and if I would then get my Lady Calthorpe, my mother-in-law, and my mother, and myself, and come before my Lady, beseeching her to be your good and gracious Lady, he thinketh ye shall have an end, for fain she would be rid of it with her honour saved, but yet money she would have. No more to you at this time, but I marvel sore that I have no letter from you, but I pray God preserve you and send me good tidings from you, and speed you well in your matters. And as for me, I have gotten me another lodging fellow, the first letter of her name is Mistress Bishop's; she recommendeth her to you by the same token that ye would have had a token to my Master Bryon.

At Norwich, the Sunday next after the feast of All Saints.

By your servant and beadswoman,

MARGERY PASTON

[1482]

III. REMONSTRANCE WITH HIS MOTHER

To my Right Worshipful Mother Margaret Paston

RIGHT worshipful Mother, in my most humble wise I recommend me to you, beseeching you of your daily blessing, and when I may, I will with as good will be ready to recompense you for the costs that my huswife and I have put you to, as I am now bound to thank you for it, which I do in the best wise I can. And, mother, it pleased you to have certain words to my wife at her departing, touching your remembrance of the shortness that ye think your days of, and also of the mind that ye have towards my brethren and sister your children, and also of your servants,

[1] Will not let it be known.

wherein ye willed her to be a mean to me, that I would tender and favour the same. Mother, saving your pleasure, there needeth not ambassadors nor means betwixt you and me, for there is neither wife nor other friend shall make me to do that, that your commandment shall make me to do, if I may have knowledge of it; and if I have no knowledge, in good faith I am excusable both to God and you; and, well remembered, I wot well, ye ought not to have me in jealousy for one thing nor other that ye would have me to accomplish, if I overlive you; for I wot well none man alive hath called so oft upon you as I, to make your will and put each thing in certainty, that ye would have done for yourself, and to your children and servants. Also at the making of your will,[1] and at every communication that I have been at with you touching the same, I never contraried anything that ye would have done and performed, but always offered myself to be bound to the same; but, mother, I am right glad that my wife is anything [in] your favour and trust, but I am right sorry that my wife, or any other child, or servant of yours should be in better favour or trust with you than myself, for I will and must forbear, and put from me that, that all your other children, servants, priests, workmen, and friends of yours, that ye will ought bequeath to, shall take to them, and this have I, and ever will be ready unto, while I live, on my faith, and never thought other, so God be my help; whom I beseech to preserve you and send you so good life and long, that ye may do for yourself and me after my decease: and I beshrew their hearts that would other, or shall cause you to mistrust, or to be unkind to me or my friends.

At Norwich, this Monday, with the hand of your son and truest servant,

JOHN PASTON

[1482]

[1] Margaret Paston died in November 1484: her will was dated February 4, 1481–82.

112. KEEPING CHRISTMAS IN MOURNING

To my right worshipful husband John Paston

RIGHT worshipful husband, I recommend me unto you; Please it you to weet, that I sent your eldest Son to my Lady Morley, to have knowledge what Sports were used in her house in Christmas next following, after the decease of my Lord her husband; and she said, that there were none Disguisings, nor Harping, nor Luting, nor Singing, nor none loud Disports; but playing at the Tables, and Chess, and Cards; such disports she gave her Folks leave to play and none other.

Your Son did his errand right well as ye shall hear after this. I sent your younger Son to the Lady Stapleton, and she said according to my Lady Morley's saying in that; and as she had seen used in places of worship [1] thereas she hath been.

I pray you that ye will assure to you some man at Caister, to keep your Buttery, for the man that ye left with me, will not take upon him to breve [2] daily as ye commanded; he saith, he hath not used to give a reckoning neither of Bread nor Ale, till at the week's end, and he saith, he wot well that he should not content it and therefore I suppose he shall not abide, and I trow ye shall be fain to purvey another man for Symond, for ye are never the nearer a wise man for him.

I am sorry that ye shall not at home be for Christmas.

I pray you that ye will come as soon as ye may; I shall think myself half a Widow, because ye shall not be at home, etc. God have you in his keeping. Written on Christmas Even.

By your MARGERY PASTON

[1484]

113. LIFE AT CAISTER

To my Master John Paston be this delivered

RIGHT reverend and worshipful Sir, in my most humble wise I recommend me to you, desiring to hear of your welfare, the which

[1] *I.e.*, families of distinction.

[2] Keep accounts.

I beseech God to preserve to his pleasure, and to your heart's desire.

Sir, I thank you for the venison that ye sent me; and your ship is sailed out of the haven as this day.

Sir, I send you by my brother William your stomacher of damask. As for your tippet of velvet it is not here; Ann saith that ye put in your casket at London.

Sir, your children be in good health, blessed be God.

Sir, I pray you send me the gold, that I spake to you of, by the next man that cometh to Norwich.

Sir, your mast that lay at Yarmouth is let to a ship of Hull for 13*s.* 4*d.* and if there fall any hurt thereto, ye shall have a new mast therefore.

No more to you at this time, but Almighty God have you in his keeping. Written at Caister Hall the 21st day of January, in the first year of King Harry the VIIth.[1]

I pray God no ladies no more overcome you, that ye give no longer respite in your matters.

By your Servant,

MARGERY PASTON

[1486]

114. THE DEATH OF SIR JOHN PASTON

To my Cousin Master William Paston

COUSIN Paston, I recommend me unto you, and have received your letter, by the which I have understanding of the death of my cousin, your father, whose soul Jesu assoil.[2] I will counsel and exhort you to take it as well and as patiently as ye can, seeing that we all be mortal and born to die. And whereas ye desire to have a letter *ad colligendum*,[3] after mine advice ye shall do well to be here with me at Michaelmas next coming; and at your then

[1] 1486.

[2] After the death of his wife Margery, in 1495, Sir John Paston married Agnes, daughter of N. Morley, of Glynde, widow of J. Hervey and of J. Isley. [F.]

[3] *I.e.*, to think upon.

coming I shall be glad to do you the best comfort and help that I can, counselling that ye in the mean time do not intermeddle in any wise with the administering of any part of your father's goods, nor with the receiving of his debts, for divers causes.

[In] the mean season look that ye be of as comfortable cheer as ye can, exhorting my lady, your mother-in-law, to be in like wise; to whom I pray you to have me recommended.

Thus fare ye heartily well. From London this 6th day of September.

Yours,

William Elect of [London] [1]

[1503]

[1] William Warham was actually Bishop of London, and Archbishop Elect of Canterbury in 1503.

SECTION II

THE FASTOLF INHERITANCE

115. FASTOLF'S GREAT CLAIM AGAINST THE CROWN

Billa de debitis Regis in partibus Franciæ Johanni Fastolf militi debitis

THESE be the Injuries, Losses, and Damages that the said Fastolf hath had, as well within the Realm of England as in other parts in manner and form as it ensueth,[1]

	£	s.	d.
First, it is to consider how that the said Fastolf hath been vexed and troubled since he came last into this land by the might and power of the Duke of Suffolk, and by the labour of his counsel and servants in divers wise, as in great oppressions, grievous and outrageous amercements, and many great horrible extortions, as it may appear more plainly by a roll of Articles thereupon made, the damages of which extend to the sum of 5000 marks . . . . =	3333	6	8
Item, taking away a manor called Dedham, in the County of Essex, to the value of 100 marks of yearly rent, with 200 marks in costs . . =	333	6	8

[1] This list is given as an instance of the impudent claims made by the Lords on national funds. Fastolf was one of the Generals driven out of France after Bedford's death, and he claims *compensation* for what he had surrendered. He acknowledges that it was his duty to attend Councils, etc., yet demands to be paid his expenses. Against his assertion that he had never fee or reward in England stands the fact that he was extremely wealthy. That the Duke of Bedford's bequests were not yet paid was largely his own fault, the Will not having been carried out by the Executors, F. being one, the rest, by 1455, were dead. He was, however, merely following the example of the Duke of York, Duke of Somerset, Earl of Warwick, etc. [Gr.]

	£	s.	d.
Item, there is cast into the King's hands by untrue forged inquisitions, three Manors of Fastolf, to the value of 100 marks yearly, and costs, the sum of 500 marks . . . . . . =	333	6	8
Item, Fastolf having the gift of the Lordship of Sillie Guillem, in the County of Maine, gotten by the said Fastolf, he was commanded by the King's Letters to deliver up the Lordship to the King's Commissioners, to damages of the said Fastolf, 2500 marks . . . . =	1666	13	4
Item, Whereas the said Fastolf had a Prisoner of his own taking, which agreed to pay him for his ransom 3200 Saluts,[1] the Prisoner was taken away from him by the Duke of Bedford, and the town of Compeyn, then lying in the French party's governance, for to be yielded to the King, and Fastolf was recompensed but to the value of 1600 Saluts in lands in Normandy, which lands he hath also lost; sum, 4000 marks . . . =	2666	13	4
Item, Fastolf is yet owing for his reward due to him for the taking of John, Duke of Alanson, at the battle of Verneuil, 4000 marks . . =	2666	13	4
Item, is due by the Last Will and Testament of John Duke of Bedford, whose soul God assoil! for Charges for safeguard and keeping of certain Fortresses, and Towns [etc.] 4599 *marks* 5*s*. 6*d*. =	3066	5	6
Sum total 21099 *marks* 5*sh*. 6 *pence* =	14066	5	6

Item, Since the last coming over of the said Fastolf into this realm [1440], by the space of 15 years and more, he hath borne great expenses, attending upon the King's Highness, and the Lords of his Council, as he hath had in commandment, and was his part to do, for the which, and for all the service that he hath done to the right

[1] A gold coin of Henry VI current in France, worth £1 5*s*. 0*d*.

noble Prince King Harry the IV Ayeul [1] to our Sovereign Lord that now is, and to the most victorious Prince and King his father, whose souls God assoil, and also to our said Sovereign Lord, he hath had neither fee nor recompence in this realm of England, but hath borne it of his own proper goods, trusting to have been considered and rewarded as other men of such deserving have been in the times of the right noble Projenitors of our said Sovereign Lords late Kings of this said Realm.

[1455]

116. FASTOLF'S CLAIM ON ALENÇON'S RANSOM

To the worshipful Sir, and my right well beloved Cousin John Paston and in his Absence to John Bocking, or William Barker

Worshipful Sir and Cousin, I recommend me to you, and like you to weet that I have a Tally [2] with my Cousin Fenn of 500 marks and more, for to be charged upon such places, as a man might have most speedy payment; and I pray you heartily to commune with the said Fenn that I might be insured of the said Tally to be exchanged, and for what reward competent tobe given upon the same, I will agree to it.

Item, I desire to know who be the Residue, the remanent of the Co-Executors of the Lord Willoughby,[3] now the Lord Cromwell is deceased; for this cause, it was so, that there was due to the Lord Willoughby and to me 10,000 marks for a Reward to be paid of my Lord Bedford's Goods, for the taking of the Duke of Alençon.

[1] Grandfather.

[2] A cleft stick, both parts of which were notched according to the sum of money advanced, and of which one part was given to the Creditor, while the other remained with the Debtor. Hence the Tallier of the Exchequer, now called the Teller. [F.]

[3] Robert, Lord Willoughby, an eminent Commander, who was present at the battle of Agincourt in 1415, and at the battle of Verneuil in 1424, where he and Sir John Fastolf took the Duke of Alençon prisoner.

And the said Lord Willoughby had but one thousand marks paid, and I one thousand marks, so 8000 remaineth yet to pay; of which Sum, 4000 must grow to the Executors of the said Lord Willoughby to dispose.

And therefore I desire that the Executors, and such as most have interest in the Lord Willoughby's Goods, may be communed with; that they make pursuit for payment of the said 4000 marks, for his part to be had, and I shall make for my part.

And [if] Master Nevile,[1] the which hath wedded my Lady Willoughby, have power, or interest to receive the Lord Willoughby's Debts, then he to be laboured unto. And my Lord of Salisbury will be a great helper in this cause.

The King, which is Supervisor of my Lord Bedford's Testament, hath written, and commanded by sundry Letters, that the said Lord Willoughby should be content [2] for his part; and so much the matter is the forwarder.

And there is one Young, a servant of the Lord Willoughby, which pursued this matter; if he were in London, he could give good information upon this matter.

I pray you write to me how my matters do, and of such novelties as ye have there, and our Lord have you in his keeping.

Written at Caister hastily, the 5th day of February, in the 34th year of King Henry VIth.

Your Cousin,

JOHN FASTOLF

[1456]

117. FASTOLF WISHES TO FOUND A COLLEGE OF PRIESTS AT CAISTER

To the worshipful, and my right well beloved Cousin, John Paston, at the Temple, or to William Barker, at Southwark, be this delivered

WORSHIPFUL Cousin, I commend me to you, and whereas I late wrote unto you, in a Letter by Henry Hansson, for the foundation

[1] Sir Thomas, younger son of the Earl of Salisbury and brother of the King-maker, Warwick.

[2] Paid.

of my College; I am sore set thereupon; and that is the cause I write now, to remember you again to move my Lords of Canterbury and Winchester for the License to be obtained, that I might have the amortizing [1] without any great Fine; in recompence of my long service continued, and done unto the King, and to his noble Father, whom God assoil,—and never yet guerdoned or rewarded.

And now since I have ordained to make the King Founder,[2] and ever to be prayed for; and for his right noble Progenitors, his Father and Uncles, methinketh I should not be denied of my desire, but the rather to be remembered and sped.

Wherefore, as I wrote unto you, I pray you acquaint me and you, for the rather speed hereof, with a Chaplain of my Lord of Canterbury, that in your absence may remember me, and in likewise with my Lord Chancellor; for seeing the King's Disposition, and also his, unto the edifying of God's service, it might in no better time be moved, etc.

My Lord of Norfolk is removed from Framlingham on foot to go to Walsingham, and daily I wait that he would come hither.

Your Cousin,

JOHN FASTOLF

[1456]

118. PRELIMINARY NEGOTIATIONS

To my right worshipful Uncle, and my right good Master, Sir John Fastolf, Knight

RIGHT worshipful Uncle, and my right good Master, I recommend me to you with all my service.

And Sir, my Brother Paston and I have communed together as touching to your College that ye would have made, and Sir, it is too great a good [3] that is asked of you for your License; for

[1] Permission to endow it with lands, in spite of the statutes against mortmain. Heavy fees were charged for such a favour.

[2] *I.e.*, so that his influence might prevent robbery of the endowment.

[3] Sum of money (see note to Letter 117).

they ask for every 100 marks that ye would amortise 500 marks and will give it no better cheap.

And Sir, I told my Brother Paston, that my Lady Abergavenny hath in diverse Abbeys of Leicestershire, seven or eight Priests singing for her perpetually, by my Brother Darcy's and my Uncle Brokesby's means, for they were her Executors; and they accorded for money and gave a 200 or 300 marks, as they might accord for a Priest.

And for the Surety [1] that he should sing in the same Abbey for ever they had Manors of good value bounden to such Person as pleased the said Brethren, Brokesby, and my Brother Darcy, that the said service should be kept.

And for little more than the King asked them for a License, they went through with the said Abbots.

And I hold this way as sure as that other; ye may commune with your Counsel thereof.

And if there be any service that I may do for you, it shall be ready at all times with the grace of God, who have you in his keeping.

Written at London, the 17th day of July.

Your Nephew and Servant,
HENRY FYLUNGLEY

[1456]

119. CHARACTER OF FASTOLF

AFTER humble and due recommendation, please it your good mastership to understand, that at making of this my poor Letter there were no novelties [2] with us, but such as ye understood full well afore your departing. . . .

Sir, I pray you, how some-ever my Master reckoneth with any of his Servants, bring not the matter in revolution in the open Court, for and it were once opened before the Judges, how that

[1] This is a curious fact, as it shows us how security was given by the Abbies, etc., to the Parties contracting for a Mass or Service, that it should be continued for ever in the same Abbey, etc. [F.]

[2] News.

any Letters Patent should be purchased of an *ante* date [1] and the default found in me, ye would be a thousand times advised and my Master F. [2] both, ere that ye would amend me so much as I should be appered thereby [3]; and therefore I beseech you be well advised how that matter be opened, for my ease.

I was not desired to write unto you of no one person, so God be my help, yourself except; but I would ye would take advice and counsel of the priest,[4] that had you so long under hands on Shor Thursday [5] when I and my fellowship, God thank you, had of you right great cheer to our great comfort and your great cost. . . .

My Master can do nothing, the which shall come in open audience at these days, but it shall be called your deed, and it is not unknown that cruel and vengible he hath been ever, and for the most part without pity and mercy. I can no more, but " vade et corripe eum " [6] for truly he cannot bring about his matters in this world for the world is not for him [7]; I suppose it will not change yet by likeliness, but I beseech you Sir, help not to amend him only, but every other man, if ye know any more misdisposed.

I can no more, but, as I can or may, shall be his servant and yours unto such time as ye will command me to surcease and leave off, if it please him.

Sir, I pray you take this Copy of your Statute, it is not examined by me, for I found it these five years passed.

Written in my sleeping time, at afternoon, on Whitsunday. . .

Your own,

HENRY WINDSOR [8]

[1456]

[1] It was a common practice to antedate Letters Patent, so that holders could claim emoluments from lands and offices from an earlier date.

[2] Fastolf.

[3] Injured—*i.e.*, neither you nor Fastolf could indemnify me.

[4] Sir Thomas Howes, Fastolf's Confessor and his wife's uncle.

[5] Maundy Thursday—the day before Good Friday.

[6] Colloquial: " devil take him ! "; literally: " go and take him ! "

[7] Circumstances are against him.

[8] A retainer of Fastolf's.

120. FASTOLF'S AFFAIRS MISMANAGED

To the right worshipful Sir, John Paston, Esquire, being in Norwich, in haste

RIGHT worshipful Sir, after due recommendation, please you to weet that I wrote a remembrance to you the day that I departed out of Norwich, by Richard, the Parson's servant of Blofield, concerning certain matters to be remembered by your wisdom for my Master's avail, which your great wisdom can well understand is right needful, as one thing in especial, that Shipdam and Spyrling ought to labour, first of any thing that belongeth, to audit the accounts of the Receipts and Dispenses of my Maister's household in Caister, since he came last into Norfolk, which as well for the provisions that is had of his own growing as in money paid; for till the said Accounts be made ordinately [1] which be of a great charge yearly, weet ye for certain my Master shall never know whether he goeth backward or forward; and many other Accomptants that maken livery [2] of provisions of Corns and Cattle to the household by the Receiver and by the Bailiffs cannot approve their Liberates [3] just, till the said household books be made up; and since it hath been kept ordinarily since my Master began to keep house this fifty year almost and when he hath been absent beyond sea, etc. it ought [to] be more readilier done and made up while he is present, and well the rather that his household meny [4] were not so whole together this forty year as be now at Caister. Also his ministers of Accounts of his chief manor of Heylesdon for three years to make up and to examine; and I assure you full simply approved [5] his Wools and his Farms.

And the third is, that so would Jesu my Master's Auditors would faithfully and plainly inform my Master of the truth of the yearly great damage he beareth in disbursing his money about Shipping and Boats, keeping an house up at Yarmouth to his great harm, and receiveth but chaffer and ware [6] for his corns and wools, etc. And then must abide a long day to make money,

[1] Methodically. [2] Delivery. [3] Accounts. [4] Family.
[5] Ignorantly managed. [6] Barter, instead of money.

of such chaffer taking he shall never be monied, nor be answered clearly of his revenues yearly, but [1] those things above said be amended betimes. In Lewis's days twelve years together my Master was wont to lay up money yearly at London and Caister, and now the contrary, *de malo in pejus.*[2]

I dare not be known of this bill, but ye may question and fele of the disposition of these matters of others, and then understand if I write justly or no; and ye, as of your motion, for my Masters' worship and profit, exhorting him, the Steward, Shipdam, and Spyrling to take a labour and a pain that this be reformed.

I pray you and require you keep this matter to yourself.

Your,

BOTONER [3]

[1457]

121. WINDSOR DESCRIBES WILLIAM WORCESTER

To my full special good Master, John Paston

WORSHIPFUL Sir, and my full special good Master, after humble recommendation, please it you to understand, that [in] such service as I can do to your pleasure, as to mine understanding, I have showed my diligence now the short season since your departing, and in special, about such a Copy of a Foundation, as your mastership commanded me to get you a Copy of; of the which I send unto you at this time, by my Brother William Worcester, three Copies written by Luket, because I had no leisure, but so much business in setting forth of my Master of the Rolls; at this time, and in all this King's days, ye can have none other according [agreeing] any thing to your intent.

And as for the names of the Poles,[4] William hath more writing than ye and I could find, found by labour made by him and me.

And also Sir, he hath caused me to examine old and many

[1] Unless. [2] From better to worse.

[3] William Worcester, Fastolf's private secretary, often used his mother's maiden name, Botoner.

[4] The De la Poles had disputed with Fastolf the right to the manor of Dedham. Worcester was apparently examining the pedigree of the De la Poles, ancestors of the late Duke of Suffolk.

Records, written by some Frenchman concerning the Manor of Dedham, that was a cumberous labour, for these Copies were full defective, as it appeareth by the correcting of them.

Item, Sir, I may say to you, that William hath gone to School, to a Lumbard called Karoll Giles, to learn and to be read in Poetry, or else in French, for he hath been with the same Karoll every day two times or three; and hath bought divers Books of him, for the which as I suppose, he hath put himself in danger [1] to the same Karoll.

I made a motion to William to have known part of his business, and he answered and said; that he would be as glad and as feyn of a good Book of French, or of Poetry as my Master Fastolf would be to purchase a fair manor; and thereby I understand, he list not to be communed withal in such matters, etc.

At this time, nothing else to your mastership, but and it please you to remember my Master at your best leisure, whether his old promise shall stand, as touching my preferring to the Boar's Head in Southwark [2]; Sir I would have been at another place, and of my Master's own motion, he said that I should set upon the Boar's Head, in the which matter I report me to William Worcester, Bokking and William Barker, and most specially to my Master's own remembrance; I know full well there can no conclusion be taken to mine avail without help of your mastership, unto the which I utterly submit me in this, and all other; and Our Lord Jesu preserve you and all yours, and send you your heart's desire with right.

Written at London on Sunday next after Saint Bartholomew's day in haste.

By your servant,

HENRY WINDSOR

[1458]

[1] Debt. [2] Presumably as manager; it was Fastolf's property.

122. FASTOLF DYING

To my Master John Paston, Esq., be this Letter presented

Jesu mercy.

RIGHT reverend Master, etc. as soon as ye may goodly come to Caister, and Yelverton [1] with you, and ye think it be to done, and send home your men and horses till ye have done here, etc. and by grace of God and your politic wisdom ye shall conclude more effectually in great matters of substance to my Master's and your worship and profit. It is high time, he draweth fast homeward, and is right low brought, and sore weaked and feebled etc. And ye must bring with you a form of a Supplication made at London, in what manner wise Master R. Popy, a cunning and a crafty man, shall present and purpose to the King for the amortising [2] of Caister to Saint Bennet's, etc. which he promitted upon a certain money, etc. and undertook it, etc. and found [at] that time no bones in the matter, etc. And now he faith he will labour and ride and do his part, etc. and he would have me help him. God bring you soon hither, etc. for I am weary till ye come. Sir Thomas the parson your own most true, etc. by my truth, and I your Beadsman, and yours at your commandment, in your Letter have no more touched of the matter, etc. to my master, etc. Every day this five days he saith, "God send me soon my good Cousin Paston, for I hold him a faithful man, and ever one man" [3] . . . .

JOHN BRACKLEY

[1459]

123. FASTOLF DEAD—FIRST STEPS

To my Master, John Paston, in Norfolk

RIGHT well beloved Brother, I recommend me to you, certifying you that on Friday last was in the morning Worcester and I were

[1] William Yelverton.

[2] For the meaning of this word see note to Letter 117.

[3] Ever one man, always steadfast.

come to London by 8 of the clock, and we spake with my Lord Chancellor [1] and I found him well disposed in all things, and ye shall find him right profitable to you, etc.

And he desired me to write you a letter in his name, and put trust in you in gathering of the goods together, and pray you to do so, and have all his [2] goods out of every place of his, and his own place, where soever they were, and lay them secretly where as ye thought best at your assignment, and till that he speak with you himself, and he said ye should have all lawful favour.

I purpose to ride to him this day for Writs of *diem clausit extremum*,[3] and I suppose ye shall have a letter sent from him self to you.

As for the Goods of Paul's [4] they are safe enough, and this day we have grant to have the Goods out of Bermondsey [5] without advice of any man saving Worcester, Plomer, and I myself, and nobody shall know of it but we three.

My Lord Treasurer [6] speaketh fair, but yet many advise me to put no trust in him; there is laboured many means to intitle the King in his Goods. Southwell is Escheator, and he is right good and well disposed.

My Lord of Exeter claimeth title in my master's place with the appurtenances in Southwark, and verily had purposed to have entered, and his counsel were with us and spake with Worcester and me; and now afterwards they have sent us word that they would move my lord to sue by means of the law, etc.

I have spoken with my Lord of Canterbury, and Master John Stokes, and I find them right well disposed both, etc.

Item, to-morrow or the next day ye shall have another letter, for by that time we shall know more than we do now.

My Lord Chancellor would that my Master [Fastolf] should

[1] Bishop Waynflete. [2] Fastolf's.

[3] This was a Writ which issued out of Chancery to the Escheator of the County, upon the death of any of the King's tenants in Capite, to inquire by a Jury of what lands he died seized, and of what value, and who was next heir to him. [F.]

[4] At St Paul's.

[5] An Abbey in Southwark, where some of his goods were deposited.

[6] James Butler, Earl of Wiltshire and Ormond. He was beheaded in 1461.

be buried worshipfully, and one hundred marks alms done for him; but this day I shall wholly know his intent; Master John Stokes hath the same conceit and alms giving.

Item, we have gotten men of the Spiritual Law with holden with us [1] what case soever happen; we have Master Robert Kent; but in any wise have all the Goods there together, and tarry for no letting,[2] though ye should do it by day-light openly, for it is my Lord Chancellor's full intent that ye should do so.

As for William Worcester he trusteth verily ye would do for him [3] and for his avail and in reason, and I doubt not, and he may verily and faithfully understand you so disposed to him ward, ye shall find him faithful to you; in likewise I understand by him he will never have other master but his old master, and to my conceit it were pity but if he should stand in such case by mine master that he should never need service, considering how my master trusted him, and the long years that he hath been with him in, and many a shrewd journey for his sake, etc.

I write you no more because ye shall [have] another letter written to morrow. Written at London the 12th day of November in haste.

By
WILLIAM PASTON

[1459]

124. BISHOP WAYNFLETE'S ADVICE

BE it remembered that for as much as Sir John Fastolf late deceased, of great affection hath put me in trust to be one of his Executors, and since it is desired [of] me to know my disposition herein, mine advice is thus, that first an Inventory be made wholly of his goods and chattels in all places, and that they be laid in sure ward by your discretions, till the Executors, or the most part of those that he put his great trust upon, speak with me, and make declaration to me of his last will, to the accomplishment whereof I will be special good Lord.

[1] On our side. [2] Hindrance. [3] Reward him.

Furthermore, as touching his burying and month's mind [1] keeping, that it be done worshiply according to his degree, and for the health of his soul, and that Alms be given in Masses saying, and to poor people, to the sum of an hundred Marks till that otherwise we speak together; and I can agree right well that his servants have their rewards betimes according to his Will, to the intent that they may be better disposed, and to pray for the welfare of his soul; taking advice of a learned man in spiritual law, for no charge of administration till the Executors come together, or the most part, that his trust was most upon, to take the administration.

WILLIAM WINTON

[1459]

[In his capacity as executor of Sir J. Fastolf, Paston took possession of Caister, Hellesdon, Cotton and other places, and established priests at Caister. Other executors meanwhile sold Caister to the Duke of Norfolk and Hellesdon to the Duke of Suffolk, and seized this property forcibly. Paston had the support of Edward IV and of the Bourchiers, but the King would not offend the Dukes and Sir John Howard, who were strong in Norfolk. Paston placed his second son John in Norfolk's household, to win favour, but without result.]

125. EARLY DIFFICULTIES

Amicabili magistro nostro Johanni Paston Armigero

FULL reverend and worshipful, after all due reverence and recommendation, your poor Priest beseecheth humbly it please your good Mastership to understand by this simple bill, that on the Friday next after the feast of the Conversion of Saint Paul last past, I was at your place at Caister to have told you what answer I had of Sir Thomas Howes, parson of Blofield, and in as much

[1] The Month's Mind was a monthly solemnity in memory of the deceased, when prayers were offered, and alms given for the health of his Soul, etc. [F.]

as ye were not at home, I told it to my mistress your wife, and God thank her of her gentleness, she made me great cheer; and moreover advised me to send you a bill thereof to London. This was his answer, when I had talked to him as I could, in like wise as ye advertised me to do; he answered again in these words, "Near is my Kirtle but nearer is my smock;" and this was his meaning, that ye should be more near us, and tender to us than he, and that ye should rather owe us good will than he, and that we should labour rather to your mastership than to him; And also, that Good [1] that he had to dispose he had beset [2] it, and of parcell, he told me, he had delivered the Abbot of Langley fourscore pounds, whereof as he said to me, ye grudged and were in manner displeased, notwithstanding ye said again to him, ye should do as much; And he said to me ye named the places where; and therefore he advised me to labour effectually to your good mastership, for ye might help us well; for he said ye had much Good of the dead to dispose, what of your father, God bless that soul, what of Berney, and what now of his good master Fastolf. And as for Sir John Fastolf, on whose soul Jesu have mercy! he said to me, ye had of his good four, four, and four more than he, in these same terms without any sum.

And after all other talkings he told me he should be with you in London hastily, and that he would say good word to you to relieve our poor place; Sir I beseech [you] be not displeased, for truly and I wist to have your heavy mastership therefore, I had lever it had been unthought. And [it] is this, that when Sir Thomas Howes and ye be soon at London, we might be so in your good grace, that our place might be brother to Langley, for that should glad us more than the commission that the Bishop of Norwich sent us on Thursday last past to gather the Dymes [3] for that is a shrewd labour for us, a great cost and a shrewd jeopardy.

Evermore that high and mighty celestial Prince preserve you body and soul, and send you comfort of the Holy Ghost well to perform all your heart's desire in all your matters to his pleasaunce and your worship, and solace to all your well-willers. Written at

[1] Property. [2] Let. [3] Tenths.

Bromholm on the Saturday next after the feast of the Conversion of Saint Paul last past.

From your Priest and Beadsman,

JOHN, Prior of BROMHOLM

[1461]

126. NORFOLK OPPOSES PASTON

To my right reverend and worshipful Master, my Master John Paston

RIGHT reverend and worshipful Master, I lowly recommend me unto your good mastership, pleaseth you to weet that I have been at Framlingham, and spake Richard Southwell to have his advice in this matter, wherein he would give me but little counsel, and said ye were strangely disposed, for ye trusted no man; and had much language, which the bearer hereof shall inform your mastership.

And as for the Letters they were delivered my Lord [1] at the Lodge, but I could not speak with his Lordship, and such time as they were delivered Fitzwilliam was there, which is now keeper of Caister, and what time as [2] my Lord had seen the Letters, he commanded him to avoid and so he did; and then my Lord sent for Southwell, and in the mean time my Lord sent a man to me and asked me where ye were, and I told him ye were with the king, and so he sent me word that an answer would be made by Southwell to the king, saying that two or three heirs [of Fastolf] had been with my Lord and shewed their evidence, and delivered it to my Lord, saying they have great wrong, beseeching my Lord that it might be reformed; wherefore he commanded me that I should go home, for other answer could I none have; so I abode [3] upon Southwell to have known my Lord's answer to the King, which answer Southwell told me was, that he writeth to the King that certain points in your Letters be untrue, and that he shall prove [at] such time as he cometh before the King, beseeching the King to take it to no displeasure, for he is advised to keep

[1] The Duke of Norfolk, who had taken possession of Caister.

[2] As soon as.

[3] Waited.

it still until the time that he hath spoken with his Highness, for he trusteth to God to shew such evidence to the King and to the Lords that he should have best right and title thereto; and so he sent a man forth to the King this day; it were right well done, ye awaited upon his man coming, that ye might know the ready intent of my Lord's writing. . . .

Thomas Fastolf [1] was there the same time that I was there, and as I am informed they have delivered my Lord certain evidence; wherefore me seemeth it were right well done, saving your better advice, to come home and seal up your evidence, and have them with you to London, to prove his title nought. There be but two or three men within the place, and if ye think it best to do it, send word, and I suppose a remedy shall be had.[2]

Also, I hear no word of Master William, nor of the Writs for the parliament. Also it is told here that Todenham [3] and Heydon have a pardon of the King, and that they shall come up to London with the Lady of Suffolk to the Coronation [4]; also as for the Letter that ye sent to Thomas Wingfield, I have it still, for he is at London; some men say he moved my Lord for to enter, and some say Fitzwilliam is in default, so I can see there is but few good.[5] Also my Master Sir Thomas Howys [6] shall send a letter to the person ye weet of, for to deliver you the gear at London the next week; my right worshipful and reverend Master, Almighty God preserve you. Written at Norwich, on the morrow after Corpus Christi day.

Your poor Servant and Beadsman,

RICHARD CALLE

[1461]

[1] Thomas Fastolf had trumped up a claim on Fastolf's property, which he transferred to the Duke of Norfolk.

[2] *I.e.*, by retaking it by force.

[3] Sir Thomas Tuddenham. He was beheaded in 1462.

[4] Edward IV was crowned on June 29, 1461.

[5] On your side.

[6] The priest.

127. A PATRON SPEAKS FOR WORCESTER

To mine wellbeloved Friend Sir Thomas Howys, Parson of Blofield

WELLBELOVED Friend I greet you well, and for as much as I understand that William Worcester, late the servant unto Sir John Fastolf, knight, whose soul God assoil, is not had in favour nor trust with my right wellbeloved friend John Paston, neither with you, as he saith, namely in such matters and causes as concerneth the will and testament of the said Sir John Fastolf; and as I am informed the said William purposeth him to go into his country, for the which cause he hath desired me to write unto you that ye would be a special good friend unto him, for the said master's sake, to have all such things as reason and conscience requireth, and that ye would be [a] mean [1] unto Paston for him in this matter, to show him the more favour at this time for this my writing, in doing of any trouble to him, trusting that he will demean him in such wise that he shall have no cause unto him, but to be his good master, as he saith, and if there be any thing that I can do for you, I will be right glad to do it, and that knoweth Almighty God, which have you in his keeping. Written at Greenwich, the 28th day of August.

J. BEAUCHAMP [2]

[1461]

128. DIFFICULTIES INCREASING

To the right reverend and worshipful Sir, and my good Master, John Paston, Esquire

RIGHT reverend and worshipful Sir, I recommend me to your good mastership, praying you to weet that I was at Blake's and spake with his Wife, and she saith he was not at home this three weeks, he rideth up the Country to take accounts of Bailiffs, and

[1] Mediator.

[2] Lord Beauchamp of Powyk, Worcestershire, a famous soldier and Knight of the Garter. He died in 1475.

that this day fev'night he should have sate in Caister by you upon accounts, and from thence he should have ridden to Lynn, and that he shall be at home on Monday at night next coming; wherefore I have left my errand with her; but she saith that he shall not mowe come [1] to you, for my Lady [2] have sent for him in great haste, both by a Letter and by a token to come to her, as hastily as he may, notwithstanding she shall do the errand to him.

As for Yelverton, I did a good feel to enquire of James Skinner when the said Yelverton should go to London; he said not this sev'night, he could not tell what day till he had spoken with his Son, his Son should come to him ere his Master should ride; I shall enquire more at Walsingham; and for God's love be not too long from London, for men say there, as I have been [informed] that my Lord of Gloucester [3] should have Caister, and there is great noise of this revel that was done in Suffolk [4] by Yelverton and Jenney [5]; and your well-willers think that if they might prevail in this, they would attempt you in others, but cease their power and malice, and preserve you from all evil, and at the reverence of God let some interposition go a-twixt you and my mistress your Mother ere ye go to London, and all that ye do shall speed the better, for she is set on great malice, and every man that she speaketh with, knoweth her heart, and it is like to be a foul noise [over] all the Country without it be soon ceased.

Also Sir it is told me, that my Lord of Norfolk is coming to Framlingham, and that ye be greatly commended in his household, therefore it were well done, me seemeth, that ye spake with him.

The Holy Trinity keep you. Written at Norwich, the Thursday after St Matthew.[6]

Your poor Priest,

[1461] JAMES GLOYS

[1] Be able to come.
[2] The Duchess of Norfolk.
[3] The King's brother, Richard; afterwards Richard III.
[4] The seizure of the manor of Cotton.
[5] Judge Yelverton and William Jenney, Paston's co-executors, who refused to acknowledge his claims as chief administrator of Fastolf's will.
[6] September 21.

129. HENRY WINDSOR WANTS HIS REWARD

To my full worshipful and special good Master,
John Paston, Esquire, abiding at Norwich

RIGHT worshipful Sir, and some time my most special good Master, I recommend me unto your good Mastership, with all my poor service, if it may in any wise suffice; and farthermore Sir I beseech you, now being in your country, where ye may daily call unto you my Master Sir Thomas Howys, once to remember my poor matter; and by your discretions to take such a direction therein, and so to conclude, as may be to your discharge, and to my furtherance; according to the Will of him that is passed unto God, whose soul I pray Jesu pardon! for truly, Sir, there was in him no fault, but in me only, if it be not as I have remembered your Mastership afore this time. For truly, Sir, I dare say I should have had as special, and as good a Master of you as any poor man, as I am, within England should have had of a worshipful man, as you are, if ye had never meddled with the Goods of my Master Fastolf.

And as much ye would have done, and laboured for me, in my right, if it had been in the hands of any other man than of yourself only. But, I trust in God, at your next coming, to have an answer, such as I shall be content with; and if it may be so; I am and shall be your Servant in that I can or may, that knoweth our Lord Jesus, whom I beseech save, and send you a good end in all your matters, to your pleasure and worship everlasting, Amen. Written at London, the 4th day of October.

As for Tidings, the King will be at London within three days next coming, and all the Castles and Holds both in South Wales and in North Wales are given, and yielded up, into the King's hand; and the Duke of Exeter [1] and the Earl of Pembroke [2] are flown and [have] taken the Mountains, and divers Lords with great puissance are after them. And the most part of Gentlemen, and men of worship are come in to the King, and have grace of all Wales. The Duke of Somerset, the Lord Hungerford, and

[1] Brother-in-law of King Edward IV, but a steady Lancastrian.
[2] Jasper Tudor, half-brother of King Henry VI.

Robert Whityngham, and other four or five Esquires, are come unto Normandy out of Scotland, and as yet they stand strait under arrest, and as Merchants that are come late thence say, they are like to be deemed and judged Prisoners. My Lord Wenlock, Sir John Cley, and the Dean of Saint Severin's, have abode at Calais these three weeks, and yet are there abiding a safe Conduct, going upon an Embassy to the French King. And Sir Walter Blount, Treasurer of Calais, with a great Fellowship of Soldiers of Calais, and many other men of the Marches, have lain, and yet do, at a Siege afore the Castle of Hammes, by-side Calais, and daily make great war, either party to other.

Item, I send unto you a copy of a Letter that was taken upon the Sea, made by the Lord Hungerford and Whityngham.

Item, we shall have a great embassy out of Scotland in all haste of Lords.

At your Commandment, and Servant,

HENRY WYNDSORE

[1461]

130. YELVERTON AND JENNEY SEIZE COTTON

To my Master Paston the elder, be this Letter delivered in haste

RIGHT worshipful Sir, I recommend me to your good mastership the cause why I write, I let you have knowledge of the men that be in Cotton-Hall,[1] how they be strangely disposed against you, for as I hear say, they make revel there, they melt lead, and break down your bridge, and make that no man may go into [the] place but on a ladder, and make them as strong as they can against you, by the supportation of Jenney, and Debenham and his Son, for they say there that Jenney hath sold the livelihood unto Debenham, and that his Son the Knight shall dwell

[1] Sir J. Fastolf's manor in Suffolk. Yelverton and Jenney seized the manor in 1461, though forestalled for a time by Richard Calle. In the absence of Paston in London, Jenney sold his interest in Cotton to Gilbert Debenham, at whose instigation a body of men took possession of the house and did much damage.

there, and therefore they have warned a Court against Monday, and now they have advised to keep it on Saturday before Monday; what they mean thereby I wot never; but as for the fellowship in the place that is there now, and have been there all this week, there is no man of substance as we hear, and there have been but seven or eight all this week, but there will be a great fellowship this night or to-morrow upon Saturday, for then they will keep the Court; and as for Edward Dale, he dare not abide well at home, they threaten him so, because he will send them no victuals, and as for myself, Edward Dale dare not let me well be there, for taking in suspicion. And as for the Tenants, they be well disposed, except one or two, so that ye will support them in haste, for they may not keep of their Cattle off the ground longer, and specially they desire to have your own presence, and they would be of great comfort. No more I write to you, but the Holy Ghost have you in keeping. Written on the Friday after my departing.

By your Servant,
WILLIAM NAUNTON

[1461]

131. PASTON RELEASED

A Letter to John Paston, Esq., from his Wife, shewing his Imprisonment in the Fleet [1]

RIGHT worshipful Husband I recommend me to you, please it you to weet that I received your Letter that ye sent me by John Holme on Wednesday last past, and also I received another Letter on Friday at night, that ye sent me by Nicholas Newman's man, of the which Letters I thank you, for I should else have thought that it had been worse with you than it hath been, or shall be, by the grace of Almighty God, and yet I could not be merry, since I had the last Letter till this day that the Mayor sent to me, and sent me word that he had knowledge for very truth

[1] Sir John Howard had caused Paston to be imprisoned in the Fleet in 1461. He was apparently released through the intervention of the King, and Howard was sent to prison instead.

that ye were delivered out of the Fleet; and that Howard was committed to ward for divers great complaints that were made to the King of him; it was talked in Norwich, and in divers other places in the country on Saturday last past, that ye were committed to the Fleet, and in good faith, as I heard say, the people were right sorry thereof, both of Norwich and in the country, ye are right much bound to thank God, and all those that love you, that ye have so great love of the people as ye have; ye are much beholden to the Mayor, and to Gilbert,[1] and to divers others of the Aldermen, for faithfully they owe you good will to their powers.

I have spoken with Sir Thomas Howes for such things as ye wrote to me for, and he promised me that he should labour it after your intent as fast as he could, and in good faith, as my brother and Playters can tell you, as by his saying to us, he is and will be faithful to you; and as for William Worcestor he hath been set so upon the hone [2] what by the parson and by others, as my brother and Playters shall tell you, that they hope he will do well enough; the Parson said right well and plainly to him.—The Parson told me that he had spoken with Sir William Chamberlayn, and with his wife, and he thinketh that they will do well enough after your intent, so that they be pleasantly intreated; and the Parson told me that he wist well, that Sir William Chamberlayn could do more ease in such matters as ye wrote of touching my Lord of Bedford,[3] than any man could do that liveth at this day; also he told me that he felt by them that they would owe you right good will, so that ye would owe them good will; the Parson hopeth verily to make you accorded when he cometh to London.

Item, my brother and Playters were with Calthorpe [4] to enquire of the matter that ye wrote to me of, what answer he gave them, they shall tell you; I sent the Parson of Hellesdon to Gurney [5]

[1] Mayor of Norwich in 1459 and 1464.

[2] From setting a razor—*i.e.*, he had been spoken to in a sharp and severe manner by the parson, Sir Thomas Howes.

[3] John, Duke of Bedford, Regent of France, died in 1435.

[4] Sir W. Calthorpe, High Sheriff of Norfolk.

[5] Thomas Gurney, Esquire, of Norwich.

to speak to him of the same matter, and he saith faithfully there was no such thing desired of him, and though he had been desired, he would neither have said nor done against you; he said he had ever found you loving and faithful to him, and so he said he would be to you to his power, and desiring me that I would not think him the contrary.

I pray you that ye will send me word whether ye will that I shall remove from hence, for it beginneth to wax a cold abiding here. Sir Thomas Howes and John Russ shall make an end of all things after your intent, as much as they can do therein this week, and he proposeth to come forwards to you on the Monday next after St Leonard's day.[1]

My Brother and Playters should have been with you ere this time, but that they would abide till this day were past, because of the Shire [court]. I spoke to my Brother William as ye bad me, and he told me, so God him help, that he hired two horses two days before that ye rode, that he might have ridden forth with you; and because that ye spoke not to him to ride with you, he said that he wend ye would [not] have had him with you.

Thomas Fastolf's Mother was here on the next day after ye were ridden, to have spoken with you for her Son, she prayeth you at the reverence of God, that ye will be his good Master, and to help him in his right, that he may have home his livelihood[2] out of their hands that have had it in his nonage; she saith that they would make him a year younger than he is, but she saith that he is more than twenty-one, and upon that she dare take an oath.

And the blessed Trinity have you in his keeping, and send you good speed in all your matters, and send ye victory of all your Enemies. Written in haste, on Soulmas-day.[3]

By yours

MARGARET PASTON

[1461]

[1] November 6. [2] Property. [3] November 2.

132. HOWES AND WORCESTER HELP YELVERTON AGAINST PASTON

To my right worshipful Master, John Paston

RIGHT worshipful Master, I recommend me unto you, etc. the cause of my writing is this, I was at Blofield on Saint Andrew's day [1] with the parson [Howes], and he understood none other but that I came to see his mastership, for it was his cheve day [2]; and there I moved unto him of the land in Southwark how I heard say when I was in Suffolk that Jenney made his avaunt that he had given you and him a chop of twenty pound of land; and incontinent he told me all the matter better than I could tell him; and as I could understand in him by my simple wit, that he was of knowledge of all the matter, for he said that Yelverton came down from the Bench, and pleaded the matter, and for cause ye were so lache,[3] and came not in time, the matter yede [4] amiss, and so I understand by him, that he is disposed to excuse Yelverton in all matters rather than you, but nevertheless make good cheer to the parson as though ye understood that he were your friend, till time ye have your intent, but beware and trust him not, but make you so strong in lordship and in the law, that ye reck not much whether he be good or bad, etc.

Item, ye be much beholden unto Thomas Greene and to Edmund Wydeville, brother to Hugh Fenn, for they report much worship of your mastership in all matters, that causes the substance of the towne to owe you service, and be well disposed unto your mastership, and that understand I every day; and if it please you, when we parted at Norwich in your place ye said unto me ye would somewhat do by my simple advice; and this is mine advice, that in any wise ye make Hugh Fenn and Thomas Greene on your counsel, if ye can find in your heart, for I dare say as I hear and understand that they owe you right good will and service, for a man may hear by the half what the whole

[1] November 30.

[2] Cheve-day, or thriving-day—the day he received the profits of his living.

[3] Negligent.

[4] Went.

meaneth; and therefore for God's love remember you well in this matter, for and it stood on my life I would do as I advise you, etc.

Item, for our Lord's love go through with William Worcester, and also please Shrews as ye think in your heart best for to do, for it is a common proverb, " A man must sometimes set a candle before the Devil; " and therefore, though it be not aldermost meet and profitable, yet " of two harms the least is to be taken."

Item, ye shall understand that the parson told me that they were summoned to come for the probate of the Testament at [the] Conversion of Saint Paul,[1] and therefore I would advise you in any wise, that ye should understand the matter wisely ere ye come home, for I suppose that Yelverton and he is confederate, and accord together. . . .

No more at this time, but God have you in his keeping both body and soul, and speed you in your matters as well as I would ye should do.

[*No signature*]

[1461]

133. JOHN RUSSE ASKS A REWARD

To the right reverend and worshipful Sir, my right honourable Master, John Paston

Right worshipful Sir, and my right honourable Master, I recommend me to you in my most humble wise, and please it your good mastership to weet, that it is said here, that my Lord Worcester is like to be Treasurer, with whom I trust ye stand right well in conceit, with which God continue; wherefore I beseech your mastership that if my said Lord have the said office, that it like you to desire the nomination of one of the offices, either of the Controuller or Searchership of Yarmouth for a servant of yours; and I should so guide me in the office as I trust should be most profit to my said Lord; and if your mastership liked to get grant thereof, that then it please you to licence one of your servants to take out the patent of the said office, and if it cost

[1] January 25.

five, or six, or eight Marks I shall truly content it again; and yearly as long as I might have the offices, or any of them, I shall give my master your son five marks toward an Hackney.[1]

It should be to me right a good mean to stand as well in the trust as in the conceit amongst merchants, with whom and with all men, I call myself a servant of yours, and so will do, if it please you, which boldeth me the more to call upon your worshipful mastership in this matter, wherein I beseech you to forgive me my boldness in this behalf. And if I knew that my Lord should have the office in certain then I would wait upon your good mastership there to obtain the patent, if it pleased your good mastership to get me the grant, etc.

No more unto you my right honourable master at this time, but Jesu I beseech send you a good conclusion in all your matters, and grant you ever your heart's desire.

Your continual Servant and Beadsman,

JOHN RUSSE

[1462]

134. ADVICE FROM RUSSE

To the right worshipful my right honourable Master John Paston

RIGHT worshipful Sir, and my right honourable Master, I recommend me to you in my most humble wise, and please your mastership to weet, that here is one Thomas Chapman, an evil disposed man alway against you, as I have informed your mastership many times, and now he hath laboured to my Lord Treasurer [Worcester] to supplant me, and brought down writing from the King and my Lord Treasurer; but, ere his writing came, Wydeville found the means, by the supportation of Master Fenn, that we had a discharge for him out of Chancery; wherefore the said Chapman proposeth to be at London in all haste, and to advertise the King and my Lord Treasurer against me, to the greatest hurt he can imagine: wherefore I beseech your master-

[1] A pacing horse.

ship considering his evil disposition to you, and also the rather at my poor instance, that ye like that my Lord Treasurer might understand that the said Chapman is of no reputation, but evil disposed to bribery of Strangers, and by colour of his office of Supervisor of the Search shall greatly hurt the Port; the said Chapman's supporters is Blakeney, Clerk of the Signet, and Avery Cornburgh, Yeoman of the King's Chamber; he hath here of Avery's twenty-four Tuns [of] Wine, whereof at the long way, he shall make the said Avery a lewd [1] reckoning; the said Chapman loveth not you, nor no man to you ward, etc.

Sir, I pray God bring you once to reign among your countrymen in love, and to be dreaded; the longer ye continue there the more hurt groweth to you; men say ye will neither follow the advice of your own kindred, nor of your counsel, but only your own wilfulness, and which, but grace be, shall be your destruction.

It is my part to inform your mastership as the common voice is, God better it, and grant you once heart's ease; for it is half a death to me to hear the general voice of the people, which daily encreaseth, etc.

Sir, I beseech your mastership to remember my mistress for the little silver, which, for certain things delivered to your use, is due to me; I have need of it now; I have bought Salt and other things, which hath brought me out of much silver, I would trust and I needed to borrow twenty pounds your mastership would ease me for a time, but this that I desire is mine own duty.[2] And Jesu grant you ever your heart's desire to your worship and profit, and preserve you my right honourable master from all adversity.

Written at Yarmouth, the 15th day of July. Here is a Carvel [3] of Caen, in Normandy, and he taketh Dutchmen,[4] and ransometh them grievously.

Your Servant and Beadsman

JOHN RUSSE [5]

[1462]

[1] Bad. [2] What is due to me. [3] A small, fast ship. [4] Germans.

[5] Russe had apparently obtained the office asked for in Letter 133.

135. ADVICE TO PLACATE SUFFOLK

To my right worshipful Master John Paston, in haste

RIGHT worshipful Husband, I recommend me to you, desiring heartily to hear of your welfare, praying you to weet, that I have spoken with Strange's wife of the matter that ye spoken to me of, and she saith plainly to me by her faith that she knew never none such nor never heard of none such, and [she] told to me in like wise as she had said to James Gloys, and she said to me if she could enquire of any other that she thought should have knowledge of any such, she should weten of them, and letten me have knowledge thereof; and if ye suppose that any other be in this Country that ye think should have knowledge of this foresaid matter, if ye will send me word thereof, I shall do my part therein.

Also I have been at Swainsthorp and spoken with Cocket,[1] and he saith that he will do like as ye bad me that I should say to him for to do. And I have spoken with the Sexton [2] and said to him as ye bad me that I should do, and he asked me right faithfully how ye sped in your matters.

I told him that ye had fair behests, and I said, I hoped that ye should do right well therein; and he said he supposed that D [3] would do for you; but he said, he was no hasty labourer in none matter, he said by his faith he wist where a man was that laboured to him for a matter right a long time, and always he behested that he would labour it effectually; but while he sued to him he could never have remedy of his matter, and then when he thought that he should no remedy have to sue to him, he spake with Fynes that is now Speaker of the Parliament, and prayed him that he would do for him in his matter, and gave him a reward; and within right short time after his matter was sped; and, the said Sexton and other folks that be your right

[1] A retainer, to whom Paston was later in debt.

[2] The sacrist, or sexton, of the priory of Norwich was the officer who had the care of the sacra, or holy things, as the church plate, copes, etc. He was likewise secretary, auditor, and chancellor of the convent.

[3] John Damme?—a neighbour from near Gresham.

well-willers have counselled me that I should counsel you to make other means than ye have made to other folks, that would speed your matters better than they have done that ye have spoken to thereof before this time. Sundry folks have said to me, that they think verily but if ye have my Lord of Suffolk's good Lordship [1] while the world is as it is, ye can never live in peace without ye have his good lordship; therefore I pray you with all mine heart, that ye will do your part to have his good lordship and his love in ease of all those matters that ye have to do, and in easing of mine heart also, for by my truth I am afraid else, both of these matters the which ye have in hand now, and of other that be not done to yet, but if he will do for you and be your good Lord. I pray you heartily send me word how ye do, and how ye speed in your matters; and I pray you as for such things as James hath a bill of, that I may have them as hastily as ye may; and that ye will vouchsafe to buy a piece of black buckram for to line with a gown for me, I should buy me a murrey gown to go in this Summer, and lay in the collar the satin that ye gave me for an hood; and I can get none good buckram in this town to line it with. The Holy Trinity have you in his keeping, and send you health and good speed in all your matters.

Written at Norwich, on the Friday next after Crouchmas day.[2]

Yours

MARGARET PASTON

[1463]

136. ORDERS FROM THE DUKE OF NORFOLK

To our right trusty and entirely well beloved Servant John Paston, the elder

The Duke of Norfolk [3]

RIGHT trusty and entirely well beloved Servant, we greet you heartily well, and specially praying you that ye will be with us

[1] The young duke, who had turned Yorkist.

[2] Crouchmas Day, or the Discovery of the Cross, was May 3.

[3] John Mowbray, the fourth Duke, son of the duke who seized Caister.

at Framlingham on Sunday next coming, that we may commune with you there, and have your sad advice in such matters as concerneth greatly to our weal, which shall be ministred unto you at your coming.

Praying you that ye fail not hereof, as our special trust is in you; and our Lord preserve you in his keeping.

Written at Framlingham, the 31st day of August.

NORFOLK

[1463]

137. ADVICE FROM MARGARET PASTON

To mine right worshipful Husband John Paston, be this delivered in haste

RIGHT worshipful Husband, I recommend me unto you, pleaseth you to weet that I sent yesterday Loveday to Norwich to speak with the Vicar of Dereham for the matter between Master Constantine and him,[1] and he saith that as for that matter Master Constantine sued him for faith and truth breaking, and he sued Master Constantine in the Temporal Court upon an obligation of ten pounds; and there was made an appointment between them by the advice of both their Counsels, before Master Robert Popy, that each of them should release other, and so they did, and the sureties were withdrawn on both parties, and each of them acquittanced other; and as for any Copy of the plea he had never none, nor he nor Master John Estgate, that was his Attorney, remembereth not that it was registered; and Master John Estgate saith, if it should be searched in the Register it would take a fortnight's work, and yet peradventure never be the nearer.

Sir Thomas Howes hath been right busy this week at Blofield, in writing and looking up of gear,[2] and John Russe hath been with him there the most part of all this week, and this day was

[1] Constantine Dalby, vicar of East Dereham in 1451. He was succeeded by Robert Sheringham in 1458.

[2] Papers.

Robert Lynne there with him; what they have done I wot not, but I shall weet if I may.

It was told me, that Sir Thomas desired of John Russe to make him a new Inventory of Sir John Fastolf's Goods; John Russe might not be spoken with yet, for the Letter that he should have written, which ye sent me word of.

Item, it is told that the Duke of Suffolk is come home, and either he is dead, or else right sick, and not like to escape; and Sir John Howard is come home; and it is said that the Lord Scales [1] and he have a Commission to enquire, why they of this country that were sent for, came not hastilier up after they were sent for.

It is reported that the King is greatly displeased therewith. At the reverence of God arm yourself as mightily as ye can against your enemies, for I know verily that they will do against you as mightily as they can with all their power.

It is told me that Sir Thomas shall come up in haste, and other such as he can make for his party.

Also for God's sake beware what Medicines ye take of any Physicians of London; I shall never trust to them because of your Father and mine Uncle, whose Souls God assoil!

The blessed Trinity have you in his keeping, and send you health and good speed in all your matters. Written in haste, on the Friday next before Saint Barnabas.[2]

By yours
MARGARET PASTON

[1464]

138. THE KING'S LICENCE

Appointment of the King for the Foundation of a College at Caister, etc.

THE King, for the sum of 300 marks (200*l.*) of lawful money of England, or of silver plate to the value thereof, granteth to John Paston the elder, Esquire, to have licence, lawfully made, to make and found a College of seven Priests and seven poor folk

[1] Anthony Woodville, created Lord Scales in 1462. [2] June 11.

at Caister, in Flegg [1] in Norfolk, for the Soul of Sir John Fastolf, Knight; they to be endued with certain rent, and otherwise after the intent and effect as is specified in a bill thereof, signed by the King; and that he shall shew his good grace, favour, and assistance to have the said foundation enacted and authorised in the Parliament next holden. . . . Also the King granteth to be good and favourable Lord to the said John Paston, and in especial in all things touching the execution of the Will of the said Sir John Fastolf, and also to be good and favourable Lord to the said John Paston, in supporting and helping him, in that the King's highness may lawfully do, in such matters as are in debate atwixt the said John Paston and William Yelverton, or William Jenney, or any other, concerning the lands and tenements, goods or chattels, that were the said Sir John Fastolf's.

And that the King shall receive an hundred pounds of the said 300 marks, what time he send for it, and the remanent as soon as the said foundation take effect; and also that his highness shall get the assent of the reverend father in God, the Archbishop of Canterbury, in such appointments as is made.

Also the King granteth that whereas this bill is not sufficiently made in clauses and terms according to the intent thereof, that his highness will take and execute the very intent thereof, notwithstanding the insufficience of any such terms and clauses in this bill. Written at Marlborough, the Monday next after the Nativity of our Lady,[2] the fourth year of the reign of the King.

[1464]

139. MARGARET URGES SPEED

To my right worshipful Master, John Paston, the oldest, be this delivered in haste

I recommend me, etc.

If it please you, I would right fain that John Jenney were put out of the Commission of the Peace, and that my brother William

[1] Flegg hundred.

[2] September 8.

Lumnor were set in his stead, for me thinketh it were right necessary that there were such a man in that county that oweth you good will, and I know verily he oweth you right good will, he was with me at Caister but late; if there be made any labour for Doctor Allen to be Justice of the Peace, I pray you for God's sake let it be letted [1] if ye may, for he will take too much upon him, if he were, I would not that he were remembered of your part, but if [2] he be spoken of of other parts; he is right great with Master Philip Lypyate and the Bailiff of Cossey.[3]

If it please you to weet that Wykes did arrest one William Dylmyn of Norwich, as Pampyng can inform you of, for certain Harness which he delivered him at Newcastle for to carry to Yarmouth by water, and there to deliver it to him again, which harness he kept still, and [he] may not be delivered, and now there is come down an Habeas Corpus for him, and [he] must appear at the Common Pleas on Friday next coming; wherefore if it pleased you that there might be taken an action in Wykes's name of trespass under such form as there may be a Capias awarded against his coming, for after that he was arrested, he did [4] Daubeney to be arrested for maintaining. . . . At the reverence of God, sloth not your matters now, and make an end of them, either purvey you to make them or to mar them in haste, for this is too horrible a cost and trouble, that ye have and have had, for to endure any while, and it is great heaviness to your friends and well willers, and great joy and comfort to your enemies.

My Lord of Norwich [5] said to me that he would not abide the sorrow and trouble that ye have abiden to win all Sir John Fastolf's good. God be your speed in all your matters. Written at Hellesdon, the 13th day of May.

I think right long to hear tidings till I have tidings from you.

Your

MARGARET PASTON

[1465]

[1] Hindered. [2] Unless. [3] Followers of Suffolk.
[4] Caused. [5] The Bishop.

140. DANGER AT DRAYTON

To my right worshipful Husband John Paston, be this delivered in haste

RIGHT worshipful Husband, I recommend me to you; please it you to weet that I have sent to Master John Smyth and to Master Stephen to have advice for the Church of Drayton; and they send me word that there must be had a Commission from the Bishop to call in the Parson Flowerdew, and that must be proclaimed in the Church of Drayton [1] three times by a Dean and after that if he appear not within six months after the first Proclamation, that then he to be deprived, and the Patron to present whom he lists, and else your presentation is not sufficient. And I have so purveyed that a Commission is had, and shall be served as hastily as it may be.

As for John Rysing I have sent to him to weet the cause that he is not brought up to London, and he saith that he called upon the Sheriff that he might be had up for [to] come to his answer, and the Sheriff told him, that he would not bring him up at his own cost; and John Andrews said that he would not have him up, and so he is still in prison at Ipswich; and so shall he be but if ye can find the better mean for to have him out; I have sent to him 13*s.* 4*d.* to keep himself therewith, he payeth for his board weekly twenty-pence; and Hopton and Smith be there still also, and they have money enough, that wheresoever they have it; Rysing deemeth that they have comfort of the other party [2] and I send you the Copy of the Warrant that they were arrested by, etc.

I spake not with my Mother since Richard Calle brought me the Letter from you touching her matter, for I might have no leisure; when I speak with her at leisure I will remember her in that matter according to your writing; and as for your Tenants of Drayton, as I can understand by them, they be right good and true hearted to you to their powers, and full fain would that ye

[1] John Flowerdew was presented to the Rectory of Drayton, Paston's manor near Hellesdon, by John Paston in 1461.

[2] Suffolk, whose manor of Cossey was near by.

had it again in peace, for they had as lief almost be Tenants to the Devil as to the Duke, except Will Herne, Piers at Sloth, and one Knott of the same Town, for they be not good.

All your Tenants at Hellesden and Drayton, except these three, be right glad that we are there amongst them, and so be many others of our old neighbours and Friends; and but if ye come home by Wednesday or Thursday in Whitsun week, I purpose me to see you in secret wise by Trinity Sunday, but if ye send to me contrary commandment ere that time; and I pray you send me your advice how ye will that we do against the next shire [court], which shall be the Monday next after Trinity Sunday, as for calling upon the Replevin that the beasts of Drayton were delivered by.

Item, Richard Calle told me that ye desired to have Master Philip's name, and his name is Philip Lypyate,[1] and I sent you a Letter by Henry Wilton's man, wherein I wrote Master Philip's name; and in the same Letter I wrote to you for Will. Lumnor; I pray you send me word if ye have it, and the blessed Trinity have you in his keeping. Written the Monday next after Ascension Day.[2]

By yours
MARGARET PASTON

[1465]

141. THE DUKE OF SUFFOLK ATTACKS HELLESDON

To my Master John Paston, in haste

PLEASETH it your mastership to weet of the rule and disposition of the Master Philip and the bailiff of Cossey, with others of my Lord of Suffolk's men, on Monday last past at afternoon, [who] were at Hellesdon, with the number of three hundred men for to have entered, notwithstanding they said they came not for to enter, but without doubt and they had been strong enough

[1] Margaret had been much troubled by Mr Philip Lypyate, the Duke of Suffolk's bailiff at Cossey.

[2] May 23.

for us, they would have entered, and that we understand enough but we [had] knowing of their coming and purveyed so for them, that we were strong enough; we had sixty men within the place, and guns, and such ordnance, so that, if they had set upon us, they had been destroyed; and there my Mistress was within and my Master Sir John, and [he] hath gotten him as great worship for that day as any gentleman might do, and so is it reported of the party and in all Norwich; and my Lord of Norwich [1] sent thither Master John Salett, and Master John Bulleman for to treat, and so they did; and the Duke's men said they had a warrant for to attach John Daubeney, Wykes, Calle, Hunworth, and Blickling and other, which they would have, and my Master Sir John answered them and said that they were not within, and though they had been, they should not have had them; and so they desired one of our men, and so Naunton stood by my Mistress and asked them whom they would have, and said if they would have him, he would go with them, and so he did, and on the next day they carried him forth to my Lord of Suffolk to Claxton, through Norwich, and there we had found a remedy for him for to have let [2] him, and he would not, but needs go forth with them; but like a gentleman he was entreated amongst them. And Harleston desired at Hellesdon to speak with my Master Sir John, and so he did, and said to him it were right well done that he rode to my Lord of Suffolk, and desired him in any wise that he should do so, and said that it was his duty so for to do, in as much as my Lord was come to [the] country, and that he would ride with him, and bring him to my Lord; and he answered and said to him, when that he understood that my Lord were his Father's good Lord and his, that then he would see his Lordship, and else he had none errand to him; and so they departed; and then appointment was taken that they should send home their men, and we should send home ours; and now my Lord of Suffolk's men come from Claxton to Norwich, and face us and fray upon us, this daily, there fell upon me before Swaine's door twelve of his men, eight of them in harness, and there they would have mischieved me, and the Sheriff letted them and other, and they make their avaunt where that I may

[1] The Bishop. [2] Hindered, stopped.

be gotten, I should die, and so they lie in wait for to mischief me, Daubeney and Wykes; and so I dare not ride out alone without a man with me, and I understand there is coming an Oyer [and] Determiner [1] to enquire of all riots, and my Lord of Suffolk and Yelverton be Commissioners; and so they say as many of us as can be taken shall be endicted and hanged forthwith; and so the people here are dismayed with their rule, wherefore that it like you to send word how my Mistress shall do at Hellesdon, and we in all other matters; and whether ye will that we fetch again the flock of Hellesdon, for they are now driven to Causton, and there go they on the heath; and my Lord of Suffolk will be at Drayton on Lammas-day, and keep the Court there, wherefore ye must seek a remedy for it, or else it will not do well.

If my Lord of Norfolk would come, he should make all well,[2] for they fear him above all things, for it is noised here that my Lord of Norfolk hath taken party in this matter, and all the country is glad of it, saying, that if he come they will wholly go with him.

And me seemeth it were well done to move my Lord in it, though ye should give him the profits of Hellesdon and Drayton for the keeping, and some money beside; for ye must seek some other remedy than ye do, or else in my conceit it shall go to the Devil, and be destroyed, and that in right short time, and therefore at the reverence of God take some appointment with Master Yelverton, and such as ye think should most hurt.

I beseech you to pardon me of my writing, for I have pity to see the tribulation that my Mistress hath here, and all your Friends, etc.

Almighty Jesu preserve and keep you. Written the Wednesday next Saint Thomas's day.[3]

Your poor Servant and Beadsman

[1465] RICHARD CALLE

[1] "Hearing and Settling." A special commission of judges on assize to deal with charges of riot and violence.

[2] The Duke of Norfolk would not oppose the Duke of Suffolk, and Calle's forecast proved true.

[3] July 7.

142. VIOLENCE OF THE DUKE OF SUFFOLK'S MEN

To my right worshipful Husband John Paston, in haste

RIGHT worshipful Husband, I recommend me to you, praying you heartily that ye will seek a mean that your servants may be in peace, for they be daily in fear of their lives; the Duke of Suffolk's men threaten daily Daubeney, Wykes, and Richard Calle, that wheresoever they may get them they shall die, and affrays have been made on Richard Calle this week, so that he was in great jeopardy at Norwich among them; and great affrays have been made upon me and my fellowship here on Monday last past, of which Richard Calle telleth me that he hath sent you word of in writing, more plainly than I may do at this time, but I shall inform you more plainly hereafter.

I suppose there shall be great labour against you and your servants at the Assizes and Sessions here, wherefore me seemeth, saving your better advice, it were well done that ye should speak with the Justices ere they come here; and if ye will that I complain to them or to any other, if God fortune me life and health, I will do as ye advise me to do, for in good faith, I have been simply [1] entreated among them; and what with sickness, and trouble that I have had, I am brought right low and weak, but to my power I will do as I can or may in your matters.

The Duke of Suffolk and both the Duchesses [2] shall come to Claxton this day, as I am informed, and this next week he shall be at Cossey whether he will come further hitherward or not, I wot not yet; it is said that he should come hither, and yet his men said here on Monday that he claimed no title to this place; they said their coming was but to take out such riotous people as was here within this place, and such as were the King's felons, and endicted and outlawed men, nevertheless they would shew no warrants whereby to take none such, though there had been such here; I suppose, if they might have come in peaceably, they would have made another cause of their coming.

When all was done and they should depart, Harleston and

[1] Meanly.   [2] His mother and wife.

other desired me that I should come and see mine old Lady,[1] and sue to my Lord, and if any thing were amiss it should be amended.

I said if I should sue for any remedy, that I should sue further, and let the King and all the Lords of this land to have knowledge what hath been done to us, if so were that the Duke would maintain that hath been done to us by his Servants, if ye would give me leave.

I pray you send me word, if ye will that I make any complaint to the Duke or the Duchess, for as it is told me, they know not the plainness[2] that hath been done in such things as hath been done in their names.

I should write much more to you but for lack of leisure.

The Trinity have you in keeping. Written the Friday next after Saint Thomas,

By your
MARGARET PASTON

[1465]

143. MARGARET PASTON AND HER YOUNGER SON HOLD COTTON AGAINST DEBENHAM

To my right reverend and worshipful Father John Paston, be this delivered

AFTER all humble and most due recommendation, as lowly as I can, I beseech you of your blessing; please it you to have knowledge that as on Sunday next before Michaelmas Day as my mother came from London ward, she came homeward by Cotton, and she sent for me, to Hellesdon, to come to her thither, and so I have been in the place ever since; and as soon as Michaelmas day was passed I began to distrain the tenants, and gathered some silver, as much, I trow, as will pay for our costs, and yet I keep here right a good fellowship, and more were promised me, which that came not to me, whereby I was near deceived, for when Debenham heard say how that I began to gather silver, he raised many men within one day and a half to the number of

[1] The dowager Duchess. [2] Brutality.

three hundred men, as I was credibly ascertained by a Yeoman of the Chamber of my Lord's [1] that oweth me good will, which Yeoman as soon as he had seen their fellowship rode strait to my Lord and informed him of it; and also he informed my Lord how that I had gathered another great fellowship, which fellowship he named more than we were by one hundred and an half and yet more; and he said unto my Lord, and my Lady, and to their Counsel that without that my Lord took a direction in the matter, that there were like to be done great harm on both our parties, which were a great disworship to my Lord considering how that he taketh us both for his men, and so we be known well enough; upon which information, and disworship to my Lord, that twain of his men should debate so near him, contrary to the King's peace, considered of my Lord and my Lady and their Counsel, my Lord sent for me and Sir Gilbert Debenham [2] to come to him to Framlingham both; and as it fortuned well my Mother came to me to Cotton not half an hour before that the messenger came to me from my Lord, which was late upon Tuesday last past at night, and the next day on the morning I rode to my lord to Framlingham, and so did Sir Gilbert also, and as soon as we were come, we were sent for to come to my Lord, and when we came to my Lord, he desired of us both that we should neither gather no fellowship, but such men as we had gathered, that we should send them home again, and that the Court should be continued [3] into the time that my Lord, or such as he would assign had spoken both with you, and Yelverton, and Jenney; and that one indifferent man, chosen by us both, should be assigned to keep the place into the time that ye and they were spoken with.

And then I answered my Lord and said, how that at that time I had my master within the Manor of Cotton, which was my Mother, and into the time that I had spoken with her, I could give none answer; and so my Lord sent Richard Fulmerston, bearer hereof, to my Mother this day for an answer, which answer he should bring to my Lord to London; for my Lord rode to London ward as yesterday, and the sooner because he

[1] The Duke of Norfolk's.

[2] For Sir Gilbert Debenham see note to Letter 130.

[3] Put off.

trusted to have a good end of this matter and all others betwixt you, which he taketh for a great worship to him ward, and a great advantage both, and he could bring this matter about, for then he would trust to have your service, all which were to him great treasure and advantage.

And this was the answer that my Mother and I gave him, that at the instance of my Lord and my Lady we would do thus much as for to put the Court in continuance, and no more to receive of the profits of the Manor than we had, and had distressed for, till into the time that she and I had word again from my Lord and you; if so were that they would neither make entries nor distrain the tenants, nor keep no Court more than we would do, and we told Richard Fulmerston that this my Mother and I did at the instance and great request of my Lord, because my Lord intended peace, which reasonably we would not he against, and yet we said we knew well that we should have no thank of you, when ye knew of it, without it were because we did it at my Lord's instance; but before this answer we had received as much silver, full nigh, as Richard Calle sent us books of, for to gather it by; and as for the possession of the place, we told him that we would keep it: and Sir Gilbert agreed, so that Yelverton and Jenney would do the same, for it was time for him to say so, for my Lord told him that he would set him fast by the feet else, to be sure of him, that he should make none insurrections into the time that my Lord came again from London.

I ween, and so doth my Mother both, that this appointment was made in good time, for I was deceived of better than an hundred men and an half, that I had promise of to have come to me when I sent for them, this promise had I before that I sent to you the last Letter the day after Saint Michael. Jenney heard say that I kept Cotton, and he rode to Nacton, and there held a Court, and received the profits of the Manor.

I beseech you that I may have knowledge in haste from you how ye will that I be demeaned in this matter and in all others, and I shall apply me to fulfil your intent in them to my power by the grace of God, whom I beseech have you in guiding, and send you your heart's desire. Written at Hemnale's Hall, in Cotton, the Thursday next before Saint Faith.

My Mother recommendeth her to you, and prayeth you to hold her excused that she writeth not to you at this time, for she may have no leisure; the bearer hereof shall inform you, whether Jenney will agree to this appointment or not, I think he dare do none otherwise.

Your Son and lowly Servant,

JOHN PASTON

[1465]

144. DRAYTON AND HELLESDON RUINED BY SUFFOLK'S MEN

To my right worshipful Husband John Paston, be this delivered in haste

RIGHT worshipful Husband, I recommend me to you, please it you to weet that I was at Hellesdon [1] upon Thursday last past, and saw the place there, and in good faith there will no creature think how foully and horribly it is arrayed but if they saw it; there cometh much people daily to wonder thereupon, both of Norwich and of other places, and they speak shamefully thereof; the Duke had by better than a thousand pound that it had never been done, and ye have the more good will of the people, that it is so foully done; and they made your Tenants of Hellesdon and Drayton with other to help to break down the walls of the place and the Lodge both, God knoweth full evil against their wills, but that they durst none other wise do for fear; I have spoken with your Tenants of Hellesdon and Drayton both, and put them in comfort as well as I can; the Duke's men ransacked the Church, and bare away all the good [2] that was left there, both of ours and of the Tenants, and left not so much but that they stood upon the high Altar and ransacked the Images, and took away such as they might find, and put away the Parson out of the Church till they had done; and ransacked every man's

[1] The Duke of Suffolk had now set up a claim to Fastolf's manors of Drayton and Hellesdon, near Norwich. After a period of quasi-legal warfare the Duke's men took possession and wrecked the buildings.

[2] Property.

house in the town five or six times, and the chief masters of robbing was the Bailiff of Eye, the Bailiff of Stradbrook, Thomas Slyford, and Porter; and Slyford was the chief robber of the Church, and he hath most of the robbery next the Bailiff of Eye; and as for lead, brass, pewter, iron, doors, gates, and other stuff of the house, men of Cossey and Causton have it, and that they might not carry they have hewn it asunder in the most dispiteous wise; if it might be, I would some men of worship might be sent from the King to see how it is, both there and at the Lodge [at Drayton], ere than any Snows come, that they may make report of the truth, else it shall not more be seen so plainly as it may now; and at the reverence of God speed your matters now, for it is too horrible a cost and trouble that we have now daily, and must have till it be otherwise; and your men dare not go about to gather up your livelihood, and we keep here [1] daily more than thirty persons for salvation of us and the place, for in very truth, and the place had not been kept strong, the Duke had come hither.

At the reverence of God, if any worshipful and profitable mean may be taken in your matters, forsake it not in eschewing of our trouble and great costs and charges that we have, and may grow hereafter; it is thought here that if my Lord of Norfolk would take upon him for you, and that he may have a Commission for to enquire of such riots and robberies as hath been done to you and other in this country, that then all the country will await upon him, and serve your intent, for the people loveth and dreadeth him more than any other Lord, except the King and my Lord of Warwick, etc.

God have you in his blessed keeping, and send us good tidings from you. Written in haste, upon the Sunday Saint Simon and Jude's Even.

By yours
MARGARET PASTON

[1465]

[1] Probably at Astley's (*cf.* Letter 146).

145. PASTON IN THE FLEET [1]

To my Cousin [2] Margaret Paston

MINE own dear sovereign Lady, I recommend me to you, and thank you of the great cheer that ye made me here to my great cost and charge and labour. No more at this time, but that I pray you ye will send me hither two ells of worsted for Doublets, to happe me [3] this cold winter; and that ye enquire where William Paston bought his Tippet of fine worsted, which is almost like silk, and if that be much finer, than that ye should buy me after seven or eight shillings, then buy me a quarter and the nail thereof for Collars, though it be dearer than the other, for I would make my doublet all worsted for worship of Norfolk, rather than like Gonner's doublet.

Item, as for the matter of the nine score pounds asked by my Lady of Bedford for the manor of West Thurrok, whereas Sir Thomas Howys saith that he hath no writing thereof, but that Sir John Fastolf purchased the said manor, and paid certain money in earnest, and afterwards granted his bargain to the Duke of Bedford, and so the money that he took was for the money that he had paid; peradventure Sir Thomas Howys hath writing thereof, and knoweth it not; for if there be any such money paid upon any bargain he shall find it in Kyrtling's books that was Sir John Fastolf's Receiver, and it was about such time as the Duke of Bedford was last in England, which, as it is told me, was the 8th year of King Harry V,[4] or the 8th year of King Harry VI,[5] and the sum that he paid for the said bargain was 300 marks. Also, he shall find the 22d year of King Harry (VI) or there about [6] in the accounts of one of Fastolf's Receivers at London, that there was taken of Sir Thomas Tyrell, and of the Duchess of Exeter, that was wife to Sir Lewis Johnes, Farmer of

[1] A semi-humorous letter, written after Margaret Paston had visited her husband in the Fleet, where, in the course of the disputes over Fastolf's will, he was imprisoned for the third time.

[2] *I.e.*, wife—either a slip or to ensure safe carriage.

[3] Keep me warm.

[4] 1420. [5] 1429. [6] 1443.

he said manor, certain money for repayment of part of the said ;oo marks. Also he shall find in years after that, or that year, ›r thereabouts that Sir John Fastolf received money of my Lord Rivers that now is, by the name of Richard Wydvile, for his own lebt due to Sir John Fastolf; wherefore, if Sir Thomas be true o his master [1] let him do his devoir [2] to make that Worcester, vhich is upheld by him with the dead's goods, be true to his naster, or else it is time for Sir Thomas to forsake him, and help o punish him, or men must say that Sir Thomas is not true; and noreover let Sir Thomas examine what he can find in this matter hat I sent him word of, which matter he shall find in the said eceiver's book, if he list to seek it.

Item, on the day after your departing, I received letters by Villiam Roos from your sons to me, and to Richard Calle, etc.

Item, I shall tell you a tale,
Pampyng [3] and I have picked your male [4]
And taken out Pieces five,
For upon trust of Calle's promise, we may soon unthrive,
And, if Calle bring us hither twenty pound,
Ye shall have your pieces again, good and round;
Or else, if he will not pay you the value of the pieces, there
To the post do nail his ear,
Or else do him some other wrongs,
For I will no more in his default borrow;
And but if the receiving of my livelode be better plied
He shall Christ's curse and mine [have] clean tried;
And look ye be merry and take no thought,
For this rhyme is cunningly wrought,
My Lord Percy [5] and all this house
Recommend them to you, dog, cat and mouse,
And wish ye had been here still,
For they say ye are a good gill.[6]

[1] *I.e.*, Fastolf. Howes and Worcester were combining against Paston.
[2] Best.
[3] One of his retainers.
[4] Trunk.
[5] Heir of the Earl of Northumberland, who was slain at Towton, now n prison as a Lancastrian.
[6] An agreeable companion.

No more to you at this time,
But God him save that made this rhyme,
Written the   of Saint Mathe,
By your true and trusty husband J. P.[1]

[1465]

146. A FRIEND AT NORWICH OFFERS SHELTER TO MISTRESS PASTON

To my worshipful Cousin, John Paston

RIGHT worshipful Cousin, I commend me to you, and for a much as there was a child dead at Astleys, and another like to b dead in the same place, what time that I rode out about my littl livelihood my Lady and I both thought pity on my mistress you wife to see her abide there, and desired her to come to my poo house unto such time as ye should a be [2] otherwise avised which if it please you I am right well apaied.

Sythen [4] I understand by my Lady that ye desire to know whether that I should abide here still or not, as to that, I hav none other place that I would abide at; and my Lady saith hov she is advised to end her life here; also she saith how ye desir to have a Stable within my place; and as to that, a faith Sir, have none, but that must needs serve for my wood; as for Chamber, ye shall have one for your men all ready; and a touching a stable, Sir John Sparham and I have gotten you on where your horse stood the last time ye were in this town and a house to lay in hay and straw, and cost you not but making of rack and a manger, and more to your ease there than here; an if ye will that it be made ready for you, send word by the bringe of this Letter. And, Cousin, as touching to payment, I canno say how ye shall be pleased with my poor fare, but after that y are come home [5] and are acquainted therewith, we shall so accor

[1] Prisoners in the Fleet could pay for rooms and comfort according t their means.

[2] Have been. [3] Decided. [4] Since.

[5] John Paston did not return to Norfolk. He was kept in London, an died there in May 1466.

as shall be pleasure to us both, with the grace of God, which have [you] in his blessed governance, and send you your Mother's blessing.

Written at Norwich, on St Martin's Even.[1]

Your poor Cousin and Friend

JOHN WYMONDHAM

And how that ever ye do,
hold up your manship.

[1465]

147. FRIAR BRACKLEY'S TESTIMONY

John Paston,[2] to his Brother Sir John Paston [3]

SIR, please it you to weet that my Mother and I communed this day with Friar Mouth, to understand what his saying shall be in the court when he cometh up to London, which is in this wise: he say that at such time as he had shriven Master Brackley, and howselled [4] him both, he let him weet that he was informed by divers persons, that the said Master Brackley ought for to be in great conscience for such things as he had done and said, and caused my father, whom God assoil! for to do and say, also in proving of Sir John Fastolf's Will [5]; to whom the said Master Brackley answered thus again; "I am right glad that it cometh to you in mind for to move me with this matter in discharging of my conscience against God"; saying furthermore to the said Friar Mouth, by the way that his soul should to, that the Will that my Father put into the court was as verily Sir John Fastolf's Will, as it was true that he should once die. This was said on the Sunday when the said Brackley weened to have died then; on the Monday he revived again, and was well amended till on the

[1] November 10.
[2] The youngest.
[3] After the death of their father in 1466 Sir John Paston remained at Court, cultivating powerful friends, while John the Youngest stayed in Norfolk.
[4] Absolved.
[5] Yelverton accused Paston of forgery in Fastolf's will. Mouth, Prior of the Grey Friars of Norwich, and Brackley overbear Howes' statement that he had helped Paston to forge the will.

Wednesday, and on the Wednesday he sickened again, supposing to have died forthwith, and in his sickness he called Friar Mouth, which was confessor unto him, of his own motion, saying unto him in this wise, "Sir, whereas of your own motion ye moved me the last day to tell you after my conscience of Sir John Fastolf's Will likewise as I knew; and now of mine own motion, and in discharging of my soul, for I know well that I may not escape, but that I must die in haste, wherefore I desire you that [you] will report after my death, that I took it upon my soul at my dying, that that will that John Paston put in to be proved was Sir John Fastolf's will"; and the said Brackley died the same Wednesday.

And whereas ye would have had Richard Calle to you as on Sunday last past, it was this Tuesday ere I had your Letter; and whereas it pleaseth you for to wish me at Eltham, at the Tournay, for the good sight that was there, by truth I have lever see you once in Caister-hall than to see as many Kings tourney as might be betwixt Eltham and London.

And, Sir, whereas it liketh you to desire to have knowledge how that I have done with the Lady Boleyn, by my faith I have done nor spoken nought in that matter, nor nought will do till time that ye come home, and ye come not this seven year; notwithstanding the Lady Boleyn was in Norwich in the week after Easter, from the Saturday till the Wednesday, and Heydon's wife and Mistress Alice both, and I was at Caister, and wist not of it; her men said that she had none other errand to the Town but for to sport her, but so God help me, I suppose that she weened I would have been in Norwich for to have seen her daughter; I beseech you with all my heart hie you home, though ye should tarry but a day, for I promise you your folk think that ye have forgotten them, and the most part of them must depart at Whitsuntide at the furthest, they will no longer abide; and as for R. Calle we cannot get half a quarter the money that we pay for the bare household, besides men's wages. Daubeney nor I may no more without coinage.

Your

JOHN PASTON

[1467]

148. DESIGNS TO SEIZE CAISTER [1]

To Sir John Paston, Knight, be this delivered in haste

I GREET you well, and send you God's blessing and mine, letting you weet that Blickling of Heylesdon came from London this week, and he is right merry, and maketh his boast that within this fortnight of Heylesdon should be both new Lords and new officers; and also this day was brought me word from Caister, that Rysing of Fretton should have heard said in divers places there, as he was in Suffolk, that Fastolf of Cowhawe maketh all the strength that he may, and proposeth him to assault Caister, and to enter there if he may, insomuch that it is said that he hath a five score men ready, and sendeth daily spies to understand what fellowship keep the place; by whose power, or favour, or supportation, that he will do this, I know not, but you wot well that I have been affrayed [2] there before this time, when that I had other comfort than I have now; and I cannot well guide nor rule soldiers, and also they set not by a woman as they should set by a man, therefore I would ye should send home your Brother or else Dawbeny to have a rule, and to take in such men as were necessary for the safe-guard of the place, for if I were there, without I had the more sadder or worshipful persons about me, and there come a meny of knaves, and prevailed in their intent, it should be to me but a villany; and I have been about my livelode [3] to set a rule therein, as I have written to you, which is not yet all performed after mine desire, and I would not go to Caister till I had done; I will no more days make thereabout if I may, therefore in any wise send some body home to keep the place, and when that I have done and performed that I have begun, I shall purpose me thither-ward, if I should do there any good, and else I had lever be thence.

I have sent to Nicholas, and such as keep the place, that they

[1] Sir John's right to the manor of Caister was confirmed by a court of audience, but Yelverton and Howes propounded yet another will and sold Caister to the Duke of Norfolk, who in 1469 laid a regular siege to it and captured it.

[2] Attacked. [3] Property.

should take in some fellows to assist and strength them, till ye send home some other word, or some other man to govern them that be therein, etc.

I marvel greatly that ye send me no word how that ye do, for your enemies begin to wax right bold, and that putteth your friends both in great fear and doubt, therefore purvey that they may have some comfort, that they be no more discouraged, for if we lose our friends it shall [be] hard in this troublesome world to get them again.

The blessed Trinity speed you in your matters, and send you the victory of your enemies, to your heart's ease and their confusion.

Written at Norwich, the Saturday next before Relick Sunday [1] in haste.

By your Mother

MARGARET PASTON

[1467]

149. DIVERSION OF CAISTER ENDOWMENT

To my right worshipful Mistress, Margaret Paston, Widow

RIGHT worshipful Mistress, after due recommendation, please your good mistresship to weet that I communed late with your entirely well-beloved son, Sir John Paston, if the foundation of my Master Fastolf's College might be at Cambridge,[2] in case it shall not be at Caister, neither at Saint Benet's, because that University lieth near the country of Norfolk and Suffolk; for, all be it my Lord of Winchester is disposed to found a College in Oxford for my said Master to be prayed for, yet with much less cost he might make some other memorial also in Cambridge, and it were of two Clerks and three or four scholars, founded at least

[1] Third Sunday after Midsummer Day.

[2] It seemed doubtful if Fastolf's intention and endowment for a new college of Priests at Caister could be carried out. Bishop Waynflete wished to divert it to his new college (Magdalen) at Oxford; Worcester proposed Cambridge as nearer to Norwich.

with the value of good Benefices and rich Parsonages, that might be purchased the advowsons with much less goods than Lordships or manors may; and I found your Son well disposed to move and excite my said Lord. Also now the Christmas week next before the feast at London, my Lord of Winchester called me to him in presence of Sir John, and desired him effectually to be my good willer; and my Master would have no words rehearsed on my behalf, and he said full well. Would Jesu, Mistress, that my good Master that was some time your husband, in my said Master Fastolf's life days, as he shewed to me, then could have found in his heart to have trusted and loved me as my Master Fastolf did, and that he would not have given credence to the maliciously contrived tales that Friar Brackley, W. Barker and others imagined untruly, saving your reverence, of me. And now ye may openly understand the soothe,[1] and your son Sir John also; and yet for all that I put never my Master Fastolf's livelihood in trouble,[2] for all the unkindness and covetousness that was shewed me, as I have declared to the bearer hereof, that I know ye trust well, to whom in this ye may give credence at this time.

Your
WILLIAM WORCESTER

And I thank you heartily for my poor woman,[3] she should come to you at your commandment late or rathe,[4] but for jealousy or misdeeming of people that have me in great await [5]; and ye know well, Mistress, better is a friend unknown than known; the world is so misdeeming and ready to make division and debate that cometh of an envious disposition. And I am right glad that Caister is and shall be at your commandment, and yours in especial, a rich jewel it is at need for all the country in time of war; and my Master Fastolf would rather he had never builded it, than it should be in the governance of any sovereign that will oppress the country. And I find the religious of Saint Benet's full unkind took away a chamber the elder Abbot had put me in possession for my solace, when I might come thither and desport

[1] Truth. [2] Property in jeopardy. [3] Wife.
[4] Early. [5] That mean to do me mischief.

me, and took [1] that chamber to Master John Smyth, that Sir Thomas Howys said to me, was none wholesome counceller in the reformation of the last testament [which] made but two Executors,[2] to have the rule alone I would he had never meddled of it, that counsel made much trouble; I pray you keep this Letter close to yourself, as I trust you and Sir James [Gloys] and also in R. Toly, that I understand him close and just.

I had no time to speak within now, late when I was but one day at Norwich, W. Barker slandered me in certain matters of good [3] to the sum of 500 marks that Reynold Harneys should keep and take one half; would Jesu Barker had said true, it might have done me much good; and mistress as I dare desire you, I pray you recommend me to my best Mistress, your Mother Agnes, for she favoured me and did me great charity, to be the better disposed to her Son Master John, and by my soul it made me the heartier to save the livelihood from trouble or from claims, as I report me to all the world, I put never manor nor livelihood of my Master Fastolf's in trouble, nor entitled no creature to no place, and ye may speak to her hereof when ye be alone.

[1468]

150. SIR JOHN ENGAGES A GARRISON TO HOLD CAISTER

To my right well-beloved Brother, John Paston, Esquire, being at Caister, or to John Dawbeney there, be this Letter delivered

RIGHT well-beloved Brother, I commend me to you, letting you weet that I have waged for to help you and Dawbeney to keep the place at Caister, four well assured and true men to do all manner of thing what that they be desired to do, in safe-guard, or inforcing of the said place; and moreover they be proved men, and cunning in the war, and in feats of arms, and they can well shoot both Guns and Crossbows, and amend and string them, and devise bulwarks, or any things that should be a strength to the place, and they will, as need is, keep watch and ward, they be sad and well advised men, saving one of them, which is

[1] Gave. [2] Paston and Howes. [3] Property.

bald and called William Peny, which is as good a man as goeth on the earth, saving a little, he will, as I understand, be a little cupschotten [1] but yet he is no brawler, but full of courtesy, the other three be named Peryn Sale, John Chapman, Robert Jack's Son, saving that as yet they have none harness come, but when it cometh it shall be sent to you, and in the mean while I pray you and Dawbeney to purvey them some.

Also, a couple of beds they must needs have, which I pray you by the help of my Mother to purvey for them, till that I come home to you; ye shall find them gentlemanly, comfortable fellows, and that they will and dare abide by their taking, and if ye understand that any assault should be towards, I send you these men, because that men of the country there about you should be frayed [2] for fear of loss of their goods; wherefore if there were any such thing towards, I would ye took of men of the country but few, and that they were well assured men, for else they might discourage all the remanent.

And as for any writing from the King, he hath promised that there shall come none, and if there do his unwares,[3] your answer may be this, how the King hath said, and so to delay them till I may have word, and I shall soon purvey a remedy.

I understand that ye have been with my Lord of Norfolk now of late, what ye have done I wot not; we say that he shall be here again this day. Moreover, I trow John Alford shall not long abide with my Lord; I shall send you tidings of other things in haste, with the grace of God, who, etc. Written on Wednesday next before Saint Martin.[4]

[1468] JOHN PASTON

151. SIR JOHN AND THE QUEEN'S CHAPLAIN

To my well-beloved Brother, John Paston, or to John Dawbeney, in his absence

RIGHT worshipful and well-beloved Brother, I commend me to you, letting you weet that Sir Thomas Howes [5] had a free

[1] High-spirited, tipsy. [2] Frightened. [3] Without his knowledge.
[4] November 11. [5] Sir Thomas Howes died in 1468.

Chapel in Caister, whereof the gift belongeth to me, which Chapel as I understand should be in the old time, ere the place at Caister were built, within the moat, wherefore I am but the better pleased; and so it is now that at the special request of the Queen and other especial good Lords of mine, I have given it to the bearer hereof called Master John Yotton, a Chaplain of the Queen's; nevertheless in time past I purposed that the Master of the College should have had it, and so ere long, I hope he shall, wherefore I think he must take possession, and that is the cause of his coming; wherefore I pray you make him good cheer; he is informed that it should be worth an hundred shillings by year, which I believe not; I think it dear enough [at] forty shillings by year; he must have it as it was had before.

Item, this day I understand that there be come Letters from my Mother and you, and Dawbeney, wherein I shall send you answer when I have seen them.

No more at this time, for within this three days I shall let you have knowledge of other matters.

Written the 17th day of March.

Whither he needeth induction, or institution, or none, I wot not; if it need, brother ye may seal any such thing as well as I. Master Stephen can tell all such things.

JOHN PASTON, Knight

[1469]

152. KING EDWARD IV TO VISIT NORWICH

To my Mother, and to my Brother John Paston

BROTHER, it is so that the King shall come into Norfolk in haste, and I wot not whether that I may come with him or not; if I come, I must do make a Livery of 20 Gowns, which I must pick out by your advice; and as for the Cloth for such persons as be in that Country, if it might be had there at Norwich, or not, I wot not; and what Persons I am not remembered.

If my mother be at Caister, as there shall be no doubt for the keeping of the place while the King is in that Country, that I may have the most part at Caister.

And whether ye will offer yourself to wait upon my Lord of Norfolk or not, I would ye did that best were to do; I would do my Lord pleasure and service, and so I would ye did, if I wist to be sure of his good Lordship in time to come. He shall have 200 in a Livery blue and tawny, and blue on the left side, and both dark colours.

I pray you send me word, and your advice by Judd of what men, and what horse I could be purveyed of, if so be that I must needs come, and of your advice in all things by writing, and I shall send you hastily other tidings.

JOHN PASTON, Knight

[1469]

153. THE KING SETTLES NOTHING

To Sir John Paston, Knight

To begin, God yield [1] you for my hats. The King hath been in this country, and worshipfully received into Norwich, and had right good cheer, and great gifts in this country, wherewith he holdeth him so well content that he will hastily be here again, and the Queen also, with whom by my poor advice ye shall come, if so be that the term be done by that time that she come into this country; and as for your matters here, so God help me, I have done as much as in me was, in labouring of them, as well to my Lord Rivers as to my Lord Scales, Sir John Wydville, Thomas Wingfield and others about the King; and as for the Lord Rivers, he said to my Uncle William, Fairfax, and me, that he should move the King to speak to the two Dukes of Norfolk and Suffolk, that they should leave of their titles of such land as were Sir John Fastolf's, and if so be that they would do nought at the King's request, that then the King should command them to do no waste, nor make none assaults nor frays upon your tenants nor places, till such time as the law hath determined with you or against you; this was said by him the same day in the morning that he departed at noon; whether he moved the King with it or not I cannot say, my Uncle William thinks nay; and

[1] Reward.

the same afternoon following I told my Lord Scales that I had spoken with my Lord his Father, in like form as I have rehearsed, and asked him whether that my Lord his Father had spoken to the King or not, and he gave me this answer, that whether he had spoken to the King or not, that the matter should do well enough.

Thomas Wingfield told me, and swore unto me, that when Brandon [1] moved the King, and besought him to show my Lord favour in his matters against you, that the King said unto him again, " Brandon, though thou canst beguile the Duke of Norfolk, and bring him about [thy] thumb as thou list, I let thee weet thou shalt not do me so; for I understand thy false dealing well enough." And he said unto him, moreover that if my Lord of Norfolk left not of his hold of that matter, that Brandon should repent it, every vein in his heart, for he told him that he knew well enough that he might rule my Lord of Norfolk as he would, and if my Lord did any thing that were contrary to his laws, the King told him he knew well enough that it was by nobody's means but by his, and thus he departed from the King.

Item, as by words, the Lord Scales and Sir John Wydville took tender your matters more than the Lord Rivers.

Item, Sir John Wydville told me, when he was on horseback at the King's departing, that the King had commanded Brandon of purpose to ride forth from Norwich to Lynn, for to take a conclusion in your matter for you; and he bad me that I should cast no doubts but that ye should have your intent, and so did the Lord Scales also; and when that I prayed them at any time to shew their favour to your matter, they answered that it was their matter as well as yours, considering the alliance betwixt you.[2] . . .

Item, the King rode through Hellesdon Warren towards Walsingham, and Thomas Wingfield promised me that he would find the means that my Lord of Gloucester [3] and himself both should shew the King the Lodge that was broken down, and also that they would tell him of the breaking down of the place. Contrary to these matters, and all the comfort that I had of my Lord Scales, Sir John Wydville, and Thomas Wingfield, my

[1] Escheator of Norwich, a relative of the Wingfields.

[2] The contract between Sir John Paston and Anne Haute (see Letter 42).

[3] Afterwards Richard III.

Uncle William saith, that the King told him [with] his own mouth, when he had ridden forth by the Lodge in Hellesdon Warren, that he supposed as well that it might fall down by the self, as be plucked down, for if it had been plucked down, he said that we might have put in our bills of it, when his Judges sat on the Oyer and Determiner in Norwich, he being there; and then my Uncle saith how that he answered the King, that ye trusted to his good grace that he should set you through with both the Dukes, by mean of treaty, and he saith that the king answered him that he would neither treat nor speak for you, but for to let the law proceed, and so he saith that they departed; and by my troth and my Lord Treasurer encourage you not more than he did us here, ye shall have but easy [1] help as on that party, wherefore labour your matters effectually, for by my troth it is needed for, for all their words of pleasure, I cannot understand what their labour in this country hath done good; wherefore be not over swift till ye be sure of your land, but labour sore the law, for by my troth till that be passed with you, ye get but easy help as I can understand. . . .

Item, my Lord of Norfolk gave Bernard, Broom, nor me no gowns at this season,[2] wherefore I waited not on him, notwithstanding I offered my service for that season to my Lady, but it was refused, I wot by advice; wherefore I purpose no more to do so. As for Bernard, Barney, Broom, and W. Calthorpe [they] are sworn my Lord of Gloucester's men, but I stand yet at large, notwithstanding my Lord Scales spoke to me to be with the King, but I made no promise so to be, for I told him that I was not worth a groat without you, and therefore I would make no promise to nobody till they had your good will first, and so we departed.

It was told me that there was out a Privy Seal for you to attend upon the King northward; and if it be so, I think verily it is done to have you from London by craft, that ye should not labour your matters to a conclusion this term, but put them [in] delay. I pray you purvey you on it, to be at home as soon as the term is done,

[1] Slight.

[2] *I.e.*, not counting them among his retainers. John Paston was a faithful follower of the Earl of Oxford.

for by God I take great hurt for mine absence in divers places, and the most part of your men at Caister will depart without abode,[1] and ye be not at home within this fortnight. I pray you bring home points and laces of silk for you and me.

JOHN PASTON

[1469]

154. CAISTER BESIEGED BY THE DUKE OF NORFOLK [2]

To Sir John Paston, be this delivered in haste

I GREET you well, and send you God's blessing and mine, letting you weet that Sir John Heveningham was at Norwich this day, and spake with me at my Mother's, but he would not that it should be understood, for my Lord [3] hath made him one of the Captains at Caister, of the people that should keep the watch about the place, that no man should succour them if my Lord departed. I desired him to favour them, if any man should come to them from me or you, and he would not grant it, but he desired me to write to you to understand, if that my Lord might be moved to find surety to recompence you all wrongs, and [whether] ye would suffer him to enter peaceably, and the law after his entry would deem [4] it you; be ye advised what answer ye would give.

Item, since that I spake with him, and the same day, a faithful friend of ours came unto me and moved me, if that my Lord might be intreated to suffer indifferent men to keep the place, and take the profits for both parties till the right be determined by the law; and my Lord for his part, and ye for your part, to find sufficient surety that you neither should vex, let, nor trouble the said indifferent men to keep peaceably the possession of the

[1] Delay.

[2] Paston's title to Caister and the other manors had been approved by King Edward IV, but the King was taken prisoner by the Earl of Warwick in 1469, and Norfolk took violent action against Caister, which had been sold to him by Yelverton and Howes under another disputed Fastolf will.

[3] The Duke of Norfolk.

[4] Award.

said place, and to take the profits unto the time it be determined by the law to his behalf, that the law deemeth it; and the said persons, that so indifferently keep possession, before their entry into the said place, to find also sufficient surety to answer the party that the law deemeth it to, of the profits during their possession, and to suffer him peaceably to enter, or any in his name, whensoever they be required by the party to whom the right is deemed of all these premises; send me word how ye will be demeaned by as good advice as ye can get, and make no longer delay, for they must needs have hasty succour that be in the place, for they be sore hurt, and have none help, and if they have hasty help it shall be the greatest worship that ever ye had, and if they be not holpen it shall be to you a great disworship; and look never to have favour of your neighbours and friends, but if this speed well; therefore pretend it [1] in your mind, and purvey therefore in haste; howsoever ye do, God keep you, and send you the victory of your enemies, and give you and us all grace to live in peace. Written on Saint Giles' even,[2] at nine of the bell at night.

Robin came home yester even, and he brought me neither writing from you, nor good answer of this matter, which grieveth me right ill that I have sent you so many messengers, and have so feeble answers again.

By your Mother

MARGARET PASTON

[1469]

155. AN ATTEMPT AT COMPROMISE

To Master Writtill

MASTER Writtill,[3] I recommend me to you, beseeching you heartily, as mine whole trust is in you, that ye do your devoir to continue truce till Friday or Saturday in the morning, by which time I hope the messenger shall come, and that ye be not driven

[1] Put it first. [2] August 31.

[3] Writtle was a servant of the Duke of Clarence, and he had apparently been sent to Caister to arrange a compromise during a truce in the siege.

to take an appointment [1] if ye can understand by any likelihood that it be able to be avoided and resisted, and that ye feel my Brother's disposition therein, as my trust is in you, praying you to remember that it resteth, as God help me, on all my weal; for, as God help me, I had lever the place were burned, my Brother and Servants [being] saved, than the best appointment that ever ye and I communed of, should by my good will be taken, if this message from the King may rescue it; and if it be so, that my Lord be removed by the King's commandment, which resteth with his honour, I may in time to come do him service, as shall recompence any grudge or displeasure that he ever had, or hath to me or mine; and ye, if it the rather by your wisdom and policy the mean above written may be had, shall be as sure of the service of my true brother and servants, and me, as ye can devise by my troth; for in good faith this matter sticketh more nigh mine heart and me than I can write unto you, and to my brother and servants more near than, as God knoweth, they wot of; wherefore master Writtill, all our welfare resteth in you, beseeching you to remember it, for this matter is to all us either making or marring.

Written at London, the next day after your departing; I shall send you more knowledge to-morrow, with God's grace.

Yours

JOHN PASTON, Knight

[1469]

156. MARGARET APPEALS TO SIR JOHN

To Sir John Paston, Knight

I GREET you well, letting you weet that your Brother and his fellowship stand in great jeopardy at Caister, and lack victuals, and Daubeney and Berney be dead, and divers other greatly hurt; and they fail [2] Gunpowder and Arrows, and the place [is] sore broken with guns of the other party, so that but they have hasty help, they be like to lose both their lives and the place, to the greatest rebuke to you that ever came to any gentleman, for every

[1] Terms for surrender.

[2] Lack.

man in this country marvelleth greatly that ye suffer them to be so long in so great jeopardy without help or other remedy.

The Duke hath been more fervently set thereupon, and more cruel, since that Writtil, my Lord of Clarence's man was there, than he was before, and he hath sent for all his tenants from every place, and others, to be there at Caister on Thursday next coming, that there is then like to be the greatest multitude of people that came there yet; and they purpose then to make a great assault, for they have sent for guns to Lynn and other places by the sea's side, that, with their great multitude of guns with other shot and ordnance, there shall no man dare appear in the place, they shall hold them so busy with their great [number of] people, that it shall not lie in their power within to hold it against them, without God help them, or have hasty succour from you; therefore, as ye will have my blessing, I charge you and require you, that ye see your brother be holpen in haste, and if ye can have none mean, rather desire writing from my Lord of Clarence, if he be at London, or else of my Lord Archbishop of York, to the Duke of Norfolk, that he will grant them that be in the place their lives and their goods; and in eschewing of insurrections and other inconveniences that be like to grow within the Shire of Norfolk, this troublous world, because of such conventicles and gatherings within the said Shire, for cause of the said place, they shall suffer him to enter upon such appointment or other like, taken by the advice of your counsel there at London, if ye think this be not good, till the law hath determined otherwise: and let him write another Letter to your brother to deliver the place up on the same appointment: and if ye think, as I can suppose, that the Duke of Norfolk will not agree to this, because he granted this afore, and they in the place would not accept it, then I would the said messenger should with the said Letters bring from the said Lord of Clarence, or else my Lord Archbishop, to my Lord of Oxford other Letters to rescue them forthwith, though the said Earl of Oxford should have the place during his life for his labour; spare not this to be done in haste if ye will have their lives, and be set by in Norfolk, though ye should lose the best manor of all for the rescue. I had lever [1] ye lost the livelihood

[1] Rather.

than their lives; ye must get a messenger of the Lords, or some other notable man, to bring these Letters; do your devoir now, and let me send you no more messengers for this matter, but send me by the bearer hereof more certain comfort than ye have done by all other that I sent before; in any wise let the Letters that shall come to the Earl of Oxford, come with the Letters that shall come to the Duke of Norfolk, that if he will not agree to the one, that ye may have ready your rescue, that it need no more to send, therefore God keep you. Written the Tuesday next before Holy Rood day,[1] in haste.

By your Mother
MARGARET PASTON

[1469]

157. SIR JOHN'S ANSWER

To Margaret Paston

MOTHER, upon Saturday last was, Dawbeney and Berney were alive and merry, and I suppose there came no man out of the place to you since that time, that could have ascertained to you of their deaths; and as touching the fierceness of the Duke or of his people, shewed since that time that Writtill departed, I trow it was concluded that truce and abstinence of war should be had ere he departed, which shall endure till Monday next coming; and by that time I trow that truce shall be taken till that day sev'night after, by which time, I hope of, a good direction shall be had; and whereas ye write to me that I should sue for letters from my Lords of Clarence and York, they be not here, and if they wrote to him as they have done two times, I trow it would not avail; and as for to labour those letters and the rescue together, they be two sundry things, for when the rescue is ready, and the cost thereof is done, for if I be driven thereto to rescue it ere they come there that should do it,[2] it shall cost a thousand scutes,[3] and as much after, which way were hard for me to take while that I

[1] September 14. [2] Whom he expected to do it.
[3] Crowns—Italian coins valued at three and a half to the pound.

may do it otherwise; but as to say, that they shall be rescued if all the lands that I have in England, and Friends may do it, they shall, and God be friendly, and that as shortly as it may goodly and well be brought about; and the greatest default earthly is money, and some friends and neighbours to help, wherefore I beseech you to send me comfort with what money ye could find the means to get or chevise [1] upon surety sufficient, or upon livelihood to be in mortgage or yet sold, and what people by likelihood your friends and mine could make upon a short warning, and to send me word in all the haste as it is needful.

But, Mother, I feel that by your writing that ye deem in me I should not do my devoir without ye wrote to me some heavy tidings, and, Mother, if I had need to be quickened with a letter in this need, I were of myself too slow a fellow; but, Mother, I ensure you that I have heard ten times worse tidings since the siege began, than any letter that ye wrote to me, and sometimes I have heard right good tidings both; but this I assure you that they that be within have no worse rest than I have, nor casteth more jeopardy; but whether I had good tidings or ill, I take God to witness, that I have done my devoir, as I would be done for in case like, and shall do till there be an end of it.

I have sent to the King to York, and to the Lords, and hope to have answer from them by Wednesday at the furthest, and after that answer shall I be ruled, and then send you word, for till that time can I take none direction; and to encomfort you, despair you not for lack of victuals nor of gunpowder, nor be not too heavy nor too merry therefore; for and heaviness or sorrow would have been the remedy thereof, I knew never matter in my life that I could have been so heavy or sorry for, and with God's grace it shall be remedied well enough, for by my troth I had lever lose the Manor of Caister than the simplest man's life therein, if that may be his salvation; wherefore I beseech you to send me word what money and men ye think that I am like to get in that country; for the hasty purchase [2] of money and men shall be the getting and rescue of it, and the salvation of most men's lives, if we take that way.

Also, this day I purpose to send to York to the King for a

[1] Borrow. [2] Procuring.

thing, which same only may by likelihood be the salvation of all; ye must remember that the rescue of it is the last remedy of all, and how it is not easy to get; and also ye send me word that I should not come home without that I come strong, but if I had had one other strong place in Norfolk, to have come to, though I had brought right few with me, I should with God's grace have rescued it by this time, or else he should have been fain to have besieged both places ere yet, and [1] the Duke had not kept Yarmouth out: but, Mother, I beseech you send me some money, for by my troth I have but ten shillings, and wot not where to have more; and moreover I have been ten times in like case, or worse, within this ten weeks.

I sent to Richard Calle for money, but he sendeth me none; I beseech you to guide the evidence that Peacock can tell you of, and to see it safe, for it is told me that Richard Calle hath had right large language of them; I would not they come in his fingers: I have no word from you of them, nor whether ye have yet in your keeping the evidence of East Beckham out of his hands, nor whether ye have sent to my Manors that they should not pay him no more money or not; also that it like you to give credence to Robin in other things.

Written the Friday next after Holy Rood day.[2]

JOHN PASTON, Knight

[1469]

158. SIR JOHN ADVISES SURRENDER, IF NECESSARY

To John Paston, and to none other

I RECOMMEND me to you, and promise you that I have and shall labour and find the mean that ye shall have honour of your dealing, as ye have hither towards, as all England and every man reporteth; and moreover I am in way for it by many divers ways, whereof there shall be one executed by this day fortnight at the furthest, and peradventure within seven days; and if ye may keep

[1] If.

[2] September 14.

it so long I would be glad, and after that if ye have not from me other writing, that then ye do therein for your safe-guard and your fellowship only, and to your worships; and as for the place, no force therefore [1]; ye know this hand, therefore needeth no mention from whom it cometh; and moreover they that be about you be in obloquy of all men; and moreover they have been written to by as special writing as might be, after the world that now is,[2] and promise you that the Duke's counsel would that they had never begun it; and moreover they be charged in pain of their lives, that though they get the place, they should not hurt one of you; there is neither ye nor none with you, but, and he knew what is generally reported of him, he or ye, and God fortune you well, may think him four times better in reputation of all folk than ever he was.

Beware whom ye make a counsel to this matter.

Also, I let you weet that I am in much more comfort of you than I may write, and they that be about you [3] have cause to be more afeared than ye have; and also beware of spending of your stuff of quarrels, powder, and stone,[4] so that if they assault you ere we come, that ye have stuff to defend you of over, and then of my life ye get no more; and that your fellowship be ever occupied in renewing of your stuff.

Written the Monday next after Holy Rood day.

I trow, though ye be not privy thereto, there is taken a truce new till this day sev'night.

[1469]

159. TERMS OF SURRENDER

The Duke of Norfolk

WHERE[AS] John Paston, Esquire, and other diverse persons have, against the Peace, kept the Manor of Caister with force, against the Will and intent of Us the Duke of Norfolk, to our great Displeasure ; which notwithstanding, at the contemplation of the

[1] It does not matter. [2] By the strongest authority that now is.
[3] The besiegers. [4] Stone bullets.

Writing of the most worshipful and reverend Father in God the Cardinal of England, and our most trusty and entirely beloved Uncle the Archbishop of Canterbury, the right noble Prince my Lord of Clarence, and other Lords of our blood, and also at the great labour and instance of our most dear and singular beloved Wife, We be agreed that the said John Paston and his said Fellowship, being in the said Manor, shall depart and go out of the said Manor without delay, and make thereof deliverance to such Persons as we will assign, the said Fellowship having their Lives and Goods, Horse and Harness, and other Goods being in the keeping of the said John Paston; except Guns, Cross bows, and Quarrels and all other Hostelments,[1] to the said Manor annexed and belonging; and to have 15 Days respite after their said departing out, to go into what place shall like them, without any Actions or Quarrel to be taken or made by us, or in our name to them, or any of them, within our Franchise or without, during the said time.

Given under our Signet at Yarmouth the 26th day of September, the 9th year of King Edward the IVth.

NORFOLK

[1469]

160. JOHN THE YOUNGEST REPORTS THE SURRENDER OF CAISTER

To Sir John Paston, Knight

RIGHT worshipful Sir, I recommend me unto you, and as for the certainty of the deliverance of Caister, John Chapman can tell you how that we were enforced thereto, as well as myself; as for John Chapman and his three fellows, I have purveyed that they be paid each of them forty shillings, with the money that they had of you and Dawbeney; and that is enough for the season that they have done you service; I pray you give them their thank, for by my troth they have as well deserved it as any men that ever bear life, but as for money ye need not to give them without ye will, for they be pleased with their wages.

[1] War-like implements.

Writtil promised me to send you the certainty of the appointments,[1] we were for lack of victuals [and] gunpowder, men's hearts, lack of surety of rescue, driven thereto to take appointment.[2]

If ye will that I come to you, send me word, and I shall purvey me for to tarry with you a two or three days; by my troth the rewarding of such folks as hath been with me during the siege, hath put me in great danger [3] for the money; God preserve you, and I pray you be of good cheer till I speak with you, and I trust to God to ease your heart in some things.

JOHN PASTON

[1469]

161. INDIGNATION OF MARGARET PASTON

To Sir John Paston, in haste, a matre

I GREET you well, and send you God's blessing and mine, letting you weet that me think by the Letter that ye sent me by Robin, that ye think that I should write to you fables and imaginations, but I do not so, I have written as it have been informed me, and will do; it was told me that both Dawbeney and Berney were dead, but for certain Dawbeney is dead. God assoil his Soul, whereof I am right sorry, and it had pleased God that it might have been otherwise.

Remember you, ye have had two great losses within this twelvemonth of him, and of Sir Thomas [4]; God visiteth you as it pleaseth him in sundry wises, he would ye should know him and serve him better than ye have done before this time, and then he will send you the more grace to do well in all other things; and for God's love remember it right well, and take it patiently, and thank God of his visitation; and if any thing have been amiss, any otherwise than it ought to have been before this, either in pride, or in lavish expences, or in any other thing, that have offended God, amend it, and pray him of his grace and help,

[1] Terms. [2] Make terms. [3] Debt.

[4] Probably Thomas Lyndes, a priest much trusted by Sir John.

and intend well to God, and to your neighbours, and though your power hereafter be to acquit [1] them of their malice yet be merciful to them, and God shall send you the more grace to have your intent in other things. I remember these clauses, because of the last Letter that ye sent me. I have sent to Harry Halman, of Sporle, to help to get as ye desired me, and he cannot get past five or eight [men] at the most, and yet it will not be, but if he come, that ye trust upon that should come, for they belong a part to him; and Richard Sharman hath assayed on his part, and he cannot get past five, for those that belong to us, they belong also to our adversaries,[2] and they have been desired by them, and they would nought do for them, and therefore they think to have maugree [3] of the other part.

As for the gentleman that ye desired me to speak with, I spake with his wife, and she told me he was not in this country, nor nought wist when he should be here; and as for the other man he has bought him a Livery in Bromholm Priory,[4] and have given up the world, etc.

Item, as for money I could get but ten pounds upon pledges, and that is spent for your matters here, for paying of your men that were at Caister, and other things, and I wot not where to get none, neither for surety nor for pledges; and as for mine own livelihood, I am so simply paid thereof, that I fear me I shall be fain to borrow for myself, or else to break up household, or both.

As for the yielding of the place at Caister, I trow Writtil hath told of the appointments how it is delivered, I would that had been so ere this time, and then there should not have been done so mickle hurt as there is in divers ways, for many of our well-willers are put to loss for our sakes, and I fear me it shall be long ere it be recompensed again, and that shall cause others to do the less for us hereafter.

I would ye should [send] your brother word, and some other

[1] Pay back.

[2] *I.e.*, the men were formally retained by both the Pastons and the other party.

[3] Ill-will.

[4] It was usual for persons growing into years, to procure by purchase or gift a retreat in some religious society, where they were treated as permanent boarders for the rest of their lives. [F].

that ye trust, to see to your own livelihood [1] to set it in a rule, and to gather thereof that may be had in haste; and also of Sir John Fastolf's livelihood, that may be gathered in peaceable wise, for as for Richard Calle he will no more gather it, but if ye command him, and he would fain make his account, and have your good mastership, as it is told me, and deliver the evidence of Beckham, and all other things that longeth to you, that he trusteth that ye will be his good master hereafter; and he saith he will not take none new master till ye refuse his service.

Remember that your livelihood may be set in such a rule, that ye may know how it is, and what is owing to you, for by my faith, I have holpen as much as I may and more, saving myself, and therefore take heed ere it be worse.

This Letter was begun on Friday was sev'night, and ended this day next after Michaelmas day; God keep you, and give you grace to do as well as I would ye did, and I charge you beware that ye set no land to mortgage, for if any advise you thereto, they are not your friends; beware betimes mine advice, etc., and I trow your Brother will give you tidings in haste.

MARGARET PASTON

[1469]

162. THE GARRISON OF CAISTER

To my Master Sir John Paston, in Fleet-street

RIGHT worshipful Sir, I recommend unto you, praying you that ye will in all haste send me word how that ye will that Sir John Styll, John Pamping, William Milisent, Nicholas Maudent, [and] T. Thomson shall be ruled,[2] and whether that they shall seek them new services, or not; and Matthew Bedford also, for he hath been with me this season, and is from my mother; and if so be that ye will have these to abide with you, or any of them, send word which that they be, for betwixt this and Hallowmas my mother is agreed that they shall have meat and drink of her

[1] Property.

[2] John seeks instruction about the disposal of the garrison of Caister, after its surrender.

for such a certain [sum] weekly as my mother and ye and I can accord when we meet, notwithstanding if ye could get Berney, or any of these said fellows, which that ye will not keep, any service in the mean season, it were more worship for you than to put them from you like masterless hounds, for by my troth they are as good men's bodies as ever live, and specially Sir John Still and John Pamping; and I were of power to keep them and all these before rehearsed, by troth they should never depart from me while I lived.

If ye send me word that I shall come to you to London for to commune with you of any matter, so God help me, I have neither money to come up with, nor for to tarry with you when I am there, but if ye send me some, for by my troth these works have caused me to lay out for you better than ten or twelve pounds, besides that money that I had of my mother, which is about an eight pound; God amend defaults, but this I warrant you, without that it be Matthew, which ye sent word by John Thresher that ye would have to await on you, there is no man that was hired for the time of this siege, that will ask you a penny.

Also, I pray you send down a commandment to Stutevylle, or to some auditor, to take accounts of Dawbeney's bills, for his Executors are sore called upon for to administer by the Bishop, or else he saith that he will sequester; Dawbeney set in his debts that ye owed him twelve pounds and ten shillings, whether it be so or not, his bills of his own hands will not lie, for he made his bills clear, or then [1] the siege came about us. As for the evidence of Beckham, my mother sent to Calle for them, and he sent her word that he would make his accounts and deliver the evidence and all together.

My mother hath sent to him again for them this day; if she speed, they shall be sent to you in all haste, or else, and ye send for me, I shall bring them with me. Send my mother and me word who ye will that [shall] have the rule of your livelihood here in this country, and in what form that it shall be dealt with. I will not make me masterfast with my Lord of Norfolk, nor with none other till I speak with you; and ye think it to be done, get me a master.

[1] Before.

Deal courteously with the Queen and that fellowship, and with Mistress Anne Hawte for Wappys [1] till I speak with you. Written on Saint Faith's Even.[2]

JOHN PASTON

By Saint George I and my fellowship stand in fear of my Lord of Norfolk's men, for we be threatened sore, notwithstanding the safeguards [3] that my fellowship have; as for me I have none, nor none of your household men, nor none will have; it were shame to take it.

[1469]

163. INTERRUPTING THE ENEMY'S COURT

To my Right worshipful Brother Sir John Paston Knight, be this delivered

RIGHT worshipful Sir, I recommend me to you in my best wise. Liketh it you to weet that I have this day delivered your mantle, your ray gown, and your cross-bows, and your Normandy bill to Kerby to bring with him to London. . . .

Item, I pray you send me some secret tidings of the likelihood of the world by the next messenger that cometh between, that I may be either merrier or else more sorry than I am, and also that I may guide me thereafter.

Item, as for Sir Robert Wingfield, I can get no ten pounds of him, but he saith that I shall have the fairest harness that I can buy in London for silver, but money can I none get.

I cannot yet make my peace with my Lord of Norfolk nor my Lady by no means [4] yet every man telleth me, that my Lady saith passingly well of me always; notwithstanding I trow that they will sue the appeal this term yet there is no man of us indicted, but if it were done afore the Coroners ere then we came

[1] May be a contraction of 'whatever happens.' Sir John did not marry Anne Haute.

[2] October 5.

[3] Safe-conducts.

[4] The Pastons were trying to come to an understanding with the Duke of Norfolk by the intercession of the Duchess.

out of the place; there is now but three men in it, and the Bridges always drawn. No more but God lant you mine herr.[1] Written the Tuesday next after Saint Agnes the first.[2]

JOHN PASTON

Item, yesterday W. Gornay entered into Saxthorp, and there was he keeping a Court, and had the tenants attourned to him; but ere the court was all done, I came thither with a man with me and no more, and there before him and all his fellowship, Gayne, Bomsted, etc. I charged the tenants that they should proceed no further in their court upon pain that might fall of it; and they letted for a season, but they saw that I was not able to make my party good, and so they proceeded further: I saw that and sat me down by the steward and blotted his book with my finger as he wrote,[3] so that all the tenants affirmed that the Court, was interrupted by me as in your right, and I requested them to record that there was no peaceable court kept, and so they said they would.

[1472]

164. SIR JOHN RECLAIMS CAISTER

To Sir John Paston, Knight, at the George at Paul's Wharf

AFTER all duties of recommendation, liketh it you to weet, that I ensure you your sending to Caister is evil taken among my Lord's folks, insomuch that some say that ye tendered little my Lord's death, in as much as ye would so soon enter upon him after his decease, without advice and assent of my Lord's counsel,[4]

[1] "God lant you mynherr," meant for a Flemish greeting—*i.e.*, God guide you, Sir [Gr.].

[2] January 21.

[3] The manor court was formerly interrupted in order to show legally that the claim to possession was contested by the Pastons.

[4] Sir John continued his efforts to regain Caister, without success until the sudden death of the Duke of Norfolk in January 1476. Sir John immediately sent a message to Caister to assert his rights there. In May the King's Counsel decided in Sir John's favour, and Caister was recovered.

wherefore it is thought here by such as be your friends in my Lord's house, that if my Lady have once the grant of the wardship of the child, that she will occupy Caister with other lands, and lay the default on your unkind hastiness of entry without her assent; wherefore in any wise get you a patent of the King ensealed before her's, and ye may, by any mean possible. Also I pray you commune with my Lord Chamberlain for me, and weet how that he will have me demeaned. It is told me for certain that there is none hay to get at Calais, wherefore if I might be pardoned for any keeping of horse at Calais till Midsummer, if it were a good turn.

The bearer hereof shall come home again from London, within a day after that he cometh thither, if ye will aught command him. I pray you send me word by him how ye do with your matters, and I pray you in any wise let me understand, by the bearer hereof, how Bowen of the Exchequer will deal with me: six-score and ten pounds it is now; and I would have seven score and ten pounds, and I to pledge it out in four or five years, or else to forfeit the manor [of Swainsthorpe]. Written at Norwich, the Tuesday next after your departing thence, the 23rd day of January, in the fifteenth year of Edward IV.

JOHN PASTON

[1476]

165. SIR JOHN JUSTIFIES HIMSELF

To John Paston, Esquire, at Norwich, be this delivered

I RECOMMEND me to you. . . .

Item, I have received a letter from you written on Tuesday last.

Item, where that some towards my Lady of Norfolk noise that I did unkindly to send so hastily to Caister as I did there is no discreet person that so thinketh; for if my Lord had been as kind to me as he might have been, and according to such heart and service as my Grandfather, my Father, yourself, and I have owed and done to my Lords of Norfolk that dead been, and yet [1] if I

[1] Even.

had wedded his Daughter, yet must I have done as I did; and moreover, if I had had any deeming of my Lord's death four hours ere he died, I must needs, but if I would be known a Fool, have entered it the hour before his decease; but in effect, they that in that matter have always meant unkindly to me, they feign that Rumour against me; but there is none that meant truly to him that dead is, that would be sorry that I had it, and in especial such as love his Soul.

Item, where it is deemed that my Lady would hereafter be the rather mine heavy [1] Lady for that dealing, I think that she is too reasonable so to be, for I did it not unwist to her Council; there was no man thought that I should do otherwise, and as to say, that I might have had my Lady's advice and leave, I might have tarried yet, ere I could have spoken with her, or yet have had any body to have moved her on my behalf. . . . It was this day before all the Lords of the Council, and among them all, it was not thought, that in my sending of Wheatley thither, immediately after the decease of the Duke, that I dealt unkindly or unfittingly, but that I was more unreasonably dealt with; wherefore, let men deem what they will, greatest Clerks are not always wisest men; but I hope hastily to have one way in it or other.

Item, I weened to have found a Gown of mine here, but it come home the same day that I come out, brought by Harry Berker Loader.[2] I would in all haste possible have that same Gown of puke furred with white Lamb. . . .

Extract from a letter five months later:

Item, blessed be God, I have Caister at my will; God hold it better than it [was] done heretofore. No more, but written the next day after Saint Peter [3] in the 16th of Edward IV.

JOHN PASTON, Kt

[1476]

[1] Unkind. [2] Carrier. [3] June 29.

SECTION III

LOCAL AFFAIRS

166. PIRATES ON THE NORFOLK COAST

To John Paston, dwelling in the Inner Inn of the Temple, at London, be this Letter delivered in haste

SON, I greet you, and send you God's blessing and mine; as for my daughter your wife [1] she fareth well, blessed be God! as a woman in her plight may do, and all your Sons and Daughters.

And for as much as ye will send me no tidings, I send you such as be in this Country; Richard Lynsted came this day from Paston and let me weet, that on Saturday last past, Dravell, half-brother to Warren Harman, was taken with enemies, walking by the Sea side, and have him forth with them, and they took two Pilgrims, a man and a woman, and they robbed the woman and let her go, and led the man to the Sea; and when they knew he was a Pilgrim they gave him money, and set him again on the land; and they have this week taken four Vessels of Winterton, and Happisborough and Eccles.

Men be sore afraid for taking of men, for there be ten great Vessels of the Enemy's; God give grace that the sea may be better kept than it is now, or else it shall be a perilous dwelling by the sea coast.

I pray you greet well your brethren, and say them that I send them God's blessing and mine. . . .

Written at Norwich, the Wednesday next before Saint Gregory.[2]

By your Mother,
AGNES PASTON

[1450]

[1] Margaret Paston.

[2] March 12.

167. HOUSE SHORTAGE IN NORWICH

To my right worshipful Master, John Paston, be this delivered in haste

RIGHT worshipful husband, I recommend me to you, praying you to weet that I have spoke with Newman for his place, and I am through with him therefore, but he would not let it in no wise less than five marks,[1] I told him that sickerly [2] ye should not know but that I hired it of him for three pounds, I said as for the noble,[3] I should pay of mine own purse, that ye should no knowledge have thereof; and this day I have had in two cartful of hay, and your stable shall be made I hope this next week. I could get no grant of him to have the warehouse; he saith if he may in any wise forbear it hereafter, ye shall have it, but he will not grant it in no covenant. He hath granted me the house betwixt the vault and the warehouse, and that, he said, he granted not you.

And as for the chamber that ye assigned to mine uncle,[4] God hath purveyed [5] for him as his will is; he passed to God on Monday last past, at eleven of the clock before noon, and Sir John Heveningham passed to God on Tuesday last past, whose souls both God assoil! his sickness took him on Tuesday at nine of the clock before noon, and by two afternoon he was dead.

I have begun your Inventory that should have been made ere this time, if I had been well at ease; I hope to make an end thereof, and of other things both this next week, and be in that other place, if God send me health. I must do purvey for [6] much stuff ere I come there, for there is neither boards nor other stuff that must needs be had ere we come there; and Richard [7] hath gathered but little money since he came from you. I have sent John Norwood this day to Greshan, Besingham, and Matlaske,

[1] £3 6*s*. 8*d*.

[2] Surely.

[3] A noble is half a mark—*i.e.*, 6*s*. 8*d*. Margaret apparently proposed to let Paston believe she had the place for £3, and to pay the odd 6*s*. 8*d*. from her own purse.

[4] Philip Berney.

[5] Provided.

[6] Cause to be provided.

[7] Richard Calle, Paston's agent.

to get as much money as he may. The blessed Trinity have you in his keeping. Written at Norwich, on the Utas day [1] of Peter and Paul.[2]

Yours,
MARGARET PASTON

[1453]

168. ROBBERS. SHORTAGE OF CLOTH

To my right worshipful Husband John Paston, be this delivered in haste

RIGHT worshipful husband, I recommend me unto you, pleaseth you to weet, that mine Aunt Moundford [3] hath desired me to write to you, beseeching you that ye will vouchsafe to chevise [4] for her at London twenty marks [5] for to be paid to Master Ponyngs, either on Saturday or Sunday, which shall be Saint Andrew's day, in discharging of them that be bounden to Master Ponyngs of the said twenty marks for the Wardship of her daughter, the which twenty marks she hath delivered to me in gold for you to have at your coming home, for she dare not adventure her money to be brought up to London for fear of robbing, for it is said here that there goeth many thieves betwixt this and London, which causeth her to beseech you to content the said money in discharging of the matter, and of them that be bounden, for she would for no good [6] that the day were broken; and she thanketh you heartily for the great labour and business that ye have had in that matter, and in all others touching her and hers, wherefore she saith she is ever bounden to be your Beads-woman, and ever will be while she liveth.

My Cousin, her son, and his wife recommendeth them unto you, beseeching you that ye will vouchsafe to be their good Master, as ye have been afore time; for they be informed that

[1] Octave. [2] June 29.

[3] Elizabeth, Margaret's aunt, and daughter of John Berney, Esq., married Osbert Mundeford, Esq., later Marshal of Calais.

[4] Borrow. [5] £13 6*s*. 8*d*. [6] At no price.

Daniel [1] is come to Rising Castle, and his men make their boast that their Master shall be again at Brayston within short time.

Furthermore, as for the matter that my son wrote to me for the box whereon was written *False Carte Sproute*, that I should enquire of William Worcester where it were; the said William was not at home since that I had his letter, but as soon as he cometh home I shall enquire of him, and send you an answer. As touching your Liveries, there can none be gotten here of that colour that ye would have of, neither murrey [2] nor blue, nor good russet, underneath 3*s*. the yard, at the lowest price, and yet is there not enough of one cloth and colour to serve you; and as for to be purveyed in Suffolk, it will not be purveyed not now against this time, without they had had warning at Michaelmas, as I am informed: and the blessed Trinity have you in his keeping. Written at Norwich, on Saint Katherine's day.[3]

By Your,

MARGARET PASTON

[1455]

169. THE VICAR'S TROUBLES

To my right reverend Mistress, Agnes Paston, be this Letter delivered in haste

RIGHT worshipful Mistress, I recommend me unto you thanking you of the great cheer that ye made me the last time that I was with you; Mistress, in all your goods and occupations that lyeth in my simple power to do in word, will, and deed, I have do my diligence and my power thereto, so I be saved before God; and have owen to your person right hearty love, for the which I am right ill acquit and it be as I understand it, for it is do me to weet, that I am sued with more of my Parishioners, for a rescue making upon the officers of the Sheriff [4]; and I take God to record that

[1] Sir Thomas Daniel, brother-in-law to Sir J. Howard (later Duke of Norfolk), an enemy of Lord Suffolk. Paston supported him at first.

[2] Mulberry colour, dark red. [3] November 25.

[4] The sheriff's officers having arrested a man during mass, the congregation rescued him: the vicar is indicted for resisting the sheriff and fled to Bromholm Priory. Williamson was vicar of Paston from 1460 to 1464.

it is wrongfully do unto us. And the great fray that they made in the time of Mass, it ravished my wits, and made me full heavily disposed; I pray Jesu give them grace to repent them thereof, that they that caused it may stand out of peril of soul.

Mistress, at the reverence of God, and as ever I may do service that may be pleasing unto you, send me justly word by the bringer of this bill how ye will that I be guided; for it is told me that, if I be taken, I may no other remedy have, but straight to prison; for the which I have sold away 20*s.* worth of Stuff, and the residue of my stuff I have put it in sure hand, for truly I will not abide the jeopardy of the suit; I have lever to go as far as my feet may bear me; nevertheless as ye command me to do, so it be not to my great hurt, I will fulfil it. No more to you at this time, but God send you that grace, that ye may come to his bliss. Written at Bromholm, in great haste.

By Your,

[1460] SIR ROBERT WILLIAMSON

170. LORD MOLYNES BARGAINS FOR GRESHAM MANOR

To the worshipful Father in God, and my right good Lord, the Bishop of Winchester

WORSHIPFUL Father in God, and my right good Lord, as heartily as I can, I recommend me to your good Lordship, to the which please it to weet, that I have received your Letter; by the which I understand the daily suit to your Lordship as of Paston,[1] as

[1] William Paston had purchased from the son of Chaucer, the poet, the Manor of Gresham, which had belonged to the Molynes family. Robert Hungerford, who married a descendant of the Molynes and became Lord Molynes, claimed the manor on the advice of John Heydon, Recorder of Norwich, and Sir Thomas Tuddenham. Paston, at first negotiated, but in 1448 Molynes took possession of the house, and in January 1450, while Paston was in London, a body of armed men attacked and captured the manor again, and did great damage. Paston appealed to Parliament, and Judge Yelverton was sent to Norfolk to suppress violence there. Paston, reinstated later at Gresham, procured an indictment against Molynes for the assault and damage, but, owing to the politics of the time, was unable to obtain justice.

for the matter betwixt him and me, wherein also I feel, that he is willed that communication and treaty should be had, betwixt his Counsel and mine now at Midsummer; to the which, my Lord, I am at the reverence of your Lordship well agreed, and have sent to my Counsel at London, after the seeing of this your last Letter as for the Treaty betwixt him and me, and that they should give full attendance to the end of the matter between the said Paston and me, as though I were present with them.

And my Lord it were too great a thing, and it lay in my power, but I would do at the reverence of your Lordship, unless that it should hurt me too greatly; which I wote well your Lordship would never desire.

And God for his mercy have you, right worshipful Father in God, and my right good Lord, in his blessed keeping.

Written with mine own hand in haste, the 13th day of June, at Teffaunt.

Very heartily,
Your
Molyns

[1448?]

171. MARGARET PASTON FORTIFIES HER HOUSE

To my right worshipful Husband, John Paston

Right worshipful husband, I recommend me to you, and pray you to get some Cross Bows and Wyndacs [1] to bind them with and Quarrels,[2] for your houses here [3] be so low that there may none man shoot out with no long bow, though we had never so much need.

I suppose ye should have such things of Sir John Fastolf, if ye would send to him; and also I would ye should get two or three short Pole-axes to keep with doors, and as many Jacks, and ye may.

[1] Windacs are what we now call grappling irons, with which the bow-string is drawn home. [F.]

[2] Square-headed metal bolts shot from cross-bows.

[3] In or near Gresham.

Partrich and his fellowship [1] are sore afraid that ye would enter again upon them, and they have made great ordnance within the house, and it is told me they have made bars to bar the doors cross wise, and they have made wickets on every quarter of the house to shoot out at, both with bows and with hand-guns; and the holes that be made for hand-guns they be scarce knee high from the plancher [2] and of such holes be made five, there can none man shoot out at them with no hand-bows.

Purry fell in fellowship with William Hasard at Quarles's, and told him that he would come and drink with Partrich and with him, and he said he should be welcome, and after noon he went thither for to espy what they did and what fellowship they had with them; and when he came thither the doors were fast sparred and there were none folks with them but Mariott, and Capron and his wife, and Quarles's wife, and another man in a black, went somewhat halting, I suppose by his words that it was Norfolk of Gimmingham; and the said Purry espied all these foresaid things.

And Mariott and his fellowship had much great language that shall be told you when ye come home.

I pray you that ye will vouchsafe to do buy for me one lb. of Almonds and one lb. of sugar, that ye will do buy some frieze to make of your child his gowns, ye shall have best cheap, and best choice of Hay's wife, as it is told me. And that ye will buy a yard of broad cloth of black for one hood for me of 44*d.* or four Shillings a yard, for there is neither good cloth nor good frieze in this town. As for the child his gowns and [3] I have them, I will do them maken.[4]

The Trinity have you in his keeping, and send you good speed in all your matters.

MARGARET PASTON

[1449?]

[1] Lord Molynes' men who were now holding Gresham Castle.

[2] Floor. [3] When. [4] Have them made.

172. LORD MOLYNES CLAIMS THE GRESHAM RENTS

To my trusty and well beloved, the Vicar and Tenants of my Lordship of Gresham

TRUSTY and well beloved Friends, I greet you well, and put you all out of doubt for all that ye have done for me; and the money that ye pay to my well beloved Servant John Partrich, I will be your warrant as for your discharge, and save you harmless against all those that would grieve you, to my power.

And as heartily as I can, I thank you of the good will ye have had, and have towards me; and as to the title of right that I have to the Lordship of Gresham [it] shall within short time be known, and by the law so determined, that ye shall all be glad that hath ought me your good will therein.

And Almighty God keep you, and by his grace I shall be with you soon after the Parliament is ended.

Written at London, on Our Lady even last past.[1]

ROBERT HUNGERFORD
LORD MOLYNS

[1449]

173. HENRY VI FAVOURS LORD MOLYNES

To our trusty and well-beloved John Paston, Esquire

By the King

TRUSTY and well-beloved, for as much as our right trusty and well-beloved the Lord Moleyns is by our special desire and commandment waiting upon us, and now for divers considerations moving us, We purpose to send him into certain places for to execute our commandments, for the which he ne may [2] be attendant to be in our Counties of Norfolk and Suffolk at the time of our Commissioners sitting upon our Commission of Oyer Determiner within the same our Counties. We therefore desire and pray you,

[1] March 24. [2] Cannot.

that considering his attendance upon us, and that he must apply him to execute our Commandment, ye will respite [1] as for any thing attempting against him, as for any matters that ye have to do, or say against him, or any other of his Servants, wellwillers, or Tenants, because of him, unto time he shall mowe be [2] present to answer thereunto; wherein ye shall minister unto us cause of pleasure, and over that, deserve of us right good thanks. Given under our Signet at our palace of Westminster, the 18th day of September.

[1450]

174. THE SHERIFF AFRAID OF LORD MOLYNES

To my right reverend and worshipful Master, John Paston, be this delivered

PLEASE it your mastership to weet, that I have spoken with the Sheriff at his place, moving to him, as for that,[3] that was left with his Undersheriff, it is your will he should send a man of his for it; for though it were more ye would gladly he should take it; he thanked you, and said his Undersheriff was at London, and himself had none deserved, and if he had he would have taken it. And when I departed from him I desired him again to send therefore, and then he said it should abide till ye came home, whereby I conceive he would have it, and be glad to take it. Moreover I remembered him of his promises made before to you at London, when he took his oath and charge, and that ye were with him when he took his oath, and other divers times—and for the promises made by him to you at that time, and other times at the Oyer Determiner at Lynn, ye proposed you by the trust that ye have in him, for to attempt and rear actions that should be to the avail of him and of his office: he would have known what the actions should be; I said I could not tell him, and then he said he would do for you that he may, except for the

[1] Delay. [2] Be able to be.
[3] A gift, doubtless of money. Molynes had been acquitted, but the men who carried out his orders at Gresham were still to be tried.

acquittal of the Lord Molyns's men, insomuch as the King hath written to him for to shew favour to the Lord Molyns and his men, and as he saith the indictment longeth to the King and not to you, and the Lord Molyns [is] a great Lord. Also, as he saith, now late the Lord Molyns hath sent him a Letter, and my Lord of Norfolk another, for to shew favour in these indictments, he dare not abide the jeopardy of that, that he should offend the King's commandment, he know not how the King may be informed of him, and what shall be said to him.

And then I said, as for any jeopardy that he should abide in any thing that he doth for you, or by your desire, ye have offered him, and will perform it, sufficient surety for to save him harmless, and therefore I supposed there would none reasonable man think but that he might do for you without any jeopardy; and then he said, he might none surety take that passed an hundred pounds; and the Lord Molyns is a great Lord, he might soon cause him to lose that and much more; then I said, by that mean, in default of a Sheriff, every man may be put from his livelihood [1]; and then he said, if it were for the livelihood men would take them the nearer for to abide a jeopardy,[2] but by his faith, as he swore, if the King wrote again to him he will no longer abide the jeopardy of the King's writing, but he trusteth to God to impannel such men as should to his knowledge be indifferent, and none common Jurors.

As me seemeth, it would do good and ye would get a commandment of the King to the Sheriff for to shew you favour, and to impannel Gentlemen, and not for to favour none such riots, etc., for he said that he sent you the Letter that the King sent him, and ye said, a man should get such one for a noble.[3]

Item, I remembered him of the promises that he made to Tymperley, and that if he would make you very true promise ye would reward him as much as he would desire, or any other reasonable man for him, and as much or more than any adversary ye have would give him; then he said he took never no money of none of them all; there was proffered him at Walsingham for the Lord Molyns twenty Nobles he had not a penny; moreover I

[1] Property.
[2] Would be cautious about risks.
[3] For 6*s*. 8*d*.—*i.e.*, of little value.

proffered him, if he would make you a promise that ye might verily trust upon him, ye would give him in hand as he would desire, or to leave a sum if he would have named it in a mean man's [1] hand, and such as he hath trust to; and then he said, if he might do for you, or if he do any thing for you, then he will take your money with a good will; and other promise I could not have of him, but that he would do for you all that he may, except for the indictments; I conceive verily he hath made promise to do his part that they shall be acquitted, but I suppose he hath made none other promise against you for the livelihood, but he looketh after a great bribe, but it is not [wise] for to trust him verily, without that he may not choose.

I suppose he had no writing from my Lord of Norfolk as he said.

I was at Framlingham for to have spoken with Tymperley, Debenham, or Berry, and they were all out; my Lord,[2] as he came from London he was at Ipswich on Monday, and when he [came] without the town towards Framlingham, he had all his men ride forth afore a great pace, for he would follow softly, and when his men were out of sight, he rode with five men to an Esquier's place of his thereby, and on Tuesday rode my lady to him; and so I did nought at Framlingham. No more at this time, but Almighty Jesu speed you, and have you in his keeping. Written at Norwich, the Thursday next after Saint Austin,[3] etc.

By your Servant,

JOHN OSBERN

[1451]

175. SIR THOMAS TUDDENHAM ACCUSES MEN FALSELY

To my right worshipful Husband, John Paston

RIGHT worshipful husband, I recommend me to you, praying you to weet that there is a great noise in this town, that my Lord of Oxford and Yelverton and ye be endited in Kent for

[1] Middleman, mediary. [2] The Duke. [3] May 26.

maintaining of the Oyer and Determiner,[1] and John Damme is indited there also of treason, because that he did Heydon inditen of treason for taking down of the quarter of the man; and the people that be against Sir Thomas Todenham and Heydon be sore afraid because of this noise, and of other language that is had both in this town and in the country, that these said Todenham and Heydon should be as well at ease, and have as great rule as ever they had.

James Gloys [2] telleth me, that he hath sent you word of Heydon's horse and of other things, more of which I was purposed to a' sent you word of. The holy Trinity have you in keeping. Written at Norwich, the Wednesday next after Saint Mathias.[3]

Yours,
MARGARET PASTON

[1451]

176. EARL OF WARWICK SOUNDS TUDDENHAM

To our right trusty, and well beloved Friend,
Sir Thomas Todenham

RIGHT truly and well beloved Friend, we greet you well, heartily desiring to hear of your welfare, which we pray God preserve to your heart's desire; and if it please you to hear of our welfare, we were in good health at the making of this Letter, praying you heartily that ye will consider our message, which our Chaplain Master Robert Hopton shall inform you of; for as God knoweth we have great business daily, and have had here before this time, wherefore we pray you to consider the Purchase [4] that we have made with one John Southcote, an Esquire of Lincolnshire, of 88*l.* by the year, where upon we must pay the last payment the Monday next after St Martin's day,[5] which sum is 458*l.* wherefore we pray you with all our heart, that ye will lend us ten or twenty

[1] For the meaning of this phrase see note to Letter 141.
[2] Margaret's chaplain.
[3] February 24.
[4] Of an estate worth £88 annually.
[5] November 11.

pounds, or what the said Master Robert wants of his payment, as we may do for you in time for to come, and we shall send it you again afore New Year's day with the grace of God, as we are a true Knight.

For there is none in your Country, that we might write to for trust, so well as unto you, for as we be informed, ye be our well willer, and so we pray you of good continuance.

Wherefore we pray you, that ye consider our intent of this money, as we will that we do for you in time to come, as God knoweth, who have you in his keeping.

Written at London, on All Soul's day,[1] within our Lodging in the Grey Friars, within Newgate.

RICHARD, EARL OF WARWICK [2]

[1450–51?]

177. THE TAILBOYS AND CROMWELL FEUD

[William Tailboys, of Sleaford, was a turbulent Lincolnshire lord. He and Lord Beaumont were supporters of the Duke of Suffolk, and so opponents of their powerful neighbours, Lords Cromwell, Welles, and Willoughby, who were terrorizing the county. This feud stirred up the local disorders of 1450.]

To my right honourable and right worshipful Lord,
Viscount Beaumount

RIGHT honourable and my right worshipful Lord, I recommend me unto your good Lordship with all my service, ever more desiring to hear of your prosperity and welfare, the which I pray God encrease and continue to his pleasure, and after your own heart's desire; and thanking you of the good Lordship that ye have shewed me at all times, beseeching you always of good continuance.

Please it your good Lordship to be remembered how afore this time Hugh Wytham hath said he would be in rest and peace

[1] November 2.

[2] Richard Neville, Earl of Warwick, afterwards famous as the "King-maker," succeeded to the title in 1449.

with me, and not to malign against me, otherwise than law and right would. That notwithstanding, upon Monday last past, he and three men with him came into a servant's house of mine in Boston, called William Sheriff, and there as he sat at his work struck him upon the head, and in the body with a dagger, and wounded him sore, and pulled him out of his house, and set him in prison without any cause reasonable, or without writ, or any other process shewed unto him; and that me seems longs not for him to do, but as he says he is indicted, and as your good Lordship knows well, and I and all my servants are in like wise, but and any man should have done it, it longs either to the Sheriff or to your Bailiff, as I conceive, and other cause he had none to him as far as I can know, but only for the maliciousness of that he hath unto me, nor I can think none other but it is so. And now, yester night my Lord Welles came to Boston with four score horses, and in the morning following, took him out of prison, saying afore all people, "False thief thou shalt be hanged, and as many of thy master's men as may be gotten," as your servant John Abbot can report unto your good Lordship, and hath taken him away with him to Tattershall, what to do with him I cannot say, but as I suppose to have him to Lincoln Castle; wherefore I beseech your Lordship in this matter to be my good Lord, and that it please your good Lordship to write a Letter to the keeper of the Castle of Lincoln, that it liked him to deliver him out of prison under a sufficient surety had for him, for and they may keep him still by this mean they may take all the servants that I have, and so I do again in like wise.

And also, as I am informed, without he be had out of prison in haste, it will be right grievous to him to heal of his hurt, he is so sore stricken; and if there be any service that your good Lordship will command me to do in any country, please it you to send me word, and it shall be done to my power with the grace of God, which have you my right honourable and worshipful Lord alway in his blessed keeping. Written at Kyme, upon Wednesday next after our Lady's day, the Assumption.[1]

Also, please it your good Lordship to weet after this Letter was made there came a man from Tattershall, unto my fen, which

[1] August 15.

ought[1] me good will, and because he would not be holden suspect, he spake with women which were milking kyne, and bad them go to a Priest of mine to Dokdyke, and bid him fast go give me warning, how that my Lord Willoughby, my Lord Cromwell, and my Lord Welles proposed then to set a Sessions, and hang the said William Sheriff, and they might bring the intent about; and so, as I and your servant John Abbot stood together, the Priest came and gave me warning hereof, which I trust for my worship your good Lordship would not should happen, for it were to me the greatest shame that might fall, but and it please your good Lordship to write to all your servants in this country, that they will be ready upon a day's warning to come when I send them word; I trust to God they shall not hang him against the law, but I, with help of your good Lordship, shall be able to let it.

By your Servant,
William Tailboys

[1450]

178. THE DUKE OF YORK. LOCAL JUSTICE

[Richard Plantagenet, Duke of York, afterwards Protector, and father of Edward IV, had been in Ireland as Lieutenant Governor. Having much popular support, he returned in 1450, after Jack Cade's rebellion, and championed the rights of the people. In particular he demanded the fair administration of justice.]

To my Master, John Paston, in right great haste

Sir, and it please, I was in my Lord of York's house, and I heard much thing more than my master[2] writeth unto you of; I heard much thing in Fleet-street; but, Sir, my Lord was with the King, and he visaged so the matter that all the King's household was, and is, afraid right sore, and my said Lord[3] hath put a bill to the King, and desired much thing, which is much after the Commons desire, and all is upon justice, and to put all those that be indicted under arrest, without surety or mainprise, and to be

[1] Owed. [2] Judge Yelverton. [3] Richard, Duke of York.

tried by law as law will, insomuch that on Monday Sir William Oldhall was with the King at Westminster more than two hours, and had of the King good cheer; and the King desired of Sir William Oldhall that he should speak to his cousin York that he would be good Lord to John Penycock,[1] and that my Lord of York should write unto his tenants that they should suffer Penycock's officers go and gather up his rent farms within the said Duke's Lordships; and Sir William Oldhall answered again to the King, and prayed him to hold my Lord excused, for though my Lord wrote under his Seal of his Arms his tenants will not obey it, insomuch [that] when Sir Thomas Hoo met with my Lord of York beyond Saint Alban's the Western men [2] fell upon him and would have slain him, had [not] Sir William Oldhall been, and therefore would the Western men have fallen upon the said Sir William, and have killed him, and so he told the King.

Sir Borle Yonge and Josse labour sore for Heydon and Todenham to Sir William Oldhall, and proffer more than two thousand pounds for to have his good Lordship, and therefore it is none other remedy but let Swaffham men be warned to meet with my said Lord on Friday next, coming to Pickenham on horseback in the most goodly wise, and put some bill unto my Lord of Sir Thomas Todenham, Heydon, and Prentice, and cry out on them, and that all the women of the same town be there also, and cry out on them also, and call them Extortioners, and pray my Lord that he will do sharp execution upon them. And my Master counsel you that ye should move the Mayor and all the Aldermen with all their Commoners [of Norwich] to ride against [3] my Lord, and that there be made bills, and put them up to my Lord, and let all the town cry out on Heydon, Todenham, Windham and Prentice, and of all their false maintainers, and tell my Lord how much hurt they have done to the City, [Norwich] and let it be done in the most lamentable wise, for Sir but if my Lord hear some foul tales of them, and some hideous noise and cry, by my faith they are else like to come to grace, and therefore Sir remember you of all these matters.

Sir, also I speak with William Norwich, and asked him after

[1] A follower of Suffolk.
[2] York's retainers from the Welsh marches.
[3] To meet.

the Lord Molyns, how he stood to my Lordward, and he told me he was sore out of grace, and that my Lord of York loveth him nought; William Norwich told me that he durst undertake for to bring you unto my Lord, and make him your right good Lord; and, Sir, my master counselled you that ye should not spare, but get you his good Lordship.

Sir beware of Heydon for he would [have] destroyed you by my faith.

The Lord Scales and Sir William Oldhall are made friends. . . .

Sir, it were wisdom that my Lord of Oxford wait on my Lord of York; in good faith, good Sir, think on all these matters; much more I had to write unto you, if I could have remembered me, but I had no leisure by my faith, hold me excused of my lewd rude writing; let John Dam beware for the Lord Molyns; and, Sir, let the City beware for he will do them a villainy, but if he may have his men; and Sir, if he come to Norwich, look there be ready to wait upon the Mayor a good fellowship,[1] for it is said here that they are but Beasts.

Sir, my Master bade me write unto you that ye should stir the Mayor and all the Aldermen to cry on my Lord that they may have justice of these men that be indicted, and that my Lord will speak unto the King thereof; and Sir, in divers parts in the town where my Lord cometh, there would be ordained many parties of Commoners to cry on my Lord for justice of these men that are indicted, and tell their names, in special Todenham, Heydon, Windham, Prentice. Sir, I send you a copy of the bill [2] that my Lord of York put unto the King, and Sir, let copies go about the city enough, for the love of God, which have you in his keeping. Written on Saint Faith's day [3] in haste.

By your Servant,

WILLIAM WAYTE [4]

[1450]

[1] A good guard for the Mayor.

[2] For this Bill see Letter 179.

[3] October 6.

[4] Clerk to Judge Yelverton.

179. RICHARD DUKE OF YORK'S PETITION TO KING HENRY FOR THE PUNISHMENT OF TRAITORS, ETC.

[Enclosure to Letter 178.]

PLEASE it, your Highness, tenderly to consider the great grudging and Rumour that is universally in this your Realm, of that Justice is not duly ministered to such as trespass, and offend against your laws; and in special of them, that been endited of Treason, and others, being openly noised of the same; wherefore, for great inconvenience that have fallen, and great is like to fall hereafter, in your said Realm, which God defend, but if [1] by your Highness provision convenable [2] be made for due reformation and punishment in this behalf; Wherefore I, your humble Subject and Liege man, Richard Duke of York, willing as effectually as I can and desiring surety and prosperity of your most royal person and welfare of this your noble Realm, counsel and advertise your excellence, for the conservation of good tranquility and peaceable rule among all true subjects, for to ordain and provide, that due Justice be had against all such that [have] been so endited, or openly so noised; Wherein I offer, and will put [me] in Devour [3] for to execute your commandments in these premises of such offenders, and redress of the said misrulers to my might and power. And for the hasty execution hereof, like it your Highness to [address] your Letters of Privy seal and Writs, to your officers and ministers, to do take, and arrest all such persons so noised or endited, of what estate, degree, or conditions so ever they be, and them to commit to your Tower of London, or to other your Prisons, there to abide without bail or mainprise [4] unto the time that they be utterly tryed, and declared after the course of your Law.

[1450]

[1] Unless.
[2] Suitable provision.
[3] Best endeavour.
[4] Surety for appearance of a prisoner.

180. PROCLAMATION IN NORFOLK

The Duke of Norfolk [1]

Be it known to all the King's true liege people, the cause of our coming into this country is, by the commandment of the King our sovereign lord, for to enquire of such great riots, extortions, horrible wrongs, and hurts, as his highness is credibly informed be done in this country, and to know in certain, by you that know the truth, by what person or persons the said great riots, extortions, horrible wrongs, and hurts be done; wherefore we charge you all, on the king's behalf our sovereign lord, that ye spare neither for love, dread, nor fear that ye have to any person of what estate, degree, or condition he be, but that ye say the sooth by whom such offences be done, and that ye spare no man that ye know guilty, and, by the faith that we owe to our sovereign lord, they shall be chastised after their desert, and it reformed as law requireth.

Also it is openly published that certain servants of the Lord Scales [2] should in his name menace and put men in fear and dread to complain to us at this time of the said hurts and griefs, saying that we would abide but a short time here, and after our departing he would have the rule and governance as he hath had afore time. We let you weet that next the king, our sovereign lord, by his good grace and licence, we will have the principal rule and governance through all this shire, of which we bear our name, while that we be living, as far as reason and law requireth, whosoever will grudge or say the contrary; for we will that the Lord Scales, Sir Thomas Todenham, Sir Miles Stapylton, and John Heydon have in knowledge, though our person be not daily here, they shall find our power here at all times to do the King our

[1] In 1452 the King sent the Duke of Norfolk to restore order in the county.

[2] In the absence of the Duke, Lord Scales had been the natural ruler of Norfolk, and under his protection other local gentry—*e.g.*, Sir Thomas Tuddenham, Sir Miles Stapleton, John Heydon—had promoted disorders. Norfolk apparently intended now to vindicate for himself the chief authority in the county.

sovereign lord service, and to support and maintain you all in your right that be the King's true liege men; for it may not be said nay, but that here hath been the greatest riots, horrible wrongs, and offences done in these parts by the said Lord Scales, Thomas Todenham, Miles Stapylton, John Heydon, and such as be confederated unto them, that ever was seen in our days; and most mischief, through their malicious purpose, like to have fallen among the King's true liege people now late at Norwich, had we not better provided therefore; and also that God fortuned us to withstand their said malicious and evil disposed purpose.

Wherefore make bills of your grievances and come to us, and we shall bring you to the King's presence ourself, whose presence will be here in all the haste with the mercy of God, and see the reformation there of his own person.

[1452]

181. THE PARTIALITY OF THE ASSIZE IN NORFOLK

To my reverend and worshipful Master Sir John Fastolf, Knight, be this Letter delivered

RIGHT reverend and worshipful Master,[1] I recommend me lowly unto you, please you to weet the Sunday, next after the feast of the Invention of the Cross,[2] the 9th day of May, at Caister, I received a letter from you by your clerk, W. Barker, the tenour whereof I shall do speed in all haste goodly; but for the more special cause of my writing at this time is to give you relation of the untrue demeaning this Oyer [and] Determiner, by the partiality of the Judges of it, for when the Counsel of the city of Norwich, of the town of Swaffham, yours, my master Inglos, Paston's, and many others Plaintiffs, had put in and declared both by writing and by word before the Judges the lawful exceptions in many wise, the Judges by their wilfulness might not find in their heart to give not as much as a beck nor a twinkling of their eye

[1] Written by Sir Thomas Howes, Fastolf's chaplain.

[2] The Discovery of the Cross, May 3.

toward, but took it to derision, God reform such partiality; and because Prisot [1] thought that if the Sessions of the Oyer and Determiner had been holden at Norwich, as they begun, he supposed it should not so fast pass to the intent of Todenham, and Heydon, and their Fellows, as it should do else in other place, but enjoined [2] to Walsingham, where they have greatest rule, there to be holden on Tuesday 4th day of May.

This knowing, my Master Yelverton, Jenney, and others might well conceive how the governance of the Oyer and Determiner should proceed, for it was the most partial place of all the shire, and thither were cleped [3] all the friends, knights, and esquires, and other Gentlemen that would in no wise do otherwise than they would, and the said Todenham, Heydon, and other oppressors of their set, came down thither, as I understand, with 400 horse and more, and considering how their well willers were there assembled at their instance, it had been right jeopardous and fearful for any of the Plaintiffs to have been present, for there was not one of the Plaintiffs nor Complainants there, but your right faithful and truly well willer John Paston. And my master Yelverton said full discreetly, and controulled the said Prisot when he said, sitting in the Guildhall of Norwich, these words to the Mayor and the Commonalty.

"A, Sir Mayor and your Brethren, as to the process of your complaints we will put them in continuance,[4] but in all other we will proceed," which words Yelverton thought right partial; and beside this the said Prisot would suffer no man that was learned to speak for the Plaintiffs, but took it as a venom, and took them by the nose at every third word which might well be known for open partiality.

And as for the Lord Scales ye know well what he is towards you, and namely [5] for Hickling matter. Also to know some of your faint friends, at the time that my Lord of Norfolk sat at Norwich upon the Oyer and Determiner, Sir John Hevingham might not find it in his heart to go four furlongs from his dwelling place to the shire house, but now he could ride from Norwich to

[1] Chief Justice of the Common Pleas. Yelverton was a Justice of King's Bench.

[2] Adjourned. [3] Called. [4] Put them off. [5] Especially.

Walsingham to sit as one of the Commissioners; as to the rule of others, that ye would have supposed your well willers, how they have behaved at Walsingham I shall send you word in all haste when Berney come home to Caister, for he is not yet come from Walsingham, but this I know well, that they found none obstacle nor impediment in their conscience in all your matter, but how they have done with Norwich, Swaffham, and Paston, I am not yet clearly informed, I suppose they are put in respite [1]; I hear say, Heydon sueth for an end to be had with the City of Norwich; and as to the names of them that passed on their acquittal against you, Broyn can well inform you, I understand that Sir Robert Conyers, Calthorp, Mundford were Captains, and Master Richard Doget also.

Of all other matters I shall send you word in all haste goodly, for at this time I had no leisure because of the hasty coming up of Hugh Fenn, whom I beseech you to feel of the demeaning of the Oyer and Determiner, for he can tell you much and he will, whether he will or nay, I cannot say; for I know well he was at Walsingham. And I beseech Almighty Jesu have you in his merciful governance.

Written at Caister the Sunday 9th day of May, in the 29th year of King Henry VI.

On the back of the letter is written:

I pray you be not displeased though I have not subscribed my name within forth, for it is of negligence saith Howys, Parson of Castlecomb.

[1451]

182. QUEEN MARGARET AT NORWICH

To my right worshipful Master, John Paston, be this delivered in haste

RIGHT worshipful Husband, I recommend me to you, praying you to weet, etc. (*here follows some account of money received, etc.*).

[1] Put off.

As for tidings, the Queen [1] came into this town on Tuesday last past after noon, and abode here till it was Thursday three [o'clock] afternoon; and she sent after my Cousin Elizabeth Clere,[2] by Sharinborn, to come to her; and she durst not disobey her commandment, and came to her; and when she came in the Queen's Presence, the Queen made right much of her, and desired her to have an husband, the which ye shall know of hereafter; but as for that, he is never nearer than he was before; the Queen was right well pleased with her answer, and reporteth of her in the best wise, and saith, by her truth, she saw no Gentlewoman since she came into Norfolk, that she liked better than she doth her.

Blake, the Bailey of Swaffham, was here with the King's Brother, and he came to me, weening that ye had been at home; and said, that the King's brother [3] desired him that he should pray you in his name to come to him, for he would right fain that ye had come to him, if ye had been at home; and he told me, that he wist well that he should send for you, when he came to London, both for Cossey and other things.

I pray you that ye will do your cost on me against Whitsuntide, that I may have something for my neck; when the Queen was here, I borrowed by Cousin Elizabeth Clere's Device, for I durst not for shame go with my Beads amongst so many fresh Gentlewomen as here were at that time.

The blessed Trinity have you in his keeping.

Written at Norwich on the Friday next before Saint George.[4]

By yours,

MARGARET PASTON

[1453]

[1] Margaret of Anjou.

[2] The wealthy widow of Robert Clere of Ormsby.

[3] Either Edmund or Jasper Tudor, half-brothers to the King, being sons of his mother Catherine, Queen of Henry V, by her subsequent marriage to Sir Owen Tudor.

[4] April 23.

183. THE DUKE OF NORFOLK ORDERS THE ELECTIONS FOR THE SHIRE

To our right trusty and well beloved John Paston, Esquire

The Duchess of Norfolk

RIGHT trusty and welbeloved, we greet you heartily well; and for as much as it is thought right necessary for diverse causes, that my Lord have at this time in the parliament such persons as belong unto him, and be of his menial [1] Servants; wherein we conceive your good will and diligence shall be right expedient; we heartily desire and pray you, that at the contemplation of these Our Letters, as Our special trust is in you, ye will give and apply your voice unto our right welbeloved Cousin and Servants John Howard,[2] and Sir Roger Chamberlayn, to be Knights of the Shire; exhorting all such others as by your wisdom shall now be behoveful, to the good exploit and conclusion of the same.

And in your faithful attendance, and true devoir in this part, ye shall do unto my Lord and Us a singular pleasure, and cause us hereafter to thank you therefore, as ye shall hold you right well content and agreed with the grace of God, who have you ever in his keeping.

Written at Framlingham Castle, the 8th day of June.

[1455]

184. ATTEMPTS TO HAVE A FREE ELECTION

To my worshipful Master John Paston, Esquire

MY Master Paston, I recommend me to you, and where [as] ye should be informed that I should say to Howard that ye laboured to be Knight of the Shire, I said never so to him; I told my Lord of Norfolk at London that I laboured divers men for Sir Roger

[1] Of his meny—*i.e.*, retainers.

[2] The Duke of Norfolk's cousin, afterwards Duke himself. He fell fighting for Richard III at Bosworth.

Chamberlayn, and they said to me they would have him, but not Howard, in as much as he had no livelihood in the shire nor conversement.[1] And I asked them whom they would have, and they said they would have you, and thus I told him, and he said unadvisedly, as he can do full well; I might not [2] say ye laboured therefore, for I heard never say ye laboured therefore by the faith I owe to God.

As for this Writ of the Parliament for Norwich, I thank you that ye will labour therein; as for my Friends there, I trust right well all the Aldermen except Brown and such as be in his danger [3]; I pray you speak to Walter Jeffrey and Harry Wilton, and make them to labour to your intent. I pray you that if ye think that it will not be, that it like you to say, that you move it of yourself, and not by my desire.[4] Some men hold it right strange [5] to be in this Parliament, and me thinketh they be wise men that so do. Written at Intwood, on Saint John's day,[6] in haste.

Your Servant,

JOHN JENNY

[1455]

185. THE DUKE PROFESSES TO ALLOW A FREE ELECTION

To my worshipful Master John Paston, Esquire

MY worshipful Master, I recommend me to you, and I thank you that it pleaseth you to take such labour for me as ye do, my servant told me ye desired to know what my Lord of Norfolk said to me when I spake of you, and he said, in as much as

[1] No property in or acquaintance with the shire. The Howard estates lay in Suffolk.

[2] Could not.

[3] In his debt, and therefore at his mercy. Brown had recently been Mayor of Norwich.

[4] *I.e.*, that if Paston thinks the election of Jenney for Norwich doubtful he would pretend Jenney had not asked him to canvass for him.

[5] Risky.

[6] June 24.

Howard might not be,[1] he would write a Letter to the Under Sheriff, that the Shire should have free Election, so that Sir Thomas Todenham were not, nor none that was toward the Duke of Suffolk; he said he knew ye were never to him ward; ye may send to the Under Sheriff, and see my Lord's Letter; Howard was as wode [2] as a wild Bullock; God send him such worship as he deserveth; it is an evil precedent for the Shire that a strange man should be chosen,[3] and no worship to my Lord of York, nor to my Lord of Norfolk to write for him; for if the Gentlemen of the Shire will suffer such inconvenience, in good faith the Shire shall not be called of such worship as it hath been. Written at Intwood, the Wednesday next after Saint John, in haste.

Your Servant,

JOHN JENNEY

[1455]

186. DISPUTED ELECTION IN NORFOLK

To my wife, Margaret Paston

I RECOMMEND me to you, letting you weet that the Under Sheriff doubteth him [4] of John Berney, wherefore I pray you bring them together, and let them accord if ye can, so that the said Under Sheriff be sure that he shall not be hurt by him nor of his country-men; and if he [5] will not, let him verily understand, that he shall be compelled to find him surety of the peace to agree on his head, and that shall neither be profitable nor worshipful; and let him weet that there have been many complaints of him by that knavish Knight Sir Miles Stapylton,[6] as I sent you word before, but he shall come to his excuse well enough so he have a man's heart. And the said Stapylton shall be understood as he is, a false shrew, and he and his wife and other have blavered,[7] here of my kindred in hoder moder,[8] but, by that time we have reckoned of old days

[1] *I.e.*, elected. [2] Mad.

[3] The Norfolk estates of the Howards had passed to the Earl of Oxford. Howard was unpopular locally, but was elected in 1455.

[4] Is suspicious of.

[5] John Berney. [6] For Sir Miles Stapleton see Letter 180.

[7] Prated. [8] Hugger-mugger, clandestinely.

and late days, mine shall be found more worshipful than his and his wife's, or else I will not for his gilt gypcer.[1]

Also tell the said Berney that the Sheriff is in a doubt whether he shall make a new election of Knights of the Shire, because of him and Grey, wherein it were better for him to have the Sheriff's good will.

Item, me thinketh for quiet of the Country it were most worshipful, that as well Berney as Grey should get a record of all such that might spend forty Shillings a year,[2] that were at the day of the election, which of them that had fewest to give it up as reason would. Written at London, on Relick Sunday.[3]

Item, that ye send about for Silver according to the old bill that I sent you from Lynn.

JOHN PASTON

[1461]

187. VIOLENCE STILL PREVALENT

Margaret Paston, to John Paston

I RECOMMEND me to you, please you to weet that I have sent to my Cousin Berney, according to your desire in the Letter that ye did write on Relick Sunday to me, whereupon he hath written a letter to you and another bill to me, the which I sent you. He told the messenger that I sent to him, that the Under Sheriff needeth not to fear him nor none of his, for he said, after the Election was done, he spake with him at the Grey Friars, and prayed him of his good mastership, and said to him that he feared no man of bodily harm, but only Twyer and his fellowship.

Item, Sir John Tatersalle, and the Bailiff of Walsingham, and the Constable, hath taken the parson of Snoring and four of his men, and set them fast in the stocks on Monday at night; and as it is said they should be carried up to the King in haste; God defend it but they be chastised as the law will. Twyer and his fellowship beareth a great weight of Thomas Denys' death in the

[1] Purse. [2] *I.e.*, those qualified to vote.
[3] Sunday following the translation of St Thomas à Becket, July 7.

Country about Walsingham,[1] and it is said there, if John Osbern had ought [2] him as good will, as he did before that he was acquainted with Twyer, he should not have died, for he might [have] ruled all Walsingham as he had list, as it is said.

Item, William Lynys that was with Master Fastolf, and such other as he is with him, go fast about in the Country and bear men a hand,[3] priests and other, they be Scots, and take bribes of them and let them go again. He took the last week the parson of Fritton, and but for my Cousin Jernyngham the younger, they would have led him forth with them, and he told them plainly if they made any such doings there, but they had the Letter to shew for them, they should have a laid on their bodies [4]; it were well done that they were met with by times. It is told me that the said William reporteth of you as shamefully as he can in divers places. Jesu have you in his keeping. Written in haste, the Wednesday after Relick Sunday.

By your,
MARGARET PASTON

[1461]

188. JUSTICE FOR MURDER

To my worshipful Husband John Paston, this Letter be delivered in haste

RIGHT worshipful Husband, I recommend me to you, please it you to weet that I am desired by Sir John Tatersalle to write to you for a commission, or an Oyer and Terminer, for to be sent down into this country to sit upon the Parson of Snoring, and on such as was cause of Thomas Denys' death, and for many and great horrible Robberies; and as for the costs thereof the country

[1] Thomas Denys, coroner of Norfolk, had complained to the King about one Twyer, of Norfolk, and Sir John Howard, a relative of the Duke of Norfolk. He was attacked and murdered by the parson of Snoring, a friend of Twyer's. Sir Miles Stapleton had tried to lay the blame on John Berney. Paston is asked to use his influence to have the prisoners tried by a special commission.

[2] Owed. [3] Accuse people. [4] Beaten them.

will pay therefore, for they be sore afraid, but the said death be chastised, and the said Robberies, they are afraid that more folks shall be served in like wise. As for the Priest and six of his men that be taken, they be delivered to Twyer, and four be with them of the Country's cost, for to be sent with to the King; and if they be brought up, at the reverence of God, do your part that they escape not but that they may have the judgment of the law and as they have deserved, and be committed to prison not to depart till they be enquired of their foresaid robbery by such a commission that ye can get, that the King and the Lords may understand what rule they have been of, not only for the Murders and the Robberies, but as well for the great insurrection that they were like a made [1] within the Shire.[2] The Priests of Caister they be straitly take heed at by Robert Harmerer and other, so that the said Priests may have nothing out of their own nor of other mens, but they be ransacked, and the place is watched both by day and night; the Priests think right long till they [have] tidings from you. At the reverence of God beware how ye go and ride, for it is told me that ye be threatened of them that be naughty fellows, that hath been inclining to them that hath been your old Adversaries.

The blessed Trinity have you in his keeping. Written in haste, the Saturday next before Saint Margaret.[3]

By your,

MARGARET PASTON

[1461]

189. SHIPS FOR THE NAVY (i)

[As Caister Castle was near Yarmouth, John Paston was concerned with the protection of the coast. He procured a commission for his son in a King's ship, the *Barge of Yarmouth*. This caused difficulty with Gilbert Debenham (whose niece Margery later married Sir John Paston the Youngest), who had already received a

[1] To have made.

[2] There is no record of what further punishment the offenders underwent.

[3] July 20.

commission for himself to arrest the barge, with its crew and provisions, for the King's service.]

To my most reverend and worshipful Master John Paston, dwelling at Hellesdon, be this delivered

Ĩhs

MOST reverend and worshipful master, I recommend me unto your good mastership, please you to have knowledge, on the Friday at afternoon next after Saint Peter, there was at the Tavern in London old Debenham and young Debenham, Thomas Edmonds and I; and there the said Thomas Edmonds fell in communication with old Debenham, and said that my Lord Treasurer [1] had put him to a great charge for the victualling of [the] Mary Talbot, saying to old Debenham, that he heard say that he had a hundred Bullocks to sell, the which the said Edmonds will buy so that they may accord of the price; then the said old Debenham answered again and said, he would, so that he might have good payment, or else the said Edmonds to be bound in an obligation to pay him at such days as they might accord; anon upon this same language, young Debenham spake to his Father, " Sir I pray you that ye will take avisement of [2] this matter till to-morrow, for I trust to your good fatherhood that ye will let me have certain of the bullocks for the victualling of the Barge of Yarmouth, and I shall find you sufficient surety for the payment thereof for Edmonds, I will that ye know that I have been there and spoke with the owner and with the master of the said barge, and they know my appointment."

Then the said Edmonds answered to young Debenham, and told him that the City of Norwich and Yarmouth hath granted, and sent writing to the King and to the Lords, that they will man and victual the said barge of their own costs from the time of her going out till her coming home; and thus the said Edmonds told him that my Lord Treasurer and all the Lords that be at London think they do right well their devoir and be worthy much thank of the King, " well," quoth young Debenham, " I had in commandment for to have the rule of the said barge, and I will be

[1] The Earl of Worcester. [2] Put off.

at Yarmouth this day four days, and man her and bring her down to the Giles of Hull, for that is my ship."

Also, he said more, without that he might have the said barge, he will not go to sea but himself and his twenty-four men, and thus, if please your mastership, he departed from the Tavern; and at his departing he told the said Thomas Edmonds, "This is Paston's labour"; then the said Edmonds answered him again, and said plainly he was to blame for to report so of your mastership, for he knoweth verily he said untruely of you and of my master your son both, and thereon he would have taken an oath; and so, if it please your good mastership, let the City of Norwich and Yarmouth have knowledge of the great cracking and boasts, and let [1] him of his purpose by the authority that they have.

Item, my master your son will have to his Jackets [2] Murrey and Tawney,[3] and that it please you some of my fellowship may speak to one of the Drapers for to ordain it against his coming home, for I trow it shall be this day fev'night ere he cometh home. . . .

No more to your good mastership at this time, but Jesu have [you] in his keeping. Written on the Saturday next after Saint Peter.[4]

By your poor servant,

J. Daubeney

[1462]

190. SHIPS FOR THE NAVY (ii)

To my Master, John Paston

Pleaseth your Mastership to weet, that I was at Scole, and spake with Arblaster and John Sadler, and with other good Yeoman of the Country, to understand how they were guided for the victualling of the Barge of Yarmouth and I understand by them that their Hundred have paid, nevertheless it is but little, there was gathered in that Hundred eighteen shillings and certain Corn; and [in] some other Hundred six Marks and corn; and so

[1] Hinder.
[2] For the livery of his men.
[3] Dark red and orange.
[4] June 29.

they have paid in all the Hundreds and Towns hereabouts, that is to say, East Flegg and West Flegg, and up to Blofield, Tunstead, and up to Stalham, I understand by the commission that Debenham hath, it is more large than Master John's, as ye shall understand, whereof I send you a Copy, which causeth me that I labour no farther therein, notwithstanding your mastership shall have knowledge what every Hundred gives and Yarmouth, both.

Written at Winterton, the morrow after I departed from your mastership.

Your poor Beadsman,

RICHARD CALLE

[1462]

191. SHIPS FOR THE NAVY (iii)

To my Master John Paston, the younger, be this delivered

SIR, I have received your Letter, wherein I understand that my master desired that my master your brother might have the guiding and governance of the Barge of Yarmouth; as to that, and men of Yarmouth had known my master's intent a fortnight ago he had been sure of it, but now it is so that Debenham hath a Commission of the King, expressed only for that ship named in his Commission, and he hath been here at Yarmouth, and spoken with the Bailiff and with the owners of the said ship, and taken such a direction that they may grant it no man but him; and moreover he hath indented with the owners of the ship what day it shall be ready, as well victualled as manned; and also he hath brought down Letters from my Lord Treasurer to all Priors [1] and Gentlemen in this Country to help him and assist him to victual and man the said ship, and his men is here daily, and goeth about and gathereth wheat, malt, money, and whatsoever any man will give. The blessed Trinity preserve you. Written at Caister, the Friday next after I received your Letter. . . .

Your Servant

RICHARD CALLE

[1] Priors of St John always helped in military defence.

192. CLAIM BY THE ABBOT OF LANGLEY ON FASTOLF'S PROPERTY

To the right worshipful Sir John Paston, Knight, be this delivered

RIGHT worshipful Sir, and tenderly beloved in our Lord God, I commend me to you, sending you knowing that I did your errand to my brother the parson of Blofield [1] on Wednesday was sev'-night, after the understanding that I had of you and from you by this bringer, which man I felt right well and favourably disposed to you ward, and more favourably will be than to any other gentleman living, the will of the dead performed, and his conscience saved, and more things said favourably for you, which I entitled in a scroll to have certified to your servant Calle, if he had come, as ye sent me word he should have done, and should as ye behested [2] me, have brought me our ferm for Hellesdon, which not done, causeth me to write, praying your gentleness that I send no more therefore, for it is unpaid for the year afore the Hallowmass that my master Fastolf died, and for the same year that he died in, and since for two years, and five shillings unpaid of a year, and come Michaelmas next shall be another year unpaid, thus is four years unpaid and five shillings, and at Michaelmas next shall be five years and five shillings.

This thus kept from Holy Church, that is Holy Church's good, may not be without great peril of foul; where the peril is God knoweth, I pray God amend it, and give them grace that have his goods so to dispose them, that they and the dead both may be out of peril, and the Trinity have you in his merciful keeping. Written at Langley, on Sunday at even late, next after Saint John's day [the] Decollation.[3]

By your well-willing,

ABBOTT OF LANGLEY

[1463]

[1] Thomas Howes. [2] Promised. [3] August 29.

193. A CLAIM BY THE CONVENT OF NORWICH

(To two gentlemen of Norfolk, unnamed)

RIGHT worshipful Sirs, We recommend us all unto you in our most hearty wise, and it is so that long and many years there hath been hanging a great variance and a grudge betwix (*a*) Agnes Paston, widow of William Paston, and her sons William and Clement and (*b*) her son John and his sons. And now the said variance continueth betwixt the said William and John that now is living, of . . . the manors of Sporle, Woodhall, Palgrave, Cressingham, Swainsthorp, and East Beckham, all in this country of Norfolk.

Liketh it you to weet that the said William Paston, Justice, in his life was a special lover and friend to our Monastery; and for singular love and trust that he had to be remembered among us after his decease, notwithstanding he died at London, yet he bequested his body to be buried, and [it] is buried in the chapel of Our Lady within our monastery. And the said William Paston, Justice, often and many times in his pleyne [1] life, the said Agnes being present, he showed unto the Prior of our Monastery that was then, called Don John Haverland, and to . . . many divers other . . . that were then old fathers of our monastery, and are now deceased; that it was his very last will, that out of the said manors should be perpetually immortised [2] a certain land or annuity of such value, that every such monk that singeth the last mass in the said Chapel, where the body of the said William Paston lyeth buried, should have that day that he sung mass there 4*d*. to pray for the souls of the said William, and of Agnes his wife, and for the ancestors, kindred, consanguinity, affinity, and friends, and for all Christian souls; and, over that, a certain sum of money yearly to be paid, to have the obit [3] of the said William and Agnes yearly kept with Dirige and Mass in the said chapel.

And it is so, that many years after the decease of the said William [the] Justice, there were many men living, both of old brethren of ours afore rehearsed, and of other that could a borne witness in this matter . . . of which men, many now be deceased;

[1] Actual. [2] Amortised. [3] Death.

and no marvel, for it is upon a 43 year past since the said William [the] Justice, died; and also the said Agnes that was his wife lived more than 30 winters after her husband, and was in singular trust with her husband, and one of his executors, and well known in this country, a woman of virtuous living and disposition, and of good discretion and conscience, and knew her husbands mind and last will, as well as any living creature.

She witnessed alway that it was her husband's last will to have this perpetual mass, and called on it all the days of her life, and also at her decease; and she said that it was the will of her husband that the annuity should go out of the said manor of Swainsthorp . . . the Executors by their common assent left a Coffer [1] with a great substance of money of the goods of the said William [the] Justice, to be kept within our monastery, and told . . . us, that the said good should never be . . . had out of our place till we were made sure of the annuity; and during all the season that the coffer with the goods was within our monastery . . . we had money yearly given us to pray for his soul and to keep his obit; when, by means devised without the knowledge of the said Agnes, or of any of our brethren, all the good that was in the said coffer was conveyed out of our monastery, and after that deed done, there was no more money given us . . . saving that the said Agnes, during her life, gave us of her own costs yearly to remember the soul . . . and this many years there hath no thing been given us, notwithstanding of our own devotion we have rehearsed his name in our beadroll every Sunday; and now it is informed us, that as well William as John hath put all their title and interest in the award of the Right Reverend Father in God my Lord of Ely, Chancellor of England, Sir Reginald Bray, Knight, and in you twain; and in as much as ye be of our country, and special friends to our monastery, that maketh me and all my brethren the more bold to show this our matter unto you; beseeching you

[1] The circumstances have been thus related: John Paston, the son of William, the Judge, procured leave to place a Coffer of his own in the same room in which that containing the goods of his family was deposited, and to which having at all times free access, he by degrees privately took out and conveyed away the valuable treasure contained in the pledged one. [F.]

both to show it both to my Lord of Ely and to Sir Reginald Bray how that we ought of right to have a grant out of the said manors . . . and all our monastery shall pray for you, and also reward you to your pleasure : and, over that, ye shall do herein such a good deed that God shall reward you. Written in our monastery, the . . . day of . . . the *2d* year of the reign of King Harry the vijth.

By JOHN, Prior of Norwich,
and the Convent

[1486]

194. A SERMON

An ancient Whitsunday Sermon, preached by Friar Brackley[1] *(whose Hand it is) at the Friars Minors Church in Norwich*

FRIENDS, this Holy time as our mother holy Church maketh mention, the Holy Ghost came from Heaven, and lighted in the Disciples of Christ, inflaming them with cunning and strengthening them with grace. And because the doctrine and preaching of them should go throughout all the world first they were to be informed and taught cunning,[2] and to be strengthened with audacity,[3] and grace, and then to be endowed [with] and given all manner of languages, that they might preach to all manner of nations, so that those nations, that they preached to, might understand them, and every nation his own tongue. And so these Apostles, after that they were inspired with the Holy Ghost, wheresoever they preached, were there never so many nations present, each nation thought that they spoke in their own language, etenim illud loquebantur variis linguis Apostoli.

Friends, three things be necessary in preaching to him that shall preach through the world as the Apostles did, that is to say, cunning, boldness, and languages; if they had had cunning and none audacity, but have feared to have preached, it should little a profited, as we have examples daily at Cambridge, exempli

[1] Dr John Brackley, a Grey Friar of Norwich, was of considerable celebrity as a preacher.

[2] Skill, knowledge.

[3] Confidence.

gratia, de Clerico quis studuit sermonem, etc. And if they have both cunning and audacity, and have none eloquency, nor copiousness of language, so that he preach that [which] his Audience is most exercised in, that they understand him, else it profiteth not.

Therefore these holy Apostles before they should preach, first they were to be confirmed and strengthened. Our Lord strengthened them by under-nemyng [1] informing, and helping culpando ut in Evangelium recumbentibus, etc.

He strengthened them with his help and grace when he breathed in them, saying " Accipite spiritum sanctum, & quorum remiseritis peccata, remittuntur eis, & quorum retinueritis retenta sunt, etc." [2] He strengthened them also by his doctrine, when he said " Petite & accipietis; si quid petieritis Patrem in nomine meo, dabit vobis." [3] How that ye should pray to God and ask, I taught you on Easter-day; therefore ye shall pray God by good working, right full labouring, and in good deeds persevering.

Friends, ye ought for to ask of God that your joy may be a full joy and perfect; we may never have a full joy in this world, whereas ever among followeth heaviness. A man joyeth sometimes in gold and silver, and in great substance of earthly goods, in beauty of women, but this joy is not perfect, but this joy is not stable, but it is mutable as a shadow; for he that thus joyeth in the beauty of his wife, it may fortune to-morrow he shall follow her to church upon a bier; but if ye will know what is a full and a very joy, truly forgiveness of sin, and everlasting bliss, whereas is never sickness, hunger, nor thirst, nor no manner of disease, but all wealth, joy, and prosperity, etc. There be three manner of joys, the one void, another half full, the third is a full joy; the first is plenty of worldly goods; the second is ghostly grace; the third is everlasting bliss. The third is everlasting bliss. The first joy, that is affluence of temporal goods, is called a vain joy, for if a man were set at a board with delicate meats and drinks, and he saw a cauldron boiling afore him with pitch and brimstone, in the which he should be thrown naked, as soon as he had dined; for [if] he should joy much in his delicious meats, it should be but a vain joy.

[1] Rebuking. [2] John xx, 22–23. [3] John xvi, 23–24.

Right so doth the joy of a covetous man, if he see what pain his soul shall suffer in hell, for the miskeeping and getting of his goods, he should not joy in his treasure, ut in libro Decalogorum, "Quidam homo dives, etc."

Semiplenum gaudium est quando quis in presenti gaudet & tunc cogitans de futuris dolet; ut in quodam libro Græco, etc. "Quidam Rex Græciæ, etc." [1] here ye may see but half a joy; who should joy in this world, if he remembered him of the pains of the other world? "Non glorietur fortis in fortitudine suâ, nec sapiens in sapientiâ suâ, nec dives in divitiis suis." [2] De quibus dicitur, qui confidunt in multitudine divitiarum suarum, quasi oves in inferno positi sunt.[3] "Qui gloriatur, in Domino glorietur."[4] Therefore let us joy in hope of everlasting joy and bliss.

Gaudete quia nomina vestra scripta sunt in cælo, ut gaudium vestrum sit plenum.[5]

A full joy is in heaven.

Et in hoc apparet, quod magnum gaudium est in cælo, quoniam ibi est gaudium quod "oculus non vidit nec auris audivit, et in cor hominis non ascendit, quæ Deus preparavit diligentibus"[6] et ideo, Fratres, variis linguis loquens, [precor] ut gaudium vestrum sit plenum, vel, habeatis gaudium sempiternum.

[*date uncertain*]

195. POSITION OF A SECRETARY

[William Worcester (or Botoner), one of Fastolf's most useful and intimate servants, acted usually as his secretary. Worcester, antiquary and scholar, left a chronicle rich in personal details. MASTER, implying the dignified M.A. degree, was a gentlemanly title which Worcester hints he had not means to support. He was a layman and married, so could not hold a benefice.]

To my Master Paston

H. R.

AFTER due recommendation with my simple service preceding,

[1] Here must have followed an anecdote, as before of the Cambridge clerk.

[2] Jeremiah ix, 23. [3] Psalms xlviii, xlix, 6, 14.

[4] Jeremiah ix, 24. [5] Luke x, 20. [6] I Corinthians ii, 9.

please your mastership to weet, that as to such remembrance that ye desire me to continue forth to the uttermost, I shall with good will, so as my Master will licence me as oft as I can the officer to have leisure to be with me, for ye know well I cannot do it alone, etc.

And whereas ye of your pleasure write me, or call me Master Worcester, I pray and require you forget that name of mastership, for I am not amended by my Master of a farthing in certainty, but of wages of household in common entant comme nous plaira,[1] by [the name of] Worcester or Botoner, I have five Shillings yearly, all costs borne, to help to pay for Bonnets that I lose; I told so my Master this week, and he said me yesterday, he wished me to have been a Priest so I had been disposed, to have given me a living by reason of [2] a Benefice, that another man must give it, as the Bishop, but [3] he would; and so I indure inter egenos ut servus ad aratrum.[4]

Forgive me, I write to make you laugh; and our Lord bring my Master into a better mood for others as [well as] for me. At Caister, the 2nd day of September.

I pray you displeasure not your Servant be so long, for my Master letted [5] him.

Your,
W. Worcester

[1454]

196. A SUGGESTED MATCH

To the worshipful Sir, and my good Master John Paston at London, in haste

Worshipful and reverend Sir, and my good master, I recommend me to you in as diligent wise as on my part appertaineth, and please you to weet that my master [6] was right well pleased

[1] *I.e.*, as agreed. [2] By means of. [3] If.
[4] *I.e.*, like a slave at the plough.
[5] Hindered. [6] Sir John Fastolf.

with your faithful labour in fulfilling the Patent for the Ward of A. B. C.,[1] and he will faithfully labour as ye have advised him by writing of John Bocking; and [to] put my master in more courage, I moved to him upon mine head, that in case be the Child were wise, that then it were a good marriage between my [mistress] your daughter and him [2]; and, Sir, my master was glad when he heard that mean, considering that your daughter is descended of him by the mother's side; and, Sir, I have enquired after the said child, and no doubt of, but he is likely and of great wit, as I hear by report of sundry persons; and it is so, as I am credibly informed, that Jeffrey Boleyn [3] maketh great labour for marriage of the said child to one of his daughters; I would well to him, but better to you; wherefore that ye diligently labour for expedition of this matter, that in case ye can find any mean there to have the said child, and we shall do faithfully or diligence in like wise here, as ye advise us, etc.

And, Sir, as ye think with advice of my master Yelverton, Jenny, and others my master's counsel therein, that the Sheriff may be rewarded,[4] and if my said master's counsel think it be to [be] done, that then ye like to take an Action upon an Atteint,[5] which ye must with them take upon you at this time in my master's absence,[6] for as ye do in that matter he will hold him content, for William Barker hath an instruction of my master's intent upon the same. And I send John Barker a copy of the panel, which I shewed you at Caister, etc.

Almighty Jesu have you eternally in his merciful governance. Written at Caister the Wednesday next after Saint Martin, anno 33 (H. VI.)

Thomas Howys

[1454]

[1] Apparently Thomas Fastolf, of Cowhawe, Suffolk, a boy about 14 whose wardship Sir John obtained, by Paston's help, and whom he treated with the same injustice as he had done his stepson, Stephen Scroop. [Gr.]

[2] Either Anne or Margery, daughters of J. Paston, the elder of whom could not have been at this time more than ten years old.

[3] Sir Geoffrey Boleyn of Salle, Lord Mayor, and later of Blickling. He was great-grandfather of Queen Elizabeth.

[4] Bribed.

[5] *I.e.*, against a jury for a false verdict.

[6] On your own responsibility.

197. THE KING'S EXACTIONS IN NORFOLK

To Sir John Paston, Knight, be this delivered in haste

RIGHT well-beloved son, I greet you well, and send you God's blessing and mine, letting you weet that I marvel that I have had no writing from you since ye sent me the letter that ye sent me before the King's coming to Norwich; in the which letter ye wrote to me that ye should have written again to me ere ye should depart out of London.

It is so that your uncle William hath paid to my cousin Robert Clere but fourscore pounds of the 100*l.* and he will no more pay, but if [1] he hath deliverance of my pledges, the which were laid to pledge for 20*l.* the which be better.[2] I wot well, because of the good will that he oweth to me, as ye know, he would be in the possession thereof.

My cousin Robert Clere was here with me this week, and told me, that if he would have delivered them, he might have had the said 20*l.* but he said he would not, till he had spoken with me; by my troth I find him right kindly disposed to you, and to me both; and so I have desired him to keep still the pledges in his possession, till I have word from you how ye are agreed with your uncle for the payment of the said money: I ween verily that ye have found him surety for all, and if ye have so done, I would ye should write to your uncle therefore, that I might have my pledges again, for I were loath that they should come in his fingers.

Item, as for Sporle Wood, before the King's coming into Norfolk, I might have had Chapmen to have bought it a great [3] for twelve score marks,[4] and now there will no man buy it a great because of the great good [5] that the people is laid to for the King; wherefore we are about to retail it as well as we may, and as well as it can be brought to; and send you word how we shall do, as hastily as I may.

As for your barley in this country, it cannot be sold above

[1] Unless. [2] Worth more. [3] Altogether.
[4] A hundred and sixty pounds. [5] Large sums.

10*d*. or 11*d*. [the comb] that is the greatest price of barley here, and but it be at a better price, I purpose for to do it malt ; and as for money, I could not get yet of Peacock but 3*l*.; he saith that by then that the outcharges be borne, and the reparation of the mill at Winterton, we are like to have but little more money beside the barley. Malt is sold here but for 13*d*. and wheat 2*s*. or 26*d*. at this time, and oats 12*d*. There is none outload,[1] suffered to go out of this country as yet; the King hath commanded that there should none go out of this land. I fear me that we shall have right a strange world; God amend it, when his will is.

I thank you for the flaggons that ye sent me; they be right good, and please me right well: I shall be as good an housewife for you as I can, and as I would be for myself. Send me word how ye do of your sickness that ye had on your eye and your leg; and if God will not suffer you to have health, thank him thereof, and take it patiently, and come home again to me, and we shall live together, as God will give us grace to do, and as I have said to you before this. I would ye were delivered of my Mistress A. H.,[2] and then I would trust that ye should do the better.

As for the books that ye desired to have of Sir James's, the best of all and the fairest is claimed; nor it is not in his inventory, I shall assay to get it for you, and I may; the price of these other books, beside that, is 20*s*. and 6*d*. the which I send you a bill of. If ye like by the price of them, and ye will have them, send me word. And also I pray you send me an answer of this letter, because I think long since I heard from you. God have you in his keeping.

Written at Norwich on the Saturday next before the Purification of Our Lady,[3] the 14th year of King Edward the Fourth.

Your mother,

MARGARET PASTON

[1475]

[1] Export. [2] Anne Haute. [3] February 2.

198. THE KING'S EXACTIONS. YOUNG SOLDIERS

Unto Sir John Paston, be this delivered in haste

RIGHT well-beloved son. . . . the King goeth so near us [1] in this country, both to poor and rich, that I wot not how we shall live, but if the world amend: God amend it, when his will is. I can neither sell corn nor cattle to no good profit. . . .

William Peacock shall send you a bill what he hath paid for you for two tasks [2] at this time; and how he hath purveyed [3] for the remanent of your corn; and also of other things that be necessary, that should be purveyed for in your absence. Send me word also whom ye will desire to do for you in this country, or elsewhere in your absence; and write to them to do for you, and they will be the better willed to do for you; and I will do my endeavour for you also, as well as I can.

The sum of money that I have received of William Peacock: First, 40*s.* of Runham. Item, of Bastwick, 20*s.* Item, of Runham, 20*s.* Item, of him for barley at Runham, 20*s.* Item, of the fishing at Bastwick, 13*s.* 4*d.* Item, for barley sold at Runham, 8*s.* Sum total, 6*l.* 1*s.* 4*d.*

Item, I have received of Richard Call, of Sporle woods, 26*s.* 8*d.* and more shall I hope for hereafter within short time; as I receive for you, I hope to give you a true account: and this is all that I have received for you yet, since ye departed hence.

God bring you well again to this country, to his pleasance, and to your worship and profit. Written at Maulteby, the 23rd day of May, and the Tuesday next after Trinity Sunday.

For God's love, and your brethren go over the sea, advise them as ye think best for their safeguard, for some of them be but young soldiers, and wot full little what it meaneth to be as a soldier, nor for to endure to do as a soldier should do. God save you all, and send me good tidings of you all. And send ye me word in haste how ye do, for I think long till I hear from you.

By your mother,

MARGARET PASTON

[1] Exacts so much. [2] Subsidies. [3] Provided.

Item, I would not in no wise that ye should sell nor set to pledge that ye have in Runham, whatsoever fortune of the remanent; for it is a pretty thing, and reasonable well paid, and near this town: I would be right sorry that ye should forbear that: I had lever ye forbore that your uncle hath to mortgage than that.

[1475]

199. DEATH OF THE DUKE OF NORFOLK

(This letter has no direction, but it is written either to John Paston or to Margaret Paston)

LIKE it you to weet, that not in the most happy season for me, it is so fortuned, that whereas my Lord of Norfolk,[1] yesterday being in good health, this night died about midnight, wherefore it is for all that loved him to do and help now that, that may be to his honour, and weal to his Soul; and it is so, that this Country is not well purveyed of Cloth of Gold for the covering for his Body and Herse; wherefore every man helping to his power, I put the Council of my Lord in comfort, that I hoped to get one for that day, if it were so that it be not broken, or put to other use; wherefore please it you to send me word if it be so, that ye have, or can come by the Cloth of Tissue, that I bought for our Father's Tomb, and I undertake it shall be saved again for you unhurt at my peril; I deem hereby to get great thanks, and great assistance in time to come; and that either Sym or Mother Brown may deliver it me to-morrow by seven of the clock.

Item, as for other means, I have sent my servant Richard Toring to London, which I hope shall bring me good tidings again, and within four days I hope to see you.

Written on Wednesday the 17th day of January, in the 15th year of Edward IV.

JOHN PASTON, Knight

[1476]

[1] John Mowbray, Duke of Norfolk, retained by Edward IV to serve him in his wars in France in 1473, died suddenly at his castle of Framlingham, on January 17, 1475.

200. A WHALE FOR THE KING

To the Right Honourable Sir John Paston, Knight, be this delivered

RIGHT reverend and honourable, after the order of all due recommendation had, I recommend me unto your mastership.[1] Sir, it is so that John Taylor of Bridgeham, Deputy in your office of the Admiralty, was with me this morning to have mine advice in this matter following, and the which is this.

There was taken against Thornham, in the King's stream, being two fathoms and a half deep upon the sea, a Whale Fish by Thornham-men labouring all night on Sunday night last was, and so have slain it and brought to land; upon the which your said Deputy hath been there as yesterday and seized my Lord's [Oxford's] part thereof, whereof the people was glad it should so be; then John a'Lowe was there, and he said to your Deputy that he would have the King's part in this wise, that the King and my Lord should part the half; Sir, the law civil saith thus, "If any fish royal be found on the sea, that is to say, Whale, Bales, Sturgeon, Porpus, or Grampus, that my Lord Admiral shall have the halverdele [2] etc.

I think my Lord hath the King's prerogative upon the sea, the which I remit to your discretion, etc.

Sir, by likelihood, without ye take heed and send thither some of yours, my Lord's part shall be little; it is a great fish and a royal; your Deputy showeth me it is eleven fathom,[3] and more of length, and two fathom [4] of bigness and deepness in the mid fish.

Sir, remember what ye have to do, there come not such a casualty in your time of your office, etc.

Wherefore this, by the information of your said Deputy, cause me to write unto you this simple bill, praying you to pardon me of the writing, for it was done in haste. Do herein now as it

[1] John Paston was Vice-Admiral for the East Anglian coast under the Earl of Oxford, Admiral of England, 1489.

[2] Half-part. [3] Sixty-six feet. [4] Twelve feet.

please you, and Almighty God have you and all yours in his keeping; beseeching you that this simple bill may recommend my poor wife unto your mastership.

Written on Candlemas day, in haste, at Wells.

Your
T. GRIGGS

[1489]

201. THE WHALE REFUSED

To my Right Worshipful Master, Sir John Paston, Knight, this letter be delivered in haste

RIGHT reverend and worshipful Sir, in the most humble wise I recommend me unto you, desiring to hear of your welfare, the which God long continue.

Sir, mine brother William recommends him unto you; and as for the letter that ye sent unto him, he hath showed mine Lord [Oxford] the intent thereof, and he thinketh himself, that it is no part of his duty to have any part of the fish, or any money that should grow thereof; nevertheless, my Lord, according as your desire was in the letter, had questioned John a'Lowe of this fish, afore the coming of John Daniel, what he had done withall; and he answered, as for the nether chavil [1] thereof he had put it in surety, and laid it in a house, because your deputy seized it to mine Lord's use, till it might be understood whether the property were in the King, or in my Lord; and so my Lord held him well content it should be so, inasmuch as the King and my Lord have commanded John a'Lowe that this foresaid chavil should be brought up to the King in all goodly haste.

Furthermore, my brother William perceived by your writing, that ye could make the remanent of the fish worth a four pound to my Lord; my Lord would ye should not trouble yourself no more withall, because he thinketh that the property is not in him. And also another, my brother William heareth say in the court, that the King and my Lord be content that the remanent of

[1] Jaw.

the fish be to the use of them of the country, the which ye shall hear the more certain thereof hereafter.

Also my brother William saith, that my Lord willed you that ye should send the return of the commission, as hastily as ye can, and marvels that ye have not sent it up ere this. . . .

And, Sir, I thank you for the letter that ye sent me; also Sir, I have fulfilled my pilgrimage, thanks be to God.

Also, Sir, we understand that it is enacted of every ten marks [1] of movable goods 20*d*. to the King, beside the tenth of every man's lands. . . .[2]

No more to you at this time, but God and the Holy Trinity have you in their keeping; and my sister Ann, with all the company, recommend them unto you.

Written at London, the 10th day of February.

By your servant,

MARGERY PASTON

[1489]

202. GIFT OF A PORPOISE

To our right reverend and worshipful and special good Master, Master Paston

RIGHT reverend and worshipful Sir, and our very loving and courteous good Master, we recommend us unto you in as faithful wise as on our part appertaineth; and heartily we thank you for your labour, and letter which ye sent to us by your servant; by the which we were ascertained of the King's pleasure; and to accomplish the same, we with the assistance of your Mastership will put us in our devoir.[3]

We were at your Manor of Caister, to have seen your Mastership, but ye were departed as well from Yarmouth yesterday, as this day from Caister.

We would have been joyous to have seen your mastership, if our fortune so had been.

Sir, we be informed that our old special good Lord of Oxford,

[1] £6 13*s*. 4*d*.

[2] For the relief of the English forces in Brittany, following the unauthorized expedition of Lord Woodville in 1488.

[3] Best endeavour.

in whom we found as great favour by the mediation of your mastership as ever we had of any creature, as we have writing to show; in recompense of which at all times since, his Lordship hath had our prayers; and now we would have waited upon his Lordship, but your Mastership knoweth well we may not be absent on Michaelmas day for divers considerations. Wherefore we beseech your good Mastership, ye like of your gentleness to recommend us unto our said good Lord, and to make our excuse to him, and to do his Lordship be presented with a Porpoise,[1] which we send you by the bringer of this; and if we had any other dainties to do him a pleasure, we would, that knoweth God, whom we beseech of his infinite mercy to preserve the King, our Sovereign Lord, and our said good Lord, and you, and all the fruits [2] of you from all adversity.

Your Lovers and Beadsmen, the old
Bailiffs of Yarmouth, and the
new Bailiffs that now shall be

[1489]

203. A HUMOROUS REQUEST TO LORD FITZWALTER FOR RABBITS

HUMBLY beseecheth your good Lordship,[3] your daily servant and beadsman, John Paston, more caitiff than knight, that it may please you of your special grace to direct out your letters, signed with your hand and sealed with your seal, to the dreadful man James Radcliff, of Billingford, Squire, farmer of your warren there; out of whose warren, no manner of man nor vermin dare take on him, for doubts of your said dreadfull [man], to take or carry away any of your game there, for fear of being hanged up among other misdoers and forfeitors, as weasels, lobsters,[4] pole-cats, basarts,[5] and main curs; that the said James shall, upon the sight of your said writing, deliver, or cause to be delivered, to

[1] A great delicacy in ancient feasts. [2] Descendants.

[3] Sir John Radcliff, Lord Fitzwalter, was lord of the manor of Billingford, in Norfolk. James Radcliff, the farmer of his warren, was evidently a kinsman.

[4] Stoats. [5] Hawks.

your said beseecher, or to his deputy, deliverer of your said letters, at his first sight of the same, six couple of black conies or running rabbits, or some black and some white, to the said number, to store with a new ground of your said beseecher at Oxnead, more like a pinfold than a park; and your said beseecher shall daily pray to God for the preservation of your noble estate long to endure.

[1490?]

204. BARTER WITH THE BISHOP OF DURHAM

To the Right Worshipful Sir, my right trusty and right entirely well-beloved Friend, Sir John Paston, Knight

IHS XTUS

RIGHT worshipful Sir, and mine especial, and of long time, approved, trusty, and faithful friend, I, in mine heartiest wise, recommend me unto you; and forasmuch as I have coals and other things in these parts, and also ye have in those parts corns, wine, and wax; and as I am informed ye be not evil-willed to deal with me, no more than I am to deal with you, in uttering,[1] and also in receiving of such things, the which might be to the profit of us both; I therefore send unto you at this time William Walter, Gentleman Usher of my Chamber, to commune with you herein; so that by deliberation such a way may be taken in this behalf, as may be to the profit of either of us, and whereby our familiarity and friendship may be increased in time to come. Whereunto, for our old acquaintance together, ye shall find me full ready, after my power, by the grace of our Lord, who ever keep you, and send you much worship and long prosperity.

Scribbled in the most haste, at my Castle or Manor of Auckland, the 27th day of January, 1489.

Your own true Lover and Friend,

JOHN DURESME [2]

[1489]

[1] Selling.

[2] John Sherwood, Bishop of Durham. A distinguished scholar and cleric.

205. A GRATEFUL HANSE MERCHANT

HONOURABLE and well-beloved Knight, I commend me unto your Mastership, and to my Lady your wife; I thank your Mastership [for] that ye have done for me; I send my Lady a little piece of Rhenish wine of the best, of ten gallons, and half an hundred oranges; I shall send her more against Pentecost, that she may have fresh; and Renold has not given me the two nobles and forty-one pence, that ye told me of, for the wine; and my service by night and by day to your commandment, if your Mastership will any thing with me, I shall be at Cley.

No more than God be with you. Written upon the Tuesday after Palm Sunday.

LUMEN HARYSON,[1]
at your commandment

[1490]

206. AN APPEAL FOR FAVOUR

To our Right Worshipful Cousin, Sir John Paston, Knight

RIGHT Worshipful Cousin, in right hearty wise I commend me unto you, and where[as] I understand by Thomas Hartford, a bowyer of Norwich, bearer hereof, [that he] hath been put to great vexation and trouble by one Thomas Hogan, shoemaker, of Norwich, and that I perceive ye have heard the matter depending in traverse betwixt the said parties; I therefore desire you that, in the right of the foresaid Thomas Hartford, ye will be unto him good master, and the better for this mine instance, as my singular trust is in you. And where[as] I conceive also that the same Thomas is noised in Norfolk for a Scotsman born; ye shall understand that I perceive well, by such honest folks as I have heard

[1] An English form of Henrikson. One of the merchants of the Hanse—the famous commercial league of German towns.

speak within the city of York, that the said Thomas was born there, and his father there inhabiting, and his godfathers and mothers, the which be right honest persons; and for that this is true, and not feigned, ye shall understand the mayor of the city of York and his brethren have made great instance unto me to write for the said Thomas; for whom I must needs do, because they are my nigh neighbours, as our Lord knoweth, who have you in his blessed safeguard.

Written in the castle of Sheriff Hutton,[1] the 24th day of April.

Your loving Cousin,

THOMAS SURREY [2]

[1490]

207. A LOVE-MATCH PERMITTED

To the right worshipful and my right entirely well-beloved Cousin and Friend, Sir John Paston, Knight

RIGHT worshipful Sir, I recommend me unto you. I write this only unto you, to advise you that I was minded that my Cousin Clippesby, bearer hereof, should well have married here in these parts, wherein your niece [3] took heavy conceit, thinking in her mind, that I was not willing that my said Cousin should marry with her.

At that time I knew not what love was betwixt them; but now I understand that both their minds are to marry together; whereunto, on my part, I am agreeable and well content, desiring and praying you to be the same; and to be the better friend unto them at this my prayer and instance. And what pleasure, as I may do unto you in these parts, shall be ready, in that I may, at your desires.

[1] Near York.

[2] Thomas Howard, Earl of Surrey, was sent North in 1489 to suppress the Earl of Northumberland's rebellion. He was made lieutenant-general north of Trent and resided in those parts for ten years.

[3] John Clippesby, of Oby, ward and step-son of Edmund Paston, married Constance, natural daughter of Sir John Paston, who died in 1479.

And I pray you to recommend me to my Cousin your niece; and Jesu preserve you.

Written at London, the first day of June.

Your own, the Prior of St John's,

Sir John Kendal

[1495]

SECTION IV

PUBLIC EVENTS

208. RELEASE OF THE DUKE OF ORLEANS

To my right reverend, and right honourable Master, John Paston, be this given

SALVETE, etc. Tidings, the Duke of Orleans,[1] hath made his oath upon the sacrament, and used it, never for to bear arms against England, in the presence of the King, and all the Lords, except my Lord of Gloucester [2]; and in proving my said Lord of Gloucester agreed never to his deliverance, when the Mass began, he took his barge, etc.

God give grace the said Lord of Orleans be true, for this same week shall he towards France.

Also Frenchmen and Picards a great number came to Arfleet (Harfleur), for to have rescued it; and our Lords with their small puissance manly beat them, and put them to flight, and blessed be our Lord, have taken the said City of Arfleet; the which is a great Jewel to all England, and especially to our Country [Norfolk].

Moreover there is one come into England, a Knight out of Spain, with a Kerchief of Plesaunce [3] enwrapped about his arm; the which Knight will run a Course with a sharp spear for his Sovereign Lady's sake, whom, either Sir Richard Wodvile, or Sir Christopher Talbot, shall deliver [4] to the worship of England, and of themselves by God's grace. . . .

[1] Cardinal Beaufort, having failed to end the French War by the Congress of Arras (1435), tried to accomplish the same object by releasing the Duke of Orleans, who had been a prisoner since Agincourt, on the understanding that he should promote a reconciliation between the two countries. Unfortunately Orleans achieved nothing.

[2] Humphrey, Duke of Gloucester, the King's uncle, who clamoured for a more vigorous prosecution of the war with France.

[3] A rich scarf, bestowed as a token by his " sovereign lady."

[4] From his vow, by jousting with him.

No more, at this time, but the Trinity have you in protection, etc. and when your leisure is, resort again unto your college, the Inner Temple, for there be many which sore desire your presence.

Written on the Feast of All Saints, between Mass and Matins.

Yours, ROBERT REPPS

[1440]

209. A SEA FIGHT

To my reverend Master, Thomas Daniel, Esquire for the King's Body,[1] *be this Letter delivered in haste*

MOST reverend Master, I recommend me unto your gracious Mastership, ever desiring to hear of your worshipful estate; the which Almighty God maintain it, and increase it unto his pleasance.

Pleasing you to know of my welfare, and of all your men, at the making of this Letter, we were in good health of body, blessed be God.

Moreover Master, I send you word by Rawly Pikering of all matters, the which I beseech you give him credence, as he will inform you of all, so sure I beseech you in the reverence of God, that ye will inform our Sovereign Lord the King of all matters, that I send you in this Letter; like as I have sent a Letter to my Lord Chancellor, and to all my Lords by the said Pickering; the which Letter, I beseech you that ye take and deliver to my Lord, and all my Lords by your own hands, and let the said Pickering declare all things as he hath seen and known.

First I send you word that when we went to sea, we took two Ships of Brest coming out of Flanders; and then after, there is made a great arming in Bretayne to meet with me and my Fellowship, that is to say, the great Ship of Brest, the great Ship of

[1] An Esquire of the King's Body was an officer of great trust, lodged near him; during the night all messages, etc., were delivered by him in person to the King. Robert Winnington, of Devonshire, had a royal commission to put down piracy and violence on the seas. He was attached to the York party and therefore writes to Daniel, Suffolk's enemy.

Morlaix, the great Ship of Vannes, with other eight Ships, Barges, and Balingers [1] to the number of 3000 men, and so we lay on the sea to meet with them.

And then we met with a Fleet of an hundred great Ships of Prusse, Lubeck, Campe,[2] Rostock, Holland, Zealand, and Flanders, betwixt Guernsey and Portland; and there I came aboard the Admiral, and bade them strike [3] in the King's name of England, and they bade me go skite [4] in the King's name of England; and then I and my Fellowship said, but he will strike down the sail, that I will oversail them by the grace of God, and God will send me wind and weather; and they bade me do my worst, because I had so few Ships and so small, that they scorned me.

And as God would, on Friday last was, we had a good wind; and then we armed us to the number of 2000 men in my Fellowship, and made us ready for to oversail them; and then they launched a Boat, and set up a Standard of Truce, and came and spake with me, and there they were yielded, all the hundred Ships, to go with me into what Port that me list and my Fellows; but they fought with me the day before, and shot at us a 1000 Guns, and Quarrels [5] out of number, and have slain many of my Fellowship, and maimed also.

Wherefore methinketh that they have forfeited both Ships and Goods at our sovereign Lord the King's Will.

Beseeching you that ye do your part in this matter, for this I have written to my Lord Chancellor, and all my Lord's of the King's Council; and so I have brought them, all the hundred Ships, within Wight [6] in spite of them all.

And ye might get leave of our sovereign Lord the King to come hither, it shall turn you to great worship, and profit, to help make our appointment in the King's name, for ye saw never such a sight of ships taken into England this hundred winters; for we lie armed night and day to keep them in, to the time that we have Tidings of our Sovereign, and his Council; for truly they have

[1] A small, light vessel; a sloop.
[2] Kampen on the Zuyder Zee.
[3] Lower the sail as a mark of deference.
[4] A slang term of contempt.
[5] Bolts.
[6] *I.e.*, into the Solent.

done harm to me, and to my Fellowship, and to your Ships, more than 2000*l.* worth [of] harm.

And therefore I am advised, and all my Fellowship, to drown them and slay them, without that we have tidings from our Sovereign the King, and his Council; and therefore in the reverence of God come ye yourself, and ye shall have a great avail and worship, for your coming to see such a sight, for I dare well say, that I have here at this time, all the chief Ships of Dutchland,[1] Holland, Zealand, and Flanders, and now it were time for to treat for a final Peace, as for these Parts.

I write no more to you at this time, but Almighty Jesu have [you] in his keeping.

I write in haste within Wight, on Sunday at night after the Ascension of our Lord.

By your own Servant,
ROBERT WENYNGTON

[1449]

210. SUFFOLK PARDONED BY THE KING

[The Duke of Suffolk became unpopular in England owing to the disasters of 1449–50 in France and the heavy taxation at home. He was believed to have plotted the death of the Duke of Gloucester in 1447. In 1450 he was impeached by the Commons on charges of gross mismanagement in France.]

To my right worshipful Master John Paston, be this delivered in haste

RIGHT worshipful Husband, I recommend me to you, desiring heartily to hear of your welfare, etc. [*Then follows some common business about his farms and tenants.*]

William Rutt, the which is with Sir John Heveningham came home from London yesterday, and he said plainly to his master, and to many other Folks, that the Duke of Suffolk is pardoned, and hath his men again waiting upon him, and is right well at

[1] Germany.

ease and merry, and is in the King's good grace, and in the good conceit of all the Lords, as well as ever he was.

There have been many Enemies against Yarmouth, and Cromer, and have done much harm, and taken many English men, and put them in great distress, and greatly ransomed them; and the said Enemies have been so bold that they come up to the land and play them on Caister Sands and in other places, as homely as they were Englishmen; Folks be right sore afraid, that they will do much harm this Summer, but if there be made right great purveyance against them.

Other tidings know I none at this time; the blissful Trinity have you in his keeping.

Written at Norwich, on Saint Gregory's day.[1]

Yours,

MARGARET PASTON

[1450]

211. SUFFOLK'S FAREWELL TO HIS SON ON HIS BANISHMENT[2]

The Copy of a notable Letter, written by the Duke of Suffolk to his Son, giving him therein very good Counsel

MY Dear and only wellbeloved Son,[3] I beseech our Lord in Heaven, the Maker of all the World, to bless you, and to send you ever grace to love him, and to dread him, to the which, as far as a Father may charge his child, I both charge you, and pray you to set all your spirits and wits to do, and to know his Holy Laws and Commandments, by the which ye shall, with his great mercy, pass all the great tempests and troubles of this wretched world.

And that, also weetingly, ye do nothing for love nor dread of any earthly creature that should displease him. And there as any

[1] March 12.

[2] King Henry VI tried to protect his friend from the fury of Parliament by banishing him for five years. On his way to the Continent he was seized and murdered (see Letter 212).

[3] John de la Pole, then a child. He is the Duke mentioned in the rest of these letters. He turned Yorkist.

Frailty maketh you to fall, beseech his mercy soon to call you to him again with repentance, satisfaction, and contrition of your heart, never more in will to offend him.

Secondly, next him above all earthly things, to be true Liege man in heart, in will, in thought, in deed, unto the King our alder-most [1] high and dread Sovereign Lord, to whom both ye and I be so much bound to; Charging you, as Father can and may, rather to die than to be the contrary, or to know any thing that were against the welfare or prosperity of his most Royal Person, but that as far as your body and life may stretch, ye live and die to defend it, and to let his Highness have knowledge thereof in all the haste ye can.

Thirdly, in the same wise, I charge you, my dear Son, alway as ye be bounden by the Commandment of God to do, to love, to worship, your Lady and Mother; and also that ye obey alway her commandments, and to believe her counsels and advices in all your works, the which dread not but shall be best and truest to you.

And if any other body would steer you to the contrary, to flee the counsel in any wise, for ye shall find it nought and evil.

Furthermore, as far as Father may and can, I charge you in any wise to flee the Company and Counsel of proud men, of covetous men, and of flattering men, the more especially and mightily to withstand them, and not to draw nor to meddle with them, with all your might and power; and to draw to you and to your company good and vertuous men, and such as be of good conversation, and of truth, and by them shall ye never be deceived nor repent you of.

Moreover, never follow your own wit in no wise; but in all your works, of such Folks as I write of above, ask your advice and counsel, and doing thus, with the mercy of God, ye shall do right well, and live in right much worship, and great heart's rest and ease.

And I will be to you as good Lord and Father as my heart can think.

And last of all, as heartily and as lovingly as ever Father blessed his child in earth I give you the Blessing of Our Lord and of me

[1] Most of all.

which of his infinite mercy increase you in all virtue and good living; and that your Blood may by his grace from kindred to kindred multiply in this earth to his service, in such wise as after the departing from this wretched world here, ye and they may glorify him eternally amongst his Angels in heaven.

Written of mine hand,

The day of my departing from this Land.[1]

Your true and loving Father,

SUFFOLK

[1450]

212. THE MURDER OF SUFFOLK

To the right worshipful John Paston, at Norwich

RIGHT worshipful Sir, I recommend me to you, and am right sorry of that I shall say, and have so washed this little bill with sorrowful tears, that unethe [2] ye shall read it.

As on Monday next after May day [3] there came Tidings to London, that on Thursday before the Duke of Suffolk came unto the Coasts of Kent full near Dover with his two Ships and a little Spinner [4]; the which Spinner he sent with certain Letters, by certain of his trusted men unto Calais ward, to know how he should be received; and with him met a Ship called Nicholas of the Tower with other Ships waiting on him, and by them that were in the Spinner, the Master of the Nicholas had knowledge of the Duke's coming.

When he espied the Duke's Ships, he sent forth his Boat to weet what they were, and the Duke himself spoke to them, and said, he was by the King's Commandment sent to Calais ward, etc. and they said, he must speak with their Master; and so he with two or three of his men went forth with them in their Boat to the Nicholas; and when he came, the Master bade him, Welcome Traitor, as men say.

And further the Master desired to wete if the Shipmen would

[1] April 30, 1450. [2] Scarcely. [3] May 4. [4] Pinnace.

hold with the Duke, and they sent word they would not in no wise; and so he was in the Nicholas till Saturday next following.

Some say he wrote much thing to be delivered to the King, but that is not verily known.

He had his Confessor with him, etc. and some say, he was arraigned in the Ship on their manner upon the Impeachments and found guilty, etc.

Also he asked the name of the Ship, and when he knew it, he remembered Stacy [1] that said, if he might escape the danger of the Tower he should be safe, and then his heart failed him, for he thought he was deceived.

And in the sight of all his men, he was drawn out of the great Ship into the Boat, and there was an Axe, and a Stock, and one of the lewdest [2] of the Ship bade him lay down his head, and he should be fairly dealt with, and die on a Sword; and took a rusty Sword and smote off his head within half a dozen strokes, and took away his Gown of Russet, and his Doublet of velvet mailed, and laid his Body on the Sands of Dover; and some say his head was set on a pole by it; and his men set on the land by great circumstance,[3] and pray.

And the Sheriff of Kent doth watch the body, and [hath] sent his Undersheriff to the Judges to weet what to do; and also to the King [to know] what shall be done.

Further I wot not, but thus far is it, if the Process be erroneous let his Counsel reverse it, etc.

I pray you let my Mistress your Mother know these tidings, and God have you all in his keeping.

I pray you this bill may recommend me to my Mistresses your Mother and wife, etc.

Written in great haste at London the 5th day of May, etc.

WILLIAM LOMNER [4]

[1450]

[1] A fortune-teller. [2] Meanest. [3] Formally.

[4] Secretary to Margaret Paston.

213. AFFAIRS AFTER SUFFOLK'S DEATH

To my right worshipful Cousin, John Paston, of Norwich, Esquire

RIGHT worshipful Sir, I recommend me unto you in the most goodly wise that I can; and for as much as ye desired of me to send you word of divers matters here, which have been opened in the Parliament openly, I send you of them such as I can.

First most especial, that for very truth upon Saturday that last was, the Duke of Suffolk was taken in the Sea, and there he was beheaded, and his body with the appurtenance set at land at Dover; and all the Folks that he had with him were set to land, and had none harm, etc.

Also the King hath somewhat granted to have the resumption again, in some but not in all, etc.

Also if ye purpose to come hither to put up your bills,[1] ye may come now in a good time, for now every man that hath any, they put them in, and so may ye if ye come, with God's Grace to your pleasure.

Furthermore upon the 4th day of this Month, the Earl of Devonshire came hither with 300 men well beseen, etc. and upon the morrow after, my Lord of Warwick, with 400 and more, etc.

Also as it is noised here, Calais shall be besieged within this seven days, etc.

God save the King, and send us peace, etc.

Other tidings be there none here, but Almighty God have you in his keeping.

Written at Leicester, the 6th day of May.

Your Cousin,

JOHN CRANE

[1450]

[1] Petitions.

214. ACCOUNT OF JACK CADE'S REBELLION

[This is the name usually given to the rising in South-east England in the summer of 1450. It was expected that the resentment of the court at the murder of Suffolk would be visited on the county of Kent, which had already suffered from extortionate taxation and grave injustices. Whole districts of the South-east rose in arms, choosing as their leader an Irish adventurer named Jack Cade. The organized force which he led to London reflected the general feeling of disgust with the incapacity of the Court and the misconduct of the war with France. Cade was captured and executed.]

To my right honourable Master, John Paston

RIGHT honourable and my right entirely beloved Master, I recommend me unto you, with all manner of due reverence in the most lowly wise as me ought to do, evermore desiring to hear of your worshipful state, prosperity and welfare; the which I beseech God, of his abundant grace, increase and maintain to his most pleasance, and to your heart's desire.

Pleaseth it your good and gracious Mastership tenderly to consider the great losses and hurts, that your poor Petitioner hath, and hath had ever since the Commons of Kent came to the Blackheath, and that is at 15 years passed [1]; whereas my Master Sir John Fastolf knight, that is, your Testator, commanded your Beseecher to take a man, and two of the best horses that were in his stable with him, to ride to the Commons of Kent, to get the Articles that they come for; and so I did; and all so soon as I came to the Blackheath, the Captain [Cade] made the Commons to take me; and for the salvation of my Master's horses I made my Fellow to ride away with the two horses; and I was brought forthwith before the Captain of Kent; and the Captain demanded me, what was my cause of coming thither, and why that I made my Fellow to steal away with the horses; and I said, that I came thither to cheer with my wife's brethren, and others that were mine Allies, and Gossips of mine, that were present there; and then was there one there and said to the Captain that I was one of

[1] This letter was written in 1465.

Sir John Fastolf's men, and the two horses were Sir John Fastolf's; and then the Captain let cry Treason upon me throughout all the field, and brought me at four parts of the field, with a Herald of the Duke of Exeter before me, in the Duke's Coat of Arms, making four Oyez at four parts of the field,[1] proclaiming openly by the said Herald that I was sent thither for to espy their puissance, and their habiliments of war, from the greatest Traitor that was in England or in France, as the said Captain made proclamation at that time, from one Sir John Fastolf knight, the which minished [2] all the Garrisons of Normandy, and Le Mans, and Maine, the which was the cause of the losing of all the King's title and right of an heritance, that he had beyond sea. And moreover, he said, that the said Sir John Fastolf had furnished his Place [3] with the old Soldiers of Normandy and habiliments of war, to destroy the Commons of Kent, when that they came to Southwark, and therefore he said plainly that I should lose my head; and so forthwith I was taken, and led to the Captain's Tent, and one axe and one block was brought forth to have smitten off mine head; and then my Master Poynyngs your brother [in law], with other of my Friends came, and letted [4] the Captain, and said plainly, that there should die an hundred or two, that in case be, that I died; and so by that mean my life was saved at that time.

And then I was sworn to the Captain, and to the Commons, that I should go to Southwark, and array me in the best wise that I could, and come again to them to help them; and so I got the Articles, and brought them to my Master, and that cost me more amongst the Commons that day than 27*s.*

Whereupon I came to my Master Fastolf, and brought him the Articles, and informed him of all the matter, and counselled him to put away all his habiliments of war, and the old Soldiers, and so he did, and went himself to the Tower, and all his meny [5] with him, but Betts and Matthew Brayn; and had not I been [there] the Commons would have brenned [6] his Place, and all his tenures; wherethrough it cost me of my own proper goods at that time more than six marks in meat and drink, and [yet] notwithstanding

[1] Presumably a captured Herald pressed into service.

[2] Reduced.

[3] Fastolf had a house in Southwark.

[4] Prevented.

[5] Company.

[6] Burned.

the Captain that same time, let take me at the White Hart in Southwark, and there commanded Lovelace to despoil me out of mine array, and so he did; and there he took a fine Gown of Muster' devillers [1] furred with fine beavers, and one pair of Brigandines [2] covered with blue velvet and gilt nails, with leg-harness; the value of the Gown and the Brigandines 8*l.*

Item, the Captain sent certain of his meny to my Chamber in your rents, and there [they] broke up my Chest, and took away one Obligation of mine, that was due unto me of 36*l.* by a Priest of Paul's, and one other Obligation, of one knight of 10*l.* and my purse with five Rings of gold, and 17*s.* and 6*d.* of gold and silver; and one harness complete of the touch of Milan; and one Gown of fine Perse [3] blue, furred with Martens; and two Gowns, one furred with Bogey,[4] and one other lined with frieze [5]; and there would have smitted off mine head, when that they had dispoiled me at [the] White Hart; and there my Master Poynyngs, and my Friends saved me, and so I was put up, till at night that the Battle was at London Bridge; and then at night the Captain put me out into the battle at the Bridge, and there I was wounded, and hurt near hand to death; and there was six hours in the battle, and might never come out thereof; and four times before that time, I was carried about throughout Kent and Sussex, and there they would have smitten off my head; and in Kent there as [6] my Wife dwelled, they took away all our Goods moveable that we had; and there would have hanged my Wife, and five of my Children, and left her no more goods but her Kirtle and her Smock; and anon after that Hurling [7] the Bishop of Rochester impeached me to the Queen, and so I was arrested by the Queen's commandment into the Marshalsea,[8] and there was in right great duress, and fear of mine life, and was threatened to have been hanged, drawn, and quartered; and so [they] would have made me [to] have impeached my Master Fastolf of Treason,[9] and because that

[1] A mixed grey woollen cloth, probably named from Moustierville.

[2] Coats of jointed mail.

[3] Sky-blue. The name of a cloth.

[4] Badger fur.

[5] A coarse, narrow cloth.

[6] Where.

[7] Commotion.

[8] Prison.

[9] Because Sir John left his House, etc., in Southwark, and retired to the Tower, instead of resisting and attacking the Rebels.

I would not, they had me up to Westminster, and there would have sent me to the Gaol House at Windsor, but my Wife's and one Cousin of mine own, that were Yeomen of the Crown, they went to the King, and got grace and one Charter of Pardon.

Per le vostre

J. PAYN

[1450]

215. THE PARLIAMENT OF 1450

To my worshipful and good Master, John Paston, Esquire

PLEASE it you to weet that Sir William Oldhall is chosen Speaker of the Parliament, and admitted by the King, etc. Item, the day of oyer and terminer shall [be] holden at Norwich, on Monday next coming, and by that cause my Lord of Oxford shall be disported [1] of his coming to the Parliament for to attend to the Sessions of oyer and terminer.[2]

Item, the Lord Moleyns had language of you in the King's presence as my Master Yelverton can tell you by mouth. Your presence should have done much ease here in your own matters and others, as your well willers think, and your absence do none ease here; nevertheless my Master Yelverton shall tell you all, etc.

Item, it is said here that the Duke of York, and the Duke of Norfolk shall not come here this sev'night.

As touching Sheriffs there are none chosen or named, and as men suppose, none shall be chosen till my Lord of York's coming, etc. Written in haste at Westminster Mercurij in sesto Sancti Martini.[3]

Yours,

JOHN DAMME,[4] and GRESHAM

[1] Diverted from.

[2] The sessions of Oyer and Terminer here mentioned were to try those who had been concerned in Cade's Rebellion.

[3] November 11.

[4] John Damme, Paston's friend, represented Norwich in this Parliament, which was memorable for its use of impeachment to bring to account the ministers of the Crown, notably Suffolk.

It is appointed that who [ever] shall sue any bill in the parliament they must be put into the Commons house before Saint Edmund's day,[1] at farthest, etc.
[1450]

216. A FACETIOUS ACCOUNT OF POLITICS

To William Wayte

RIGHT faithful and wellbeloved brother William Wayte, I commend me to you, as the Lord may to his tenant, praying you effectually to recommend me to my singular good master [2] and yours, excusing me that I write not to him, for I dare not involve me in the same; And as for tidings here, I certify you that all is nought, or will be nought; the King [Henry VI] borroweth his expences for Christmas; the King of Arragon, the Duke of Milan, the Duke of Ostrich,[3] the Duke of Burgoyn [4] would have been assistant to us to make a conquest,[5] and nothing is answered nor agreed in manner, save abiding the great deliberation that at the last shall spill all together,[6] etc.

The Chief Justice hath waited [7] to have been assaulted all this sev'night nightly in his house, but nothing come as yet, the more pity, etc. An Oyer and Determiner goeth into Kent, and Commissioners my Lord the Duke of York, Bourchier, my master (that will not come there) *de proditionibus*, etc.,[8] but Kent prayeth them to hang no men when they come.[9]

Other tidings as yet can I none tell you, save Ulveston is Steward of the Middle Inn, and Isley of the Inner Inn, because they would have offices for excuse for dwelling this time from their wives, etc. Sir Thomas Todenham lost his Primer at the Tower-hill, and sent his man to seek it, and a good fellow wished it in Norfolk, so he would fetch it there, etc. Men ween that

[1] November 20.

[2] Sir John Fastolf: Wayte and Bocking were his servants. The address is jocular.

[3] Austria. [4] Burgundy. [5] *I.e.*, in France.

[6] Except in much talking and doing nothing.

[7] Expected. [8] For treasons.

[9] *I.e.*, the assize would be a farce.

Norfolk men were hardier than they be.[1] God grant, and, at the reverence of God, help too that an outas [2] and clamour be made upon the Lord Scales, praying him, for weal of the country, neither sustain nor help him [Tuddenham] nor Heydon in no wise, and that ye cry upon my master and yours that he obey not the *Certiorari* [3] as yet, as you may see by his letter from my master, rudely and in haste by me endited, of which I pray excuse, etc. And pray Blake to do Swaffham men say somewhat to the matter. I weet well Todenham and Heydon will not come there at this time, as it is verily reported, etc. " Mitte sapientem,[4] etc." Brayn and I shall be with you on Sunday next at even with the grace of Jesu, to whom I betake you. In haste at London the 2nd day of January.

By
J. Bocking

[1451]

217. POLITICAL NEWS

To my Master Paston

Worshipful Sir, and my good Master, after due recommendation with all my true service preceding, like you weet, that as to Novelties, etc., the Prince [5] shall be created at Windsor upon Pentecost Sunday, the Chancellor, the Duke of Buckingham, and many other Lords of estate, present with the Queen.

As to my Lord [of] York, he abideth about York till Corpus Christi Feast be passed, and with great worship is there received.

And certain Justices, Prisot, Bingham, Portington, etc. be thither for execution of Justice upon such as have offended in causes criminal.

[1] *I.e.*, wished Tuddenham and his primer both in Norfolk: people think Norfolk men would not have put up with Tuddenham in the old times.

[2] Outcry.

[3] To be certified; first word of a writ calling for a case to be tried in a superior court.

[4] Literally: " Send a wise man."—the opening phrase of some proverbial expression.

[5] Edward, infant son of Henry VI and Margaret of Anjou, to be created Prince of Wales. York was Protector and Salisbury Chancellor.

It is said, the Duke of Exeter is here covertly, God send him a good counsel hereafter.

And the Privy Seal [1] is examined how, and in what manner, and by what Authority, privy Seals were passed forth in that behalf, which is full innocent and right clear in that matter, as it is well known.

The Frenchmen have been afore the Isles of Jersey and Guernsey and a great Navy of them, and 500 be taken and slain of them by men of the said true Isles, etc.

Sir Edmund Mulso is come from the Duke of Burgundy; and he saith, by his Servants' report, that he will not discharge the Goods of the Merchants of this land, but so be [2] that Justice be done upon the Lord Bonville, or else that he be sent to him to do justice himself, as he hath deserved, or satisfaction be made to the value.

Your matter is ensealed as of the thing ye wot of.

I can no more for haste and lack of leisure, but our Lord keep you. Written hastily the 8th day of June.

I send a letter to Master Berney to let you see for the Governance in Yorkshire.

BOTE H R. NER [3]

[1454]

[The English defeat at Castillon in Guienne in 1453 brought the Hundred Years War to an end, leaving only Calais in English hands. Bedford, Gloucester, Suffolk, and Beaufort were dead: the leading parts were now played by Richard, Duke of York, Somerset, and Queen Margaret of Anjou. Henry VI, suffering from recurrent fits of insanity was a figure-head in the hands of his dominating consort. The birth of their son, Edward, in 1453 ended York's hopes of succession, but in 1454 Parliament appointed him Regent during the King's insanity. With Henry's restoration to health York's protectorate ended, and Somerset was restored to power. In these circumstances Duke Richard resolved to appeal to arms, and the Wars of the Roses began.]

[1] Duke of Exeter. [2] Unless.

[3] William Botener, otherwise Worcester, secretary to Sir John Fastolf. He here signs his name in a very particular manner, inserting H R between *Bote* and *ner*. Perhaps it is meant to show his loyalty to King Henry. [F.]

218. THE KING RECOVERS

To my well beloved Cousin John Paston, be this delivered

RIGHT well beloved Cousin, I recommend me to you, letting you weet such tidings as we have.

Blessed be God! the King is well amended, and hath been since Christmas-day; and on Saint John's day,[1] commanded his Almoner to ride to Canterbury with his offering, and commanded the Secretary to offer at Saint Edward's.

And on the Monday afternoon, the Queen came to him and brought my Lord Prince with her, and then he asked what the Prince's name was, and the Queen told him Edward; and then he held up his hands, and thanked God thereof.

And he said, he never knew him till that time; nor wist not what was said to him, nor wist not where he had been, whilst he hath been sick till now; and he asked who were Godfathers, and the Queen told him, and he was well apaid.[2]

And she told him that the Cardinal[3] was dead; and he said, he knew never thereof till that time; and he said, one of the wisest Lords in this land was dead.

And my Lord of Winchester, and my Lord of Saint John's,[4] were with him on the morrow after Twelfthday, and he speak to them as well as ever he did; and when they came out, they wept for joy.

And he saith he is in Charity with all the world, and so he would all the Lords were.

And now he saith Matins of Our Lady, and Evensong, and heareth his Mass devoutly.

And Richard shall tell you more tidings by mouth.

I pray you recommend me to my Lady Morley[5] and to Master Prior,[6] and to my Lady Felbrigg, and to my Lady

[1] December 27. [2] Content.
[3] John Kemp, Archbishop of Canterbury, Cardinal, died 1453.
[4] Lord Prior of the Order of St John of Jerusalem.
[5] Daughter of the Earl of Suffolk.
[6] Probably the Prior of Bromholm.

Heveningham, and to my Cousin your Mother, and to my Cousin your Wife.

Written at Greenwich, on Thursday after Twelfthday.

By your Cousin,

EDMUND CLERE [1]

[1455]

219. MEMORIAL OF THE DUKE OF YORK AND THE EARLS OF SALISBURY AND WARWICK TO HENRY VI [2]

MOST Christian King, right high and mighty Prince, and our most redoubted Sovereign Lord, we recommend us as humbly as we suffice unto your high Excellence, where unto please it to weet that for so much as we hear and understand, to our greatest sorrow earthly, that our Enemies of approved experience, such as abide and keep themselves under the wing of your Majesty Royal, have thrown unto the same, right studiously and right fraudulently, many ambiguities and doubts of the faith, legiance, and duty, that God knoweth, we bear unto your Highness, and have put them in as great devoir as they could to enstrange us from your most noble presence, and from the favour of your good grace; which good grace to us is, and ought to be, our singular and most desired joy and consolation. We at this time be coming with grace, as your true and humble liege men, toward your said high Excellence, to declare, and shew thereto at large, our said faith and legiance, intending, with the mercy of Jesu in the said coming, to put us in as diligent and hearty devoir and duty as any your liege men alive to that at [3] may advance or prefer the

[1] " Edmund of the King's house " had a place in the royal household, then resident at Greenwich. He was brother-in-law of " my cousin, Elizabeth Clere." [Gr.]

[2] This memorial was drawn up just before the battle of St Albans, but Lord Somerset and his friends would not allow it to be presented to the King.

[3] Which.

honour and welfare of the said Majesty Royal, and the surety of the said most notable Person, the which [we] beseech our blessed Creator to prosper [with] as great honour, joy, and felicity as ever had any Prince earthly, and to your said Highness so to take, accept, and repute us, and not to please to give trust or confidence unto the sinister, malicious, and fraudulent, labours and reports of our said enemies, unto [1] our coming to your said most noble presence, whereunto we beseech humbly that we may be admitted as your liege men, to the intent to shew us the same, whereof yesterday we wrote our Letters of our intent, to the right reverend father in God, the Archbishop of Canterbury, your Chancellor of England, to be shewed to your said Highness, whereof, for so much as we be not ascertained whether our said intent be by his fatherhood shewed unto your said good grace or not; we send thereof unto this closed a Copy of our said Letters of our disposition towards your said high Excellence, and the honour and weal of the land, wherein we will persevere with the grace of our Lord.

[1455]

220. THE FIRST BATTLE OF ST ALBANS

[With the termination of his protectorate, and the Somerset party in power, York decided to secure his position by force of arms. With an army recruited in the North he advanced on London. A vain attempt at negotiation at St Albans was followed by the battle, in which York was completely victorious, Somerset and other Lancastrian nobles being slain.]

Unto my worshipful and well beloved Cousin, John Paston, be this Letter delivered in haste

RIGHT worshipful and entirely well beloved Sir, I recommend me unto you, desiring heartily to hear of your welfare.

Furthermore letting you weet, as for such Tidings as we have here, these three Lords be dead, the Duke of Somerset, the Earl

[1] Until.

of Northumberland, and the Lord Clifford; and as for any other men of name, I know none, save only Cotton of Cambridgeshire.[1]

As for any other Lords, many of them be hurt, and as for Fylongley [2] he liveth, and fareth well, as far as I can enquire, etc.

And as for any great Multitude of people that there was, as we can tell, there was at most slain six score; and as for the Lords that were with the King, they and their men were pilled and spoiled out of all their Harness and Horses; and as for what Rule we shall have yet I weet not, save only there be made new certain Officers.

My Lord of York, Constable of England; my Lord of Warwick is made Captain of Calais; my Lord Bourchier is made Treasurer of England; and as yet other Tidings have I none.

And as for Our Sovereign Lord, thanked be God, he hath no great harm.

No more to you at this time, but I pray you send this Letter to my Mistress Paston, when ye have seen it; praying you to remember my Sister Margaret against the time that she shall be made a Nun.

Written at Lamehith [3] on Whitsunday, etc.

By your Cousin,

JOHN CRANE

[1455]

221. AFTER ST ALBANS [4]

To William Worcester be this Letter delivered in haste

SIR, I recommend me to you, and as for Tidings ye may inform mine Master, [Fastolf] that for new there is none but that he hath knowledge of.

But that the King, the Queen and the Prince remove to Hert-

[1] Vice-Chamberlain to Henry VI. [2] A nephew of Fastolf.

[3] Lambeth.

[4] After his victory at St Albans York craved forgiveness of the King and was restored to favour.

ford tomorrow without fault; my Lord of York to the Friars at Ware; my Lord of Warwick to Hunsdon; the Earl of Salisbury to Rye; and there they shall abide to the time the Parliament begins.

The Duke of Buckingham is come in, and sworn that he shall be ruled, and draw the line with them; and thereto he and his Brothers [1] be bound by recognizance in notable sums to abide the same.

The Earl of Wiltshire [2] sent to the Lords, from a place of his called Petersfield, a Letter desiring to know if he should come, and abide about the King's Person as he did before, and if he should not, then that they would license him to go into Ireland, and live there upon his lands, etc.

And before this done, the Lords were advised to have made him to do as the Duke of Buckingham hath done and no more; but what that will fall now thereof, no man can tell as yet.

The Baron of Dudley is in the Tower, what shall come of him God wot.

The Earl of Dorset [3] is in ward with the Earl of Warwick.

It was said forsooth, that Harper and two other of the King's Chamber, were confederated to have sticked [4] the Duke of York in the King's Chamber, but it was not so, for they have cleared them thereof.

But London upon the same tale [hath] arisen, and every man to harness on Corpus Christi even [5] and much ado there was.

Sir William Oldhall abideth no longer in Sanctuary than the Chief Justice come; for at that time he shall go at large and sue all his matters himself, etc.

The Baron Dudley hath impeached many men; but what they be, as yet we cannot weet.

Sir Philip Wentworth was in the Field, and bore the King's Standard, and cast it down and fled; my Lord of Norfolk saith, he shall be hanged therefore, and so is he worthy; he is in Suffolk now, he dares not come about the King.

[1] The Bourchiers.

[2] James Butler, Earl of Ormond and Wiltshire. He fled disgracefully from St Albans.

[3] Son of Somerset, afterwards Duke. [4] Stabbed. [5] June 5.

Edmund Stendal was with Wenlock there in the field and foully hurt.

Fylongley is at home at his own place with his wife, and shall do right well, but we have a great loss of his absence this term, for it will be long ere he come this term, I am afraid.

All the Lords that died at the Journey are buried at Saint Alban's.

Other things be none here, but ye shall see by Thomas Scales' Letter the rule of the Frenchmen, etc.

God speed us well in our matters this term, I pray to God, who have you in his keeping, etc.

W. B.[1]

[1455]

222. SEQUEL OF ST ALBANS

Unto my most faithful Brethren, John Bocking, and William Worcester, and to either of them

WORSHIPFUL Sir, and my most heartily and best beloved Brother, I recommend me unto you in more lowly wise, than I can either think or write; and with all my service and true heart thank you of your gentle Letters, full brotherly written unto me at many times of old, and in especial of late time passed. And truly brother, I thank Almighty God of your welfare, of the which the Bearer of this my poor Letter certified me of, etc.

And Sir, as touching all manner of new Tidings, I know well ye are avarous [2]; truly the day of making of this Letter, there were none new, but such [as] I heard of, ye shall be served withal.

As for the first, the King, Our Sovereign Lord, and all his true Lords stand in health of their bodies, but not all at Heart's ease, as we amongst others marvel.

Two days afore the writing of this Letter there was language between my Lords of Warwick and Cromwell afore the King; insomuch as the Lord Cromwell would have excused himself of all the stirring or moving of the male journey [3] of St Albans; of the which excuse making, my Lord Warwick had knowledge,

[1] William Barker, a legal agent of Fastolf.

[2] Desirous.

[3] Evil fight.

and in haste was with the King, and swore by his Oath, that the Lord Cromwell said not truth, but that he was the Beginner of all that journey at St Alban's; and so between my said two Lords of Warwick and Cromwell there is at this day great grudging, insomuch as the Earl of Shrewsbury hath lodged him at the Hospital of St James [1] beside the Mews [2] by the Lord Cromwell's desire, for his safeguard.

And also all my Lord of Warwick's men, my Lord of York's men, and also my Lord of Salisbury's men, go with harness, and in harness, with strange weapons, and have stuffed their Lords' Barges full of weapons, daily unto Westminster.

And the day of making of this Letter there was a Proclamation made in the Chancery on the King's behalf; that no man should neither bear weapon nor wear harness defensible, etc.

Also the day afore the making of this Letter, there passed a Bill both by the Kings, Lords, and Commons, putting Thorp, Joseph, and my Lord of Somerset in all the default,[3] by the which Bill, all manner of actions that should grow to any person or persons, for any offences at that journey done, in any manner of wise should be extinct and void, affirming all things done there, well done; and nothing done there never after this time to be spoken of; to the which Bill many a man grudged full sore now it is passed.

And if I might be recommended, unto my special Master and yours, with all lowliness and true service, I beseech you heartily as I can.

No more, but our Lord have you both in his perpetual keeping.

Written at London on Saint Margaret's Even [4] in haste; and after this is read and understood, I pray you burn or break [5] it, for I am loth to write any thing of any Lord, but I must needs, there is nothing else to write. Amen.

Your own,

[1455] HENRY WINDSOR

[1] St James's Palace.

[2] A place for the keeping of hawks, now the royal stables.

[3] Putting all the blame upon. Thorp had been Speaker, an opponent of the Duke of York. William Joseph was apparently a servant in the royal household.

[4] July 19.

[5] Tear.

223. DISTURBANCES IN THE WEST

To my right worshipful Master, John Paston, at Norwich, be this delivered

PLEASE it your Mastership to weet [*here follows an account of some Law business, etc.*].

Here be many marvellous tales of things that shall fall, this next month, as it is said; for it is talked, that one Doctor Grene a Priest, hath calculated and reporteth, that before St Andrew's day next coming, shall be the greatest battle that was since the battle of Shrewsbury [1] and it shall fall between the Bishop's Inn of Salisbury and Westminster Bars; and there shall die seven Lords, whereof three should be Bishops.

All this and much more is talked and reported, I trust to God it shall not fall so!

Also there is great variance between the Earl of Devonshire, and the Lord Bonvile,[2] as hath been many day, and much debate is like to grow thereby; for on Thursday (23rd of October) at night last passed, the Earl of Devonshire's Son and Heir came with sixty men of arms, to Radford's Place in Devonshire which was of counsel with my Lord Bonvile; and they set an house on fire at Radford's gate, and cried and made a noise, as though they had been sorry for the fire; and by that cause Radford's men set open the Gates and yede [3] out to see the fire; and forthwith the Earl's Son aforesaid entered into the place, and entreated Radford [4] to come down of his Chamber to speak with them promising him that he should no bodily harm have; upon which promise he came down, and spoke with the said Earl's Son; in the mean time his meny rob his chamber, and rifled his hutches,[5] and trussed such as they could get together and carried it away on his own horses; then the Earl's Son said: " Radford, thou must come to

[1] Where the Percy rebellion was crushed by Henry IV in 1403.

[2] The eldest son of the Earl of Devonshire fought Lord Bonvile in a regular pitched battle near Exeter. Bonvile retired to the city, and the Earl of Devonshire attacked the city and the cathedral.

[3] Went.

[4] Nicholas Radford was an eminent Lawyer. [F.]

[5] Coffers.

my Lord my Father." He said he would, and bade one of his men make ready his horse to ride with them; which answered him, that all his horses were taken away; then he said to the Earl's Son: "Sir, your men have robbed my Chamber, and they have mine horses, that I may not ride with you to my Lord your Father, wherefore I pray you, let me ride for I am old, and may not go."

It was answered him again, that he should walk forth with them on his feet; and so he did till he was a flight shot or more from his place, . . . and forthwith came nine men again upon him and smote him on the head and felled [him and] cut his throat.

This was told to my Lord Chancellor this forenoon. . . . [The King is] at Hertford, and some men are afraid that he is sick again, I pray God. . . . In haste at London on Saint Simon's day and Jude.[1]

Your poor,
JAMES GRESHAM [2]

[1455]

224. THE GREAT RECONCILIATION

[With the King's recovery again in 1456, York was relieved of his office as Protector; two years of comparative peace followed, and in March 1458 a great ceremony of reconciliation took place at St Paul's.]

To my Right Worshipful Master, Sir John Fastolf

RIGHT Worshipful Sir, and my right good Master, I recommend me to you in my full humble wife.

Please you to wete, as to Novelties here being, Christopher Barker writeth to you more along.[3]

The King came the last week to Westminster, and the Duke of York came to London with his own Household only, to the

[1] October 28.

[2] His Seal has on it a Grasshopper; a Device afterwards borne by Sir Thomas Gresham, the Founder of the Royal Exchange, the Vane on the top of which is a Grasshopper. [F.]

[3] At large.

number of 140 Horse, as it is said; the Earl of Salisbury with 400 Horse in his Company, four score Knights and Squires.

The Duke of Somerset came to London [the] last day of January with 200 Horse, and lodgeth without Temple Bar.

And the Duke of Exeter shall be here this week with a great Fellowship and strong, as it is said.

The Earl of Warwick is not yet come, because the wind is not for him; and the Duke of Exeter taketh a great displeasure that my Lord Warwick occupieth his office, and taketh the charge of the keeping of the Sea upon him.

Item, as for tidings of beyond Sea, I hear none certain, but that the French King [1] should have married his Daughter to the King of Hungary which had the discomfiture upon the Turks; and the said King is deceased within this six weeks, ere the Espousal was made, but he ordained ere he died that the French King's Daughter should be named Queen of Hungary during her life.

Right worshipful Sir, I beseech the blessed Trinity have you in his governance.

Written at London the first day of February, in the 36th year of King Henry VIth.

My Brother promised me a certain sum when I married, and I shall have it of my Sister if I may.

Your Humble Servant,

William Botoner, called Worcester

[1458]

[1] Charles VII. Ladislaus V of Hungary was actually poisoned on the eve of his marriage to Magdalen, daughter of Charles VII, in 1457.

[The continued lack of ' strong governance ' and the alienation of the powerful Nevilles from the Lancastrians as the result of an attempted murder of Warwick, caused York again to take up arms in 1459. In October York was routed at Ludlow by the army of Henry VI, commanded by Somerset and Exeter, and the Yorkist lords fled from the country in confusion after being attainted by the Parliament of Coventry.]

225. THE PARLIAMENT OF COVENTRY

To my right worshipful Masters, William Yelverton Justice, John Paston, and Henry Filongly, and to each of them

RIGHT worshipful Sirs, I recommend me to you, and like it you to know, that my Lord Chancellor [1] is a right good and tender Lord in all your matters, and so will continue and my Lord Treasurer [2] in like wise. . . . As for any particular matters, the Parliament, as yet, abideth upon the great matters of Attainder and Forfeiture,[3] and so there be many, and diverse particular bills put in, but none ready, nor touching us, as nigh as we can harken. . . . The Chief Justice [4] is right well and hearty, and sayeth full well and kindly of my Master, whom Jesu for his mercy pardon, and have you in his blessed governance. Written at Coventry the morrow after St Nicholas. I came to this town of Coventry, such day sev'night as the parliament began; and as for such things as I could harken after, I send to William Worcester a great bill of tidings to shew you and all.

Yesterday in the morning, came in the Earl of Pembroke [Jasper Tudor] with a Good Fellowship; and the Duchess of York [5] came yester evening late, as the Bringer hereof shall more plainly declare [to] you, to whom ye like to give credence.

The Bishop of Exeter [G. Neville] and the Lord Grey of Ruthin have declared them full worshipfully to the King's great pleasure.

Playters and I [have] written you a Letter by Norffolk, Yeoman for the King's mouth.

Your,
JOHN BOKKING

[1459]

[1] William Waynflete, Bishop of Winchester.
[2] James, Earl of Wiltshire.
[3] *I.e.*, of the Yorkists.
[4] Sir John Fortescue.
[5] Cecily, daughter of the Earl of Westmoreland.

[The following list of those of the Duke of York's party who were attainted by Parliament is pinned to the above letter.

The Duke of York.
his sons the Earl of March and the Earl of Rutland.
(R. Neville) the Earl of Warwick.
(R. Neville) the Earl of Salisbury.
The Lord Powys.
The Lord Clinton.

Countess of Salisbury.
Sir Thomas Neville.
Sir John Neville.
Sir Thos. Haryngton.
Sir Thos. a Parre.
Sir John Conyers.
Sir John Wenlock.

Sir William Oldhall.
Edward Bourchier.
John Denham (and eight others).

As for the Lord Powys, he come in[1] and had grace as for his life, but as for his goods, the forfeiture passed.

As nearly all of the above had fled the country they lived to fight again, and the forfeiture of their property to the Crown lasted but for a few months. F.]

[In the summer of 1460 the Yorkist lords returned to England and entered London. King Henry was in the Midlands, and the Yorkists advanced to meet him, and at Northampton on July 10 the Lancastrians were totally defeated. The King was taken prisoner, Queen Margaret fled to Scotland, and Henry was compelled to recognize York as heir to the throne.]

226. AFTER THE BATTLE OF NORTHAMPTON

To the right worshipful Sir and Master, John Paston, Esquire, at Norwich, be this Letter delivered in haste

RIGHT worshipful Sir and Master, I recommend me unto you; please you to weet, the Monday after our Lady day there come hither, to my Master's place, my Master Bowser, Sir Harry Ratford, John Clay, and the Harbinger of my Lord of March, desiring that my Lady of York might lie[2] here until the coming of my Lord of York, and her two Sons, my Lord George, and my Lord

[1] Surrendered. [2] Stay.

Richard, and my Lady Margaret her Daughter, which I granted them in your name to lie here until Michaelmas.

And she had not lain here two days but she had tidings of the landing of my Lord [1] at Chester.

The Tuesday next after, my Lord sent for her that she should come to him to [Hereford] and thither she is gone; and she hath left here both the Sons, and the Daughter, and the Lord of March cometh every day to see them.

Item, my Lord of York hath diverse strange Commissions from the King, for to sit in diverse towns coming homeward; that is to say, in Ludlow, Shrewsbury, Hereford, Leicester, Coventry, and in other diverse Towns, to punish them by the [2] faults to the King's Laws.

As for tidings here, the King is away at Eltham and at Greenwich to hunt, and to sport him there biding [3] the Parliament, and the Queen and the Prince abideth in Wales always, and [there] is with her the Duke of Exeter, and others with a few meny [4] as men say here.

And the Duke of Somerset he is in Depe [5] and with him Master John Ormond, Whittingham, Andrew Trollop, and other diverse of the Garrison of Guisnes, under the King of France's safe conduct, and they say here, he purpose him to go to Wales to the Queen. And the Earl of Wiltshire is still in peace at Ottery [Devon] at the Fryers, which is Sanctuary. . . .

Item, Master Poynings hath entered on a two or three places upon the Earl of Northumberland,[6] and he standeth in good grace of the King, my Lord of March, my Lord Warwick, and my Lord of Salisbury,[7] most part of the Country about his livelihood holdeth with him; and my Mistress your sister is not delivered as yet, God give her good deliverance.

No more to you at this time, but and ye will command me any service I may do, it is ready, and Jesu have you in his blessed

[1] Duke of York. [2] For their. [3] Until.

[4] Followers. [5] Dieppe.

[6] Had taken possession of some of the lands claimed by the Earl of Northumberland, who was a Lancastrian and the Yorkist Earls now favour Poynings.

[7] The King was in the hands of the three earls: March, Salisbury, and Warwick.

keeping; and I beseech you, this Letter may commend me to my Mistress your Mother, and my Mistress your wife, and all your household.

Written at London, the 12th day of October,

Your own Servant,

CHRISTOPHER HANSSON

[1460]

[Queen Margaret did not remain long in Scotland. She returned in 1460, raised an army in Wales and the North, advanced against the Yorkists, and decisively defeated them at Wakefield Green. Richard of York was himself slain, while the Earl of Salisbury and other prominent nobles were executed. The King, however, in London, was in Warwick's hands.]

227. AFTER THE BATTLE OF WAKEFIELD

To his Right Worshipful Brother, John Paston

RIGHT reverend and worshipful Brother, I recommend [me] to you, certifying you that your letter was delivered me the 23d day of January about the noon season, and Richard Calle rode in the morning, and therefore I broke your Letter, if [1] there were any after matter. . . .

My Lord Fitzwalter is ridden northwards, and it is said, in my Lord of Canterbury's house, that he hath taken 200 of Andrew Trollop's men. And as for Colt, and Sir James Strangwyse, and Sir Thomas Pykering, they be taken or else dead; the common voice is, that they be dead.

Hopton and Hastyngs be with the Earl of March and were not at the Field [of Wakefield].

What word, that every one have from my Lords that be here,[2] it is well done, and best for you to see, that the Country be always ready to come both footmen and horsemen, when they be sent for; for I have heard said, the farther Lords [3] will be here sooner

[1] Lest. [2] Warwick and the Yorkists.

[3] Edward, son of the late Duke of York, and other Yorkists then in Wales.

than men ween, I have heard said, ere three weeks to an end; and also that ye should come with more men, and cleanlier arrayed than any other man of your Country should; for it lie the more upon your worship, and toucheth you more near than other men of your country, and also ye be more had in favour with my Lords here. In this Country every man is well willing to go with my Lords here, and I hope God shall help them, for the People in the North rob, and steal, and be appointed to pill [1] all this country, and give away mens Goods and Livelyhoods, in all the South Country, and that will ask a mischief. My Lords, that be here, have as much as they may do to keep down all this Country, more than four or five shires,[2] for they would be up on the men in the North, for it is for the weal of all the South. I pray you recommend me to my Mother, and that I prayed her of her blessing; I pray you excuse me to her, that I write her no letter, for this was enough to do. I dare not pray you to recommend me to my Sister your wife, and the messenger I trow be so wise he can not do it. Ye must pay him for his labour, for he tarried all night in this town for this letter.

Written the 23d day of January in haste, when I was not well at ease.[3] God have [you] in his keeping.

By Clement Paston,
Your Brother

[1461]

228. FEAR OF THE QUEEN'S NORTHERN ARMY IN NORFOLK

A Letter to John Paston, Esquire, from his Wife

Please it you to weet that it is let me weet by one that oweth you good will, that there is laid await upon you in this Country, if ye come here at large, to bring you to the presence of such a Lord in the North as shall not be for your ease, but to jeopardy of your life, or great and importable loss of your goods; and he that hath

[1] Pillage.
[2] London and Home Counties.
[3] Apparently written when Queen Margaret's victorious army was marching southward after Wakefield.

taken upon him this enterprize now, was Under Sheriff to Giles Saintlowe; he hath great favour hereto by the means of the Son of William Baxter that lieth buried in the Grey Friars; and as it is reported the said Son hath given great Silver to the Lords in the North to bring the matter about, and now he and all his old fellowship put out their sins, and are right flygge [1] and merry, hoping all thing is and shall be as they will have it; also it is told me that the father of the bastard in this Country [2] said that now should this Shire be made sure for him and his heirs, and for the Baxter's heirs also, whereby I conceive they think that they have none enemy but you, etc.

Wherefore like it you to be the more wary of your guiding for your person's safe-guard, and also that ye be not too hasty to come into this Country till ye hear the world more sure. I trow the bearer of this shall tell more by mouth, as he shall be informed of the rule in this Country. God have you in his keeping. Written in haste, the second Sunday of Lent, by candle light at even.

By yours, etc.,

MARGARET PASTON

[1461]

229. BETWEEN TWO KINGS

[This letter is without either date, name, or direction lest some one of the Lancastrian party should get possession of the letter and so discover the sentiments of the Pastons respecting public affairs. F.]

I RECOMMEND me to you, and let you weet, that notwithstanding tidings come down as ye know, that people should not come up till they were sent for, but to be ready at all times; this notwithstanding, most people out of this Country [3] have taken wages, saying, they will go up to London; but they have no Captain nor Ruler assigned by the Commissioners to await upon, and so they straggle about by themselves, and by likeliness, are not like to come at London half of them; and men that come from London say, there have not passed Thetford not passing 400; and yet the

[1] Ripe. [2] Possibly John Heydon. [3] Norfolk.

Towns and the Country that have waged them shall think they be discharged [1]; and therefore if these Lords above wait after more people in this Country, by likeliness it will not be easy to get without a new Commission, and Warning, and yet it will be thought right strange, of them that have waged people, to wage any more, for every town hath waged, and sent forth, and are ready to send forth, as many as they did, when the King [2] sent for them before the field at Ludlow; and they that are not gone, be going in the same form.

Item, there was shrewd [3] rule toward in this Country, for there was a certain person forthwith after the Journey [4] at Wakefield gathered Fellowship to have murdered John Damme, as is said.

And also there is at the Castle of Rising, and in other two places made great gathering of People, and hiring of Harness, and it is well understood, they be not to the King-ward [5] but rather the contrary, and for to rob.

Wherefore my Father is in a doubt, whether he shall send my Brother up or not, for he would have his own men about him, if need were here; but notwithstanding, he will send up Dawbeney,[6] his Spear, and Bows with him; as Stapleton and Calthorp or other men of worship of this Country agree to do; wherefore demean you in doing of your Errands thereafter; and if ye shall bring any message from the [Yorkist] Lords, take writing, for Darcort's message is not verily believed, because he brought no writing.

Item, this country would fain take these false Shrews,[7] that are of an opinion contrary to the King, and his Council, if they had any authority from the King to do so.

Item, my Brother is rode to Yarmouth for to let Bribers [8] that would have robbed a Ship under colour of my Lord of Warwick, and belong nothing to them-ward.

JOHN PASTON
[*the Youngest*]

[1461]

[1] Have done their share.
[2] Henry VI?
[3] Bad.
[4] Fight.
[5] Edward IV?
[6] His agent.
[7] Disloyal intriguers.
[8] Hinder robbers.

[Three months after Wakefield, the son of Richard of York, was proclaimed King as Edward IV, and the Lancastrians were heavily defeated at Towton. From this time Henry VI remained a prisoner.]

230. NEWS OF TOWTON

To my Master John Paston in haste

PLEASE you to know and weet of such tidings, as my Lady of York hath by a Letter of Credence, under the sign manual of our Sovereign Lord King Edward; which Letter came unto our said Lady this same day Eastern Even at xj o'clock, and was seen and read by me Willm Paston.

First, Our Sovereign Lord hath won the field [1]; and upon the Monday next after Palm Sunday, he was [received] into York with great Solemnity and Processions. And the Mayor and Commons of the said City made their means to have grace by Lord Montagu, and Lord Berners,[2] which before the King's coming into the said City, desired him of grace for the said City, which granted them grace.

On the King's part is slain Lord Fitzwalter, and Lord Scroop sore hurt; John Stafford, Horne of Kent be dead, and Humphrey Stafford and William Hastyngs made Knights with others; Blount is knighted, etc.

On the [contrary] part is dead Lord Clifford, Lord Nevyle, Lord Welles, Lord Wylloughby, Anthony Lord Scales, Lord Harry, . . . the Earl of Northumberland, Andrew Trollop with many others, gentle and commons, to the number of twenty thousand.

Item, King Harry, the Queen, the Prince, Duke of Somerset, Duke of Exeter, Lord Roos be fled into Scotland, and they be chased and followed, etc. We send no ere [3] unto you because we had none certain till now; for unto this day London was as sorry City as might [be]; and because Spordams had no certain tidings, we thought ye should take them a worth [4] till more certain.

[1] Towton, March 29, 1461.

[2] John Neville, Lord Montagu; Sir John Bourchier, Lord Berners.

[3] No sooner.

[4] As you would.

Item, Thorp Waterfield is yielded as Spordams can tell you.

And Jesu speed you; we pray you that this tidings my Mother may know.

By your Brother,
W. Paston
[1461] Th. Playters

231. AFTER TOWTON

To my Master, John Paston, Esquire

Please your Mastership to weet, that I have spoken with Essex, in the matter that ye weet of, and find him by his talking well disposed. . . .

Item, as for tidings, it is noised and told for truth of men of worship, and others, that the Earl of Wiltshire is taken, Doctor Morton, and Doctor Makerell, and be brought to the King at York. Master William also spoke with a man that saw them. Item, Sir I hear of Sir John Borceter and Christopher Hanson that Harry the Sixth is in a place in Yorkshire is called Coroumber, such a name it hath, or much like.[1]

And there is Siege laid about, and divers Esquires of the Earl of Northumberland have gathered them together a five or six thousand men, to bicker with [2] the siege, that in the mean while Harry the Sixth might have been stolen away at a little Postern on the back side; at which Bicker [3] be slain four thousand men of the North. Sir Robert Ogle and Conyers [4] lyeth the siege on our side, and they it is that have done this act. Some say the Queen, Somerset, and the Prince should be there. Item, it is talked now for truth, the Earl of Northumberland is dead. Item, the Earl of Devonshire is dead justly.[5] Item, my Lord Chancellor is to York. Item, the King and the Lords come not here before Whitsuntide, as it is said.

Item, Sir, soon upon the Chief Baron's coming I shall send you

[1] Error for Kirkcudbright? [2] Interfere with. [3] Fight.
[4] The "Robin of Redesdale," who rebelled. [5] Recently.

a Letter with God's Grace, who preserve you, and have you in his blessed keeping.

Your,
THOMAS PLAYTERS

At Cockermouth was the Earl of Wiltshire taken, and these other Doctors. Item, some men talk Lord Welles, Lord Wylloughby, and Scales be on live.[1]

[1461]

232. THE WEDDING OF MARGARET OF YORK TO CHARLES, DUKE OF BURGUNDY

[The princess ordered Sir John to attend her. The Court of Charles the Bold was the most splendid in Europe.]

To my right reverend and worshipful Mother, Margaret Paston, dwelling at Caister, be this delivered in haste

RIGHT reverend and worshipful Mother, I recommend me unto you as humbly as I can think, desiring most heartily to hear of your welfare and heart's ease, which I pray God send you as hastily as any heart can think.

Please it you to weet, that at the making of this bill, my Brother, and I, and all our Fellowship, were in good hele, blessed be God.

As for the Guiding here in this country, it is as worshipful as all the world can devise, and there were never Englishmen had so good chear out of England, that ever I heard of.

As for Tidings here, but if it be of the Feast, I can none send you; saving, that my Lady Margaret [2] was married on Sunday last past [3] at a Town that is called The Damme, three miles out of Bruges, at five of the clock in the morning; and she was brought

[1] Alive.

[2] Margaret, sister of King Edward IV. Warwick was anxious that Edward IV should ally with France. The Burgundian territories under Charles the Bold extended over the whole of the Netherlands.

[3] July 3, 1468.

the same day to Bruges to her dinner; and there she was received as worshipfully as all the world could desire; as with procession with Ladies, and Lords, best beseen of any people, that ever I saw or heard of. Many Pageants were played in her way in Bruges to her welcoming, the best that ever I saw; and the same day my Lord, the Bastard,[1] took upon him to answer 24 Knights and Gentlemen within 8 days at Justs [2] of Peace; and when that they were answered, they 24 and himself should turney with other 25 the next day after, which is on Monday next coming; and they that have justed with him into this day, have been as richly beseen, and him self also, as cloth of Gold, and Silk, and Silver, and Goldsmiths work might make them; for of such Gear, and Gold, and Pearl, and Stones, they of the Duke's Court, neither Gentlemen nor Gentlewomen, they want none; for without that they have it by wishes, by my truth, I heard never of so great plenty as here is.

This day my Lord Scales [3] justed with a Lord of this country, but not with the Bastard; for they made promise at London, that none of them both should never deal with other in arms; but the Bastard was one of the Lords, that brought the Lord Scales into the field; and of misfortune an horse struck my Lord Bastard on the leg, and hath hurt him so sore, that I can think he shall be of no power to accomplish up his arms; and that is great pity, for by my truth I trow God made never a more worshipful Knight.

And as for the Duke's Court, as of Lords, Ladies and Gentlewomen, Knights, Esquires, and Gentlemen, I heard never of none like to it, save King Arthur's Court. And by my truth, I have no wit nor remembrance to write to you, half the worship that is here; but what lacketh, as it cometh to mind, I shall tell you, when I come home, which I trust to God shall not be long tofore. We depart out of Bruges homeward on Tuesday next coming, and all folk that came with my Lady of Burgoyn out of

[1] Anthony, Count de la Roche, a natural son of Duke Philip the Good, commonly called the Bastard of Burgundy. He was famous for chivalrous accomplishments.

[2] Jousts.

[3] Anthony Woodville, Lord Scales and later Earl Rivers. He was also famous for fashionable chivalry.

England, except such as shall abide here still with her, which I wot well shall be but few.

We depart the sooner, for the Duke hath word that the French King is purposed to make war upon him hastily, and that he is within four or five days journey of Bruges, and the Duke rideth, on Tuesday next coming, forward to meet with him; God give him good speed, and all his; for by my truth they are the goodliest fellowship that ever I came amongst, and best can behave them, and most like Gentlemen.

Other Tidings have we none here, but that the Duke of Somerset, and all his Bands departed well beseen out of Bruges a day before that my Lady the Duchess came thither, and they say here, that he is to Queen Margaret [1] that was, and shall no more come here again, nor be holpen by the Duke.

No more, but I beseech you of your blessing as lowly as I can, which I beseech you forget not to give me every day once; and Mother, I beseech you that ye will be good Mistress to my little man, and to see that he go to school.

I sent my Cousin Dawbeney 5*s*. by Calle's man, for to buy for him such gear as he needeth; and Mother I pray you this bill may recommend me to my Sisters both, and to the Master, my Cousin Dawbeney, Sir James,[2] Sir John Stylle, and to pray him to be good Master to little Jack, and to learn him well; and I pray you that this bill may recommend me to all your Folks, and to my Well Willers; and I pray God send you your heart's desire.

Written at Bruges the Friday next after Saint Thomas.

Your Son and Humble Servant,

J. PASTON, the Younger

[1468]

[Edward IV, resentful of control by Warwick, married Elizabeth Woodville and raised her kinsmen to rank and power. King and King-maker became bitter enemies. Following a revolt by " Robin of Redesdale," who defeated Edward IV, Warwick imprisoned the King, but could not keep him in captivity, owing to his strong supporters.]

[1] Margaret of Anjou, wife of Henry VI.

[2] Sir James Gloys, the priest.

233. EDWARD IV RETURNS TO LONDON

To Mistress Margaret Paston, be this delivered

RIGHT worshipful Mother, I commend me to you, and beseech you of your blessing and God's; thank you for your tenderness and help both to me, my brother, and Servants. . . .

The King is come to London,[1] and there came with him, and rode again [in company with] him, the Duke of Gloucester, the Duke of Suffolk, the Earl of Arundel, the Earl of Northumberland, the Earl of Essex; the Lords Harry and John of Buckingham, the Lord Dacre [W. Fiennes], the Lord Chamberlain [Hastings], the Lord Mountjoy [Blount], and many other Knights and Esquires; the Mayor of London, 22 Aldermen, in scarlet, and of the Craftsmen of the Town to the number of 200, all in blue.

The King came through Cheap, though it were out of his way, because [otherwise] he would not be seen; and he was accompanied in all people with 1000 horse, some harnessed and some not.

My Lord Archbishop [of York] came with him from York, and is at the Moor [2] and my Lord of Oxford rode to have met the King, and he is with my Lord Archbishop at the Moor; and came not to town with the King. Some say that they were yesterday three miles to the King-wards from the Moor; and that the King sent them a Messenger, that they should come when that he sent for them.

I wot not what to suppose therein.

The King himself hath good language of the Lords of Clarence, of Warwick, and of my Lords of York and of Oxford, saying, they be his best friends; but his household men have other language, so what shall hastily fall I cannot say. My Lord of Norfolk, shall be here this night. I shall send you more when I know more.

Item, if Ebysham [3] come not home with my Uncle William, that then ye send me the two French Books, that he should have written, that he may write them here.

JOHN PASTON, Knight

[1469]

[1] After his imprisonment by Warwick in 1469.
[2] His seat in Hertfordshire. [3] A transcriber of Books.

234. THE WELLES RISING [1]

To my Cousin, John Paston

THE King came to Grantham, and there tarried Thursday [March 15] all day, and there was headed Sir Thomas Dalalaunde and one John Neille a great Captain; and upon the Monday next after that at Doncaster, and there was headed Sir Robert Welles, and another great Captain; and then the King had word, that the Duke of Clarence, and the Earl of Warwick, was at Esterfield, 20 miles from Doncaster; and upon the Tuesday [March 20] at nine of the bell, the King took the field, and mustered his people; and it was said, that were never seen in England so many goodly men, and so well arrayed in a field; and my Lord [Duke of Norfolk] was worshipfully accompanied, no Lord there so well; wherefore the King gave my Lord a great thank.

And when the Duke of Clarence, and the Earl of Warwick heard that the King was coming to themward, incontinent they departed, and went to Manchester in Lancashire, hoping to have had help and succour of the Lord Stanley; but in conclusion, there they had little favour, as it was informed the King; and, so men say, they went westward, and, some men deem, to London.

And when the King heard they were departed and gone, he went to York, and came thither the Thursday next after, and there came in to him all the Gentlemen of the Shire; and, upon Our Lady Day, made Percy Earl of Northumberland, and he that was Earl afore,[2] Marquis Montagu; and so the King is purposed to come Southward, God send him good speed.

Written the 27th day of March.

FOR TRUTH

[1470]

[1] A Lancastrian rising in Lincolnshire, headed by Sir R. Welles, in March 1470, was defeated by Edward IV. The King turned on Warwick, who fled to France.

[2] John Neville, Earl of Northumberland, brother to the Earl of Warwick; apparently even at this time the King dared not punish him. The restoration of Percy offended the new Marquis, who lost by it.

235. WARWICK AND CLARENCE PREPARE TO INVADE ENGLAND

To J. Paston, etc.

BROTHER, I commend me to you, etc.

As for tidings, my Lord Archbishop [of York] is at the Moor, but there is beleft with him diverse of the King's servants; and, as I understand, he hath licence to tarry there till he be sent for. There be many Folks up in the North, so that Percy [1] is not able to resist them; and so the King hath sent for his Feodmen [2] to come to him, for he will go to put them down; and some say, that the King should come again to London, and that in haste; and as it is said, Courtneys be landed in Devonshire, and there rule.

Item, that the Lords Clarence and Warwick will assay to land in England every day, as Folks fear.[3]

I pray you let not John Mylsent be long from me, with as much [money] as can be gathered; and also that ye write to me of all things that I have written to you for, so that I may have answer of every thing.

Other things Batchelor Walter, bearer hereof shall inform you. Written at London, the Sunday next before Saint Lawrence's day.[4]

Also my brother Edmund is not yet remembered; he hath not to live with, think on him, etc.

JOHN PASTON, Knight

[1470]

[1] The restored Earl of Northumberland.

[2] Retainers.

[3] Warwick was welcomed by Louis XI of France, who reconciled him to Margaret of Anjou, herself a refugee there. Louis equipped a small force, which he sent to England under Warwick's leadership.

[4] August 10.

236. PROCLAMATION BY EDWARD IV

To our well-beloved William Swan, Gentleman

Rex Edwardus. By the King

TRUSTY and well beloved we greet you well, and for so much as we be credibly ascertained that our ancient enemies of France and our outward rebels and traitors be drawn together in accord, and intend hastily to land in our country of Kent, or in the parts thereof near adjoining, with great might and power of Frenchmen utterly to destroy us and our true Subjects, and to subvert the common weal of the same our Realm.

We straitly charge and command you, upon the faith and liegeance that ye bear unto us, that ye a-ready you with all the fellowship ye can make, and as soon as ye may understand that they land in our said county or nearby, that ye draw thither, as we have commanded other our Subjects to do, and put you in uttermost devoir with them to resist the malice of our said enemies and traitors; and if they and ye be not of power so to do, that then ye draw you to our city of London, by which time we trust to be there in our own person or nearby; and if we be not that, that then ye do farther all ye shall be commanded by our Council there, upon the pain above said.

Given under our Signet, at our City of York, the 7th day of September.

[1470]

[Warwick marched on London while Edward IV was in the North. He brought the unhappy Henry VI from his prison in the Tower, and placed him again on the throne. Edward IV fled to Flanders to his brother-in-law, Charles the Bold.]

237. HENRY VI RESTORED

To my right worshipful Mother, Margaret Paston, be this delivered

AFTER humble and most due recommendation, as lowly as I can, I beseech you of your blessing. Please it you to weet, that, blessed be God, my Brother and I be in good hele; and I trust that we shall do right well in all our matters hastily; for my Lady of Norfolk hath promised to be ruled by my Lord of Oxford [1] in all such matters as belong to my brother and to me; and as for my Lord of Oxford, he is better Lord to me, by my truth, than I can wish him in many matters; for he sent to my Lady of Norfolk by John Bernard only for my matter, and for none other cause, mine unweeting, or without any prayer of me, for when he sent to her I was at London, and he at Colchester, and that is a likelihood he remembered me.

The Duke and the Duchess sue to him as humbly as ever I did to them; insomuch that my Lord of Oxford shall have the rule of them and theirs, by their own desires and great means.

As for the Offices, that ye wrote to my brother for and to me, they be for no poor men; but I trust we shall speed of other offices meetly for us. For my Master the Earl of Oxford biddeth me ask and have. I trow my brother Sir John shall have the Constableship of Norwich Castle, with 20*l.* of Fee, all the Lords be agreed to it.

Tidings, the Earl of Worcester [2] is like to die this day, or to morrow at the farthest; John Pilkington, M. W. at Clyff, and Fowler are taken, and in the Castle of Pomfret, and are like to die hastily, without they be dead. Sir Thomas Montgomery and Joudone be taken, what shall fall of them I cannot say.

[1] John de Vere, a staunch Lancastrian.

[2] John Tiptoft, Lord Treasurer and Lord Constable, absconded on the departure of his Royal Master, but was taken in Weybridge Forest, in Huntingdonshire, concealed in a tree; and being brought to the Tower was there beheaded upon a charge of cruelty. [F.] As Constable he condemned men not according to English Law, and earned the title of "The Butcher of England."

The Queen that was,[1] and the Duchess of Bedford [2] be in Sanctuary at Westminster; the Bishop of Ely with other Bishops are in Saint Martin's; when I hear more, I shall send you more; I pray God send you all your desires. Written at London on Saint Edward's even.

Your Son and humble Servant,
J. PASTON

[1471]

[In March 1471 Edward IV returned to England with forces supplied by Charles the Bold. A landing at Cromer was avoided, owing to the vigilance of the Earl of Oxford and his preparations for defence, so the King steered northward and landed at Ravenspur to fight the triumphant Barnet-Tewkesbury campaign, which firmly re-established his throne and his grip on England.]

238. EARL OF OXFORD OPPOSES THE LANDING OF EDWARD IV

To my right dear and well beloved Brother, Thomas Veer

RIGHT dear and well beloved Brother, I commend me heartily unto you; certifying you that I have received your writing, directed now last unto me, by my servant William Cooke, by which I understand the faithful guiding and disposition of the Country to my great Comfort and Pleasure; which I doubt not shall redound to the greatest praising and worship that ever did till any Country. . . . I have disposed me with all the power that I can make in Essex and Suffolk, Cambridgeshire and other places, to be on Monday next coming at Bury, which purpose I intend to observe with God's Grace towards you into Norfolk, to the assistance of you and the Country, in case Edward with his Company had arrived there, and yet I shall do the same notwithstanding; for if he arrive Northward, like as ye weet by likelyhood he should, I cast [3] to follow and pursue him, and where[as] ye desire that I should send you word what disposition shall be taken in the Coun-

[1] Elizabeth Woodville, Queen of Edward IV.
[2] Mother of Elizabeth Woodville.
[3] Intend.

try where ye be, I desire you, that ye, by the advice of the Gentlemen which be there, chuse three or four and send them to me at Bury on Monday next; and then I and they, with my Council, shall take a direction for the surety of all that Country by God's grace; by whom I shall send then to you relation, whether ye shall remain still there yourself, or resort to me with all those that be accompanied with you, and Jesu preserve you. At Hedingham the 14th day of March.

By your loving Brother,

OXYNFORD [1]

[1471]

239. CLARENCE DESERTS WARWICK FOR EDWARD IV

To the right worshipful and special Singular Master, Sir John Paston, knight, be this delivered

AFTER due recommendation had, with all my service, etc. [*Here follow Copies of Indictments and Appeals procured against Sir John Paston, and his Servants;—and likewise other Law business.*]

As for tidings, here in this Country be many Tales, and none accord with other; it is told me by the Under Sheriff, that my Lord of Clarence is gone to his Brother late King; insomuch that his men have the Gorget [2] on their breasts, and the Rose over it. And it is said, that the Lord Howard hath proclaimed King Edward King of England in Suffolk.

Yours, and at your Commandment,

JAMES GRESHAM

[1471]

[In March 1471 Edward IV advanced from Ravenspur, on the Humber, towards London, without opposition. He was welcomed by the citizens, and marched out to meet Warwick. He was completely victorious at the battle of Barnet, the King-maker himself being among the killed.]

[1] John de Vere, Lancastrian, joined Warwick in 1470.

[2] A gorget—plate-armour for the neck—appears as a badge of Edward IV, who also gave collars to his supporters.

240. AFTER THE BATTLE OF BARNET

To my Mother

[John the Youngest fought under the Earl of Oxford on the Lancastrian and Warwick's side.]

MOTHER, I recommend me to you, letting you weet, that, blessed be God, my brother John is alive and fareth well, and in no peril of death; nevertheless he is hurt with an Arrow on his right arm, beneath the elbow; and I have sent him a Surgeon, which hath dressed him, and he telleth me, that he trusteth that he shall be all whole within right short time.

It is so that John Milsent is dead, God have mercy on his Soul! and William Milsent is alive, and his other Servants all be escaped by all likelihood.

Item, as for me, I am in good case blessed be God; and in no jeopardy of my life, as me list myself; for I am at my liberty if need be.

Item, my Lord Archbishop [1] is in the Tower; nevertheless I trust to God, that he shall do well enough; he hath a Safeguard for him and me both; nevertheless we have been troubled since, but now I understand, that he hath a Pardon; and so we hope well.

There was killed upon the Field, half a mile from Barnet, on Easter day, the Earl of Warwick, the Marquis Montagu, Sir William Tyrell, Sir Lewis Johns, and divers other Esquires of our Country, Godmerston and Booth.

And on the King Edward's party, the Lord Cromwell [Bourchier], the Lord Say [R. Fiennes], Sir Humphrey Bourchier of our Country, which is a sore mourned man here; and other people of both Parties to the number of more than a thousand.

As for other tidings, [it] is understood here, that the Queen Margaret is verily landed and her Son, in the West Country, and I trow that as to-morrow or else the next day, the King

[1] George Neville, Archbishop of York.

Edward will depart from hence to her-ward, to drive her out again.[1]

Item, I beseech you that I may be recommended to my Cousin Lomner, and to thank him for his good will to me-ward, if I had had need, as I understood by the Bearer hereof; and I beseech you on my behalf to advise him to be well ware of his dealing or language as yet, for the world, I assure you, is right queasy [2] as she shall know within this month; the People here feareth it sore.

God hath shewed himself marvellously like him that made all, and can undo again when him list; and I can think that by all likelihood shall shew himself as marvellous again, and that in short time; and, as I suppose, oftener than once in cases like.

Item, it is so, that my Brother is unpurveyed [3] of money, I have holpen him to my power and above; wherefore, as it pleaseth you, remember him, for [I] cannot purvey for myself in the same case.

Written at London the Thursday in Easter week.

I hope hastily to see you. All this bill must be secret. Be ye not adoubted [4] of the world, I trust all shall be well; if it thus continue, I am not all undone, nor none of us; and if otherwise then, etc. etc.

[*No signature*]

[1471]

241. BEFORE TEWKESBURY. EARL OF OXFORD TO HIS COUNTESS

To the right reverend and worshipful Lady

RIGHT reverend and worshipful Lady, I recommend me to you, letting you weet that I am in great heaviness at the making of this Letter; but thanked be God, I am escaped myself,[5] and

[1] Queen Margaret landed at Weymouth, on the day of Warwick's defeat. She recruited in the South West and made for Wales. She was overtaken by Edward IV, her army routed at Tewkesbury on May 4, 1471, her son killed or put to death, and she herself taken prisoner. From now until his death in 1483 Edward IV's position was unassailable.

[2] Unsettled.

[3] Not provided.

[4] Suspicious.

[5] From Barnet.

suddenly departed from my men; for I understand my Chaplain would have betrayed me; and if he come into the Country, let him be made sure, etc.

Also ye shall give credence to the Bringer of this letter, and I beseech you to reward him to his costs; for I was not in power at the making of this letter to give him, but as I was put in trust by favour of strange people, etc.

Also ye shall send me in all haste all the ready money that ye can make; and as many of my men, as then come well horsed, and that they come in diverse parcels.

Also that my best horses be sent with my steel saddles, and bid the Yeoman of the horse cover them with leather.

Also ye shall send to my Mother, and let her weet of this letter, and pray her of her blessing, and bid her send me my Casket, by this token; *that she hath the Key thereof, but it is broken.*

Also ye shall send to the Prior of Thetford, and bid him send me the Sum of Gold that he said that I should have; also say to him by this token; *that I shewed him the first Privy Seal, etc.*

Also let Paston, Felbrig, and Brews, come to me.

Also ye shall deliver the bringer of this letter an horse, saddle, and bridle.

Also ye shall be of good cheer, and take no thought, for I shall bring my purpose about now by the grace of God, Who have you in keeping.

O——D

[1471]

242. JOHN THE YOUNGEST BEFORE TEWKESBURY

A Letter of John Paston, Esq., to his Mother

AFTER humble and most due recommendation, in as humble wise as I can, I beseech you of your blessing, praying God to reward you with as much pleasure and heart's ease as I have lateward caused you to have trouble and thought; and, with God's grace, it shall not be long-to or-than [1] my wrongs and other

[1] Before.

men's shall be redressed, for the world was never so like to be ours as it is now; wherefore I pray you let Lumnor not be too busy as yet [in procuring pardons from Edward IV].

Mother, I beseech you, and ye may spare any money, that ye will do your alms on me and send me some in as hasty wise as is possible; for by my truth my leechcraft [1] and physic and rewards to them that have kept me and conducted me to London hath cost me since Easter day more than five pounds, and now I have neither meat, drink, clothes, leechcraft, nor money but upon borrowing; and I have assayed my friends so far, that they begin to fail now in my greatest need that ever I was in. Also, mother, I beseech you, and my horse that was at leechcraft at the Holt be not taken up for the King's hawks,[2] that he may be had home and kept in your place, and not to go out to water, nor no whither else, but that the gate be shut, and he to be chased after water within the place, and that he have as much meat as he may eat; I have hay enough of mine own, and as for oats, Dollys will purvey for him, or who that doth it, I will pay; and I beseech you that he have every week three bushels of oats, and every day a pennyworth of bread; and if Botonor be not at Norwich, and Sym keep him, I shall give him well for his labour.

Also that Philip Loveday put the other horse to grass there, as he and I were accorded.

Item, that Botoner send me hither the two shirts that were in my casket, and that he send me hither forty shillings by the next messenger that cometh to London.

Item, that Mistress Broom send me hither three long gowns, and two doublets, and a jacket of plunket [3] camblet,[4] and a murrey [5] bonnet, out of my coffer. Sir James [Gloys] hath the key, as I sent her word before this.

Item, that such other writings and stuff as was in my casket, be in your keeping, and that nobody look [over] my writings.

Item, that the horse that Purdy hath of mine, be put to some good grass in haste; and if it please you to have knowledge of our royal person, I thank God I am whole of my sickness, and trust

[1] Medical attention. He was recovering from a wound received at Barnet.
[2] *I.e.*, as dead flesh.
[3] Blue.
[4] A rich cloth.
[5] Mulberry, dark red.

to be clean whole of all my hurts within a sev'night at the farthest, by which time I trust to have other tidings; and those tidings once had, I trust not to be long out of Norfolk, with God's grace, whom I beseech preserve you and yours for my part. Written the last day of April.

The Bearer hereof can tell you tidings, such as be true for very certain. Your humblest Servant,

JOHN OF GELSTON [1]

[1471]

243. AFTER TEWKESBURY. JOHN GETS A PARDON FROM EDWARD IV

To my Most Worshipful Mother, Margaret Paston, be this delivered in haste

RIGHT Worshipful Mother, I recommend me to you, and as lowly as I can, I beseech you of your blessing. Please you to understand that this Wednesday Sir Thomas Wingfield sent to me, and let me weet that the King had signed my bill of pardon, which the said Sir Thomas delivered me; and so by Friday, at the farthest, I trust to have my pardon ensealed by the Chancellor, and soon after, so as I can furnish me, I trust to see you, if so be that any of the King's house come into Norwich.

I would fain my grey horse were kept in mew,[2] for gnats. Also, Mother, I beseech you that Dollys and his fellow may be sent to, that I may have my money, ready against that I come home, which is due to be paid, for this matter hath cost me [much] the setting on. Also that it may please you that Purdy at Hellesdon may be sent to for the horse that he hath of mine, and that the horse may be kept well, and have as much meat as he will eat betwixt this and [the time] that I come home; and that Jack's nag have meat enough also. Also and Sir Thomas Wingfield come to

[1] Gerlyston, Gelderstone, or Gelston had been the home of Margaret Paston's mother and her second husband, R. Garneys. Probably on her death it had become John's property. [Gr.]

[2] Shut up.

Norwich, that he may have as good cheer as it please you to make unto that man, that I am most beholden to for his great kindness and good-will; for he taketh full my part against my greatest enemies, Brandon [1] and his brother William; for at my first coming to Sir Thomas Wingfield, both William Wingfield and William Brandon the younger were with Sir Thomas, and had great words to mine own mouth, and in chief William Wingfield; and wheresoever he may meet me on even ground, he will do much, but and we meet evenly, no fears, so I have your blessing.

I pray you, without it be to my Lady Calthorpe, let there be but few words of this pardon. No more, but I pray God preserve you and yours. Written the Wednesday before Mary Magdalen.[2] By your humblest Son,

JOHN PASTON

[1471]

244. ADVICE FROM SIR JOHN

To Mrs Margaret Paston, or to John Paston, Esquire, her Son, in haste

RIGHT well beloved Brother, I commend me to you, letting you weet, that I am in welfare I thank God, and have been ever since that I spake last with you; and marvel sore, that ye sent never writing to me since ye departed; I heard never since that time any word out of Norfolk; ye might at Bartholomew fair [3] have had Messengers enough to London, and if ye had sent to Wykes, he should have conveyed it to me. I heard yesterday, that a Worsted man of Norfolk, that sold Worsteds at Winchester, said, that my Lord of Norfolk and my Lady were on Pilgrimage at Our Lady [of Walsingham] on foot, and so they went to Caister; and that at Norwich one should have had large language to you, and called you Traitor, and picked many quarrels to you; send me word thereof; it were well done, that ye were a little surer of

[1] William Brandon, the younger, nephew of the Wingfields, was standard-bearer to Henry VII at Bosworth, where he fell. For Edward IV's slight to the elder Brandon see Letter 153.

[2] July 22.

[3] The famous fair in Smithfield.

your pardon than ye be, avise you,[1] I deem ye will hereafter else repent you.

I understand that Bastard Fauconbridge [2] is either headed, or like to be, and his brother both; some men say he would have deserved it, and some say nay.

I purpose to be at London the first day of the term, send me word whether ye shall be there or not.

Item, I would weet whether ye have spoken with my Lady of Norfolk, or not, and of her disposition and the household's to me and to you-wards, and whether it be a possible [thing] to have Caister again and their Good Wills, or not.

And also I pray you understand what Fellowship and Guiding is in Caister; and have a Spy resorting in and out, so may ye know the secrets amongst them.

There is much ado in the North, as men say; I pray you beware of your Guiding, and in chief of your language, so that from henceforth, by your language no man perceive, that ye favour any person contrary to the King's pleasure.

I pray you recommend me to my Mother, and beseech her of her blessing on my behalf.

Item, I pray you send me word, if any of our Friends or Well-willers be dead, for I fear that there is great death in Norwich, and in other Borough Towns in Norfolk; for I ensure you, it is the most universal Death that ever I wist in England; for by my truth, I cannot hear by Pilgrims that pass the country, nor none other man that rideth or goeth any country, that any Borough Town in England is free from that Sickness; God cease it, when it please him.

Wherefore for God's sake, let my Mother take heed to my young Brethren, that they be not in none place where that Sickness is reigning, nor that they disport not with none other young people, which resorteth where any sickness is; and if there be any of that sickness dead or infect in Norwich, for God's sake, let her send them to some friend of hers into the country, and do ye

[1] Take care; consider.

[2] Thomas Neville, natural son of Lord Falconbridge. He led a raid on London against Edward IV, surrendered, and was pardoned, but he was beheaded in 1471 when Edward felt secure.

the same by mine advice; let my Mother rather remove her household into the country.

I had almost spoken with Mrs Anne Hault, but I did not, nevertheless this next term I hope to take one way with her or other; she is agreed to speak with me, and she hopeth to do me ease, as she saith.[1]

I pray you send me word how ye do with my Lady Elizabeth Bourchier, ye have a little chafed it, but I cannot tell how; send me word whether ye be in better hope or worse.

I hear say that the Earl of Oxford's Brethren be gone out of Sanctuary. Sir Thomas Fulford is gone out of Sanctuary, and a great Fellowship fetched him, a three score, and they say, that within five miles of London he was 200 men, and no man weeteth where he is become, not yet. The Lords Hastings and Howard be in Calais, and have it peaceably; and Sir Walter Wrottesly and Sir Jeffrey Gate be coming thence, and will be at London this day as it is said.

Written at Waltham beside Winchester the day next Holy Rood day.[2]

JOHN PASTON, Knight

[1471]

245. SIR JOHN'S OPTIMISM

To my most honourable and Tender Mother Margaret Paston, be this Letter delivered

MOST Worshipful and kind Mother, I commend me to you, and beseech you of your daily blessing and remembrance. Please it you to weet, that I have my Pardon,[3] as the Bearer hereof can inform you, for comfort whereof I have been the merrier this Christmas; and have been part thereof with Sir George Browne,[4] and with my Lady mine Aunt his wife; and before Twelfth I came to my Lord Archbishop [of York], where I have had as

[1] For Anne Haute see Letter 42.
[2] September 14.
[3] Granted in December 1471.
[4] Second husband of Elizabeth Paston (formerly wife of R. Poynings). He resided at Betchworth Castle, Surrey.

great Cheer, and been as welcome as I can desire; and if I had been in surety that Caister were had again, I would have come home this day.

[*Here follow directions about Caister, and a hope that it might be had again by the latter end of the term, when he would come home, and put his lands and houses into order.*] And I beseech you to remember my Brother to do his devoir that I may have again my stuff, my books, and vestments, and my Bedding howsoever he do, though I should give 20ty Scutas [1] by his advice to my Lady Brandon, or some other good Fellow.

As for any tidings there be none here, save that the King hath kept a royal Christmas; and now they say, that hastily he will North, and some say, that he will into Wales, and some say, that he will into the West Country. As for Queen Margaret, I understand that she is removed from Windsor to Wallingford, nigh to Ewelm, my Lady of Suffolk's Place in Oxfordshire.[2]

And men say, that the Lord Rivers shipped on Christmas Even into Portugal ward; I am not certain.

Also there shall be a Convocation of the Clergy in all haste, which men deem, will avail the King [3] a Dime [4] and an half, some say. I beseech God send you good health and greater joy in one year than ye have had these seven. Written at the Moor the 8th day of January, in the 11th of Edward IV.

By your Son,

JOHN PASTON, Knight

[1472]

246. CLARENCE AND GLOUCESTER

To John Paston, Esquire, be this Letter delivered

BROTHER, I commend me to you, and pray you to look up my *Temple of Glass*,[5] and send it me by the Bearer hereof.

Item, as for tidings, I have spoken with Mrs Anne Hault, at a

[1] Crowns (three and a half to the pound).

[2] She remained a prisoner till 1475, when Louis XI paid her ransom of fifty thousand crowns.

[3] Pay him a tax of. [4] Tenth (*dixième*). [5] A poem by Lydgate.

pretty leisure, and blessed be God, we be as far forth as we were tofore, and so I hope we shall continue; and I promised her, that at the next leisure, that I could find thereto, that I would come again and see her; which will take a leisure as [I] deem now, since this observance is over done; I purpose not to tempt God no more so.

Yesterday the King, the Queen, my Lords of Clarence, and Gloucester, went to Shene to pardon; men say, not all in charity; what will fall, men cannot say.

The King entreateth my Lord of Clarence for my Lord of Gloucester; and as it is said, he answereth, that he may well have my Lady his Sister in Law, but they shall part no livelode as he saith, so what will fall can I not say.[1]

This day I purpose to see my Lady of Norfolk again, in good hour be it!

There is proffered me Merchants for Sporle wood, God send me good Sale, when I begin; that poor Wood is sore menaced and threat.

Yet wot I not whether I come home before Easter or not, I shall send you word; no more, etc.

Written the first Tuesday of Lent.

JOHN PASTON, Knight

[1472]

247. THE DEFEAT OF CHARLES THE BOLD AT GRANSON [2]

To Mrs Margaret Paston, at Norwich, to her son John Paston, Esquire, and to each of them

I RECOMMEND me to you, like it you to weet, that I am not certain yet whether my Lord [Hastings] and I shall come into England

[1] Clarence, having married a daughter of Warwick, intended to keep the entire inheritance and is said to have made Anne, Prince Edward's widow, hide in disguise in a mean street in London. His brother, Gloucester, marrying her, was entitled to half Warwick's estates, but obtained the whole on Clarence's disgrace and death. [Gr.]

[2] The powerful kingdom of Charles of Burgundy (brother-in-law of Edward IV), served to maintain a balance of power in France. His

the week before Easter, or else the week after Easter; wherefore Mother, I beseech you to take no displeasure with me for my long tarrying, for I must do none otherwise for displeasing of my Lord.

I was nothing glad of this journey, if I might goodly have chosen; nevertheless saving that ye have cause to be displeased with me for the matter of Koketts, I am else right glad, for I hope that I am far more in favour with my Lord than I was tofore.

Item, I send you, Brother John, a Letter herewith, which was brought hither to Calais, from the George at Paul's Wharf; I deem it cometh from my brother Walter.

Item, if ye intend hitherwards, it were well done that ye hied you, for I suppose that my Lord will take the view of all his Retinue here, now before his departing; and I think that he would be better content with your coming now, than another time; do as ye think best, and as ye may.

Item, where[as] Master Fytzwalter made me to write to you to advise you to tarry, I remit that to your discretion.

As for tidings here, we hear from all the world, first, the Lord Rivers was at Rome right well and honourably, and other Lords of England, as the Lord Ormond, the Lord Scrope, and at their departing twelve miles on this half Rome, the Lord Rivers was robbed of all his Jewels and Plate, which was worth 1000 Marks or better, and is returned to Rome for a Remedy.

Item, the Duke of Burgundy hath conquered Lorrain and Queen Margaret [1] shall not now by likelihood have it; wherefore the French King cherisheth her but easily [2]; but after this conquest of Lorrain, the Duke took great courage to go upon the Land of the Swiss to conquer them, but they bearded [3] him at an onset place, and hath distressed him, and hath slain the most part of his Vanward, and won all his Ordnance and Artillery,

victorious career was checked in an expedition against the Swiss in 1476–77, and in the last of three battles he was killed at Nancy. The decline of Burgundy increased the power of the King of France, and so endangered the English possession of Calais.

[1] Margaret, widow of Henry VI. The preoccupation of the French King now enabled him to give less support to Margaret's interests.

[2] Neglectfully. [3] Faced.

and moreover all Stuff that he had in his Host; except men and horse that fled not, but they rode that night twenty miles; and so the rich Salets, Helmets, Garters, Nowches [1] gilt, and all, is gone, with Tents, Pavillions and all, and so men deem his pride is abated; men told him, that they were froward Carles,[2] but he would not believe it, and yet men say, that he will to them again, God speed them both.

Item, Sir John Myddleton took leave of the Duke to sport him, but he is set in prison at Brussels.

I pray you send me some word, if ye think likely that I may enter Caister when I will, by the next Messenger.

Written at Calais, in reasonable health of body and soul, I thank God, the 21st day of March, in the sixteenth year of Edward IV.

John Paston, Knight

[1476]

248. THE DEATH OF CHARLES THE BOLD

To John Paston, Esquire, at Norwich, in haste

I recommend me to you, letting you weet, that yesterday began the great Council,[3] to which all the Estates of the Land shall come to, but if [4] it be for great and reasonable excuses; and I suppose the chief cause of this Assembly is, to commune what is best to do, now upon the great change by the Death of the Duke of Burgundy, and for the keeping of Calais, and the Marches, and for the preservation of the Amities taken lately, as well with France as now with the Members of Flanders; whereto I doubt not there shall be in all haste both the Dukes of Clarence, and Gloucester, whereof I would that my brother Edmund wist. . . .

It is so that this day I hear great likelihood, that my Lord Hastyngs shall hastily go to Calais with great Company; if I think it be for you to be one, I shall not forget you.

[1] Clasps. [2] Enterprising men.

[3] In February 1477 the King convoked a great council to consider the effects of the death of Charles the Bold.

[4] Unless.

Item, this day the matter between Mrs Anne Haulte and me hath been sore broken both to the Cardinal [Bourchier], to my Lord Chamberlain, and to myself, and I am in good hope; when I hear and know more, I shall send you word.

It seemeth that the World is all quavering, it will reboil somewhere, so that I deem young men shall be cherished, take your heart to you, I fear that I cannot be excused, but that I shall forth with my Lord Hastings over the Sea, but I shall send you word in haste, and if I go, I hope not to tarry long. . . .

I shall hastily send you word of more things.

Written at London, the 14th day of February, in the 16th year of Edward IV the Friday afore Fastingong.[1]

JOHN PASTON, Knight

[1477]

249. NEWS FROM FRANCE

Unto the Right Worshipful Sir John Paston, Knight

MASTER Paston, after all due recommendation, and hearty desire to hear of your good Hele, please it you to weet. . . . As for tidings in these parts, the French King [2] lieth at siege at St Omers, on the one side of the Town a mile off, but he hath no great Ordnance there; and they of the town skirmish with them every day, and keep a passage half a mile about the town; and the French King hath brenned [3] all the Towns, and fair Abbeys, that were that way about St Omers, and also the Corns which are there.

And also, as it is said for certain, the French King hath brenned Cassell, that is my old Lady of Burgundy's Jointure,[4] and all the Country thereabout, whereby she hath lost a great part of her livelihood; and that is a shrewd [5] token that he meaneth well to the King our Sovereign Lord, when he intendeth to destroy her.

Moreover Sir Philip de Crevecœur hath taken them that were

[1] Lent.
[2] Louis seized many possessions of Burgundy on the death of Charles.
[3] Burned.
[4] Margaret, sister of Edward IV, widow of Charles of Burgundy.
[5] Evil.

in Fynes within this four days to the number of 14 persons, and the remanent were fled, and he had them to the French King, and he hath brent all the place, and pulled down the Tower, and a part of the wall, and destroyed it.

And as it is said, if the French King cannot get St Omers, that he intendeth to bring his Army through these Marches into Flanders, wherefore my Lord hath do broken [1] all the passages, except Newham Bridge, which is watched and the Turnpike shut every night.

And the said French King within these three days railed greatly of my Lord to Tyger Poursuivant,[2] openly before two hundred of his Folks; wherefore it is thought here, that he would feign a quarrel to set upon this town, if he might get advantage.

And as I understand, the Emperor's Son is married at Ghent as this day; and there came with him but four Hundred Horse, and I can hear of no more that be coming in certain; and in money he brought with him an hundred thousand Ducats,[3] which is but a small thing in regard for that he hath to do; wherefore I fear me sore, that Flanders will be lost; and if St Omers be won, all is gone in my conceit; nevertheless they say there should come great power after the Emperor's Son,[4] but I believe it not, because they have been so long of coming.

At Calais, the Sunday next after the Assumption.

Your,

EDMUND BEDYNGFELD

[1477]

[Edward IV died in April 1483, followed by the brief, three months' reign of his son, Edward V, who, with his brother Richard of York, was murdered in the Tower by the orders of their uncle, Richard, Duke of Gloucester, who had been made Protector during the minority of the King. Gloucester was now crowned King as Richard III.]

[1] Caused to be broken. [2] A herald.

[3] The gold ducat was worth ten shillings, the silver, five shillings.

[4] Maximilian, son of the Emperor Frederick III, married Mary, daughter and heir of Charles the Bold, Duke of Burgundy, the richest heiress of her time.

250. THE ACCESSION OF RICHARD III PROVOKES INSURRECTIONS

To my right well beloved Friend John Paston, be this delivered in haste

RIGHT well beloved Friend, I commend me to you. It is so that the Kentishmen be up in the Weald, and say that they will come and rob the City, which I shall let [1] if I may.

Therefore I pray you, that, with all diligence, ye make you ready and come hither, and bring with you six tall fellows in harness; and ye shall not lose your labour, that knoweth God, who have you in his keeping.

Written at London, the 10th day of October.

Your Friend,

J. NORFOLK [2]

[1483]

251. PROCLAMATION OF RICHARD III AGAINST HENRY TUDOR [3]

RICHARD R.

Richard, etc. wisheth health, we command you, etc.

FORASMUCH as the King, our Sovereign Lord hath certain knowledge that Piers (Courtney), Bishop of Exeter, Jasper Tydder,[4] Son of Owen Tydder, calling himself Earl of Pembroke, John, late Earl of Oxford, and Sir Edward Wodevile, with others diverse, his Rebels and Traytors, disabled and attainted by the authority of the High Court of Parliament, of whom many be known for open Murderers, Advowterers,[5] and Extortioners,

[1] Prevent.

[2] John, Lord Howard, Duke of Norfolk. He was slain at Bosworth in 1485.

[3] Henry Tudor, Earl of Richmond, claimed the throne as representing the Lancastrians, through the Beauforts, descendants of John of Gaunt, father of Henry IV.

[4] Tudor.

[5] Adulterers.

contrary to the pleasure of God, and against all truth, honour and nature, have forsaken their natural country, taking them first to be under the obeysance of the Duke of Bretagne, and to him promised certain things, which by him and his Council, were thought things too greatly unnatural and abominable, for them to grant, observe, keep, and perform, and therefore the same utterly refused.

The said Traitors seeing the said Duke and his Council would not aid nor succour them nor follow their ways, privily departed out of his Country into France, and there taking them to be under the obeysance of the King's ancient Enemy, Charles, calling himself King of France, and to abuse and blind the Commons of this said Realm, the said Rebels and Traytors have chosen to be their Captain one Henry Tydder, Son of Edmund Tydder, son of Owen Tydder, which of his ambitious and insatiable covetise encroacheth and usurpeth upon him, the name and title of Royal Estate of this realm of England; whereunto he hath no manner of interest, right, title or colour, as every man well knoweth; for he is descended of bastard blood, both of father's side, and of mother's side; for the said Owen the Grandfather, was bastard born; and his mother was daughter unto John, Duke of Somerset, son unto John, Earl of Somerset, son unto Dame Catherine Swynford, and of their indubitable Avoutry [1] gotten; whereby it evidently appeareth, that no title can nor may in him, which fully intendeth to enter this realm, proposing a conquest, and if he should atchieve his false intent and purpose, every man's life, livelihood, and goods, shall be in his hands, liberty, and disposition; whereby should ensue the disheriting and destruction of all the noble and worshipful blood of this realm for ever.

And to the resistance and withstanding whereof every true and natural Englishman born, must lay to his hands for his own surety and weel.

And to the intent that the said Henry Tydder might the rather atchieve his false intent and purpose by the aid, support, and assistance of the King's ancient enemy of France, [he] hath, covenanted and bargained with him, and all the Council of

[1] Adultery.

France, to give up and release in perpetuity all the right, title, and claim, that the King of England have had, and ought to have, to the Crown and Realm of France, together with the Duchies of Normandy, Anjou and Mayne, Gascoign and Guysnes, Cassell, and the towns of Calais, Guysnes, Hammes, with the Marches appertaining to the same, and exclude the Arms of France out of the Arms of England for ever. . . .

The King our Sovereign Lord willeth, chargeth, and commandeth, all and every of the natural and true subjects of this his Realm, to call the premises to their minds, and like good and true Englishmen to endow themselves with all their powers for the defence of them, their wives, children, and goods, and hereditaments, against the said malicious purposes and conspirations, which the said ancient, enemies have made with the King's said Rebels and Traitors, for the final destruction of this land, as is aforesaid.

And our said Sovereign Lord, as a well willed, diligent, and courageous Prince, will put his most royal person to all labour and pain necessary in this behalf, for the resistance and subduing of his said enemies, rebels, and traytors, to the most comfort, weel, and surety of all his true and faithful liege men and subjects.

And over this our said Sovereign Lord willeth and commandeth all his said Subjects, to be ready in their most defensible array, to do his Highness service of war, when they by open proclamation, or otherwise shall be commanded so to do, for resistance of the King's said Rebels, Traitors, and enemies.

Witness myself at Westminster, the 23d day of June, in the second year of our Reign.

[1485]

[Henry Tudor landed, with the Earl of Oxford, at Milford Haven. Richard III met them at Bosworth in August 1485. Richard, fighting desperately, was killed, and the throne passed to the victor, who was crowned as Henry VII.]

252. BEFORE BOSWORTH

To my well-beloved Friend John Paston, be this bill delivered in haste

WELL beloved Friend, I commend me to you, letting you to understand that the King's Enemies be a-land, and that the King would have set forth as upon Monday, but only for our Lady Day [Aug. 15]; but for certain he goeth forward as upon Tuesday, for a Servant of mine brought to me the certainty.

Wherefore I pray you, that ye meet with me at Bury [St Edmunds], for, by the Grace of God, I purpose to lie at Bury as upon Tuesday night; and that ye bring with you such Company of tall men as ye may goodly make at my cost and charge, besides that which ye have promised the King; and, I pray you, ordain them Jackets of my Livery, and I shall content you at your meeting with me.

Your Lover,

J. NORFOLK

[1485]

253. KING HENRY'S INSTRUCTIONS TO CAPTURE LORD LOVEL

To my right trusty and well beloved John Paston, Sheriff of Norfolk and Suffolk

RIGHT trusty and well beloved, I recommend me unto you; and forasmuch as I am credibly informed, that Francis, late Lord Lovell,[1] is now of late resorted into the Isle of Ely, to the intent by all likelihood, to find the ways and means to get him shipping and passage in your coasts, or else to resort again to Sanctuary, if he can or may.

[1] An adherent of Richard III, attainted in 1485 after the accession of Henry VII. He escaped and later joined the rebellion of Lambert Simnel in 1487.

I therefore heartily desire and pray you, and nevertheless, in the King's name, straitly charge you, that ye in all goodly haste endeavour your self, that such watch, or other means be used and had in the Ports, and Creeks, and other places, where ye think necessary by your discretion, to the letting of his said purpose; and that ye also use all the ways ye can or may by your wisdom, to the taking of the same late Lord Lovell; and what pleasure ye may do to the King's Grace in this matter, I am sure is not to you unknown; and God keep you.

Written at Lavenham, the 19th day of May.

MARGARET OXYNFORD

[1486]

254. LAMBERT SIMNEL'S RISING

Unto my Right Worshipful Cousin, John Paston, Esquire, for the body (to the King's Majesty, prout patet alibi per ejus literam [1])

RIGHT worshipful Cousin, I recommend me unto you as heartily as I can, letting you weet I was with my Lord Steward [J. Ratcliffe, Lord Fitzwalter], as on Monday last past, by the desire of them that I might not say nay to; I heard all that was said there, but they got none advantage, word, nor promise of me, but they thought, in as much as they were the best in the shire, that every man ought to wait and go with them; whereto it was answered, that our master,[2] next the King having his commission, must needs have the gentlemen and the country to await upon him by the vertue of the same; but it was thought I ought not to obey no copy of the commission, without I had the same under wax,[3] wherein hath been great argument, which I understood by report a fortnight past; and that caused me to send unto my Lord to have the very commission, which he sent me, and a letter, whereof I send you the copy herein closed.

[1] Literally: " as is obvious elsewhere through his letter."

[2] Earl of Oxford.

[3] *I.e.*, seal.

As for you, ye be sore taken in some place, saying that ye intend such things as is like to follow great mischief; I said I understood none such, nor things like it; and it is thought ye intend not to go forth this journey,[1] nor no gentleman in that quarter but Robert Brandon, that hath promised to go with them, as they say.

I understand Sir William Boleyn and Sir Harry Heydon were at Thetford into Kent ward, but they returned into Norfolk again; I think they will not go this journey, if the King need. Sir Harry was at Attleborough on Saturday; I ween he had advice there to turn again; wherefore, Cousin, it is good to understand the certainty what gentlemen intend to go; and be assured to go together, that I may have word; my Cousin Hopton hath promised that he will be one. As for Wiseman, he saith he will be the same, but I can have no hold. Furthermore, Cousin, it is said, that after my Lord's departing to the King ye were at Barkway, which is construed that ye had been with the Lady Lovel, but wrath said never well; and inasmuch as we understand my Lord's [Oxford's] pleasure, it is well done [that] we deal wisely thereafter. And, next to the King, I answered plainly, I was bound to do him service, and to fulfil his commandment to the utmost of my power, by the grace of God, who ever preserve you to his pleasure. Written at Oxburgh, the 16th day of May.

Your Cousin,

EDMUND BEDINGFELD [2]

[1487]

[1] Lambert Simnel, claiming to be Earl of Warwick, crossed from Ireland and led a small revolt against Henry VII in 1487. He was defeated at Stoke-on-Trent, near Newark.

[2] Bedingfield and John Paston were knighted after Stoke field.

255. THE EARL OF OXFORD SATISFIED

The Earl of Oxford [1] *to Sir Edmund Bedingfeld*

[Enclosed with last letter.]

WHEREAS I understand by your late writing unto me that ye have right well endeavoured you to the execution of the King's commission and commandment, in preparing yourself with the gentlemen, and other of the country, to be ready to do the King service, which I have showed unto the King's Highness, so that his Grace is right well content, and right thankfully accepteth the same, understanding the right good minds and disposition of you, and of other gentlemen there towards his Grace; howbeit his Highness will not as yet put you to any further labour or charge for so much as his rebels and enemies [2] be into Ireland; nevertheless his Grace will that the country be ready at all times to do his Highness service upon reasonable warning, for so much as the King's Grace intendeth to make provision to send an army into Ireland in haste, not knowing as yet whether that ye, and other about you, shall be desired to bear any charge thereto or no. And whereas it is marvelled that ye had not the King's Commission, under his Great Seal, I send it to you with this my writing, willing you not to proceed farther to any execution thereof till such time as ye have otherwise in commandment, alway thanking heartily the gentlemen, and all other, for their good wills towards me.

[1487]

[1] John de Vere, Earl of Oxford, joined Warwick in 1470, escaped from Barnet, and led another Lancastrian attempt at St Michael's Mount, Cornwall, in 1473. In 1484 he joined Henry VII, after whose accession he obtained great power. He was a patron of John Paston.

[2] Lambert Simnel.

256. ENGLISH HELP FOR BRITTANY AGAINST FRANCE

To Sir John Paston be this Letter delivered

AFTER all due recommendation, please it you to understand that my Lord [1] hath been with the King in Windsor at St George's Feast; and there at the same feast were both the Embassadors of Bretaigne and of Flanders, as well from the King of [the] Romans as from the young Duke [2]; but I cannot show you the certain whether we shall have with them war or peace; but I understand for certain that all such Captains as went to the sea in Lent, that is to say, Sir Charles Somerset, Sir Richard Hawte, and Sir William Vampage maketh them ready to go to the sea again, as shortly as they can; to what intent I cannot say.

Also, whereas it was said that my Lord Wodevile and other should have gone over into Bretaigne, to have aided the Duke of Bretaigne, I cannot tell of none such aid; but upon that saying there came many men to Southampton, where it was said that he should have taken shipping, to have waited upon him over; and so when he was countermanded, those that resorted thither, to have gone over with him, tarried there still, in hope that they should heve been licensed to have gone over; and when they saw no likelihood that they should have license, there was 200 of them that got them into a Bretaigne ship, the which was late come over with salt, and bad the master set them a land [3] in Bretaigne; and they had not sailed not past five leagues but they espied a Frenchman; and the Frenchman made over to them; and they fared as though they would not have meddled with them, and all the Englishmen went under the hatches, so that they showed no more but those that came to Southampton with the ship, to cause the Frenchmen to be the more glad to meddle with them; and so the

[1] Oxford.

[2] Philip, son of Maximilian and Mary of Burgundy, was now Duke of Burgundy (including Flanders). He and his father professed to help Brittany against Charles VIII of France. Henry VII sent troops to Brittany to oppose France.

[3] On land.

Frenchman boarded them, and then they that were under the hatches came up, and so took the Frenchmen, and carried the men, ship and all, into Bretaigne.

Also, there was there an ambassador from the King of Scots [1] who is now put in great trouble by his son, and other of the lords of his land. . . .

Written at Hedyngham, the 13th day of May, with the hand of your brother.

WILLIAM PASTON [2]

[1488]

257. THE KING'S LETTER TO THE EARL OF OXFORD

The King to my Lord of Oxenford

" RIGHT trusty and entirely beloved Cousin, we greet you well; inasmuch as it hath liked God to send us good tidings out of Bretaigne, such as we doubt not but that ye be desirous to understand; we write unto you of them, as they be come to our knowledge, and as followeth.

" The Lord Malpertuis, now late with us in ambassade from our dear Cousin the Duchess of Bretaigne, shipped at our port of Dartmouth, and arrived at St Paul de Lyon in Bretaigne, on Palm Sunday [3] at 4 in the afternoon, from whence he wrote us the disposition and the state of the country there, and of the landing and the demeaning of our army.

" We received his writing on Monday last at evensong time; and because he was of Bretaigne born, and favourable to that party, we ne gave [4] such trust to his tidings, as was thought to us surety to write to you thereupon.

" This day after high mass cometh unto us from out of Bretaigne aforesaid, and with a new ambassade from our said Cousin, Falcon one of our Pursuivants,[5] that ratifieth the news of the said Lord Malpertuis, which be these.

[1] James III.
[2] William Paston was in Oxford's household.
[3] April 12.
[4] Did not give.
[5] Heralds.

" After the garrison of Frenchmen in the town of Gyngham [1] had certainty of the landing of our army, they drew down the Fauxbourgs [2] of Gyngham, and made them meet to defend a siege; but as soon as they understood that our said army journeyed towards them, they left the same Gyngham, where our said army arrived the Thursday next before Palm Sunday, and was received with procession, lodged and received, and refreshed in the town four days; and going towards the said Duchess, they must pass to the castle and borough of Monconter; in that castle was also a garrison of Frenchmen, which incontinently, upon word that our said army drew towards them, the Frenchmen did cast down great part of the walls and fled from thence; in that castle and borough our said army kept their Easter. The castle of Chauson, adjoining near to the town of Saint Brieu was also garrisoned with Frenchmen, that castle they set on fire, and so fled. The towns of Hennebone and Vannes were garrisoned with Frenchmen, which brake down the walls of the towns, and put themselves to flight. The inhabitants about Brest have laid siege thereunto, and gotten the Base Court of the Frenchmen [3] ere the departing of our said Pursuivant. The garrison of the town of Concarnell, which is one of the greatest strengths of all Bretaigne, was besieged in like wise, and driven to that necessity, that they within offered, ere his said departing, to avoid the town with staff in hand; how that is taken, or what is more done since, we cannot tell.

" Our said Cousin, the Duchess, is in her city of Rennes; our right trusty Knight and Counsellor, Sir Richard Edgcombe, [is] there also, having chief rule about her; and the Marshal of Bretaigne a-readieth him to join with them in all haste with a good band of men. Many noblemen of that country repair to our said army to take their party.

" These premisses in substance we have by writing, as well from the chief Captains of our said army, as from our Comptroller aforesaid. And that our said army, blessed be God! hath among themselves kept such love and accord, that no manner of fray or

[1] Guingamp.

[2] Suburbs—*i.e.*, destroyed the suburbs to improve their position.

[3] The castle courtyard from the French.

debate hath been between them since the time of their departing out [of] this our realm.

"Given under our signet, at our Castle of Hertford, the 22d day of April."

Sir, this is the copy of the letter that the King sent to my Lord of Oxenford of tidings out of Bretaigne.

By your brother,
William Paston

[1489]

258. HENRY VII VISITS THE EASTERN COUNTIES

To his Brother Sir John Paston, Knight, be this Letter delivered

Sir, I recommend me unto you, letting you weet that [*here follows some Account relative to a Grant from the Crown, etc.*].

As for my Lord Treasurer he was not with the King of all the council time, the which was ended on the 3d day of March. And thither came my Lord of Northumberland, the first day of March, and departed the even afore the making of this letter; and hath endented with the King for the keeping out of the Scotts, and warring on them; and [he] shall have large money, I cannot tell the Sum for certain.

Also there is a Rover taken at Bristol, one Cowper, as I ween, and he is like to be hanged, and he confesseth more of his Fellows. Also Edward Heestowe of Dover is apeached of Treason of many strange points; and his accuser and he were both afore the King, and then they were taken apart; and he himself confessed it, that his accuser accused him of, and many other things more than he was accused of.

And he had many Lords and Gentlemen to answer for his truth, and his demeaning afore time, for as I heard say, both the King in a manner, nor none of the other Lords, nor Gentlemen, believed not his accuser, till that he confessed it himself, and so he is in the Tower, and like to be dead.

As for the King's coming into the Country, on Monday come fortnight he will lie at the Abbey of Stratford, and so to Chelmsford; then to Sir Thomas Montgomery's; then to Hedingham; then to Colchester; then to Ipswich; then to Bury; then to Dame Anne Wingfield's, and so to Norwich; and there will he be on Palm Sunday Even; and so tarry there all Easter, and then to Walsingham; wherefore ye had need to warn William Gogney and his Fellows to purvey them of wine enough, for every man beareth me on hand, that the Town shall be drunk dry, as York was when the King was there.

Sir, Master Sampson recommend him unto you, and he hath sent you a Ring by Edmond Dorman; and besides that, he required me to write unto you, that it were best for you to purvey you of some Gentlemeny Things against the King's coming, for sure he will bring you Guests enough, and therefore purvey you thereafter. Also, he sendeth you word, that it is my Lord's mind, that my Sister, with all other goodly Folks there about, should accompany with Dame Elisabeth Calthrop, because there is no great Lady there about, against the King's coming; for my Lord [1] hath made great boast of the fair and good Gentlewomen of the Country; and so the King said, he would see them sure.

Sir, my Lord hath sent unto the most part of the Gentlemen of Essex to wait upon him at Chelmsford, where, as he intendeth, to meet with the King, and that they be well appointed, that the Lancashire men may see, that there be Gentlemen of so great substance that they be able to buy all Lancashire.[2] Men think that ye among you will do the same.

Your Country is greatly boasted of, also the Inhabitors of the same. I beseech you to remember my horse that you promised me. God keep you.

Written at Sheen in haste, the 7th day of March, with the hand of your Brother.

William Paston

[1489]

[1] Oxford.

[2] Oxford's strength lay in Essex. The Stanleys of Lancashire had at one time been Yorkists and joined Henry VII only at the last moment.

259. THE EARL OF OXFORD WANTS WINE AND RETAINERS

To my right worshipful and my well-beloved Counsellor, Sir John Paston, Knight

RIGHT worshipful and right well-beloved Counsellor, I recommend me to you. And whereas I understand by your writing that a great ship is perished with you in those parts, and that ye have been greatly occupied about the saving of the goods of the same; and that the merchants thereof be disposed to put their wines to sale, of the which ye may buy a ton for one hundred shillings and little more. I may buy in this country for four pounds; wherefore if ye may buy there any better cheap, I pray you to purvey for me, such as ye seem necessary.

And forasmuch as ye may not be here with me at this time, I desire and pray you to prepare and ordain yourself with as many men in harness as ye goodly may, to do the King service in my company, at the King's charge and costs, so as ye and they may be with me at Cambridge upon Tuesday next coming; and that ye fail not hereof, as my right special trust is in you.

Written at my castle of Hedingham, this 6th day of May.

OXENFORD

[1489]

260. WARNING THAT THE EARL AND THE KING WILL NOT ACCEPT EXCUSES

To his Brother Sir John Paston

SIR, I recommend me unto you, and whereas ye desire that I should send you word of such tidings as Philip Lewes and Windsor bringeth from the court; they be come thence both, but we hear of no tidings that they bring, but that yonder folks abide still about the place whereas this unhappy deed [1] was done, and not

[1] The murder of the Earl of Northumberland by Yorkshiremen who rebelled upon the levy of the tax voted by Parliament in May 1489.

with no great number, they say not with past 5 or 600, when they were most; however they have made proclamations in the country, to meet with other of their affinity, as on Tuesday last past, as it appeareth in the copy of their proclamation hereafter following.[1]

Also they show the King intendeth to hold over his journey, and Philip Lewes is ridden again to the King, and shall bring with him money for all their wages that shall be in my Lord's retinue, as you and six of Sir William Bolein's servants and other.

Sir, Master Clopton saw your letter,[2] and a saith he knew my lord's mind such, that he durst not move him with it. There was Sir William Say, (but Clopton would not it should be known of none other but yourself); he sent my lord, by a servant of his, 40*l.* to have excused him, and it would not be taken, and that I marvel of. Howbeit he brake thus far to my lord: he asked him how many he appointed you to bring with you; and he answered him twenty; and then he showed him your charges that ye have had; my lord said he might have men enough, and their wages shall be paid for.

Clopton answered, how that it would cost you large money beside their wages to horse them and harness them; and how that, to say the truth, ye were not well at ease.

Notwithstanding all this, my lord willed that ye should come to him to Cambridge on Tuesday at night with as many as ye might, and ye and he should do well enough. So Clopton thinketh that, and ye bring a dozen with you it is sufficient; howbeit that Sir Edmund Bedingfield, Sir Thomas Tyrell,[3] and Sir Richard Lewes have been with my lord, and each of them have offered to meet with my lord at Cambridge with thirty men apiece of them; so I would not ye should be so far under them; wherefore I think best that ye purvey you so as and ye should go forth yourself, for I can perceive none otherwise. My bedfellow Cornwallis [4] is married

[1] For this proclamation see Letter 261.

[2] The excuse for not appearing at Cambridge (see Letter 259).

[3] Possibly the younger brother of Sir James Tyrell, the supposed murderer of Edward V and his brother in the Tower, but perhaps a gentleman of Essex.

[4] This was most probably William Cornwallis, Esq. The term ' bedfellow ' was often used in this age by one friend speaking of another, as persons of the highest quality in the days here spoken of frequently slept together. [F.]

in the north, and he came as yesternight strait out of the country, and he saith none otherwise, but as I have written here before in this letter.

Ye shall have for yourself and for each of your servants horsed and harnessed 20 shillings in hand at Cambridge for a month, and I trust we shall have done ere twenty days to an end, with the grace of God, who have you in keeping. At Hedyngham.

By your brother,

William Paston

[1489]

261. THE REBELS' PROCLAMATION

[Enclosure with Letter 260]

To be known to all the north parts of England, to every lord, knight, esquire, gentleman, and yeoman, that they shall be ready in their defensible array, in the east part, on Tuesday next coming, on Alderton Moor, and in the west part on Cately Moor the same day, upon pain of losing of their goods and bodies; for to gainstand such persons as are about for to destroy our sovereign Lord the King and the Commons of England, for such unlawful points as Saint Thomas of Canterbury died for. And this to be fulfilled and kept by every like commoner upon pain of death.

And this in the name of Master Hobbe Hyrste,
Robin Good Fellow's brother, he is, as I trow.

262. EDICTS AGAINST SMUGGLING AND PIRACY

The King to the Earl of Oxenford

HENRY R.

Right trusty and right well-beloved Cousin, we greet you well, etc. In that ye desire all the Doggers [1] of those parts should have our license to depart in the voyage towards Iceland, as they have

[1] Fishing boats, trading mainly with Iceland.

been accustomed to do yearly in time past, and that ye will undertake they shall have with them no more quantities of grains than will only suffice for their victualling and expenses.

We let you weet that our full entirely beloved Cousin, the King of Denmark, hath showed and complained unto us by divers his letters, that when our subjects come to the said Iceland, being in his obeysance, they steal, rob, and extort his subjects there, against right and conscience; wherefore, the said Doggers finding sufficient surety before you, such as ye will answer unto us, that they shall not have with them no grains more than shall only suffice for their victualling, nor other thing with them that is forbidden; and that also they shall not, in going, coming, nor in their being at the said Iceland, take nothing but that they truly pay or agree for, and friendly entreat our said Cousin's subjects, without any robbing or extorting them in their bodies nor goods; we be content the said Doggers make their voyages thither at their liberties, every our writing or commandment made unto the contrary notwithstanding; and else we will that our restraint of their thither going stand still in his strength and virtue.

Given under our Signet, at our Manor of Shene the 6th day of April.

JOHN VERE, Earl of Oxynford, Great Chamberlain and Admiral of England, Viscount Bulbec, and Lord Scales, to all them that this present writing shall see or hear, greeting; and for as much as I late have received the King our Sovereign Lord's Letters, bearing date the 6th day of this month of April, according to a copy of the same signed with mine hand, which my right trusty servant John Rowe, Marshal of my Admiralty, hath for to show.

Know ye, that I, the said Earl and Admiral, have assigned and deputed my said servant to see our said Sovereign Lord's letters plainly executed, according to the tenor of the same; and by this present writing have given to him full authority and power to put under arrest all such Doggers as be disposed to make the voyage towards Iceland, to such time as they have found surety afore me, according to our said Sovereign Lord's commandment, for their demeaning in the said voyage.

Given under mine Signet and Sign Manual, the 10th day of

April, the 6th year of the reign of our said Sovereign Lord King Harry the VIIth.

OXYNFORD

[1491]

263. PIRACY ON NEUTRALS FORBIDDEN

To the right worshipful and right entirely well beloved Counsellor, Sir John Paston, Knight

RIGHT worshipful and right entirely well-beloved Counsellor, I commend me to you; and whereas I understand, by your writing to me delivered by this bearer, the robbery and despoiling of certain Corvers of Holland and Zeeland, done by the ship called the Fool, whereof Robert Spenser was master, as well in herring, victual, and tackling, as ye be informed by three persons of the same ship, and of the intent and disposition of the master and fellowship of the same, which show, as ye write, that Berkeley, as well with that ship as with a prize that he hath bought, late taken of the Frenchmen, were disposed and determined to do much harm, whereupon ye have endeavoured you to break the same; howbeit that the said Berkeley hath been late with me, and found surety in a hundred pounds to answer to all such demeaning, when he shall be called; and thereupon I wrote to you to suffer him, his men, and ships, to depart at liberty; yet nevertheless, considering your large writing, I cannot be content in my mind till such time as I may hear both you and Berkeley together; willing therefore that you do keep the ships and goods in surety, and to be with me yourself, . . . bringing with you such three persons as have certainty of this matter. And so I have written to Berkeley to answer to the same; and God keep you. Written this . . . day of October. Also if there be any of the Dutchmen . . . [make?] any suit for their goods, that ye then cause one of [them?] to show and claim their own.

OXYNFORD [1]

[1491]

[1] Oxford was Lord High Admiral of England, and Sir John Paston his Vice-Admiral for the Norfolk coast.

264. PERKIN WARBECK [1]

To our right honourable and especial good Master, Sir John Paston, Knight, this Letter be delivered in haste

RIGHT worshipful Sir, we recommend us unto your good Mastership, certifying you that Robert Albon of Yarmouth, with many more of our neighbours, this Saturday are coming home from Canterbury, and Robert Albon hath spoken with the English Captains of the King's rebels there, part of them that are taken; and Robert Albon and his company saith, that there were taken and slain to the number of sevenscore, whereof were five Captains, four of them he named over; Mountford, Whight, Belt, and Corbet; he could not tell the fifth Captain's name; and they told him that they have appointed to have a town of strength, for they would have had Sandwich, and the country had not resisted them; and so Belt said unto Robert Albon he wist well that he was but a dead man, and for as much as he wist that he was of Yarmouth, he showed him that they would have Yarmouth, or they shall die for it, as Robert saith to us. And this is a matter of truth, and therefore we desire and pray your good Mastership, that we may have your mighty help of aid and succour, and that it will please you to commune with Master Mayor of Norwich, to move him of his succour, but in especial, that we may have your Mastership among us, with such strength of your good counsel, as your Mastership shall think most best for the King's pleasure, and for the surety of us all, for we put us in devoir to furnish the town with all that we can do, for we know none other but that they may be here, by possibility, this night or to-morrow at night at the farthest.

No more to you, but Jesu preserve you. Written at Yarmouth, in haste, this Saturday the 11th day of July.

By your own the Bailiffs of Yarmouth, with our Brethren the Commons of the same town.

[1495]

[1] Perkin Warbeck, a Fleming, professed to be Duke of York and a son of Edward IV. He made a landing in Kent, where his force was exterminated. The men of Yarmouth were afraid of a landing there, threatened by one of the prisoners. In 1497 Warbeck made another landing, was defeated at Exeter, confessed his imposture, and was executed.

265. HENRY VII AND PHILIP OF BURGUNDY

To the Right Worshipful Master Robert Darcy and Master Giles Alington, being at the George in Lombard Street, be this delivered in haste

RIGHT Worshipful Masters, I recommend me unto you, certifying you that the King's Grace and the King of Castile [1] met this day, at three of the clock, upon Elworth Green, two miles out of Windsor, and there the king received him in the goodliest manner that ever I saw, and each of them embraced other in [his] arms.

To show you the King's apparel of England, thus it was, his horse of bay, trapped with needle work; a gown of purpure velvet; a chain with a George of Diamonds, and a hood of purpure velvet, which he put not off at the meeting of the said King of Castile; his hat and his bonnet he availed,[2] and the King of Castile in case like.

And the King of Castile rode upon a sorrelled hobby,[3] which the king gave unto him; his apparel was all black, a gown of black velvet, a black hood, a black hat, and his horse-harness of black velvet.

To show you of the king's company; my Lord Harry of Stafford [4] rode in a gown of cloth of tissue, tucked, furred with sables; a hat of goldsmith's work, and full of stones, diamonds and rubies, riding upon a sorrelled courser barded with a bard [5] of goldsmith's work, with roses and dragons red; and my Lord Marquis [of Dorset] riding upon a bald sorrelled horse, with a deep trapper full of long tassels of gold of Venice, and upon the crupper of his horse a white feather; with a coat upon his back, the

[1] Philip, Duke of Burgundy and heir of Maximilian, and his wife Juana of Castile, now King and Queen of Castile and Leon, were shipwrecked near Weymouth, on their way from Flanders to Spain. Henry VII entertained them for three months with the greatest magnificence.

During the time that these royal personages remained here, Henry concluded several treaties with them for his own and his kingdom's advantage. He likewise obtained the delivery of Edmund de la Pole, Duke of Suffolk, son of Elizabeth, the sister of Edward IV. [F.]

[2] Took off.

[3] Chestnut-coloured pony.

[4] Eldest son of the Duke of Buckingham.

[5] Covering for the breast and flanks of a horse.

body goldsmith's work, the sleeves of crimson velvet, with letters of gold.

My Lord of Kent upon a sorrelled horse, bald; the harness of Venice gold, with a deep fringe of half a yard of length. My Lord of Kent's coat was one bar of cloth of gold and another of crimson velvet, purled with a demy manche [1] cut off by the elbow. These be the lords that bare the bruit.[2]

Sir Hugh Vaughan upon a bay horse trapped with crimson velvet full of gilt bells, a gown of black velvet, and a chain of gold bawdrick wise [3] worth five hundred pounds. These be the spears: Master St John upon a black horse, with harness of cloth of gold, with tassels of plunket [4] and white; a coat of plunket and white, the body of goldsmith's work, the sleeves full of spangles.

John Carr and William Parr, coats like, the horses gray, of Parr, trapped with crimson velvet, with tassels of gold, and bells gilt. Carr's horse bay, with an Almayne harness of silver, an inch broad of beaten silver, both the coats of goldsmith's work the bodies, the sleeves one stripe of silver, the other gilt.

Edward Neville upon a gray horse trapped with black velvet full of small bells; his coat the one half of grain velvet, the other of white cloth of gold; these two the rutters [5] of the spears, with other divers well appointed.

On the King of Castile's party, the Lord Chamberlain Chief, I cannot tell his name as yet, his apparel was sad,[6] and so was all the residue of his company, with cloaks of sad tawny and black, guarded, some with velvet and some with sarsenet,[7] not passing a dozen in number.

It is said there are many behind, which shall come with the Queen of Castile, which shall come upon Tuesday.

When the King rode forth to Windsor Castle, the King rode ever upon the right hand of the King of Castile; however the King's Grace offered him to take him upon the right hand, the which he refused.

And at the alighting the King of Castile was off his horse a good

[1] Decorated with a half-sleeve.
[2] Were most talked of.
[3] Worn like a belt.
[4] Blue.
[5] Throwers.
[6] Dark coloured.
[7] Fine woven silk.

space ere our King was alighted; and then the King's Grace offered to take him by the arm, the which he would not, but took the King by the arm, and so went to the King of Castile's chamber, which is the richestly hanged that ever I saw; seven chambers together, hanged with cloth of Arras wrought with gold as thick as could be; and as for three beds of state, no king christened can show such three.

This is as far as I can show you of this day, and when I can know more, ye shall have knowledge.

From Windsor this Saturday at five of the clock.

By Yours,

William Makefyr

Windsor
January 17, 1506